Joint Ventures in the People's Republic of China

Joint Ventures in the People's Republic of China

THE CONTROL OF FOREIGN DIRECT INVESTMENT UNDER SOCIALISM

Margaret M. Pearson

PRINCETON UNIVERSITY PRESS

PRINCETON, NEW JERSEY

Copyright © 1991 by Princeton University Press
Published by Princeton University Press, 41 William Street,
Princeton, New Jersey 08540
In the United Kingdom: Princeton University Press, Oxford

Library of Congress Cataloging-in-Publication Data

Pearson, Margaret M., 1959–
Joint ventures in the People's Republic of China : the control of
foreign direct investment under socialism / Margaret M. Pearson.
p.   cm.
Includes bibliographical references (p.   ) and index.
1. Joint ventures—China.   2. Investments, Foreign—China.
I. Title.
HG5782.P43   1991   338.8'8851—dc20   90-19955

ISBN 0-691-07882-3 (cl) (alk. paper)

This book has been composed in Linotron Caledonia

Princeton University Press books are printed
on acid-free paper and meet the guidelines for
permanence and durability of the Committee on
Production Guidelines for Book Longevity
of the Council on Library Resources

Printed in the United States of America by Princeton University Press,
Princeton, New Jersey

1   3   5   7   9   10   8   6   4   2

For Steve

CONTENTS

TABLES AND FIGURES

ACKNOWLEDGMENTS

THE ORIGIN of this book was the doctoral dissertation I wrote while at Yale's Department of Political Science. The study of control of foreign investment by the Chinese state seemed only natural, for at the time China was just beginning to experiment with foreign investment. The study also made sense in that it was at the intellectual nexus of two of my primary fields of study, Chinese politics and international political economy. To work at the interstices of two subfields of the discipline is extremely stimulating, but it can also be fraught with dangers. Those who were most responsible for keeping me from falling through the intellectual cracks were my diverse group of dissertation advisors, Hong Yung Lee, Thomas J. Biersteker, and James C. Scott.

The research of course could not have proceeded without the help of those people I interviewed anonymously and who provided the core of the data used in this study. I learned a tremendous amount from the Chinese and foreign managers in joint ventures, Chinese officials, and various foreign "experts" involved in the negotiation and operation of joint ventures during the 1980s. As a group, these men and women were extremely generous with their time and their thoughts. Those at the two joint ventures I studied intensively impressed me particularly with their insight and candor.

During the research and writing of the thesis, I drew intellectual support from several people in addition to my graduate advisors. Vivienne Shue and Nicholas Lardy, through their graduate courses, were influential in shaping the way I think about China's politics and economy. True to the old saw that much if not most learning in graduate school comes from other students, I benefited much from stimulating discussions with my fellow graduate students in the China area at Yale: Kevin O'Brien, Daniel Kelliher, Arlene Macleod, Al Yee, and Melissa Ennen. Others who made helpful comments at various stages of the project included Vivienne Shue, Ian Shapiro, Stanley Rosen, and Peter N. S. Lee. A seminar I presented at the University of Southern California's Center for International Studies helped crystallize some of the main ideas. Dorothy J. Solinger gave the draft manuscript a very careful reading and made most valuable and constructive comments. She and several anonymous readers, whether or not they realized it, engaged me in just the sort of dialogue that an author needs and, indeed, craves.

I am grateful for the financial and technical support I received throughout the dissertation and book process. John Bryan Starr and Mark Shelden, and the International Asian Studies Program at the Chinese University of Hong Kong, provided an inviting and peaceful environment for field research. The Information Center at the U.S.-China Business Council provided much valuable data in the United States. Several people assisted with valuable research and editorial functions: Amy Chow in Hong Kong; I. Neel Chatterjee, Michael John Lytle, and Scott Lush at Dartmouth College; and Sally Seymour. Very generous support from a postdoctoral fellowship at the Center for International Studies at the University of Southern California and the Burke Research Initiation Grant at Dartmouth allowed me to do what was necessary to revise the dissertation. Margaret Case at Princeton University Press was patient and adept at guiding the manuscript to publication.

I owe a very important debt to my undergraduate teacher and advisor at Smith College, Steven M. Goldstein. His model of intellectual excellence combined with humor and kindness sets a very high standard for those of us inspired by him to pursue academic life. My family and friends, even when they could not understand why it was taking so long, never stopped calling, writing, and pestering.

By far my greatest thanks go to my husband, Steven Gunby, who influenced nearly everything having to do with this project (except the typing), and for the better. His unflagging commitment—both to getting my ideas out into the world and to getting this project out of our hair—kept me more or less sane and moving ahead. It is to him that this book is dedicated.

ABBREVIATIONS

AMC	American Motors Corporation
AWSJ	*Asian Wall Street Journal*
BOD	board of directors
CASP	The "Campaign Against Spiritual Pollution"
CCP	Chinese Communist Party
CCPIT	China Committee for the Promotion of International Trade
CITIC	China International Trade and Investment Corporation
CJV	contractual joint venture
DGM	deputy general manager
DIC	department in charge [*zhuguan bumen*]
EJV	equity joint venture
EOE	export-oriented enterprise
EPZ	export processing zone
FBIS	*Foreign Broadcast Information Service*
FDI	foreign direct investment
FETAC	Foreign Economic Trade Arbitration Commission
GM	general manager
GMW	*Guoji Maoyi Wenti* [*Intertrade*]
JFRB	*Jiefang Ribao* [*Liberation Daily*]
JJDB	*Jingji Daobao* [*Economic Reporter*]
JJGL	*Jingji Guanli* [*Economic Management*]
JJYJ	*Jingji Yanjiu* [*Economic Research*]
JPRS	*Joint Publications Research Service*
JV	joint venture
JVITL	Joint Venture Income Tax Law
LO	labor organization
MOFERT	Ministry of Foreign Economic Relations and Trade
NCUSCT	National Council for U.S.-China Trade
NEP	New Economic Plan (Lenin)
NFRB	*Nanfang Ribao* [*Southern Daily*]
NYT	*New York Times*
OEZ	open economic zone
SAEC	State Administration for Exchange Control
SCMP	*South China Morning Post* (HK)
SEZ	special economic zone
SMIDC	Shenzhen Municipal Industrial Development Corporation
SSB	State Statistical Bureau
SSZH	*Shenzhen Tequ Bao* [*Shenzhen Special Zone Herald*]

SWB	*Summary of World Broadcasts*
TAE	technologically advanced enterprise
TITIC	Tianjin International Trade and Investment Corporation
TKP	*Ta Kung Pao* (HK)
TNC	transnational corporation
UNCTC	United Nations Centre on Transnational Corporations
UNIDO	United Nations Industrial Development Organization
WSJ	*Wall Street Journal*
WWP	*Wen Wei Po* (HK)

Joint Ventures in the
People's Republic of China

INTRODUCTION AND OVERVIEW

IN A DRAMATIC shift in foreign economic policy, the Chinese leadership, in late 1978, announced that China would "open to the outside world." As part of this new "open" policy, China embarked on a strategy to use private foreign capital to spur economic development. The post-Mao leadership believed that by absorbing foreign direct investment China would gain access to new sources of capital, advanced technology, and management skills, as well as to international markets that would absorb China's exports and provide foreign exchange to finance China's import needs.

Because China's leaders had followed a policy of self-reliance since the mid-1960s and, since the revolution in 1949, had viewed private foreign capital as antithetical to socialist developmental goals, the post-Mao policy shift was particularly dramatic. The policy of self-reliance had been rooted in the historically and ideologically grounded belief that private foreign direct investment in China would lead to a number of negative results. China's leaders doubted China's ability to capture its share of the economic benefits generated by foreign investment. They also feared loss of state control over the country's development path, loss of political independence, and the potential for foreign influences to contaminate traditional and socialist values. The "open" policy formulated in the late 1970s did not reject the view that foreign direct investment has potential negative effects. Instead, the policy was based on the view that present-day China could use its strengths to reap the benefits the leadership identified with foreign direct investment, while guarding against the perceived problems; the post-Mao leadership believed China could "selectively absorb the good things and boycott the bad things from abroad."[1] The primary strength that would allow China to control the effects of foreign investment, the leaders believed, was the existence of a consolidated socialist state. In particular, the leadership intended to apply to the foreign sector the same tools of the socialist state that it had relied upon to control the domestic economy—the state plan, extensive government participation in and regulation of the economy, and preceptoral controls to combat "unhealthy" cultural tendencies.

At the core of the attempt to use foreign capital to spur economic development while maintaining control over that capital was the use of equity joint ventures. The government strongly favored this form of direct investment because it believed that partial state ownership of equity joint ventures would afford China an additional means of control. Because foreign companies were familiar with this form from their investments in other countries, leaders reasoned further, the companies would be willing to invest in China under similar terms. Leaders also believed that, as part owners of equity joint ventures, foreign investors would be more committed to their success and hence would more willingly supply ventures with advanced technology and management. As a consequence of this favored status, equity joint ventures constituted one of the most significant channels for foreign investment during the 1980s. This book examines the Chinese government's effort to control the terms of foreign investment in these equity joint ventures from the origin of the policy in 1979 to the resurgence of the more conservative leadership in the spring of 1989.

The book has three underlying goals. The first is primarily descriptive. Because the foreign investment policy represents a major part of the post-Mao reforms, it is important for the study of contemporary China to understand the government's goals of both absorbing and controlling foreign investment, and how it has attempted to realize these goals. Despite the substantial attention given to China's "open" policy, there has been no comprehensive analysis of the precise contours of China's foreign investment program, and changes in that program over time, from the perspective of the state's efforts to control the terms of investment. The first purpose of this study is therefore to document this important element of the post-Mao reforms and of China's deepening participation in the international economy by providing a thorough description of the measures the Chinese government adopted to control equity joint ventures, and by showing how the original controls changed over time.

The second goal is to understand the various forces that shaped foreign investment policy throughout the 1980s, that is, the factors that influenced the formulation and implementation of the "open" policy and that caused it to evolve as it did. Both internal and external forces molded the foreign investment policy. Important among the internal forces (those that emanated from within and are indigenous to China) was the capacity or bargaining power that the Chinese state could bring to bear in negotiating over foreign investment. Also crucial in shaping the policy were the dynamics of China's domestic politics—the historical and ideological legacies that influenced the attitudes of political leaders, the mixture of consensus and divisiveness that characterized the Chinese leadership, and change in the character of the leadership and in the dominant official outlook toward foreign investment since the late 1970s—and the nature of China's domestic economy. The foremost external factor that molded the foreign investment policy, especially the manner in which the policy evolved over time, was the norms and terms of the international investment regime that China, as a player in the international economy, had to accept. In particular, China had to bargain with foreign firms that had substantial power, even relative to China's socialist state. As is true in many host countries, the foreign investment policy was influenced by foreign perceptions of the attractiveness of China's investment environment and by pressures from foreign investors, operating via accepted bargaining norms, to adapt to the needs of investors.

The third aim of this book is to examine how effective China actually was at meeting its goals. It draws on the internal and external factors to explain when China was able to establish and maintain strong controls over foreign investment at the same time that it absorbed significant quantities of such investment, and when it was not. It also seeks to explain why in some ways, again as a result of internal and external pressures, the government's policy toward foreign investment evolved over the course of the 1980s, and why in other ways the policy did not change. This work does *not* focus on how much China has benefited economically from foreign investment; it does not question that China obtained significant economic benefits from foreign investment. Rather, the book seeks to examine how well China's socialist state carried out a foreign investment policy that called for extensive controls over foreign capital at the same time that the state tried to derive substantial benefit from that policy.

As important as this third question is for China, it is at least as significant for other developing countries. China's experience can inform our understanding of the extent to which host states in developing socialist countries are able simultaneously to reap the benefits and control the terms of foreign direct investment.[2] Numerous studies have found serious deficiencies in the ability of the state in capitalist developing economies to control foreign investment to their satisfaction.[3] These failures have led some critics of foreign investment, implicitly and explicitly, to suggest that socialist governments are better positioned to both benefit from and control foreign investment. Yet no previous studies have analyzed systematically whether a strategy that depends on tools of a socialist state is feasible, or whether the existence of a socialist state can enhance a host country's bargaining position sufficiently to meet the goals of these states.

China may represent the best test case for beginning to answer these broader questions about the ability of socialist states to manipulate their positions in the international economy. A number of China's attributes put it in a much better bargaining position than virtually all other developing countries. It possessed as consolidated a socialist regime, undiluted by a private national bourgeoisie or managerial class oriented toward foreign direct investment, as existed during the 1980s. Moreover, China's bargaining power was enhanced significantly by the foreign perception of a huge potential domestic market. If China could not maintain the control that it and most socialist states have wished from foreign investment, serious questions must be raised about the ability of other socialist states that do *not* possess these qualities to an equal degree to reach these same goals.

This book is organized into six chapters. Chapter 1 establishes the framework necessary for understanding China's foreign investment policy. It introduces the internal and external factors that were crucial to the establishment of the foreign investment policy and its evolution over the course of the 1980s. It also outlines the view, held by many critics of foreign investment, that a socialist state may be better able than a nonsocialist government to control the terms of investment. In doing so, the chapter establishes the Chinese experience as a critical case for determining the capacity of socialist states to control their interaction in the world economy. Chapter 2 examines the post-Mao leadership's outlook toward foreign investment to discern what specific concerns it held about foreign investment in the early years. The chapter identifies concerns at three levels: national, regional, and enterprise. It emphasizes the importance of Chinese perceptions of past foreign aggression in China and the ideological legacies of anti-imperialism and self-strengthening in the original formulation of the policy to absorb and control foreign capital. The chapter also analyzes the reformist rationale for the "open" policy, a rationale that asserted China's ability to control foreign investment and at the same time legitimized the view that China's policy toward foreign investment would be flexible.

Chapter 3 begins to establish what actually happened to China's foreign investment policy over the course of the 1980s. It argues that, throughout the decade, as the reformers became more dominant, the official perception of the dangers of foreign investment decreased, while the emphasis on benefits to be derived from it strengthened. It traces the actual pattern of investment in equity joint ventures through three phases: 1979 to mid-1983, late-1983 to mid-1986, and late-1986 to the end of 1988. By examining statistical data on the pattern of investment during the 1980s, the chapter finds that foreign capital flowed into joint ventures and other forms of investment at an uneven pace and, judging from official statements and actions, at a level lower than desired by the reformers. This lack of success in attracting foreign capital at the desired level placed significant stress on China's ability to retain controls that foreign investors disliked. The chapter argues that the disincentive effect of controls, the reformers' desire to increase the level of investment, and the changing composition of the leadership, spurred the liberalization of the investment environment starting in the second phase. This chapter also compiles statistical data on equity joint ventures from 1979 to 1989, presenting information to be drawn upon in subsequent chapters.

The next two chapters detail China's establishment of controls at the national, regional, and enterprise levels during the early phase, and the Chinese government's ability to maintain those controls during the second and third phases. Chapter 4 examines the government's use at the national level of Chinese law, general principles, control over procedures, sectoral controls, and state plans, as well as stringent controls over specific issues of foreign investment (including access of foreign firms to the domestic market, foreign exchange, profit repatriation, domestic content, and transfer of technology). The chapter also identifies regional controls designed to direct investment into the coastal areas of China and to control the spread of what the government perceived to be negative effects from these regions. Chapter 5 analyzes Chinese controls at the enterprise level by examining policies set up in the early years to avoid foreign managerial control of joint ventures. Both chapters find that the government was effective at maintaining stringent controls over a number of issues. But at all levels the government also encountered significant difficulties in implementing many controls and, moreover, was pressed to liberalize the investment regime in significant ways.

The concluding chapter draws on the analysis presented in the previous chapters to assess China's overall ability to control the terms of foreign investment. In discussing the ways in which China was effective at implementing and maintaining strong controls, the chapter argues that although this result was due in part to its socialist controls and to the continued salience to reformers of some of the original concerns, it also was due to a factor wholly unrelated to socialism: the lure of China's domestic market. Chapter 6 also argues that the problems of policy implementation and the deliberate erosion or liberalization of controls throughout the 1980s were significant. It summarizes how both internal and external factors pressured the government to liberalize controls; direct pressure from foreign investors and their governments to loosen controls and the ability of potential foreign investors to withhold capital were accompanied by the growing influence of reformers and the evolution in their views toward a greater willingness to trade off controls in order to obtain the desired level of foreign investment. Finally, this chapter generalizes from the implications of China's experience to other socialist and nonsocialist nations. It concludes that, despite the potential bargaining strengths of socialist states, China's experience suggests that the hopes of other socialist countries, such as Vietnam, that have embarked on strategies similar to China's, are unlikely to be realized. That China, with its strong socialist state and the attraction of its large domestic market, has experienced significant problems in its joint venture program suggests that other centralized socialist developing countries will have substantial difficulty gaining benefits from and at the same time controlling foreign direct investment to the extent desired.

## Chapter One

THE POLITICAL ECONOMY OF
FOREIGN INVESTMENT IN CHINA:
ISSUES AND FRAMEWORK

DEVELOPING countries such as China that incorporate foreign capital into their development plan frequently employ a dual-edged strategy: they try at once to absorb enough capital to provide the desired developmental benefits, but at the same time they try to maintain state control over the terms of investment. The strategy is an attempt to reap what these governments perceive to be benefits of investment and avoid what they view to be negative results. The success of such a strategy depends on the host state's capacity to control the terms of investment. That capacity is in turn influenced by the domestic political and economic systems, on the one hand, and the international economy, on the other. This chapter discusses the factors, both political and economic, internal and external, that can influence a host state's capacity with respect to this strategy, and develops a framework to understand and evaluate China's attempt to control foreign investment over the course of the 1980s.

One major factor that influences the capacity of a host state is its bargaining strength vis-à-vis foreign investors. The Chinese government's need to enter into a bargaining relationship with foreign investors—a relationship that is governed by international norms—creates a crucial exogenous source of pressure on China; the international environment establishes the "rules of the game" to which China must adhere if it is to attract foreign investment. Yet within the context of these externally generated norms, the host state and the foreign investors each possess considerable potential bargaining strengths and weaknesses that they can bring to bear in the negotiation process. The first part of this chapter details the strengths of the Chinese state and foreign investors in China. In particular, it outlines the argument suggested by some scholars and host governments that socialism such as was found in China in the 1980s can significantly enhance a country's bargaining power.

Bargaining theories emphasize the importance of understanding thoroughly each actor in the bargaining relationship in order to discern its interests and behavior. The remainder of this chapter addresses that need by examining the actors and the environment in which they operate. The second and third parts examine China's domestic political and economic systems, thereby introducing the major domestic factors that have influenced the foreign investment controls. The discussion of Chinese politics in the second section suggests the ways in which characteristics of post-Mao politics, as well as long-standing features of Chinese political life, affected the goal of absorbing and controlling foreign capital, and the state's capacity to bargain with foreigners in a unified manner. The third section examines those technical features of China's economy and its positioning in the international economy that influenced the investment environment. In the fourth part, the focus returns to the behavior of foreign investors to discuss the motivations of these firms for investing in China and the main conflict of interests foreign firms had with the Chinese government.

Before embarking on the discussion of the forces influencing China's ability to control foreign investment, it is worthwhile to place the issue of Chinese control over foreign investment in the context of the broader debate from which it arises: whether foreign direct investment is, on balance, positive or negative for the economic, social, and political life of developing nations.[1] Proponents of foreign investment believe that such investment results in net economic benefits—such as a net inflow of capital and technology and the creation of economic value (revenues, profits, and so on)—for both the investor and the host country. Proponents who take a "neoclassical" economic view believe further that both partners can best reap benefits from investment in a relatively uncontrolled investment environment.[2] Critics of foreign investment argue that foreign direct investment, on balance, is not beneficial to host country development. Rather, they argue that transnational corporations capture a disproportionately large share of the benefits of foreign investment, at the expense of host countries. Although these critics disagree among themselves over whether any economic development can occur where foreign participation in the economy is extensive, they generally agree that host countries would be better off without foreign investment, or with foreign investment occurring only on very limited terms. Since the early 1970s, critics of foreign investment in developing countries also have argued that, not only the interests and behavior of transnational corporations (TNCs) and processes inherent in the international economy, but also domestic factors, especially host country class structures and the nature of host states, pose constraints for Third World development.[3]

Critics of foreign investment differ, however, over the proper responses to problems they associate with foreign investment, and over the degree to which host countries can improve the terms of investment.[4] Those critics writing from orthodox Marxian and "world systems" perspectives argue that one country can do little to change the terms of investment without significant historical progression away from what they see as capitalist domination of the international economy toward socialism on a global scale. Other critics agree that systemwide change is unlikely, but have tried to visualize the prospects for host country development without foreign capital, and prior to what they hope will be the advent of global socialism. They have prescribed autarky or regional integration, often under a socialist regime.[5] Another group of critics hoped for salvation in a now defunct program for a "New International Economic Order," believing rich and poor nations could formally agree to structural change.

Policymakers in many developing countries, in agreement with the position of a number of United Nations development agencies, adopted yet another view, particularly in the 1970s. Although leaders in these countries believe that foreign direct investment produces some negative results, they have found the potential benefits of such investment—as a source of capital accumulation, advanced technology, management skills, and access to international markets—to be significant. They do not accept that the negative results of investment are inextricable from or outweighed by the potential benefits. Rather, they have attempted to limit the negative effects by establishing controls over a wide range of variables.[6] While leaders of developing countries have attempted to engage in the world economy while limiting the negative effects, these leaders reject the argument that an individual developing country does not have the ability to influence the terms of interaction in the global capitalist economy. They have witnessed the failed attempts to industrialize under a strategy of national or regional self-reliance; they are unwilling to accept the political ramifications (especially popular dissatisfaction over low consumption levels) and economic problems (such as capital shortages and materials bottlenecks) that other countries have experienced under these strategies. As will be discussed in chapter 2, the strategy adopted in China in the late 1970s was consistent with this view.

BARGAINING POWER AND HOST STATE CONTROL
OF FOREIGN INVESTMENT

A Theory of Bargaining

Studies of host country attempts to control foreign investment often suggest that the extent to which a host country can assert control in relation to foreign firms depends upon its bargaining power and the possibility for increasing it. A country's ability to bargain with TNCs, in turn, depends in large part on the nature of the host state. Standard bargaining power scenarios posit that each party brings to negotiations a set of attributes or strengths that it can use to influence an outcome.[7] Because both the relative strengths of each side and the issues under consideration vary, each instance of bargaining will be unique. Analyses of bargaining between host countries and foreign firms therefore describe a mode of interaction or a process, rather than a precise set of outcomes. Certain consistencies in the relative bargaining power of the host government and foreign investors nonetheless can lead to similar outcomes across different cases.

Underlying standard bargaining models for foreign investment is the view that foreign direct investment is not a zero-sum proposition; rather, despite the myriad potential conflicts between partners, there is a range of conditions within which the interests of a host country and a foreign investor may converge to generate an outcome that makes each side better off. Bargaining scenarios presume that, because each party is free to opt out of the negotiation when it can make no gains against the status quo, bargaining will lead to gains for each side.[8] Although the strengths of the negotiating parties are by no means necessarily equal, no party need enter negotiations unless it can gain. The norm of bargaining also presumes that, because both sides must gain, neither can unilaterally control the outcome at the expense of the other. The impossibility of unilateral control contains an important if simple point for assessing a host government's capacity for controlling investment: where the interests of the parties diverge, each side will have to make concessions or trade-offs to reach an agreement and thereby to gain the benefits that are possible through cooperation.

If they are to participate in the international economy, host countries and investors alike must accept the international norm of bargaining over the terms of investment.[9] The bargaining scenario is significant for China because it presents norms to which China, too, must adhere. As an accepted means of international economic interaction, the bargaining norm allows China to use its assets and powers to attract foreign capital on favorable terms. It also gives play to the substantial power of foreign firms. The issue of the comparative bargaining power of parties to the negotiations thus becomes important for understanding China's ability to control the terms of foreign investment.

The Potential Strengths and Weaknesses of China's Socialist State in Controlling Foreign Capital

In the 1970s, studies of foreign investment in developing capitalist countries began increasingly to focus on the capacity of host states to formulate and implement controls over foreign investment.[10] These studies identified a variety of possible regulatory mechanisms, including taxes, limits on foreign currency flows, restrictions on joint venture sales in the domestic market, requirements for local ownership and management (often in joint ventures), monitoring of technology transfer, and state approval at various stages of the investment process. They also noted that, as a partner in foreign investment projects, the state could have a direct channel of control over operations.[11] Although the ability to actually carry out regulations such as these would depend upon a variety of factors (as discussed subsequently), the *potential* for host state control was deemed to be significant.

Yet the actual ability of host states to draw on these potential control mechanisms to enhance their bargaining power was found to be mixed in capitalist developing countries. Some successes in controlling foreign investment were evident. For example, the Mexican government gained a number of favorable terms in its negotiations with TNCs in the automobile industry when the interests of the Mexican government and the TNCs converged. The Mexican government gained TNC cooperation for a plan to produce parts in Mexico for export (rather than for domestic sale) when, in the 1970s, the trends toward Japanese global markets and fuel-efficient vehicles spurred international automakers to examine global sourcing more seriously. Similarly, the Nigerian state, through its indigenization policy, was able to enhance local control by enforcing Nigerian majority ownership of most enterprises with foreign capital, and through greater government control of key sectors, notably banking.[12] Both Mexico and Nigeria, then, were able to gain more control over foreign investment through state bargaining with TNCs and state regulation of investment.

But many of these same studies of capitalist developing economies showed that host states in these countries had considerable difficulty formulating and implementing effective controls over foreign investment, and that their bargaining power remained relatively weak.[13] The studies pointed to several reasons for this difficulty. They implicitly or explicitly criticized the assumption of the standard bargaining scenario that the outcome of host-TNC bargaining is neutral, and argued that the scenario fails to emphasize sufficiently the factors that regularly bolster the bargaining position of TNCs. The study of Nigeria, for example, revealed investors' strategies to counteract the 1972 indigenization decree by having local but mainly "silent" Nigerian owners and managers act as "fronts" for foreign owners, who maintained effective power despite the appearance of indigenous control.[14]

Others argued that weaknesses in state power vis-à-vis TNCs also came from forces within the host country itself. They argued that host state efforts to control foreign investment had been strongly influenced by the presence of a national bourgeoisie or comprador class, or by continuing colonial ties. In Nigeria, for example, local business interests opposed the government's 1977 indigenization decree, and supported the successful efforts of TNCs to keep local partners "silent." Local business interests also undermined the state's efforts to formulate the 1972 indigenization policy. In Mexico, the state's orientation since the 1920s had been to support a national bourgeoisie; thus, not only was the state subject to pressure from private interests (such as the auto industry's business associations), but the interest of the state itself was judged to coincide frequently with private interests, at the expense of broader "national" interests. Direct participation in foreign investment projects by a capitalist-oriented state has been seen to create further state-investor alliances that enhance state control, not over foreign capital but over domestic groups, such as independent labor organizations.[15] These studies concluded, then, that host states lack the structural unity to implement controls, that they lack independence from domestic societal forces that may have interests in common with foreign investors, or that the state has an interest in preserving an environment that is favorable to capitalism and hostile to controls that might hinder foreign participation.

Although critical of the ability of capitalist host states to control the terms of foreign investment, some studies have implicitly or explicitly suggested that socialism in some form would overcome the problems experienced in capitalist developing countries, and would provide a substantial increase in host bargaining power. Authors of the study of the Mexican auto industry, for example, concluded that extensive state ownership of Mexican automobile firms could have helped to prevent distortions that occurred with foreign investment:

> State ownership [of Mexico's automobile sector] could have been used to achieve goals that the private sector would not have achieved, even with vigorous regulatory efforts of a more traditional sort. A state-owned firm could wield significant market power. As an oligopolistic buyer or seller, it could force prices down among other members of an oligopoly by operating at lower profits, or even at a loss. As a sole source of inputs for private manufacturers, it could raise or lower their costs of production. State ownership could give the state power to influence the degree of product differentiation, the kind of technology used, and other aspects of production, with less regard to profit maximization. As a shareholder in a private firm, it might be able to direct the conduct of the firm more effectively from within than it could with the use of regulatory tools. Finally, state ownership could give state officials inside knowledge of an industry that would be invaluable for reshaping industry structure or regulating firm conduct.

Influential *dependencia* writers from Latin America have also prescribed socialism.[16] Yet no thorough studies exist of the particular capabilities of socialist states in controlling foreign capital.

Several elements of a socialist form of government can be hypothesized to contribute to the bargaining power of a developing country and therefore to contribute to a state's ability to control foreign investment. A number of these strengths are identifiable in light of the literature on states in nonsocialist developing countries, and specifically are strengths that writers have noted to be absent in these countries. As a socialist country, China in the late 1970s to a large degree possessed these strengths. China also had a number of attributes that were unrelated to its socialist economic and political structures.

When China initiated its "open" policy, one of the attributes that was related to the country's socialism was the absence of a continuing foreign influence from the nineteenth- and early twentieth-century era of colonial expansion. The 1949 socialist revolution eliminated the influence of Western and Japanese colonial powers that had been present since the Opium Wars of the mid-nineteenth century. The ouster of Soviet advisors and capital in 1960, and the ensuing period of isolation, further deepened China's independence from foreign powers. China's historical conditioning contrasted with that of former colonies which, despite decolonization, continued to be strongly influenced in the business sphere by a foreign presence. A potential second strength, also related to China's socialism, was structural. By the time of the "transition to socialism" in 1956, the Chinese Communist Party (CCP) had eliminated the material basis of China's small capitalist class through both physical means and confiscation of private capital. This was, again, unlike the experience of other developing countries, such as Mexico and Nigeria, where the local private business class effectively undermined control efforts of the host state. When China "opened to the outside world" in the late 1970s, then, there were entrenched interests of neither foreign nor private capital to influence the policy from within. These historical and structural features allowed the government to start to absorb investment from a highly controlled position in which it could choose, at least initially, the precise areas for the liberalization of control over investment and the pace of such liberalization.

The first two strengths arose from the absence of structures or influences that could have limited China's ability to control foreign capital. The third grew from structures that did exist. China had socialist political and economic structures in the late 1970s that strengthened the government's bargaining position in negotiating foreign contracts and overseeing operations. The state's monopoly over joint venture approvals had potential to allow it to determine the range of terms for foreign investment contracts. The state also was positioned to supervise individual bargaining sessions at the firm level; the negotiating process could be controlled by state organs and personnel subject to central supervision. The state's extensive penetration of the economy, moreover, could allow for state control over the operations of foreign-backed projects. Because joint ventures were formed with state-owned enterprises, the socialist state had the opportunity to directly foster its own ends and to control the role of foreign capital in China's development. Socialist planning mechanisms also offered ready organizations and personnel to determine the role and function of foreign investment in China's economy. Line ministries, finance bureaus, and party bureaucracies were positioned to regulate and oversee foreign-backed operations. For example, China's foreign currency bureaucracy had monopoly authority over foreign exchange transactions, and China's state economic bureaucracy, which traditionally regulated marketing, was in a strong position to allow or disallow marketing by foreign-backed firms.

Although state participation in joint ventures and the existence of planning mechanisms are often associated with socialist states, they need not be. Some degree of state intervention and planning is commonplace in developing capitalist economies, as is government ownership of strategic sectors. Conversely, the authority of the planning mechanism in socialist countries frequently exhibits gaps, so that complete central control is never achieved in practice. The difference between planned socialist economies and those capitalist economies characterized by some state ownership and planning, although one of degree rather than kind, is important: in socialist economies the state routinely pervades, and is sanctioned to pervade, most aspects of the economy. What is also potentially unique about a socialist country dominated by planning is the existence of a will or interest, supported by ideology, to enact economic policies strong enough to control foreign investment. A socialist state such as that found in China in the late 1970s and 1980s is *more* likely, for example, to be able to manipulate foreign capital to promote state ends directly, and to control any possible negative distributive consequences of outside investment. Hence, in the late 1970s the organizational structure for control over bargaining was bolstered by ideological support for a state monopoly over China's bargaining with and control over the foreign sector.

A fourth possible strength relates to the timing of the Chinese leadership's decision to absorb foreign capital. Because China embarked on its strategy to simultaneously absorb and control foreign capital late compared to many nonsocialist countries, it was the beneficiary of a "demonstration effect" among host countries. The dissemination of information about the positive and negative experiences of other host countries and the guidance China received from international organizations presumably made China more able to achieve its goals.

Finally, the prospect that China would open what investors had long believed to be its huge potential domestic market made China a highly desirable location for new investment, and hence was an extremely strong positive lure for foreign investors. As is discussed subsequently, the "market of one billion" was the primary reason why most foreign investors were interested in China, although Hong Kong manufacturers were also attracted by the relatively cheap, proximate labor. China could use this strength particularly when bargaining with firms in industries in which international competition to enter new markets was fierce. The ability to lure foreign firms with the prospect of access to its domestic market, which was relatively unsaturated by either domestic or foreign producers, was perhaps the greatest strength at the disposal of the Chinese leaders. It was, of course, a strength that was unrelated to China's socialism.[17]

Substantial potential weaknesses were also evident in China's bargaining position in the late 1970s. These weaknesses often paralleled the strengths of foreign firms. The most important source of China's weakness, and of TNC strength, arose from a simple but crucial factor inherent in the bargaining dynamic: the government's ability to attract investment, and impose controls over foreign investment, depends upon the attractiveness of the host environment. Investors are less willing to endure controls when they gain few benefits. If the web of controls as a whole is too strong—if it allows too few benefits to investors—investors can ultimately withhold investment. Because in the late 1970s and early 1980s foreign firms were investing anew in China, moreover, it was possible for them to withhold initial investment to try to induce concessions from Chinese negotiators; potential investors did not yet have the liability of a "sunken" investment which, particularly in extractive industries, could have limited their maneuverability in bargaining. Thus, although China possessed the strong lure of the market, the need to maintain an attractive market suggests that China could not wholly ignore the disincentive effect of controls.[18] It also suggests that for some sectors, such as the extractive sector, China as a new entrant to the foreign investment field was in a worse position to bargain than countries where existing investors would make concessions to protect "sunken" investments.[19]

Second, the technology, international markets, and management skills that the Chinese leadership very much wanted were frequently found in industries in which only a few firms dominated. In many of these industries China had few alternatives, and hence its ability to bargain with any one firm was limited.[20] China's foreign policy stance in the late 1970s also limited its search for capital and skills to the capitalist world. Although the Soviet Union possessed some of the benefits China sought, in the late 1970s China's strategic opposition to that country eliminated it as a source of investment. Even with a Sino-Soviet rapprochement in the late 1980s, the common Chinese belief that Western technology is superior to that of the Eastern bloc translated into a continuing preference for Western investment.

Third, although the potential internal market, and to a lesser extent natural resources (especially oil), were powerful incentives, much was staked on them; they were the only positive incentives China had to offer

Western and Japanese investors employing advanced technology—one type of investor China very much hoped to attract. Other Asian countries provided better bases for export production, for they could offer labor that was more highly skilled and had experience in shifting quickly to the demands of the world market. Chinese enterprises generally did not offer the special knowledge of industries or other "synergies" most multinational investors look for in a joint venture partner. As discussed in more detail below, China did offer certain attributes, notably inexpensive rent and labor, and proximity relative to Hong Kong and Taiwan, that attracted Hong Kong and Taiwan capital.

TNCs had considerably more experience bargaining with host governments than China had bargaining with transnationals in the late 1970s. Although Chinese negotiators could be expected to gain the experience that would allow them to move up a "learning curve," their lack of such experience in the early years of the foreign investment policy likely weakened their ability to gain the most favorable outcome possible. Furthermore, foreign firms could bring to bear the pressure of their home governments. This pressure was potentially very strong, especially as the Chinese government tried increasingly to form military and economic ties with the United States in the 1978–1981 period. Comparatively rich TNC negotiating experience and the support of home governments were the fourth and fifth potential disadvantages for China in the late 1970s.

Finally, even with the centralized governmental structure that exists in socialist countries, the state is unlikely to be *completely* unitary or even coordinated in its bargaining position. The possibility of a nonunitary actor requires a close examination of the complexity of the bargainer and, in the case of host countries, of *internal* political factors that weaken a state's ability to transform its power attributes to actual outcomes. As discussed further in the second part of this chapter, in China during any period, local or ministerial actors within the state can be expected to influence the Chinese bargaining position and to try to limit the effectiveness of formal controls in accordance with their own interests. Intra-bureaucratic and central-local bargaining occurs in policymaking largely because adherence to and implementation of policy is dependent upon a number of bureaucratic and local actors with varying interests. Cooperation of these actors is important to the success of any policy set forth by the center because, particularly in a period of decentralization, they command resources they may use to further or hinder the policy. Centralized planned economies face some unique problems of their own, including a system "overload" for a central apparatus trying to implement many complex policies, a physical inability to monitor closely local level implementation, the consequent reliance on simplistic performance indicators, and unintended consequences that arise from the appearance of contradictory goals within one policy or the interaction of one policy with others.[21] Despite potential for greater state unity in bargaining when compared with nonsocialist countries, internal factors that existed in China in the late 1970s had the potential to weaken the Chinese state's ability to achieve its desired outcomes.

China thus possessed a set of bargaining strengths, which grew in part out of its socialist structure, and a set of weaknesses, which often coincided with the strengths of foreign firms. Some of China's attributes—especially the organizational structure and ideological support for state control of economic activity—arose out of its socialism, and are not found in nonsocialist countries. Even some countries with planned socialist economies and supporting ideologies do not possess all the attributes associated with Chinese socialism, notably the absence of colonial ties or the remnants of a national business class. Most importantly, other socialist countries do not possess a domestic market of the sheer size of China's. China's weaknesses, moreover, were rather typical of socialist countries that wish to attract international investment. They all must engage in international bargaining with TNCs, often with oligopolies that possess the technology they desire, and that have more extensive experience in such bargaining. They all possess cracks in their otherwise relatively unitary state structures. Few socialist countries can do better than China did in supplying abundant, cheap labor for production of exports, despite China's problems in this area. Given China's attributes, and the absence of weaknesses unique to China among the socialist countries, China appears to have been well positioned in the 1980s to control the terms of foreign investment, and to test the capacities of socialist states that have subsequently chosen to embark on similar paths.

To fully understand the capacity of a host state to control foreign investment, however, it is not enough to list the assets of host countries and foreign firms; other factors complicate the bargaining dynamic. As implied previously, a host country's bargaining power can be relatively weaker or stronger depending on certain characteristics of the sector or industry of the firm with which it is negotiating. A host country's strength depends particularly on the degree to which an industry's technology is disseminated and standardized, and the strength of the oligopolistic rivalry and competition for new markets within the industry. In new, high-technology industries or industries where technology changes rapidly, frequently only one firm or several firms monopolize the technology. In these situations, the firm's bargaining power may be strengthened, as the alternatives for the host government are few. Moreover, the more crucial an industry is politically and economically to the host country, the less latitude that country has to bargain.

In contrast, in industries where a number of alternative firms possess a standardized technology (usually a few major oligopolies), where firm rivalry is strong, and whose world markets are extensively penetrated, the alternatives, and hence the bargaining power of the host state, are greater. Certain industries with technologies that are fairly standardized elsewhere in the world, such as automobiles, electronics, pharmaceuticals, and elevators, have in fact been very anxious to invest in China. Firms in these industries, investing defensively to prevent competitors from preempting new markets, believe they cannot afford *not* to enter China.[22] Defensive competition between the few members of the industry theoretically allows the Chinese government to utilize its monopoly over access to the domestic market to enhance its bargaining position.

Moreover, the capacity to control foreign investment is not a static capability; the relative power of the host state and a foreign investor often shifts over the life of an investment, though not uniformly. Studies of foreign investment in the extractive sectors of developing countries have argued that bargaining power over such projects shifts to the host country as the costs of disengagement rise, as the investment is "sunken," and as the investor's technology and know-how disseminate to host competitors. In contrast, studies of manufacturing industries have argued that the host state's power is greatest at the point of initial investment, when it can more easily set the terms of the investor's entrance to the domestic market. The relative power of the manufacturing foreign investor increases after investment, however, because the state continues to rely upon the investor for products, capital, technological aid, parts, and employment. Because a substantial proportion of the foreign investment projects in China is in manufacturing, this literature suggests that for the first years of the foreign investment policy, China's bargaining power may have been at its peak but that it may have weakened over time. For all sectors, moreover, even though a host country may gain some bargaining power as it moves up the "learning curve," investors can often reverse or nullify the host advantage through a variety of strategies (as occurred in Nigeria).[23]

One additional point must be made regarding the bargaining context of China's effort to control foreign investment. In establishing a framework for understanding China's bargaining capabilities, it is necessary to distinguish between two levels at which bargaining occurs: the firm level and the state level. Emphasis on firm-level bargaining is especially appropriate for analysis of investment in those nonsocialist developing countries where the state's role is minimal, or where local private entities (such as local partners, in the case of joint ventures) have much latitude in negotiations. Analysis of bargaining at the firm level is important for China too, for this is where negotiations over investment contracts, and contacts with foreign business interests, have been most direct. But it is also crucial to emphasize (as has been done in the previous discussion) the more generalized, nonproject specific role of states, especially socialist states, in bargaining with foreign investors, for to a large degree, the state is the source of the strength of and changes in a country's bargaining power. The state's capacity to bargain with investors manifests itself largely in laws and policies governing the overall terms of foreign investment, and changes in the relative bargaining position of a host state can be traced easily—more easily than through private negotiations over individual projects—through changes in laws and policies over time. Changes in bargaining power at the state level can also be expected to strongly influence bargaining that occurs at the firm level, moreover, particularly as joint foreign–Chinese investment projects virtually always have involved state enterprises as the Chinese partner.[24] This study examines changes in the bargaining position of the Chinese government over time as these changes manifested themselves at both the firm and, especially, the state level.

· · ·

Applied to China, then, bargaining theories suggest that although China brought to the bargaining process weaknesses as well as strengths, on the whole China's potential strengths were enviable. The combination of three features—the relatively centralized control of the economy, the absence of a national bourgeoisie, and the huge potential market—in one socialist country meant that China was better situated to control the terms of foreign investment than was any other developing socialist country considering foreign investment in the late 1970s and 1980s. Yet although China was able to offer both the "carrot" of the potential market and the "stick" of the extensive regulatory regime, China's socialism could neither change the rules of the bargaining norm nor eliminate the bargaining strengths of foreign investors. China could not unilaterally dictate the terms of investment, and was constrained especially by the need to provide a good environment for investment. The Chinese government's capacity to control the terms of investment was also influenced strongly by factors in its own domestic environment; the domestic political situation and the domestic economic structure both were important forces affecting China's bargaining strengths and the government's willingness to control foreign investment. The next section examines these internal factors that influenced the foreign investment policy.

THE EFFECT OF DOMESTIC POLITICS ON THE FOREIGN INVESTMENT POLICY

Two sets of domestic political issues are crucial to understanding the ability of China's socialist government to control foreign investment. The first set of issues concerns the dynamics of China's political elite and the influence of these dynamics on the policy. Specifically, it concerns the conflicts between reformers and conservatives over the "open" policy, the consensus that formed among various groups behind the original investment policy, and the shift in the relative power of reformers and conservatives throughout the 1980s. The second set of domestic political issues concerns the specific regulatory mechanisms available to Chinese leaders to control foreign investment in the 1980s. The Chinese reformers relied upon both new and old mechanisms of control over foreign investment, many of which were effective. But over the course of the decade, the will and capacity of the reformers to use these controls weakened (although it did not completely dissipate) particularly as the overall economic reform program reduced the role of the state in the economy. At the same time, traditional factors that have long undermined central control in China— *guanxi* (connections), bureaucratism, and localism—weakened the state's centralized controls over foreign investment.

The Divided Chinese Leadership and the Rise of Reformers

When Deng Xiaoping announced the "open" policy in late 1978, he did so in the face of mixed views within the leadership. As in many other realms, those who most supported the policy came into conflict with those who were wary of it. Analysts frequently interpret China's divisive leadership dynamic in terms of ideological tendencies.[25] The tendency view posits that three relatively distinct groups had coexisted in the high echelons of the CCP and the government bureaucracy since the late 1950s: "conservatives," "radicals," and "reformers." Historically, policies have swung between ideas advocated by each of the three groups or an alliance of two groups, creating policy cycles.[26]

Each of these three groups has at times been influential in the economic sphere since the 1949 revolution. Those labeled "radicals" found their way into leadership positions during the Cultural Revolution. They were wary of reliance upon foreign sources of development and espoused a vision of radical self-reliance and equalitarianism. Radicals have been in eclipse since the demise of Hua Guofeng in 1978, however, and were of little *direct* significance to the formulation of the "open" policy, although the specter of radical politics could not have been far from the minds of those formulating the policy.[27] "Conservatives" have been both prime supporters and beneficiaries of China's centralized economic structure. They, too, have been wary of dependence on the West as a source of development but, as we shall see, some of their concerns about greater economic ties to the West were met by the policy that was originally implemented. Conservatives were the dominant leadership force in the era of Soviet-style planning (1950s) and, in conjunction with reformers, were influential

during the late 1970s. Although they re-emerged in some realms following the crushing of the student-led demonstrations in the spring of 1989,
conservatives lost much of their earlier influence as the decade wore on,
while the reformers became more dominant. The reformers, under Deng
Xiaoping, initiated sweeping policy changes beginning in the late 1970s,
adopting methods that for China were unorthodox in order to foster economic efficiency and rapid industrial development. In particular, they advocated greater use of market forces in agricultural and industrial policy,
and more extensive participation in the international economy.[28]

Although tendency analysis has important explanatory power, the politics of foreign investment cannot be explained purely in terms of leadership divisions, for such a model ignores or dismisses evidence that members of different elite groups share a range of values. It ignores, for example, evidence that China's top leaders of the late 1970s and early 1980s,
regardless of ideological tendency, shared both a common formative history and a deep concern for protecting China's sovereignty. Substantial
evidence of compromise in economic policymaking also contradicts a pure
tendency view.[29] Moreover, a pure tendency view ignores that, although
different groups placed emphasis on different values (conservatives on economic order, radicals on egalitarianism and self-sufficiency, and reformers on efficiency), and differed with respect to trade-offs among these values, those in each group would prefer to enhance all the values of the
three groups *if* those values did not contradict each other; ideally, the core
values could all be maximized.[30] A more satisfactory interpretation of the
leadership dynamic behind the foreign investment strategy thus draws on
elements of both tendency and consensual views of Chinese politics, and
also recognizes the changes within and between groups over time.[31] The
combination of elements of these two views suggests that members of
different groups share a core set of values. Importantly, when the "open"
policy was initiated in 1979, reformers shared two of the same concerns
about foreign investment that the tendency model commonly attributes to
conservatives: protection of Chinese sovereignty, and maximization of
China's share of any benefits generated by foreign investment. Consensus
on the importance of these values led to a shared belief in the need for
strict controls over foreign capital.

Despite this consensus on the need for controls between conservatives
and reformers in the late 1970s and early 1980s, they were divided over,
first, the relative weight to be assigned to the dangers and benefits of the
"open" policy and, second, whether it was possible for China to guard
against the risks of foreign investment to protect the shared values.[32] Reformers placed a higher value on the potential economic benefits to be
gained from foreign direct investment (capital, technology, management
skills, and access to international markets), and were willing to go further

than conservatives to capture these benefits. They also asserted that the concerns about foreign contamination and loss of sovereignty they held in common with conservatives could and should be met by the tools of a socialist state. In contrast, conservatives, though anxious to promote modernization, were less certain of the value of foreign capital, technology, and management, and were more concerned that foreign investment would harm China.

It is essential to note that the original plan for foreign investment in the late 1970s attempted to satisfy the values of *both* promoting rapid growth and efficiency through efforts to absorb external capital and technology and, simultaneously, to guard against loss of control to outside forces: China would permit foreign investment, but only on terms over which the Chinese government maintained substantial control and captured a just share of the benefits. While conservatives were wary of the reformist *means* to modernization—foreign capital and technology—the solution of the reformers seemed to meet the conservative and reformist concern about control of the terms of investment. The reformist view that it could maximize the shared conservative and reformist value for Chinese control over the terms of investment provided the basic rationale for the policy. (This rationale is discussed further in chapter 2.) Thus, by offering a concrete vision for China's economy—something the conservatives did not do at the time—and by positing a way to meet the concerns about negative results of foreign investment—thereby blunting conservative criticism—the reformers were able to institute the "open" policy.

Although they did not mount a major effort to overturn the policy, conservatives continued through the early 1980s to raise questions about the danger of engagement with the outside world and the introduction of market forces. These questions served to keep up the pressure on reformers to maintain strong controls. Yet the leadership environment evolved, thereby changing the political dynamic and its effect on the "open" policy. Deng Xiaoping attempted gradually to change the configuration of elite conflict, to reduce the political obstacles posed by the conservatives. He attempted to transform the state elite and bureaucracy by introducing a group of younger cadres who were dependent for their own careers on the success of the economic reforms and, hence, were loyal to his program. Reflecting the reformist bias for expertise, the cadres promoted at all levels were to be better educated and more professionally competent than those in the previous cadre corps, many of whom had come to power during the Cultural Revolution on the basis of political loyalties to Mao. The influence of reformers extended to key state enterprises, including those that entered joint ventures, as managers closely tied to former policies were replaced with others who were more technically competent and sometimes formally trained. Deng also encouraged and obtained the retirement of older cadres in power, many of whom were conservatives or radicals associated with previous policies.[33]

As of 1983, Deng's efforts had reduced the overall influence of conservatives in Chinese politics, especially in the area of foreign economic policy. Although conservative-reformist conflict continued to exist on a number of important issues, it had greatly declined with regard to the foreign investment policy by 1983. In addition to the fact that the formulation of the policy tried to meet conservative concerns, two other factors led to the decline in conflict. As a result of Deng's political maneuvering, those bureaucracies that had primary control over foreign investment, especially the Ministry of Foreign Economic Relations and Trade (MOFERT), were for the most part controlled by reformers. Moreover, it appeared that, with the exception of concern over "unhealthy tendencies," conservatives became an even less virulent source of opposition to the policy over time.[34] This assessment was lent support, in retrospect, by the efforts to keep the "open" policy intact even after more conservative leaders returned to power in June 1989.

The one area where public pressure by conservatives remained concerned what were termed, generally, "unhealthy tendencies" (at various times called "spiritual pollution" and "bourgeois liberalization"). These included, for example, consumerism, smuggling, corruption, and prostitution. Concern over unhealthy tendencies was evident in the Campaign Against Spiritual Pollution (CASP) of 1983, in the Campaign Against Bourgeois Liberalization (CABL) in 1986, and in the second CABL that followed the events at Tiananmen in June 1989. Reformers, like conservatives, criticized unhealthy tendencies and associated them with the "open" policy (as discussed further in chapter 2). But, especially in the 1983 and 1986 campaigns, conservatives went further to suggest that these problems might warrant significant revision of the "open" policies. Reformers were determined that the broad scope of the campaigns not threaten the "open" policy. They argued that unhealthy tendencies in the cultural realm should not threaten the basic economic policy, and quickly squelched the campaigns.[35] By 1989, when conservatives had regained influence in many areas, criticisms of "bourgeois liberalization" were applied to foreign political and social norms, but largely avoided foreign economic ties.

As influential for the "open" policy as the decline of conservative opposition was another change in elite politics: the outlook of the reformist leadership itself evolved over time. As is discussed in more detail in chapter 3, the relative weighting by reformers of the desire for benefits of foreign investment, on the one hand, and cautions about negative results of such activity, on the other, changed to favor the former even more strongly. Several interrelated judgments on the part of the reformers supported this evolution: an increased desire for the benefits reformers perceived investment to bring; the view that China was absorbing too little foreign capital to capture those benefits; the knowledge that, with the decline of both the conservative leadership itself and its opposition to foreign investment, it was less risky *politically* to de-emphasize controls; and the knowledge that great disaster, particularly serious threats to national sovereignty, had not befallen China since the advent of the "open" policy. Thus, although the concerns the reformers had originally shared with conservatives did not completely dissipate, they were increasingly outweighed by the desire for the benefits of foreign investment.

The dynamic of China's ruling elite during the 1980s, then, influenced the policy in two basic ways. First, at the initiation of the policy, the need to meet the shared concerns of conservatives and reformers about possible negative results of foreign investment led to a policy that would incorporate strong controls on foreign investment and simultaneously would attempt to attract such investment. But, second, the changes over the course of the 1980s in the relative power of conservatives and reformers, as well as the changes in the views of both groups, created an environment where the emphasis on the need for benefits became pre-eminent, and set the stage for liberalization of the investment environment.

The Decline of Controls Available to the Leadership and Traditional Constraints on Central Controls

The issue of state controls over foreign investment is also an important part of the domestic political context of foreign investment. Since 1949, although different leadership groups used somewhat different policy tools, the state bureaucracy and the party organization had been the main vehicles for carrying out party directives. Whether by exhortation, directive, or material inducements, the state plan controlled producers. These bureaucratic methods were consistent with the historical precedent in China of a relatively centralized state apparatus, as well as with Leninist views of the socialist state. Moreover, especially during the Cultural Revolution but also at other times, the Chinese Communist Party had emphasized that an individual's "correct" (as defined by the party) thought and action should motivate, and was the barometer of, social change and economic development. Ideological persuasion, especially in the form of political study, was a primary means of leadership control over individuals and politics.[36]

Yet in the late 1970s and early 1980s, the reformers began to discuss and experiment with types of controls over politics, economics, and individuals other than those used by the Maoist regime. In particular, the period witnessed the beginning of a decline in the emphasis on traditional ideological and planning mechanisms of state control over society. The role of the plan was to be decentralized, and a limited degree of autonomy was to be allowed in economic and cultural realms. In legitimating greater autonomy, reformers also enhanced the legitimacy of expertise and experts. They argued that party- or state-defined "truths" should give way to "objective laws," which could be discovered by "seeking truth from facts," or looking to concrete circumstances to determine the proper course of action.[37] The reformist effort to inject certain "objective" economic laws, particularly comparative advantage and the division of labor, meant that economic control mechanisms increasingly took the form of market allocation and economic inducements (such as taxation) rather than central directives and planning. The limited adoption of rules of legal due process also reflected the new emphasis on objective laws. Reformers also asserted they would move away from reliance on ideological exhortation toward use of economic inducements for behavior; they repudiated many of the more extreme methods, particularly mass ideological campaigns and extreme politicization of the work force. This shift was in part an attempt by post-Mao leaders to reverse the decline in the party's own authority that had resulted from popular disillusion with its arbitrary use of power, particularly during the Cultural Revolution. The party sought to reassert its leadership role, but at the same time to limit its function to one of broad guidance in nonpolitical areas, particularly economic production. The discussion of reduction of state controls that was occurring in this period presaged an important overall decline in state controls, including many of those that the government applied to foreign investment, throughout the 1980s.

But despite some move away from "politics-in-command" and central planning, reformers did not totally repudiate statist controls. Statist economic controls over foreign direct investment remained, and the government continued to utilize ideological and political education, though at a less intensive level and in a more limited scope, in the effort to combat "unhealthy tendencies." Nonetheless, changes throughout the 1980s in state–society relations and, especially, changes in the mechanisms of state domination of the economy strongly affected the Chinese state's ability to control foreign investment. The government's capacity to control foreign investment relied in large part upon the use of the traditional tools of the state plan, the socialist bureaucracy, and the ideological leadership of the party, tools that were weakened in the overall economic reforms. The codification of new civil laws and use of regulation by the market replaced traditional controls in some realms.[38] But new controls designed to replace older ones were not directed consistently at the same end as the former controls: extensive state control over the economy. These changes in the traditional tools would diminish the comprehensiveness and effectiveness of the controls over foreign capital.

Central state control over the economy had never been total in China, even in the 1950s heyday of central planning. Several long-standing features of Chinese politics that had often undermined the state's ability to implement policies in the past persisted in the post-Mao era: *guanxi*, bureaucratism, and localism. The use of *guanxi* (or connections) in bureaucratic relations predated the 1949 revolution. This concept refers to networks of personal ties and obligations between people within and among organizations, and to decisions that are made or influence that is exerted on the basis of these networks. Governmental decisions or bureaucratic relations based on *guanxi* contrast with Weber's ideal-typical "rational-legal" model of bureaucracy, which separates private and official spheres, although elements of the two types may exist simultaneously in practice.[39] In theory, dependence on personal ties could supplement state control over enterprises, insofar as the state actors upon whom enterprises rely could exert authority via these informal channels. Yet *guanxi* generally functions poorly as a mechanism of central control. It is in essence an exchange relationship rather than a hierarchical one. Although *guanxi* may exist within the context of a hierarchy, obligations are incurred in two directions; authority exerted by officials over the economy via informal networks may work in the interest of local officials (who may themselves have their enterprise's money or their own reputation at stake) and not in the interest of the state or of socialist goals, as central authorities define them. Thus, the informal dynamic of *guanxi*, endemic to Chinese bureaucratic behavior, was positioned to dilute the hierarchical lines of authority upon which the Chinese leadership relied to control foreign investment.

Two other long-standing features of Chinese politics that had the potential to affect unified central control over foreign investment were bureaucratism and localism. Intrabureaucratic and central-local bargaining, which has been studied increasingly by scholars in recent years, is prevalent in the formulation and implementation of policy in China. With regard to the "open" policy in particular, the general presence of bargaining behaviors would lead us to expect that the various bureaucracies involved in approving and overseeing foreign investment projects would have differing interests in foreign investment activities, and would disagree over the parameters of an acceptable contract. Once formal bargaining is completed, moreover, controls may not be implemented fully by local officials or managers. Local controls could also counteract the efforts of the central government, causing contradictory standards to be set for investors.[40]

·   ·   ·

The complex political environment of post-Mao China therefore was positioned to strongly influence the Chinese government's ability to simultaneously attract and control foreign investment. The relationship between reformers and conservatives both at the outset of the policy and as it evolved during the 1980s, as well as the overall trends toward reform of state-society and state-economy relations, affected the political outlook on foreign investment. At the same time, the traditional political features of *guanxi*, bureaucratism, and localism, all of which have the capacity to work against unified, centralized control by the Chinese state, remained salient parts of post-Mao political life. These weaknesses in the unity of the socialist state were not unique to China, nor did they occur in China more than could be anticipated in other socialist states embarking on a similar foreign investment policy. Rather, all socialist states can be expected to exhibit such weaknesses, albeit in forms characteristic of that state. In particular, the decline in traditional state controls over the economy that in China has gone hand in hand with the decision to allow foreign investment can be expected elsewhere.[41] Moreover, patron-client ties, bureaucratism, and localism are far from unique to China. Weaknesses in the Chinese state's capacity to control foreign investment that arose from its domestic political dynamic, then, did not put China in a worse position to control the terms of foreign investment than other socialist countries.

THE ECONOMIC ENVIRONMENT FOR STATE CONTROL

In addition to the political environment, the economic environment both in China and internationally was positioned to influence the Chinese government's capacity to control foreign investment. As discussed previously, the economy was in one way a strong positive asset in attracting foreign investment, for the foreign perception of China's huge untapped domestic market was a bargaining chip Chinese negotiators could use to gain favorable investment terms. Yet despite these assets, a number of features common to developing countries, both socialist and nonsocialist, made the economic environment in which foreign investment occurred harsh, and provided significant disincentives for foreign investment. The nature and extent of these problems are introduced briefly here, and developed more fully in later chapters.[42]

At the most fundamental level of the economy, China's infrastructure had—and continues to have—serious problems. Although existing transportation facilities (roads, railways, airways, and ports) by and large covered the geographical area of the country, they did not have enough capacity to efficiently carry the volume of goods they had to transport over both short and long distances. The transport sector was also marked by managerial and technical inefficiency. China's economy further suffered from shortages of strategic goods. Energy (coal, oil, and electricity) in particular was in short supply throughout the 1980s. Provision of energy and other key industrial materials to both industry and consumers was irregular, a problem of both supply and transportation. At the same time, there was inefficient usage of energy and industrial products, further straining demand.[43] Under such conditions of shortage, the state plan served an important positive function to the extent that it was a more reliable means of providing needed inputs to those covered by the plan, including foreign-invested enterprises, than private procurement in poorly functioning markets.

The productivity performance of Chinese industrial labor in foreign-backed enterprises was mixed, with some foreign partners satisfied and others finding lower productivity than in a number of Asian countries with which China competes for investment.[44] Although wages (the basic wage, bonuses, and subsidies) paid to Chinese workers were comparatively low, correspondingly low productivity for skilled labor frequently removed much of the wage-based advantage. (This problem was less relevant for low-skilled labor used in assembly and processing production.) Moreover, the prevalent practice by local officials of levying extra labor "taxes" and fees for foreign-backed enterprises added labor-related costs to the originally competitive wage. High costs for skilled labor in China, and the generally low quality of Chinese goods by international standards, meant that China was not an attractive export base for most large TNCs. Managerial capacity in Chinese industry was also the source of problems. Formal management training declined during the Cultural Revolution (1966–1976), leaving uneducated a generation of young adults who normally would have moved into management positions during the 1980s. Moreover, those Chinese managers who received training before the Cultural Revolution were trained to operate under conditions of a planned economy, not an economy that relies upon domestic and international market signals. For both these reasons, the Chinese reform effort was hindered by the low level of management. Foreign-backed enterprises found it difficult to recruit Chinese managers trained in production and managerial techniques the investors wished to use, and who had experience producing for international markets.

The technical quality of goods produced in China was often relatively poor. National standards for grades, sizes, and so on, of production materials sometimes did not exist or, where they did exist, were not followed rigorously. Nor did existing national standards correspond to international standards. For many foreign investors, these problems of quality and standardization meant that the goods they produced in China were not easily exported. Even if those lower quality goods could be exported, foreign firms often would not readily put their brand name on substandard products. Moreover, the poor quality and standardization of goods produced in China's domestic market meant that it was difficult for foreign investors to utilize domestic sources of production inputs. Where they imported equipment and materials to fit their production specifications, they often found that the necessary parts and supports were unavailable in China. Problems of standardization and quality thus raised costs and lowered the competitiveness of more sophisticated Chinese joint venture goods on international or Asian markets.[45] Although the Chinese government made efforts to move toward greater standardization of production beginning in the early 1970s, the problem remained throughout the 1980s.

Perhaps the most difficult problem of China's economic environment for foreign investors during much of the decade was foreign exchange. China's domestic currency, *renminbi*, is nonconvertible, thereby preventing earnings derived from sales on the domestic market from being converted readily to hard currency. Moreover, the Chinese government was careful to maintain a high level of foreign exchange reserves, strongly curbing imports when reserves dropped to what they perceived to be dangerously low levels (as occurred in 1985). In addition to dealing with foreign exchange requirements established by the Chinese government (discussed in chapter 4), currency nonconvertibility meant foreign investors had to find other ways of earning the foreign exchange they required to import materials and repatriate profits. The government made some efforts to improve this situation, but it remained problematic in the eyes of many investors.

The difficulties in the economic environment would have been less severe for China if it were the only destination for foreign capital in the developing world or in Asia. But this was obviously not the case; despite the advantage of China's market, China was competing with other countries for foreign investment.[46] The competition among developing countries for foreign investment manifested itself in a competitive liberalization of those investment controls many countries had enacted in the 1960s and 1970s. This trend was evident in socialist countries (particularly countries in Eastern Europe, Angola, and Nicaragua), in nonsocialist countries (such as Indonesia, Guinea, and Mexico), and in mixed economies (such as India). Within Asia, developing countries competed for foreign investment on the basis of tax rates and customs treatment, for example.[47] This meant that China had to compete with other countries to provide an attractive environment—something difficult to do given the poorly developed domestic economy.

Overall, then, the difficult economic environment that investors in China faced could be expected to present disincentives for investment. The efforts of other developing countries, particularly in Asia, to provide competitive or more favorable terms also meant that, for some types of projects, investors had an alternative to China.

MOTIVATIONS OF FOREIGN INVESTORS AND POINTS OF CONFLICT
BETWEEN CHINESE AND FOREIGN INTERESTS

Bargaining models predict that, under the proper conditions, Chinese and foreign sides can reach agreement in negotiating over the terms of projects. Agreements are more difficult to reach, of course, when the goals and motivations of the two sides differ. By identifying the goals of foreign investors, and the discrepancies between these goals and those of the Chinese government, it is possible to identify potential points of conflict between the two sides. Analysis of where Chinese or foreign interests prevail can indicate how successful the state has been at controlling foreign investment. This section lays out the goals of foreign investors and identifies the major points on which these goals conflict with Chinese goals.

Foreign firms invest in China for many of the same reasons they invest in any overseas location, although some of the standard reasons are more important in China than they are in other locations.[48] During the 1980s, the foremost motivations for Western and Japanese TNCs to invest in China were the prospect of gaining access to what they perceived to be a huge domestic market in China and, reflecting the oligopolistic rivalry in the structure of many of these investors, preempting competitors from gaining a large share of that new market first.[49] For Western firms, the lure of the China market remained strong during the first several years of the foreign investment policy, to the advantage of the Chinese government. In the second half of the decade this view came more and more to be tempered—though not thoroughly negated—by greater understanding of the technical difficulties of operating in China's economy.

Because of the desire to gain access to China's domestic market, and because of the problems of international competition discussed previously, Western firms were not especially keen to use China as a base for exports. Even without these goals and problems, Western firms that already had strong market positions in Asia were unenthusiastic about exporting goods from China that would undercut their existing sales. Short-term profits also were not a major incentive for Western investors due to the recognition of inefficiencies of China's economic structure, and the fact that domestic markets had to be developed before substantial profits could be made there. These firms were willing to forgo immediate profits from the joint ventures themselves in exchange for the hope the ventures would offer them a "foot in the door." There was also a widespread view among Western firms that the Chinese would remember "old friends"— firms that had made a commitment to China's modernization even when the conditions were not optimal—and hence that losses in the short term would translate into long-term profits.[50]

Motivations of Japanese and Hong Kong investors differed somewhat from those of U.S. and European firms. Although Japanese firms were willing to engage in direct trade with China, and made tremendous profits doing so in the 1970s and 1980s, many were relatively less willing to engage in direct investment. The Japanese government also discouraged direct investment in China. Japanese firms had less faith than Western firms in the long-term profitability of joint ventures, and were skeptical that China's legal framework, despite China's continual addition of regulations, was adequate to safeguard investment. Japanese firms also believed they had a long-term reason to avoid direct investment in China: by transferring valuable technology and management skills they would be fostering the growth of a future dominant economic and political actor in the region. This reluctance by the Japanese to form joint ventures changed somewhat in the mid-1980s as the revaluation of the *yen* pushed up the price of Japanese exports, and Japanese manufacturers increasingly began to explore China as a location for lower cost manufacturing.[51]

Although many Hong Kong firms, like Western and some Japanese firms, wished to gain a foothold in the domestic market, they also sought immediate profits through lower costs for low-skilled labor and land, and a better labor supply than were available in Hong Kong. Some in the Hong Kong business community, also reflecting the notion of "old friends," believed investment would bring them better treatment when the PRC regains control of the colony in 1997. Much of the investment from Hong Kong was in small assembly and processing plants that produced simple goods, such as toys, textiles, plastic flowers, and handbags in Guangdong and Fujian provinces (including the Special Economic Zones—SEZs). These plants essentially represented a shifting of low-skill jobs from Hong Kong across the border to the SEZs and coastal provinces where, even with the frequent imposition of arbitrary local fees, wage rates for the low-skill workers were lower than in Hong Kong. Chinese sites also offered more factory space than was available in crowded, high-rent Hong Kong, allowing manufacturers to increase their capacity for orders and inventories. The majority of ventures with Hong Kong partners produced goods for re-export, rather than for sale in the Chinese domestic market. Given the extremely competitive Hong Kong business environment, Hong Kong investors were willing to move their operations with the prospects of relatively small savings.[52] It should be noted that some Hong Kong projects were fronts for Taiwanese and South Korean investors who, because of political restrictions, could not publicly invest in the mainland. Taiwanese and South Korean investment, which became more widespread beginning in 1988, seems to have been motivated by many of the same factors that motivated Hong Kong investment.

Although the reasons that foreign firms entered equity joint ventures rather than other forms of investment in China were often idiosyncratic, several factors stood out.[53] In a positive sense, the legal and policy environment for equity joint ventures was more well defined throughout the 1980s, and hence was somewhat less risky than other forms. Joint ventures also offered foreign firms more direct control over the technology they transferred than did simple licensing or sales agreements, in theory allowing firms to limit the dissemination of proprietary technology. They also allowed a degree of management control by expatriate managers, though of course not to the degree provided by wholly foreign-owned enterprises, and allowed investors to learn about Chinese markets from within China. Several negative factors tended to restrict the choice of foreign firms to equity joint ventures. Chinese negotiators often encouraged equity joint ventures over other forms. Although the joint venture policy was not a forced indigenization policy, the Chinese government viewed wholly foreign-owned operations less favorably until the late 1980s. Chinese policy to discourage imports at various times (such as in 1986) pushed U.S. and European companies immediately toward direct investment agreements rather than through a more standard sequence in which exports to the host country precede investments.[54]

There were clearly areas of strong compatibility between foreign goals for foreign investment and the Chinese goals of absorbing foreign capital, advanced technology and management skills, and opening export markets. Most obviously, both hoped joint ventures would be economically successful. Both had interests in promoting the use of Chinese materials rather than imports. That Western firms invested in joint ventures not for immediate profits but primarily as a means of building a presence for future access to Chinese markets might at first glance suggest that relatively few conflicts would occur over day-to-day operations of investments themselves, as foreign partners tried to learn about the Chinese market and to build long-term relationships and a good reputation in China. Yet the goals of these investors conflicted in a number of ways with those of the Chinese government. The most obvious, and probably most important, discrepancy was over the issue of access for foreign firms to China's domestic market. Investors' strong desire for such access conflicted with the desire of the reformers to have joint ventures export and open international markets for China, and to prevent joint ventures from creating a drain on foreign exchange. The difficulties of exporting that arose from China's economic infrastructure reinforced the bias of foreign investors against selling abroad. Conflicts also surrounded several other issues: the Chinese attitude that the balancing of foreign exchange was important conflicted with a foreign view that foreign exchange concerns should not hamper production; the Chinese desire to gain advanced foreign technology conflicted with the desire of most TNCs to limit the dissemination of their proprietary technology; and Chinese efforts to learn foreign management skills in an environment of equality conflicted somewhat with the typical desire of foreign investors to manage their overseas operations. On these and a number of other issues, the discrepant interests of the two sides translated into a source of pressure from foreign investors on the reformers to change controls to better meet the goals of investors. The full range of these conflicts will become evident with the detailed exploration of China's controls on foreign investment in chapters 4 and 5.

CONCLUSION: THE PROSPECTS FOR CHINESE CONTROL OVER FOREIGN INVESTMENT— THE CRITICAL CASE OF CHINA

The previous discussion of the external and internal factors shaping China's joint venture policy—the bargaining strengths and controls available to China, the economic environment for foreign investment, the motivations and goals of foreign investors, and domestic politics—sets forth a framework for understanding China's capacity to control foreign capital. The discussion of host country bargaining strengths and tools of control suggests that both capitalist and socialist developing countries have available to them a number of bargaining strengths and tools to control foreign direct investment, such as controls on foreign currency flows and requirements for local ownership. Despite these strengths and tools, however, a number of studies have found that capitalist developing countries have not been successful in formulating and implementing effective controls. Some studies have prescribed socialism, arguing that it will equip the state with additional tools to control investment and additional bargaining strengths to employ in negotiations with foreign investors. According to these studies, socialism also should allow a host state to avoid the problem, encountered by nonsocialist states, of a national bourgeoisie or colonial elite that dilutes state bargaining power. If this prescription is correct, China in the 1980s should have been well positioned to accomplish its goal of simultaneously absorbing and controlling foreign investment. Its position was further enhanced by the fact that it, more than any other developing country, possessed a crucial "carrot" with which to lure investors, a huge potential domestic market. China's bargaining strengths and tools were of course not absolute, but even so the country was in a better position than virtually any other developing socialist country to control the terms of foreign investment. As such, the Chinese case provides an excellent "critical case study" of whether socialism enhances the bargaining power of developing countries to the degree that they can assert the significant degree of control they hope for over the terms of investment.[55]

The bargaining strengths and tools available to China did not, by themselves, determine China's ability in the late 1970s and 1980s to carry out the strategy of simultaneously absorbing and controlling foreign investment; the three other factors discussed in this chapter influenced the policy as well. Foreign investors had their own motivations for investment, which determined in large part the areas in which they would resist controls. With regard to the domestic environment, the poor infrastructure, relatively poor labor and managerial skills, the poor quality of output, and the fact that China faced stiff competition for investment from its Asian neighbors all harmed the attractiveness of China as an investment destination. These problems were by no means unique to China, but they nevertheless were a disincentive to investors. Moreover, although the size and perceived attractiveness of China's domestic market helped mitigate against these perceived flaws, this attraction in itself caused pressures. The goals of Western and Japanese investors to gain access to this market conflicted with the Chinese goal of encouraging the foreign sector to export.

The discussion of domestic politics suggests that the nature of the Chinese leadership elite also had a powerful effect on the equity joint venture policy. Indeed, a complex political dynamic was played out during the late 1970s and the 1980s. In the late 1970s, a delicate accommodation was reached between conservatives and reformers over the strategy for foreign investment. Although the two groups differed in their valuation of the risks and benefits of investment, both agreed that if investment should be allowed it must be controlled. This accommodation laid the foundation for the establishment of a strict investment environment in the late 1970s and early 1980s. The forces behind the reformer-conservative accommodation evolved in two major ways during the 1980s, however: the conservative source of resistance to foreign direct investment declined; and the reformers, though not abandoning most of their concerns about foreign investment, came to value such investment more highly and became sensitive to the disincentive effect they perceived controls to have on the volume of investment China was attracting. As a result of these two domestic political trends, the impetus for controls was greatly weakened. The policy was further affected by the decline in traditional controls of the Chinese socialist state that came as part of the economic reforms. As will be discussed in chapters 3, 4, and 5, the change in the leadership's outlook, and in particular the disappointment of reformers over the volume of foreign capital flowing into China, played a crucial role in the changes that occurred during the 1980s in the policies toward equity joint ventures.

Given the significance of the domestic political forces, not only in creating the initial set of controls over foreign investment, but also in the impact of their change over time, it is important to examine the origins and contents of these views in greater depth. That examination is the goal of the following chapter.

Chapter Two

THE CHINESE OUTLOOK
AT THE OUTSET OF THE
FOREIGN INVESTMENT POLICY

While learning advanced [foreign] science and
technology, China will on no account import the
capitalist system, which is built on the exploitation
of man by man, or its decadent ideology
and way of life.
—Xinhua, "Socialist Road Fundamental to
China's Modernization"

We can cooperate with capitalism economically but,
politically and ideologically, we should by no
means accept decadent capitalist elements.
We should wage a thoroughgoing and protracted
struggle against them.
—Shen Shi, "Views on a Number of Issues in
Building Special Economic Zones"

IN LEGITIMIZING the use of foreign investment, the reformers argued that, in contrast to the past or to other developing countries, the Chinese socialist state had the capability to guard against the perceived negative effects, while absorbing the benefits. Despite the newfound justification for using foreign capital, the lessons the post-Mao leadership drew from China's experience with foreign powers in the nineteenth and early twentieth centuries left it, in the late 1970s, with a strong legacy of concerns about the potential negative impact of foreign direct investment. This legacy shaped the outlook of reformers and conservatives toward China's engagement in the international economy, and led to the expression of concrete concerns about foreign investment. This chapter examines this historical legacy and how it was manifested in the leadership's view of the outside world and of foreign investment during the early years of the policy. It also analyzes the ideological reformulations the government used to justify foreign investment in reaction to—and sometimes in spite of—these legacies.

THE HISTORICAL LEGACY OF
FOREIGN AGGRESSION AND CHINA'S RESPONSES

In the spectrum of alternating dynastic grandeur and corrosion that characterizes Chinese history, China in the early nineteenth century fell toward the latter end of the spectrum; the era was characterized by imperial corruption, overpopulation, famine, and rebellion. The Qing court was not only unable to deal effectively with internal problems, it was at a loss for how to resist incursions by a Western world that, in the 1830s, for the first time posed a serious threat to China.[1]

Foreign pressures, in conjunction with the domestic forces of decline, sparked two major kinds of reaction in China. These reactions, in various forms and degrees, continue to manifest themselves in post-Mao China. The first reaction was anti-foreignism, which much later evolved to incorporate anti-imperialism as well. It was characterized by an extreme hostility toward a foreign political, military, and economic presence in China and, as exemplified by the Boxer Rebellion (1898–1901), was often mass-based.[2] The second type of reaction was embodied in the late-nineteenth-century intellectual movement that called for China's "self-strengthening" against foreign aggression through selective use of foreign ideas and goods. China's traditional disregard for foreign "barbarians" was replaced, for some elites, by the perception that the best strategy for building a powerful nation was to adapt certain positive elements of foreign systems to China's own strengths. Self-strengtheners at the end of the nineteenth century introduced the ambiguous *ti-yung* formula, which called for Chinese learning as the essence (*ti*) of modernization, but for incorporation of foreign learning for practical use (*yung*). Although the legacy of self-strengthening was submerged during much of the Maoist era, both reactions have constituted highly influential legacies for the post-Mao government's attitude toward the outside world.

The Historical Legacy of Foreign Military, Political, and
Economic Encroachment in China

When the Qing court attempted to suppress the profitable opium trade with South Asia and the West in the 1830s, Britain's military response demonstrated the weakness of the Qing government and the strength of foreign resolve to force China into the arena of international trade. With the First Opium War (1839–1842), a period of extended military and political encroachment by foreigners began, and economic encroachment continued through the opium trade. The aggressive foreign stance was codified in the 1840 Treaty of Nanjing, the first in a series of "unequal treaties" between foreign and Qing governments. Although during this period foreign powers never came dangerously close to ousting the Qing rulers, the pattern of interaction nevertheless was one in which foreign powers demanded, and the Qing government conceded, terms that increased foreign authority over crucial aspects of Chinese political and economic life and weakened imperial rule.[3] The Qing government was forced to cede to foreigners sovereign rights to strategic Chinese territories and authority over economic activity. The Treaty of Nanjing, signed with and essentially dictated by Britain, levied indemnities against the Qing regime, forced the cession of Hong Kong Island, and opened the first five treaty ports (Guangzhou, Xiamen, Fuzhou, Ningbo, and Shanghai).

After the Nanjing Treaty, China was subsequently forced to grant privileges similar or identical to those claimed by Britain in 1840 to France, Belgium, Sweden, Norway, Russia, and the United States, all of whom had acquired "most favored nation" status.[4] In the aftermath of the joint Qing-foreign repulsion of Taiping forces from Shanghai during the 1850s, moreover, China was forced to give up authority over local tariffs to American and British officials, giving foreigners further control of maritime customs. The Shanghai International Settlement and French Concessions were also opened at this time. Foreigners gained extraterritorial political authority in these areas, thereby excluding China as the sovereign power. Foreigners further demanded large indemnities, the opening of eleven additional treaty ports (including Tianjin and interior ports along the Yangtze River), and a number of other authorities as terms of settlement for the Second Opium War (1856–1860). Later, the Sino-British Yantai (Chefoo) Convention opened four more port as well as certain interior areas to foreigners. By the end of the century, Western governments controlled most of the key port cities along China's coast, as well as many interior areas.[5] Japan, long considered by Chinese dynastic rulers to be a mere vassal state, began in the latter part of the nineteenth century to demand treatment on par with Western governments. These demands reached new strength in the Treaty of Shimonoseki, which settled the 1894–1895 Sino-Japanese War. This treaty followed the familiar formula imposing territorial concessions—China ceded Taiwan, the Pescadore Islands, and the Liaodong Peninsula—and huge indemnities. It also granted to the Japanese rights to build industrial plants in the treaty ports. Again, the economic privileges accrued to the other foreign powers involved.

Foreign military aggression continued well into the twentieth century, and was aided by national disintegration and the outbreak of warlordism that followed the overthrow of the Qing Dynasty in 1911.[6] For example, Russia and Japan, in secret treaties concluded with each other in 1907, partitioned Manchuria into spheres of influence.[7] The large-scale Japanese invasion and occupation of Manchuria in 1931, and the eventual spread of the Japanese to other areas, further entrenched foreign influ-

ence. Even as late as 1945, the foreign powers sanctioned foreign occupa-
tion of China: the Yalta Pact negotiated between Britain, the Soviet
Union, and the United States opened the way for Soviet occupation of
Manchuria.[8]

Foreigners frequently used military and political means to secure economic benefits. Most important, they used "unequal treaties" and their
extraterritorial status in the treaty ports to gain economically. Foreign
public and private interests gained directly from indemnities that were
imposed by foreign governments under the Sino-Japanese War treaty
and, later, the Boxer Protocol (1901), for example. Moreover, starting
with the 1858 Treaty of Tianjin, foreign trade vessels gained authority to
carry domestic trade along the Chinese coast and inland waterways (cabotage). Unequal treaties and the treaty ports also became the primary windows for foreign economic activity in the form of trade and investment.
Economic penetration in the form of foreign direct investment in China
was fairly negligible until after the Sino-Japanese War (1894–1895). (One
estimate places total American investment in China in 1875 at only $7
million.) After the war, and reflecting the *ti-yung* strategy, the Qing government began to encourage limited foreign investment and partnerships
in mining and railways in the belief that investment would aid construction of the national economy and help rebuild China's ability to meet foreign threats. During the 1902–1914 period, foreign investment rose from
a total of $503 million to $1.06 billion, and reached a peak of $2.68 billion
in 1936. Japan and Britain continued as the largest investors throughout,
with 50% and 35%, respectively. Foreign investment projects at this time
included infrastructure (railways, transport, coal mining, and pig iron),
services (banking, real estate, and trade), utilities, and manufacturing.
Prior to 1937, 70.2% of total foreign direct investment was in trade, finance, real estate, and general government loans, while 29.8% was in
communication and transportation, manufacturing, mining, and public
utilities, although the share that went into manufacturing (especially textiles) increased over time. Foreign capital was concentrated in Shanghai
and northeast China; these two areas accounted for over 80% of investment in the mid-1930s.[9]

The economic impact of foreign economic activity in China during this
period has been debated extensively outside of China. The dominant view
among American economists who have studied foreign economic activity
in pre-revolutionary China is that its impact on significant economic indicators was likely positive but, in any case, was small. Moreover, some
have argued that even though the volume of investment increased following the 1895 Sino-Japanese War, the overall inflow of foreign capital to
China was low compared with foreign investment in other countries at
that time.[10] More important for this study than the absolute volume and

impact of trade or investment during the treaty port era is the Chinese *perception* that these activities had harmful consequences, and the perception (generally held both inside and outside of China) that they were based on illegitimate means and infringed on China's sovereign rights. As the post-Mao leadership (both reformers and conservatives) read the history of foreign involvement in the economy (including the history of joint ventures and wholly foreign-owned enterprises), it was the negative impact that dominated the texts and their attention.

The government perceived foreign economic activity to have harmed China in a number of ways.[11] For example, indemnity payments placed a serious burden on the Qing government's finances. The sting was felt even more—and raised strong resentment—when the government had to borrow from foreign governments and banks to meet indemnity demands. Loans to meet indemnity payments were made under the condition that China guarantee them with revenues from the government salt monopoly and the customs service (which earlier treaties had placed under foreign authority). This extended foreign claims on Qing fiscal resources even more.[12] The right to cabotage, obtained in the Treaty of Tianjin, was perceived by the Chinese as harmful to both China's finances and sovereignty; by giving foreign traders greater access to inland markets, it allowed foreigners a right that is usually restricted under international law to domestic carriers. Japan's possession of China's important enterprises in the occupied areas, and placing of all joint-run enterprises under Japanese jurisdiction, were perceived as further encroachments on China's economy, as was Japan's grant to non-Chinese courts of a role in interpreting contracts and disputes in joint companies. By assuming the privileges secured by the Japanese following the Sino-Japanese War, Western corporations also began to invest in manufacturing joint ventures and wholly owned enterprises in the treaty ports. Because foreign corporations situated in these concessions held extraterritorial rights, they were out of reach of the weak Chinese government's authority. Foreign mining corporations, for example, were registered under the corporation law of the treaty signatories, and as such they were not subject to Chinese law. Qing control over the foreign sector of the Chinese economy eroded even further as foreigners used political and criminal means for economic gain.[13]

Within jointly run enterprises set up at this time, the Chinese partners had little authority. In most cases the foreign side retained effective managerial control, even where Chinese partners held majority equity.[14] The weakening Qing government, in the face of loss of control in the foreign areas, abolished in 1902 prohibitions on foreign management and foreign majority ownership that had been designed to prevent foreigners from controlling Chinese corporations. The result was that non-Chinese agents gained control of mining and railway construction industries. Foreign governments passed additional laws stipulating that expatriates should manage foreign operations established in China.[15] Finally, Chinese analysts argued that the level of profits returned to foreigners who invested in China were excessive, and a further sign of foreign exploitation. This is supported by some studies in the West, including one that argues that the capital inflow was only 57% of the capital outflow from 1902 to 1931, and hence that there was a significant net outflow.[16]

In 1929, the Nationalists gradually began to re-assert a degree of control by negotiating tariff autonomy. During World War Two, they secured abrogation of the "unequal treaties" and concluded equal and reciprocal treaties with Britain and the United States, which were interested in obtaining support against Japan. More substantial state control over foreign economic activity was achieved only after the defeat of the Japanese in 1946, and the gradual consolidation of the communist government beginning in 1949. A foreign presence by capitalist investors in China continued even after the revolution, but on terms that reflected increasing capacities of the newly formed government to control investment. Prior to 1967, the PRC government and overseas Chinese partners operated over 100 enterprises involving private foreign capital. These enterprises were established in 1951 in Guangdong and Fujian provinces, and in Tianjin and Shanghai. Although most catered especially to the demand of overseas Chinese for special goods, there were also textile and paper mills, rubber factories, sugar refineries, and hydroelectric plants. The ventures were tax exempt, but allowed only limited profit repatriation and, after 1967, paid no dividends and eventually closed. No longer able to operate profitably, foreign firms withdrew.[17] The policy was even more restrictive for Western firms than for overseas Chinese partners. Until 1954, the Chinese government had engaged in a policy of what one scholar has called "hostage capitalism" toward Western business interests. Under this policy, the government refused to permit foreign businesses to close with compensation. Simultaneously, through wage, tax, and other policy levers, the government reduced the profit-making capabilities of the firms. To gain closure permits, foreign firms had to transfer funds from abroad to China, a form of "reverse compensation." Through these measures, jobs for Chinese workers were protected and paid at the expense of foreign firms, and firms accrued liabilities that could eventually offset assets when China was ready to socialize the economy.[18]

China's experience with Soviet participation in the postrevolutionary economy was more mixed. On the one hand, joint stock companies that had been formed with the Soviet Union under protection of the unequal treaties were dissolved by 1955, when full ownership returned to China. On other projects, the Chinese invited new aid from the Soviet Union, which was considered an allied socialist country, in order to spur development under the First Five-Year Plan. The Soviet government sent complete sets of equipment (including technical blueprints), monetary aid, and hundreds of technical and management advisors to help with more than 300 projects, including the building of hydroelectric power and heavy industrial plants. The Chinese government even entered into joint ventures with the USSR to develop civil aviation, mineral, oil, and nonferrous metal industries, and received technical and financial assistance from Eastern European countries.[19]

The Chinese government turned away from the Soviet model in the late 1950s. Tensions grew between the Chinese and Soviets on a number of political and ideological fronts, as well as over the economic results of cooperation. In the ensuing Sino-Soviet split, the Soviets suddenly withdrew from China their technicians and personnel, who took many of the blueprints for numerous half-completed projects with them. Chinese leaders made the best of a bad situation and launched a new development program, arguing that the Soviet emphasis on capital-intensive and urban-oriented production did not fit China's labor-rich, agricultural economy. They also were critical of the results of technology transfer efforts, finding that the complete sets of Soviet technical equipment that had been transferred were poorly absorbed and required continual Soviet aid to keep them operative. In the eyes of some Chinese, technology transfer became inextricably associated with dependence on foreign imports.[20] Others complained that the return on investment in joint Sino-Soviet projects was too low. Although post-Mao Chinese analysts infrequently cited this experience, the reformers and conservatives could not but have been aware that their most recent episode with intense foreign involvement in their economy was costly and left them highly vulnerable.[21]

Foreign political and economic activity in China was thus extensive after the Opium Wars. Although the experiences were varied in the seriousness of their impact on China, the Chinese perception of these actions has been that they were negative. These experiences left in the dominant ideology the view that interaction with foreigners was potentially very harmful for China and must be regarded with suspicion.

Chinese Reactions to Foreign Incursions: Anti-Foreignism and Anti-Imperialism, and "Self-Strengthening"

The economic and political activities of foreigners raised two fundamental responses from within China: anti-foreignism, which evolved into anti-imperialism, and the desire for "self-strengthening." Anti-foreign attitudes developed in China on a large scale during the second half of the nineteenth century, and were expressed frequently in mass demonstrations and violence against foreigners. The oft-noted attitude that Chinese culture is superior to foreign cultures has a long tradition in China, but virulent anti-foreignism first became widespread as a mass force by the 1860s, and was especially strong in the Boxer Rebellion (1898–1901). Although in the Boxer Rebellion attacks were made primarily on churches and missionaries, the underlying conflict was not merely with foreign religions, but also with the general threat to Chinese culture.[22]

Following the Boxer Rebellion, anti-foreign activity was redirected from religious and cultural realms toward economic and political realms; anti-foreignism in the early twentieth century increasingly was characterized by anti-imperialism—the desire for an end to the economic and political presence of foreign powers in China—and calls for equality with other nations. Early in the twentieth century, the Chinese government and, increasingly, the gentry demanded restoration of China's rights to control railroads, mines, and maritime customs, and expressed great frustration when such restoration did not occur. Hostility toward foreign enterprises became even stronger during the late 1910s and 1920s. Protests by intellectuals and students against imperialism in general, and the treaty port system, foreign financial power, and foreign investment in particular, continued as part of the May Fourth Movement, which began in 1919. Gentry and merchant classes, and eventually workers, also opposed the competitive strength foreign businesses gained under the protection of the unequal treaties. They viewed the foreign sector as a threat to domestic enterprises, and encouraged "buy Chinese" boycotts of foreign products.[23]

Criticism of economic aggression, as well as military, political, and psychological aggression, were major tenets of the Nationalists under Sun Yat-sen and, later, Chiang Kai-shek. Indeed, as part of the overall economic plan during the Republican period, especially during the anti-Japanese war and the postwar period, the Nationalists argued that foreign investment, although it was to be allowed, must be regulated to meet the goals of the government.[24] Anti-imperialism mixed with nationalism was also central to the Chinese Communist Party's (CCP) ideology. Like the Nationalists, the CCP conceived of imperialism as the force underlying China's economic, military, and cultural subordination to the foreign powers. But unlike Sun and Chiang, and in line with Lenin and the Comintern, Mao Zedong based his understanding of imperialism on analysis of a global class struggle underlying "monopoly capitalism." In Mao's view, imperialism worked to turn China into a semifeudal and semicolonial society.[25]

Mao's solution was to carry out two inextricable revolutions: the first, a "bourgeois democratic" revolution to overthrow domestic feudal classes (primarily the landed gentry and rich peasants), and the second, a national, anti-imperial revolution to overthrow foreign interests. During and after these revolutions, the CCP drew on anti-imperialist ideology, particularly "anti-U.S. imperialism," as a rallying point in both foreign and domestic politics. Mao's "paper tiger" theory of U.S. imperialism—the view that, despite their terrifying appearance, imperialist forces were basically weakening and were for China more a problem of psychology than reality—implied some confidence in postrevolutionary China's capacity to fight against imperialism. Yet his prescription for handling foreign imperialists, for the most part, consisted of dissociating from them externally and struggling against their domestic counterparts. His policy of self-reliance rejected economic cooperation with capitalist nations or corporations as exploitative (although, as noted previously, a small degree of Western and overseas Chinese investment remained through the 1950s and 1960s). The assertion made during the Cultural Revolution (1966–1976) that the presence of capitalist elements within China could bring about "reversion" to capitalism heightened antagonism toward contacts with "imperialists."

The second reaction that grew out of the foreign presence in the nineteenth century was "self-strengthening," the archetype being the self-strengthening movement of the late Qing (1860–1894).[26] Unlike the anti-foreign reaction, which had strong mass backing, self-strengthening was an elite reaction led by a handful of reformist officials. The catchphrase of the movement, ti-yung—Chinese learning as the essence (ti), foreign learning for practical use (yung)—embodied the desire to maintain Chinese culture (consistent with anti-foreignism) but at the same time to use technical skills and products developed in the West to fight the West and save China. The self-strengtheners emphasized, first, the use of foreign technology and advisors, but not investment, to modernize armaments. They later stressed a more general development of China's infrastructure industries and railways, and especially the improvement of China's navy.

The immediate cause of failure of the self-strengthening movement was opposition by the Empress Dowager Cixi. But the movement failed in more than a political sense; even while intact, it also failed to achieve its goals. The emphasis on foreign imports and advisors was not matched by efforts to ensure that the technology was absorbed. Training of Chinese technicians fell short both in terms of the quality of training and the numbers of people trained. The program was neither systematic enough nor carried far enough to meet the foreign threat successfully. More fundamentally still, there were problems inherent in the ti-yung formulation itself. The point at which foreign technology and learning would begin to impinge upon the Chinese ti was a highly ambiguous one. The determination of this point and decisions as to the costs to China's essence of increasing the foreign presence, were subjective judgments, subject to political manipulation.

Despite its failure as a policy in the late nineteenth century, the movement initiated among many Chinese intellectuals the belief that Western (and Japanese, eventually) ideas and techniques could be used simultaneously to meet the foreign challenge and to modernize China. Self-strengthening re-emerged, albeit in a somewhat different guise, in the nationalist May Fourth Movement in the form of Chen Duxiu's calls to adopt Western science and democracy ("Mr. Science" and "Mr. Democracy") to modernize China. Mao Zedong, too, despite his later calls for extreme self-reliance, in 1956 endorsed the idea that China must "study all the good points of foreign countries, their politics, their economics, their science and technology, and their literature and art."[27]

THE REFORMIST OUTLOOK

The legacy of these two reactions to the period of foreign intervention, anti-foreignism and anti-imperialism, and self-strengthening, strongly influenced the outlook of both conservatives and reformers at the time they formulated the foreign investment policy, and were clearly manifested in the strategy of simultaneously absorbing and controlling foreign capital. The reformist view that the positive elements of foreign investment may be distilled from the negative elements had obvious, but unacknowledged, parallels with the *ti-yung* formula of the self-strengtheners. Indeed, the comments of one nineteenth-century advocate of this strategy could be applied readily to express the post-Mao reformers' version of self-strengthening: "[W]e should send people to travel to all countries to enlarge their points of view and enrich their store of information, to observe the strengths and weaknesses, the rise and fall of other countries; to adopt all the good points of other nations and to avoid their bad points from the start."[28] Just as the idea of self-strengthening kept a tenacious hold in China, so too did the ambiguity of its two goals: protection of Chinese essence and modernization using Western norms, for the self-strengtheners or, in present terms, obtaining the benefits of foreign help without the costs. The ambiguity of the self-strengthening movement presaged the difficult question that ultimately had to be faced by the reformers: how could China maximize both goals, and where would it need to suffer costs in exchange for benefits?

Anti-imperialist analysis of past aggression also influenced reformers and conservatives as they conceived the foreign investment policy. These historical sentiments continued to underlay suspicions about engaging in activities with foreign capitalists, and motivated the desire to guard against potential negative results of foreign investment. Hu Yaobang, as party secretary, made it clear that lessons from the post–Opium War era continued to be relevant for post-Mao China when he claimed in 1985, on the fortieth anniversary of the Japanese invasion, that it would be many decades before China would forget Japan's pre-1945 role. Another Chinese analyst of foreign investment in the 1980s also recognized the importance of the historical experience in his statement that "reviewing the more than half century before Liberation, Chinese-foreign joint ventures under unequal treaties were not handled with equality and mutual benefit, but rather [reflected] imperial plunder and exploitation of the Chinese people's blood vessel."[29]

That leaders embraced some elements of the anti-imperialist reaction in the early years of the "open" policy was evident at the initiation of the policy in the cautious view of foreign investment and in the espousal of some of the values that were promoted during the Maoist era. Key among the values expressed by the post-Mao leadership were commitments to promote economic "self-reliance" (albeit in a reformulated version), sovereign independence and equality for China, socialist economic development, and "socialist spiritual civilization." In addition, the leadership's outlook was characterized by a reluctance to wholeheartedly embrace all elements of foreign systems.

Self-reliance (*zili gengsheng*) has been a flexible term in postrevolutionary China, and has been used to mean different things at different times.[30] Proponents of self-reliance during the Cultural Revolution decade prescribed a model for economic development that, by isolating China from exploitative capitalist and foreign forces, was to evenly raise the economic standard of the population as a whole. They believed China would achieve development by depending on the labor and talent of the Chinese people, and by intensively mobilizing local resources behind the accumulation of capital and the development of indigenous technology. As will be seen in the next section, the reformers refashioned the Maoist concept of self-reliance to legitimate some engagement in the international economy in the late 1970s and early 1980s. Yet even the reformulated concept of self-reliance continued to limit China's interactions with the international economy, for it continued to stipulate that specific uses of capital and technology would be decided upon within China and according to China's needs, as determined by the government. Foreign capital and technology should enhance the indigenous capacity for production, exports, investment, and growth. Simultaneous with using foreign technology, China also would continue to develop its own technology. The aim was to maintain the foreign sector in a subordinate position, to "make foreign things serve China" in the *ti-yung* tradition. Although there were tensions between the goal of self-reliance and the use of foreign capital and technology, as long as China relied primarily on its own resources, the two were not considered incompatible.[31]

China's insistence that it be dealt with according to the principles of independence and "equality and mutual benefit" (*pingdeng huli*) in economic and military affairs with foreigners was another key element of the post-Mao outlook. These two principles have been central tenets of post-revolutionary Chinese foreign policy generally, and were retained in the post-Mao strategy of integration into the international economy. The great sensitivity to maintaining independence clearly reflected the memory of past foreign aggression. The centrality of this value to China's "open" policy was highlighted by the reformist assertion that political independence underlies China's very ability to gain effectively from participation in the international economy without suffering great exploitation. Thus, political independence was considered necessary for modernization. The goal of maintaining equality for China reflected a desire to avoid China's subordination, or the appearance of subordination, to other countries, as leaders perceived to have occurred during the era of "unequal treaties." Similarly, the call for "mutual benefit" reflected in large part the view that the vast majority of China's experiences with foreigners from 1840 to 1949 worked to China's detriment. "Equality and mutual benefit" also expressed nationalist pride: "As long as [these values] are not infringed upon, we cannot say that the dignity of socialism has been infringed upon."[32]

A third element of the post-Mao outlook was that use of foreign capital should support the commitment to building China's own version of socialism—"socialism with Chinese characteristics"—and in the long run, to building communism.[33] Specifically, the belief was that socialism must be achieved in both the material and the "spiritual" realms. At the material level, the transition to communism and its principle of distribution according to need was seen to require a high level of development of production forces and an abundance of material wealth. Thus, in Deng Xiaoping's view, "the fundamental task of the socialist phase [of economic construction was] to develop the productive forces" and create wealth for the country and for individuals.[34] The "open" policy in this view contributes to socialist construction because it utilizes modern technology and organization to strengthen industry and agriculture, and hence quickens the pace of development. Yet at the same time all plans for socialist construction must accommodate China's special characteristics, for example, a poor infrastructure and a large population with limited arable land, and must not be dictated by foreign needs.[35] Other fundamental components of socialism, such as the predominance of social ownership and the state sector, distribution according to work, a substantial role for the planned economy (albeit a more decentralized planning system and wide use of markets), and extensive welfare functions, were to be retained.[36]

The need to build a "socialist spiritual civilization" was espoused by both reformers and conservatives, although, as discussed in chapter 1, the latter group at various times during the 1980s tried to use campaigns against "unhealthy tendencies" as a means to undermine the economic reforms pushed by the former. The task of building a "socialist spiritual civilization" was seen to involve fighting against corrupting values that accompanied increased exposure to the outside world and domestic use of markets. Discipline, self-sacrifice for the good of others and the state, collectivism, moral and professional integrity, patriotism, "socialist humanitarianism," hard work, and good manners were often listed as communist values. Education, science, and public health also were emphasized. Party members, who particularly should exemplify this behavior, were to lead the creation of a spiritual society through ideology and propaganda work.[37] The concept of "socialist spiritual civilization" also encompassed notions of what communist morality was *not*: liberal bourgeois morality or "corrupt capitalist ideology." Specifically, it was not characterized by overemphasis on self-interest, competition, or profit-seeking, or by a factional mentality among leaders. Nor did it encourage a society where "the relationship between man and man is one between the exploiter and the exploited and money is everything."[38]

Breaking with the orthodox Marxist view that superstructural development at a given stage grows out of substructural development at that stage, and instead reflecting the Maoist view, the Chinese leadership asserted that a communist party should promote communist values in the superstructure even prior to the transition to communism. Indeed, some active promotion of communist morality in the superstructure, especially among party members, was viewed as a spur to economic construction.[39] According to the reformist view, efforts to promote communist morality did not mean that political or ideological work should take precedence over economic work in the society at large; yet the government believed there was no reason to expect that even when a socialist material civilization was completed, China would "spontaneously get abundant spiritual wealth and lofty moral values" without consciously instilling the values appropriate to a high level of socialism.[40] Consequently, the promotion of communist values was viewed to be an important task for the party. Two further points about efforts to promote a "socialist spiritual civilization" are worth noting. First, although not stated publicly by the Chinese leadership, the party's emphasis on upholding state-defined morals can also be seen as an effort to protect the party's authority as arbiter of national values. Second, espousal of the idea that it was the party's duty to foster the growth of "socialist spiritual civilization" contradicted the simultaneous effort (discussed in chapter 1) of the reformers to remove the party role from everyday life and move away from "politics-in-command." Indeed, the efforts to combat "unhealthy tendencies" and build a "socialist spiritual civilization" in effect were carved out as an exception to this general reform.

Anti-foreign and anti-imperialist concerns, directed primarily against the economic threat posed by Western capitalism, remained a central part of the leadership's outlook. Although anti-imperialist rhetoric and anti-foreign demonstrations appeared less frequently after the mid-1970s, evidence of continued anti-imperialist sentiment surfaced at the mass level in the anti-Japanese student demonstrations in 1985, in which students protested the huge trade deficit with Japan and the rise in corruption and "unhealthy tendencies" generally, calling the situation a "second occupation."[41] This apprehension was expressed within the leadership in analyses of the international economy in the early years of the "open" policy. Although the reformers rejected the radical self-reliance model and at times emphasized positive aspects of capitalism—such as advanced technology and the overall high level of "productive forces"—they, and conservatives, continued to regard industrialized nations as potentially exploitative and rife with contradictions between the advanced, socialized productive forces and private ownership. For example, capital was said to be "by nature avaricious, and in order to reach the greatest degree of profit it will not even stop at taking chances which go against the law."[42] As in Lenin's and Mao's theories of imperialism, some post-Mao analyses argued that the export of capital transmits capitalism to capital-importing countries. Some analysts also argued that the contradictions between developing countries and imperialists were growing and that the contradictions were leading inexorably to the demise of capitalism and the advent of worldwide socialism.

A few reformers even stated that joint ventures, a form of capital export, are a product of the later phase of imperialism, when international capital must concede to some reduction in control over investments in order to obtain profitable returns. While international joint ventures have "promoted scientific and technological exchange between different countries and nationalities and promoted the development of productive forces in society," they have also "inevitably increased the value of capital and spread bourgeois ideology."[43] Thus, while joint ventures were viewed as offering less of a threat than other forms of capital export, they too were viewed as replete with threats. This danger put the impetus on the Chinese leadership to take precautions, as reflected in Hu Yaobang's statement that "[i]n no circumstances must we forget that capitalist countries and enterprises will never change their capitalist nature simply because they have economic and technical exchanges with us."[44]

The view that imperialism and attendant "bourgeois values" would threaten "Chinese values," "socialist values," and the socialist system thus was expressed frequently by both reformers and conservatives in the early years of the "open" policy.[45] The perception of dangers arising from engagement with international capital dictated that China must try to guard against the perceived dangers of foreign participation in its economy.

CHINA'S TURN TO THE OUTSIDE WORLD
IN THE LATE 1970s: THE RATIONALE

Against the historically based view that foreign participation could harm China's economy, the Chinese leadership's announcement in 1978 that it would allow private foreign corporations to invest on Chinese soil marked a striking change in the official outlook of the previous decades.[46] As discussed previously, from the Chinese revolution in 1949 to the late 1970s, private foreign investment in general was considered antithetical to the socialist goals of the PRC.[47] Even as late as 1977, one year before the policy was announced, the *Peking Review* reaffirmed the anti-imperialist line on investment by foreigners in China: "We do not allow foreign capital to exploit China's resources nor do we run joint enterprises with foreign countries, still less beg them for foreign loans."[48] For foreign investment suddenly to be allowed in 1979, some effort to legitimate it was clearly necessary. The reformers attempted to justify their decision to use foreign investment primarily by arguing that it was a necessary step to solve *economic* problems. But if the "open" policy was to be *ideologically* palatable and politically viable to large portions of the Chinese leadership (including the more conservative cadres), and to the population as a whole, the justification had to do more than cite economic problems; it had to respond to the nationalistic and anti-imperialist concern that the acceptance of foreign investment would harm China. The following sections detail the economic and ideological elements of the official rationale offered by the reformers in the early years of the "open" policy.

It should be noted that the rationale was not fully in place prior to the initiation of the foreign investment policy, however; that theory apparently was developed simultaneously with, and in some cases even following, decisions regarding what was required, in practice, to reform the economy. This was true, for example, of the rationalization for opening the Shenzhen SEZ: local leaders pressed for and were allowed by central authorities to organize the zone based on the need for export earnings and a view of the opportunities that this economic format presented. The ideological justification (based on Lenin, as discussed below) was not articulated until 1980–1981. Similarly, ideological debates over absorbing foreign investment to develop China's offshore oil reserves followed the decision that foreign capital and technology were needed if China was to rapidly explore and develop petroleum reserves on the continental shelf.[49] But although initially theory followed practice in some cases, a rather full justification eventually appeared.

The Economic Rationale

A strong motivating force behind the adoption by reformers of the "open" strategy was their recognition of the deep economic troubles that China faced in the 1970s. Despite impressive economic gains since 1949, there was some evidence that China's total factor productivity was lower than in many developing countries, and perhaps even declined after 1957.[50] Reformers were also troubled that China had a low standard of living compared with other countries in Asia and the West. Recognition of China's relative poverty made reformers hesitant to continue financing development at the expense of domestic consumption. State budget deficits also hindered domestic funding of infrastructure and industrial projects that were desperately needed but extremely expensive. Low technological and managerial sophistication in industry, and shortages of foreign exchange to pay for technology and other imports, were additional obstacles to industrial development. These economic problems, together with Sino-Soviet tensions and a capitalist world eagerly eyeing the huge Chinese market, pushed China toward significant domestic reforms, and to participation in the international economy.[51]

In terms familiar to neoclassical economists, and reminiscent of self-strengtheners, the reformers argued that foreign direct investment, and joint ventures specifically, would offer China four things that could spur development and were lacking in China's own economy: new sources of capital; advanced technology; advanced management skills; and, by tapping into the existing markets of foreign partners, access to international markets. The belief was that, because Western technology and management were more "advanced," their use could lead to greater productivity and efficiency, and could cut consumption of raw materials and energy while raising the quality of goods produced. The reformers also reasoned that foreign companies would be more willing to transfer sophisticated technology and management skills and to share access to overseas markets if, through shared management, they were to have direct responsibility for the profits they would generate.[52]

China's reformers avoided using China's self-strengthening movement of the late nineteenth century as a positive economic model for the post-Mao policy. Despite the fact that the precedent for the current strategy hearkens back to the earlier reaction, the view that the self-strengthening movement was a failed effort by a corrupt imperial regime rendered that movement illegitimate as a possible model.[53] Yet the reformers used a number of other comparative and historical arguments to bolster their rationale. Chinese economic journals pointed to the positive elements of the experience of Eastern European nations (Hungary, Romania, and Yugoslavia), and other Asian countries (including Taiwan), with international joint ventures.[54] As one reformer argued, "international experience proves that the rational use of foreign capital is an effective means of accelerating economic development. In the process of their economic development, almost all of the developed countries in the world today used foreign capital; nor has there been any country which attained high-speed economic development without using foreign capital."[55] Another analyst raised Sun Yat-sen as an historical Chinese authority on the need to use foreign capital from other more developed countries in the face of China's lack of capital and skills. Sun, according to this author, wrote that use of foreign capital would not impair China's sovereignty as long as the Chinese were unified and determined to defend their own territory.[56]

Lenin provided what was perhaps the most important external model for the reformers. In the early 1920s and as part of the New Economic Plan (NEP), Lenin invited foreign investment in a number of "concession" areas in order to promote industrialization. Lenin argued that such a retrenchment was necessary even though he believed foreigners would try to exploit the Soviets. To avoid excessive exploitation, Lenin argued, the Soviets would need—and had the ability—to control the activities of foreign investors. The Chinese reformers, especially in the early 1980s, often used Lenin's endorsement of foreign concessions to build support for foreign investment in the SEZs. Continuing to use the Soviet Union as a model of a socialist state's capabilities, they also cited the success of international economic cooperation that occurred under Stalin. As one Chinese analyst argued with regard to the Stalin period, "the dictatorship of the proletariat and the public ownership of the means of production established in the Soviet Union were a powerful guarantee of its economic independence."[57]

Yet reformers in China did not follow the NEP closely in one important sense. Lenin viewed NEP and the foreign concessions as *temporary, expedient* measures. They were deliberate steps backward that would allow the Soviet Union to develop its economy to the point (which according to Marx would be reached under capitalism) where it would be prepared for the transition to socialism. Significantly, however, the reformers de-emphasized Lenin's view that the foreign investment program under NEP would be temporary. Nonetheless, even though China's reformers substantially modified the NEP model, they also derived substantial benefit from the mantle of legitimacy it, and the Stalinist example, provided.

The Ideological Rationale

Because the decision to use foreign investment was such a radical change from the prior ideology, a justification based on economic need alone was insufficient to meet concerns of both conservatives and reformers. Reformers therefore reformulated several tenets of the prior ideology to justify the change. The first reformulation involved the concept of national self-reliance. After Mao's death in 1976, news reports began to assert that a concept of self-reliance which led China to isolate itself from the international economy was a distortion, attributable to the "Gang of Four," of the true meaning of the concept. Indeed, reformers argued, the closed-door policy had hindered China's economic development. Not all aspects of the Maoist version of self-reliance were repudiated; for example, the reformers continued to argue that China's economy was large enough to provide many basic needs (such as grain, energy, and raw materials). But in contrast to the earlier version, the reformers argued that striving for self-reliance does not dictate isolation from the international economy. Instead, China should use foreign technology, aid, and capital to help build a strong and even more self-reliant economy; as long as the foreign sector conforms to the state plan and remains subordinate to the domestic economy, foreign investment does not compromise China's sovereignty or its essential independence. Reformers thus viewed foreign investment not as antithetical to self-reliance but as complementary to and even supportive of it. As Zhao Ziyang stated in late 1982, "the aim of our foreign economic and technical exchange is of course to raise our capacity for self-reliance. . . . Under no circumstances should we waver on this point."[58]

The reformulation of self-reliance attempted to redefine the debate on the development alternatives available to China, while responding to the political need to uphold the value of economic independence which underlay the goal of self-reliance. While the Maoist version of self-reliance was seen as the only alternative to dependence and exploitation, the new version implied that China could interact with the rest of the world to some point along a continuum, and still remain essentially independent. To support this view, reformers in the late 1970s invoked Mao's early speeches in which he endorsed study of foreign ideas and technology to strengthen China.[59] This reformulation was of course consistent with the legacy of self-strengthening. Yet in the post-Mao reformulation of self-reliance, as in the idea of self-strengthening, an important problem was left unresolved. The reformers did not clarify the point at which the line between self-reliance and dependence, or "fawning on foreigners," existed. This lack of precision left vague a key policy question: at what point would use of foreign technology and ideas harm China's independence, and China's essence? It also gave reformers considerable leeway in interpreting the legitimate scope of the "open" policy.

The reformulation of self-reliance was part of a broader ideological shift toward a view of a capitalist world that is less threatening.[60] While reformist and conservative leaders both asserted that a single capitalist world economy existed, the latter considered participation in this system to be potentially detrimental to China's socialist development, whereas the former viewed participation to be natural, inevitable, and, under certain circumstances, beneficial. To support their view, reformers made several additional arguments that engagement with the world economy was legitimate. They emphasized that the historical relationship between capitalism and socialism legitimates the use by socialist countries of forces developed under capitalism. They argued that the historically objective expansion of "productive forces" under capitalism had socialized production to a global scale and created an integrated world economy, making isolated development impossible. Rather than negate what had developed under global capitalism or focus on the contradictions between the two systems, reformers argued, socialism in China must be based on the material foundation of capitalism. If socialist modernization and, ultimately, communism are to occur, China must inherit the positive productive forces of capitalism. These positive forces were considered not inherently capitalist but, instead, "fruits of civilization" that grew up in capitalism. The argument was an eclectic one. It implied the more orthodox Marxian interpretation of historical development that socialism can only be achieved on the basis of capitalist development. Yet it also endorsed the idea that a degree of interdependence is a natural, inevitable, and often even beneficial phenomenon that China should not try to shun under socialism.[61]

Advocates of a more isolationist version of self-reliance had in the past argued that comparative advantage and the international division of labor had a "bourgeois" class basis and were tools for oppressing the developing world. The reformers, to the contrary, asserted that comparative advantage and the international division of labor are "objective" economic forces. Although they may have developed under capitalism, the ability of these laws to promote efficiency could also benefit China.[62] Consistent with acceptance of comparative advantage was the acceptance of the view that foreign investment, a capitalist force, could benefit China. This also meant accepting the corollary views that such investment is not a zero-sum game and that cooperation between capitalists and socialists is possible. As one reformist trade official from Guangdong asserted in 1980, "foreign investors aim at gaining profits, and [we] aim at realizing the construction of socialist modernization. For the sake of our respective targets, there is a possibility of economic cooperation."[63]

Once China's reformist leaders adopted as inevitable, objective, and useful the ideas of comparative advantage and the international division of labor, the prescription for participation in the world economy followed easily. Claiming that they were bringing China in line with objective economic fact, the reformers argued that China should take advantage of the opportunity that such participation was giving it: "Today, when the productive forces and science and technology are developing on an unprecedented scale, not only have production and consumption long become worldwide, but capital, technology, news, skilled personnel, and knowledge have also become worldwide. Any nation that wants to become developed cannot close itself to international intercourse."[64] Thus, acceptance of "objective" laws made economic ties between capitalist nations and socialist China theoretically permissible, and justified China's participation in the international economy.

That reformers accepted these "objective" laws did not mean they deemed the laws to be completely neutral or beneficent, however. Some reformers continued to argue that use of the international division of labor and comparative advantage would distort development in colonial areas or single product economies.[65] Consistent with their emphasis on self-reliance (and with economic policies and practices of most Western countries), reformers stopped short of suggesting that China should produce *solely* according to its comparative advantage. Although they believed that China could gain by utilizing its comparative advantage, such as in the textile and tourism sectors and in labor, they simultaneously wished to *change* China's comparative advantage, thereby removing China from the world's poor nations to a place among the advanced industrialized nations.

The acceptance of the international norms of bargaining also meant that China would be expected to make trade-offs of some values in the course of negotiations in order to achieve the overall benefits of foreign investment. With the acceptance of trade-offs, reformers showed that they were, in theory, prepared to accept less than complete control over the terms and benefits of investment. The understanding that China would have to pay a nontrivial price for the overall benefits it gained was reflected in the statement of the Guangdong official quoted previously: "[W]hen private investors outside China enter into whatever form of economic cooperation within China, their aim is to gain profit. There must be exploitation; this point was clear to us long ago. To realize the Four Modernizations and develop the socialist economy, we shall tolerate a certain degree of exploitation."[66]

In addition to arguing why foreign investment was ideologically legitimate in socialist China, the reformers also tried to meet remaining concerns about possible negative effects of foreign investment. They asserted that two factors, independence from foreign or colonial domination and a socialist system, would minimize the risks of investment to an acceptable level. On the factor of independence, one article argued broadly that "it is clear that whether an international division of labor can bring a country genuine economy of social labor and a sound development of its economy depends on the internal as well as external conditions of a country. An international division of labor can play its proper role and a lopsided single product economy can be avoided only when the colonies and dependencies have won political independence, removed the internal and external obstacles to their economic development, and established foreign economic relations based on equality and mutual benefit."[67] Reformers argued that China possessed the political independence that would allow it to benefit from the international division of labor.

Equally important for the reformers' contention that China in the late 1970s could control its participation in the world economy were their assertions as to why a socialist state makes a difference. The reformist assertions were fully consistent with the arguments discussed in chapter 1 that socialism can help developing countries better control the terms of investment. The reformers argued, first, that a socialist state has stronger tools to regulate foreign investment. The strength of these tools grows out of the regulatory and bureaucratic authority of the state plan over the economy, and the communist party's tradition of combating negative cultural influences. Reformers further asserted that enterprises that are either "national capitalist" (joint ventures) or fully capitalist (wholly foreign-owned enterprises) take on a qualitatively different form when they are subordinate to a socialist economy and must follow the regulations established in a socialist state. In joint ventures in particular, the Chinese partner would always be a state enterprise, allowing direct state control over foreign capital.[68] Second, reformers argued that a socialist state makes a difference because it has the will to manipulate foreign investment for its own ends. They asserted that the aims of the socialist state in using capitalism are different from those of capitalist states; while in the Chinese view, the sole aim of capitalists is profit of the corporation, the Chinese goal would be to use capitalist methods for the benefit of socialist modernization.[69]

Finally, the reformers argued that foreign investment in China would not threaten a "capitalist restoration." In doing so, they refuted arguments made by critics of foreign investment that such investment would create a new comprador class within China. Reformers also refuted similar arguments, made by the "Gang of Four" during the Cultural Revolution, that contact with "bourgeois ideology" and values could bring about a capitalist restoration within the party through the growth of a new class of bureaucratic capitalists. These ills, the "Gang of Four" had argued, dictated the long-term strategy of class struggle against enemies in society and within the party itself.[70] The post-Mao leadership (both reformers and conservatives) explicitly rejected the view that the use of foreign capital would reflect—or necessitate—class struggle; indeed, reformers declared in 1978 that class struggle in China had ended with the completion of the "socialist transformation" in 1956, thereby undermining the radical argument that foreign capitalist forces would threaten the socialist purpose of the foreign investment policy or create a new capitalist class within China. The reformers also intended to undermine the argument that use of former Chinese capitalists in key positions in the "open" sector would threaten socialism. Indeed, the reformers hoped to rely heavily for skills and investment capital on members of the Chinese business class who had fled China prior to or after the 1949 revolution, and on those "former capitalists" who remained behind and had been rehabilitated by Deng Xiaoping.[71]

One analyst, echoing many others who wrote in the early 1980s, precisely characterized the reformist view of why China's situation in the 1980s differed from that of other countries: "We must see that after the importation of foreign capital, not a few countries' economies became abnormal and lopsided and their people became impoverished. The fundamental reason was that these countries lost their political independence and could not use foreign capital freely; on the contrary, they were subject to control by foreign capital. We are a socialist country, politically independent, and fully equipped with the political premise to use foreign capital."[72] Thus, according to another, "because we are implementing the 'open' policy under the socialist system and the leadership of the Communist Party, we are also able to selectively absorb the good things and boycott the bad things from abroad. We must absolutely not give up eating for fear of choking."[73]

Overall, then, the view of a less threatening international economy, acceptance of "objective" economic laws, belief that benefits can be gained from foreign investment and, most important, confidence in the capacity of an independent, socialist China to control the terms of investment, made up the core of the reformers' justification for using foreign capital in the late 1970s and early 1980s. Rather than wholly exonerating foreign investment, they viewed it as a package consisting of both beneficial and negative elements that could be separated through correct policy. Moreover, by elevating the capacities of the socialist state, they asserted that use of foreign capital would not sacrifice the goal of socialism but, rather, would foster it. The justification allowed the reformers to argue that China could avoid the problems it encountered during the Treaty Port era, and encouraged the idea that China could "pay off" foreign investors at a fairly low price.

CHINESE LEADERSHIP CONCERNS ABOUT POTENTIAL NEGATIVE EFFECTS OF FOREIGN CAPITAL

This section details the specific concerns that were expressed by the Chinese leaders at the initiation of the "open" policy, identifying threats against which the "open" policy would need to attempt to guard. Concerns were perceived as potentially affecting three levels of society: national, regional, and enterprise levels.[74] Most of the concerns discussed here were held broadly by both reformers and conservatives when the "open" policy was initiated in the late 1970s. In some cases, however, the dangers were perceived as more intense, and expressed more vehemently, by conservatives, but were de-emphasized by reformers, who argued that China's socialist state rendered the concerns moot.

National Level

At the national level, the Chinese leadership believed foreign investment had the potential to generate negative effects in three major areas. There was concern that outside forces would have undue influence over the direction of *economic* development, and that as a result China would not reap a "just" share of potential or actual benefits (such as profits) generated by foreign investment. There also was the *political* concern that foreign investment would threaten China's independence and sovereignty. Finally, there was concern that the "national *culture*" (a combination of traditional and socialist values) might be contaminated by contact with the outside world. None of these concerns, or those expressed about the regional or enterprise levels, were unique to China's leaders; rather, they shared similar experiences and ideology with much of the developing world, and experiences of other developing countries influenced the Chinese leadership's caution toward foreign investment.

With regard to the first concern, loss of economic control, Chinese leaders stressed the following potential negative results:

Loss of control over the general direction of development (particularly the industries and sectors to be emphasized), and over the uses for and scope of foreign capital[75]

Loss of control over the domestic market, with joint ventures monopolizing market share, or providing undue competition for developed Chinese enterprises[76]

Extraction by foreigners of "excessive" profits through unsavory accounting practices, low wages, and transfer pricing[77]

Net drain of foreign exchange[78]

Transfer to China of outdated, excessively expensive, insufficient, and/or inappropriate technology[79]

Absence of backward linkages to the domestic economy, particularly the use of domestic supplies[80]

There also was a general wariness of being "duped" by foreign investors.[81] This sensitivity was notable especially with regard to the issues of division of profits and transfer of technology, as evidenced by the critical attention given to several instances of transfer or sales of extremely outdated technology to Shenzhen SEZ during the early years of its existence.[82]

The second broad concern, which grew out of the legacy of anti-imperialism, was that foreigners, through ownership of assets located in China, would be able to translate control over investments into political power. Once in such a position, foreigners might deprive the Chinese government of its authority to direct the economy toward its own goals, and possibly even threaten its political authority. Conservative leaders in particular worried that neither the times nor the country had changed drastically enough to eliminate concerns about foreign domination.[83] Reformist leaders countered this with their argument that China's socialism, and its ability to protect China's political independence, rendered foreign political intervention through channels of foreign investment highly unlikely.[84]

The third type of concern, contamination of the national culture by foreigners and foreign systems, also had clear antecedents in China's antiforeign tradition. Reactions in the Chinese press to the "open" policy echoed this concern by raising questions about the influence of what were termed "bourgeois values," "spiritual pollution," and, generally, "unhealthy tendencies" on the population as a whole and especially on Chinese youths. Although the concern was often expressed in terms of contamination by capitalism, the more basic concern was a cultural one. Cultural concerns were voiced regularly in statements of both reformers and conservatives. Agreement of many liberals and conservatives on this issue was to be expected insofar as many who were considered economic reformers, notably Deng Xiaoping and others in the older generation of the leadership, were at the same time "conservative" on political and social matters. Indeed, few of the values labeled "decadent" during the conservative-run 1983 Campaign Against Spiritual Pollution (CASP) were defended subsequently as good, with the exception of certain personal fashions such as Western-style suits, cosmetics, and hair styles. Thus, there was apparent consensus on this concern, despite the fact that the reformers eventually brought a halt to the campaign when conservatives began to use it to criticize the overall economic reforms.[85]

General discussions in the press offered a sense of how the problem was perceived by both reformers and conservatives. "Spiritual pollution" or "unhealthy tendencies" were viewed as an inculcation of unwanted values by party cadres and the general population. During the CASP, Deng Xiaoping offered a grand theory definition of "spiritual pollution" as "the spreading of decadent and declining ideologies of the bourgeoisie and other exploiting classes, and the spreading of sentiments of distrust regarding the cause of socialism and communism and the leadership of the Communist Party."[86] After the end of the CASP, another official suggested that "bourgeois" influences from outside China could affect individual ideas and lifestyles, encouraging "pleasure-seeking without doing work, egoism, and gaining by exploiting others."[87] Working exclusively for personal gain and profiteering at the expense of others also were criticized. One conservative commentator complained that "all kinds of capitalist notions of looking for money in everything are running rampant." Desire for material goods such as fashions, jewelry, and cosmetics were eschewed as "sugar-coated bullets," although criticism in this vein declined after the end of the CASP.[88] Other problems attributed to the negative influence of capitalist societies, particularly gambling, prostitution, pornography, and drug use, were the subject of consistent criticism from reformers and conservatives. The attitude of "fawning on foreigners" also was viewed harshly.[89]

Economic crime and corruption also fell under the rubric of "unhealthy tendencies."[90] Criminal activity involving both the domestic and the foreign sectors of the economy increased dramatically following the initiation of the domestic economic reforms and the "open" policy in the late 1970s. The higher incidence of economic crime first was reported mostly in and around the SEZs, but became widespread as reforms were expanded to include large areas outside the zones. The press was full of accounts of smuggling and of the growing black market in consumer goods and foreign exchange. Some cases of bribery by foreigners and accounting discrepancies involving foreign investment projects also were reported.[91] Moreover, reforms in foreign and domestic economic policy were accompanied by an increase in reported incidents of corruption (such as graft, bribery, and accounting fraud) within the party. One official, for example, stated that "the outlook of 'seeing only money' and the 'money worship' ideological trends are corrupting some of our [party] people."[92] Cadre corruption was a major concern of the party leadership because the party was to be a model of socialist morality. Threats to its "communist purity" were thus considered serious threats to the socialist system, for popular perceptions that the party was corrupt would seriously undermine the legitimacy and authority of the party.

Further concerns were expressed that contacts by Chinese individuals both with foreigners and with elements of capitalism would transmit unwanted values. Leaders were uncomfortable with the prospect of unmonitored contacts between foreign business representatives and Chinese individuals. As one article from Shenzhen commented, "because we are more open to the outside, our personnel's contacts with Hong Kong and foreign traders are expanded, and the possibility of receiving bad (*bu liang*) influences is increased."[93] Reformers in the top leadership did not take the view that foreign cultural influences were an acceptable by-product of the more open economy, and they did not judge cultural practices that grew up outside China and often under capitalism as "objective" forces, as they did with "objective" economic laws. If they had argued this successfully, the issue of "unhealthy tendencies" would have become much less salient. The fact that foreign cultural influences remained on the list of concerns of at least older leaders of both conservative and reform camps indicates that such an objectivization of the phenomenon remained unacceptable.

Regional Level

The regional level encompasses the Special Economic Zones (SEZs) and the open coastal regions that were designated as locations in which foreign investment is to be emphasized. (These areas are described more fully in chapter 3.) The concerns expressed about foreign investment in these regions frequently were the same as those voiced at the national level, as the regions to some degree were microcosms of what was occurring elsewhere in China. This section focuses on those concerns that were directed specifically (though not necessarily solely) at the regional level.

When the SEZs first became operational in the early 1980s, they were the focus of much concern about potential negative results in the economic, political, and cultural spheres. The expansion of permissive policies to a number of major, populous coastal cities in the mid-1980s enhanced such fears.[94] With regard to the economy, concern was voiced that the zones would fail to spread any of the economic benefits they accrued— particularly technology and management skills, and linkages with internal markets—to inland areas. Although this concern was not voiced in the earliest days of the policy, emphasis on "internal linkages" in the early and mid-1980s reflected the growth of this concern. A degree of concern was also expressed that the special status granted to these regions would generate larger regional disparities than already existed. This is not to say, however, that inequality was completely opposed by reformers. The reformers argued that confusing "socialism" with "egalitarianism on the basis of universal poverty," as they claimed the "Gang of Four" did, impedes modernization. Lifting the population out of poverty, they maintained, required that some people or areas be allowed to get rich first, for "getting rich in common does not mean getting rich simultaneously."[95] In particular, the emphasis on rapid development of the coastal areas sanctioned regional disparities between coastal and inland areas. Nonetheless, some discussion of regional parity occurred, spurred on in part by conservatives and in part by those in inland areas who perceived themselves as removed from the benefits of the "open" policy.

The primary political concern at the regional level was that the SEZs would become modern equivalents of the foreign concessions of prerevolutionary China, replete with the decadence of the treaty ports and the loss of Chinese sovereignty. Leaders from inland regions also voiced concern about the political privilege that would accrue to the coastal areas by virtue of their stronger economic status, that is, about political inequality.[96] Moreover, conservatives and reformers alike were sensitive to evidence of "unhealthy tendencies" in the cultural realm. The "capitalist flavor" of the zones reportedly upset a number of senior CCP members, as well as some high- and middle-ranking army cadres. Even if the prospect of new foreign concessions were judged to be acceptable when weighed against benefits that would accrue to the whole economy from the special regions, concern was voiced that undesired forms might unintentionally spread to and contaminate the rest of Chinese society. There also was concern that Shenzhen in particular was unable to prevent foreign values and foreign criminals (such as Hong Kong triad members) from entering under the aegis of the "open" policy and gaining a foothold in China.[97] Indeed, some of these fears were realized in the form of a dramatic increase in criminal activity and corruption, and in what some leaders perceived as excessive consumerism by Shenzhen residents, especially youths.[98]

Enterprise Level

Joint ventures themselves were the locus of substantial concerns about control over economic decisionmaking, and about the maintenance of "equality and mutual benefit" between Chinese and foreign partners. The level of the enterprise was the point at which the tension between the desire to attract and control foreign capital was most evident; although they were a major focus of concerns, foreign-backed enterprises were also where the concrete benefits of the foreign direct investment policy most obviously accrued. Hence, any need to choose between benefits and costs of foreign investment was most evident at the enterprise level. Though few explicit statements appeared in the public media expressing concerns about dangers at the enterprise level, foreigners involved in negotiating and operating joint ventures readily cited evidence that their partners were highly sensitive to several enterprise-level issues, such as how best to divide ownership and managerial control, and how to manage the venture's personnel and social welfare matters.[99]

One enterprise-level concern that was voiced frequently through the mid-1980s was that key decisions in a joint venture would be made unilaterally by foreign management. Published articles reflected concern that, especially through foreign ownership, a foreign partner would impose its own, competing interests on the local partner in such decisions as pricing, international marketing, wages, and profit distribution. This could result in loss of both economic control and economic benefits for the Chinese side.[100] Second, there was concern that granting authority to foreign managers could threaten political and social welfare functions that were designed to protect the interest of the workers under the socialist system and that were integral to all workplace "units" (danwei), including joint ventures, in China. These functions included political and ideological study for party cadres, trade union activities, health care, and child care.[101] In essence, this was a concern that Chinese workers employed in joint ventures might be exploited by working directly for foreign managers or in a firm run in part according to the interests of foreign investors. The need to maintain investment conditions, especially low wages, that would attract foreign capital did give Chinese enterprises certain incentives to ignore the interests of Chinese labor. However, because in China there was a strong precedent for guaranteeing workers certain protections and benefits, personnel matters in joint ventures were considered to be a realm requiring strong input from the Chinese side. Specifically, there was concern that in an effort by the foreign side to keep production costs low, Chinese workers would be paid "unequally" and hence "exploitatively," or would be fired or punished without due cause.[102] Although Chinese leaders did not set forth a precise definition of exploitation, the issue of payment of Chinese managers and staff was extremely sensitive, and at times was carried into board meetings of operative joint ventures.[103] Finally, reflecting the possibility of threats to "socialist spiritual civilization" that have been described for the national level, concern was expressed that party members and workers in joint ventures could be affected by possible "corrosion" from contact with foreign investors.

CONCLUSION

The Chinese leadership's decision to open to the outside world in the late 1970s was not made in a vacuum. It had to contend with a daunting historical legacy of economic, military, and political encroachment, and resulting ideologies of anti-foreignism and anti-imperialism. It also had to avoid explicit association with the model of self-strengthening that was viewed as a failed effort by a corrupt imperial regime and an illegitimate model. A key question therefore was how the leadership, which as during the self-strengthening movement wanted benefits the outside world could offer, would reconcile these negative legacies with the need to absorb foreign capital.

The official justification for the "open" policy did not reject the view that China must be wary of the outside world. Rather, reformers asserted a new conceptualization of how China would deal with the outside world. In the postrevolutionary era, they asserted, China was a fully independent and sovereign country that was not in danger of crumbling under pressure from outside. Moreover, socialism provided China with tools to control foreign investment, and generally enhanced its bargaining power. Thus, China in the late twentieth century could avoid the harm predicted by history and ideology by bringing to bear the powers of its consolidated socialist state to control foreign investment. The government had therefore come to view participation in the world economy as much less threatening for new China than it had been in the past; China could draw what it desired from the capitalist world and limit harm to acceptable levels.

The new conceptualization not only legitimated the decision to allow foreign investment, it also allowed the reformers flexibility in bargaining with foreign investors. While the rationale explained why China could meet its goal of limiting harm, the flexibility in the rationale allowed China room to adapt to foreign pressures, and therefore to meet the parallel goal of absorbing foreign capital. Flexibility was evident particularly in two ways. First, the reformulation of the concept of self-reliance, which asserted that China could utilize foreign investment but still remain essentially independent if foreign capital were kept in a position subordinate to the state sector, left unresolved the question of the precise definition of "subordinate"—the point at which foreign participation would violate self-reliance. As had been true of the self-strengtheners, the reformers never clearly established where use of foreign capital would force China across the line between independence and self-reliance, on the one hand, and dependence on foreigners, on the other. Second, flexibility was inherent in China's acceptance of the norms and processes of bargaining over the terms of foreign investment. The acceptance of bargaining justified the fact that China would need to engage in a process that would require it to trade off some values in order to capture the benefits of investment. But because the norm stopped short of determining the outcome of negotiations, the reformers left themselves room to adapt to specific bargaining situations, and to determine the extent of trade-offs China would make, without violating key tenets of the original rationale.

The absence of a delineation between independence and dependence, and the legitimation of trade-offs, thus set the stage for relaxation of controls over investment. Indeed, the flexibility proved to be critical in determining the course of controls during the 1980s; as various forces from inside and outside of China pressed on the reformers to change the policy, the flexibility in the original rationale facilitated the ability of reformers to respond to these forces. Chapters 3, 4, and 5 focus on the issue of the originally strict controls, the effectiveness of the government in implementing these controls, and the evolution of controls over time in response to these pressures.

## Chapter Three

THE PATTERN OF
FOREIGN DIRECT INVESTMENT
IN CHINA, 1979–1988

AT THE INITIATION of the foreign investment policy, the reformers, cognizant of China's past experiences with the outside world, reasoned that the strengths of China's socialism positioned it to reap the benefits offered by engagement in the world economy and, specifically, would allow China to both absorb foreign investment and control the terms of investment sufficiently to avoid harm. Chapters 4 and 5 describe the attempts of China's government to use its strengths to control the terms of investment. They argue that although the Chinese government began with a very strict set of controls, and was able to maintain controls in a number of areas, it was not always successful in implementing these controls. The chapters also argue that the various forces influencing foreign direct investment encouraged reformers to exercise the flexibility left them in the initial conceptualization of the "open" policy, resulting in a loosening of the original controls in many areas over the course of the 1980s.

The present chapter lays the groundwork for understanding the actual evolution of controls over foreign investment that is discussed in the following chapters, and especially the liberalization of controls. The first part of this chapter discusses the changes in the reformist outlook toward foreign investment that occurred over the course of the decade, changes that led the leadership to place greater emphasis on the problems of attracting foreign investment and to give less attention to many of the original concerns. The second part lays out in broad terms the overall process of liberalization. It describes the relationship between the evolving political context for investment, foreign reactions to China's regulatory environment and economic infrastructure, and the actual flow of foreign investment in China. Furthermore, it traces the dynamics of this relationship as it unfolded—and created pressures for liberalization—in three phases in the decade from 1979 to 1988.

The third part serves a somewhat different purpose. It gives a basic definition and description of equity joint ventures, and establishes the importance of this and other forms of direct investment in China's overall economic modernization strategy. It also presents a compilation and analysis of statistical data on equity joint ventures, including data to be drawn upon in chapters 4 and 5, on features such as the size of ventures, the origins of the investment, and the sectors and regions in China that have received the most foreign capital. It is presented here in compiled form for use by readers seeking a complete overview of the pattern of investment in equity joint ventures as they have actually been set up in the first decade of the foreign investment policy.

CHANGES IN THE REFORMIST VIEW OF FOREIGN DIRECT INVESTMENT DURING THE 1980s

The concerns the reformers shared with conservatives at the initiation of the joint venture policy led to the original set of strict controls established in the first half of the 1980s. During the decade, however, although these concerns did not completely disappear, the outlook of the reformers toward foreign investment evolved noticeably. This evolution was a major force precipitating the liberalization of controls over foreign investment.

Change in the reformist outlook grew in part out of other changes occurring at the same time. Many of the post-Mao economic reforms were based on the premise that the level of central control over the economy that had existed over much of the preceding period had been an obstacle to development. It was not surprising, then, that reforms to reduce central governmental control over the economy in general were extended to the foreign sector. The evolution in views toward the "open" policy also grew out of the reformers' assessment of what was occurring in the policy itself. By the middle of the decade, the reformers could review the first several years and find that foreign investment had not caused major disasters; China's sovereignty was intact, and the economy had not come to be dominated by foreigners. The absence of strong conservative pressure to maintain controls removed another important factor that had argued for controls in the early years; as was discussed in chapter 1, conservatives voiced little public opposition to the foreign investment policy after the early years, except on the issue of unhealthy tendencies. Conservative pressures were replaced by pressures from foreign investors to liberalize what they viewed as a harsh investment environment.

Not only did the reformers come to face a set of pressures that was very different from those that existed at the outset of the policy, it was also evident that they made a positive assessment of the results of the early years. They became increasingly committed to obtaining these benefits, even at the expense of controls. One clear sign of this growing commitment was the opening of more and more cities and regions to foreign investment, starting in 1984 with the fourteen coastal cities (as discussed in the third part of this chapter). These changes were also evident in the reformers' public statements about the foreign investment policy. The prior emphasis in public statements and the media on the dangers of imperialism and the possible risks of foreign investment declined noticeably after the early years. Anti-imperialist language was less frequent, moreover, and discussions of the capacity of socialism to guard against such problems largely disappeared from the press. Instead, the reformers began to cite, as the major problem of the policy to attract foreign investment, China's failure to absorb enough foreign capital, technology, and managerial expertise to allow it to gain the perceived benefits. The new emphasis was evident in a 1987 statement by Deng Xiaoping, in which he asserted that China had been insufficiently "bold" in absorbing foreign investment and technology:

> To settle this problem, we should deal with it in two aspects: on the one hand, we should open the door still wider to the outside world, create a more favorable environment for investment and be bold in using foreign capital; on the other hand, it is hoped that foreign parties would be more open-minded in technology transfer. The logic here is very simple indeed. It won't do if foreign parties invest here but without gaining profits. As too high cost makes it impossible to gain profits, we cannot but be resolute to improve the environment for investment. In other words, terms for both opening and investment should be reasonable. This means that excessive profits are also unjustifiable. *The key issue is now the unfavorable environment.* [Emphasis added][1]

The statement is notable not only for the expressed commitment to improving the investment environment, but also for the mild treatment of the foreign responsibility for the poor level of technology transfer.

Reformers also placed even more emphasis on those elements of the original rationale that argued for China's participation in the international economy, particularly the "objective" economic laws of comparative advantage and the international division of labor, and the concept of global interdependence. The drive to use foreign capital to develop China's coastal areas into export-oriented zones was perhaps the most important example of how comparative advantage had become a central economic tenet of reformers.[2] To the extent that ideological legitimacy based on "socialist" theories was still important, the reformers drew on different theories. After about 1983, the use of Lenin's NEP as a legitimate socialist model was de-emphasized in favor of Deng Xiaoping's view that China was building "socialism with Chinese characteristics" and Zhao Ziyang's view that China was in the "initial stages of socialism." These new theories minimized even further the NEP view that use of foreign capital was a temporary expedient.[3] As with the reformulation of self-reliance and acceptance of bargaining, the theories of Zhao and Deng on China's overall development were vague and hence could be interpreted flexibly.

The specific concerns of reformers about foreign investment also changed over time, in tandem with changes in the general outlook on foreign investment. As economic reformers saw that many of the dangers they originally perceived did not in fact come to pass, and as the need to improve the investment environment took primacy, many of the earlier concerns received less attention.[4] When the possible risks of foreign investment were raised at all in the mid- and late 1980s, discussions focused much more on how China could overcome the risks than on the foreign source of the risk itself. The tone of discussions of controls became milder, and the solutions discussed were more often focused on how to use positive incentives to induce the desired behavior from investors, or on preceptoral controls emphasizing education and socialist ethics; rather than further restrictions on investment itself, the solutions were aimed at controlling any negative impact.[5]

The shift away from the original outlook, rationale, and concerns was by no means total, however. The basic strategy of simultaneously absorbing and controlling foreign investment remained, and the belief that, by drawing on socialism the "open" policy would enhance rather than hinder China's socialist development and self-reliance, occasionally was reiterated.[6] Reformers continued to perceive controls to be necessary, particularly controls over technology transfer, foreign exchange, and domestic marketing. They also continued to see foreign investment as a risk to China's spiritual life; concern about unhealthy tendencies continued to resonate with most reformers, especially those of the older generation.[7] Nonetheless, the decline in emphasis on these issues was marked. Reflecting the pressures from outside China to loosen controls, examination of benefits achieved in the early years, and the declining role of conservatives in foreign economic policymaking, the changing view of the reformers was an important factor precipitating the change in controls over foreign investment that occurred throughout the decade.

TRENDS IN THE FLOW OF FOREIGN INVESTMENT DURING THE 1980s

The evolution of the outlook of the reformers clearly facilitated their will and capacity to change the investment policy itself. They in fact did change the policy, in three broad stages. This section discusses the major changes in the investment policy as it occurred in these stages, and the major reasons for these changes.

As could be expected, given that China started with no foreign capital when the foreign investment policy was initiated, foreign investment grew over the 1979–1988 period; tables 3-A and 3-B illustrate the fact that the number and volume of investment in all forms of foreign direct investment, and in the specific form of investment preferred by the government, equity joint ventures, rose significantly from 1979 to the late 1980s. Cumulative pledged foreign direct investment was $15 billion by the end of 1985, and $27 billion by the end of 1988. Investment pledged to equity joint ventures also grew substantially, from zero in 1979 to a total of nearly

TABLE 3-A
Pledged and Utilized Foreign Direct Investment (All Forms), 1979–1989

Year	Number of Projects Pledged	Value of Projects Pledged ($billions)	Value of Projects Utilized ($billions)	Utilized Value as a % of Pledged[a]
1979–82	922	4.61	1.37	30
1983	470	1.73	0.64	37
1984	1856	2.65	1.26	48
1985	3073	5.93	1.66	28
1986	1498	2.84	1.87	66
1987	2233	3.71	2.31	62
1988	5945	5.30	3.20	60
1989	5784	5.60	3.30	59
TOTAL	21,781	32.37	15.61	48

Sources: 1979–1988: MOFERT Almanacs, for 1984 to 1989. 1989: FBIS-CHI-90-017 (25 January 1990), p. 29.
[a] Utilized value as a percentage of pledged value.

$10 billion by the end of 1988.[8] Yet it is also evident that the absorption of foreign capital, and particularly the annual rate of growth, was quite volatile; tables 3-A and 3-B and figures 3.1 and 3.2 show that the absorption of pledged foreign direct investment in equity joint ventures and in all forms of direct investment proceeded unevenly. Steady growth occurred in the number of equity ventures from 1979 through 1982. But as figures 3.1 and 3.2 show, the rate of growth in the value of investment in equity joint ventures rose dramatically in 1983 and 1984, and then declined precipitously in 1985 and 1986. Figure 3.1 shows that a decline in the growth rate of pledged investment in all forms occurred a year later, in 1986, and was steeper than the decline for joint ventures that had occurred in 1985. Growth in both measures renewed, but at a more moderate rate, again in 1987. Investment in all forms fell significantly again in 1989, reflecting the reaction of Western firms to the events at Tiananmen.

These trends in the flow of investment are closely related to three phases in the regulatory environment for equity joint ventures: 1979 to mid-1983; late 1983 to mid-1986; and late 1986 to the end of 1988.[9] The start of each new phase was marked by a major effort by the reformers to establish or modify, in a major new law or set of regulations, the regulatory environment for joint ventures. The relationship between these major laws, the trends in the rate of growth of investment, and the perceptions of both the Chinese government and foreign investors, explains the changes in the Chinese policy to control foreign investment throughout the 1980s.

TABLE 3-B
Pledged and Utilized Investment in Equity Joint Ventures, 1979–1988

Year	Number of Projects Pledged	Value of Projects Pledged ($billions)	Value of Projects Utilized ($billions)	Utilized Value as a % of Pledged
1980	26	0.040[a]		
1981	28	0.043[a]		
1982	29	0.044[a]	0.034[b]	77
[1979–1982]	[83]	[0.127[c]]	[0.099[c]]	[73]
1983	107	0.19	0.07	37
1984	741	1.07	0.25	23
1985	1412	2.03	0.58	29
1986	892	1.38	0.80	58
1987	1395	1.95	1.49	76
1988	3909	3.13	1.98	63
TOTAL 1979–1988[d]	8539	9.88	5.27	53[e]

Sources: 1979–1988: MOFERT Almanacs, for 1984 to 1989.

[a] Values are estimated assuming equal sizes of investment per joint venture signed in each of these three years.

[b] Figure from Lardy 1987, p. 37.

[c] Derived from the 1984 Almanac by subtracting figures for 1983 from cumulative figures for 1979–1983. N. R. Chen (1986), pp. 8–9 provides other figures of $141 million for the value of pledged investment in EJVs and $103 million for the value of utilized investment in EJVs in 1979–1982.

[d] 1989 figure for number of pledged EJVs is 3663. FBIS-CHI-90-017 (25 January 1990).

[e] Utilized value as a percentage of pledged value, 1979–1988.

The first of the three major laws marking each phase was the Joint Venture Law.[10] Promulgated in mid-1979, it was the first formal statement of commitment to foreign investment by the Chinese government, and established the principles of and procedures for investment. The Joint Venture Law provided an important signal to investors, for it legitimated the right of foreigners to invest and profit—the minimum needed to give some security to potential investors. Very soon after the promulgation of this law, foreign business representatives thronged to China to investigate the potentially lucrative situation. Some foreign investors did take advantage of the new opportunities being offered by the reformers; by the end of 1982, eighty-three equity joint ventures had been approved with an aggregate value of $127 million in pledged investment.

But in its fifteen short, general articles, the Joint Venture Law fell far short of guiding both Chinese and foreign partners in crucial legal and operational matters. Although the vagueness of the law was compensated

FIGURE 3.1
Rate of Growth of Foreign Direct Investment, 1983–1989

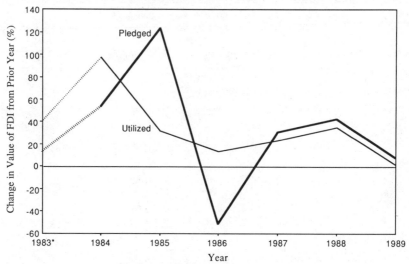

*Growth rate for 1983 over 1982 estimated based on aggregate 1979-82 figures.

FIGURE 3.2
Rate of Growth of Equity Joint Ventures, 1982–1988

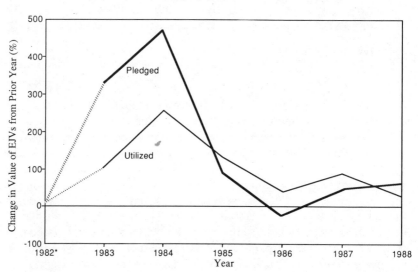

*Growth rate for 1982 over 1981 estimated based on aggregate 1979-81 figures.

for somewhat by the gradual addition of supplementary regulations (including regulations on investment in the SEZs, labor use, foreign exchange expenditures, and taxation of joint ventures), and although investors were glad that the new rules helped clarify the investment environment, they correctly read this trend to indicate that China was building a regulatory environment that was quite restrictive.[11] The confidence of foreigners was further affected by the government's retreat in 1980 from its original, highly ambitious domestic construction plans; for example, the Chinese government's cancellation of large contracts for the steel plant being constructed at Boashan in cooperation with Japanese companies exacerbated the existing wariness of Japanese investors. Hence, despite some progress in attracting foreign investment, and enthusiasm about the "China market," the perception held by foreign investors was problematic.

By 1983, the reformers recognized that the regulatory environment for foreign investors had to be improved if China was going to attract capital at a level that would support the Four Modernizations. They hoped to relieve the doubts of many potential investors through promulgation of another major piece of legislation on joint ventures in September 1983. The Joint Venture Implementing Regulations initiated a second regulatory phase (late 1983 to mid-1986). When these regulations were announced, Yuan Mu indicated clearly that a central purpose was to improve the investment environment in order that investment might be increased: "The Chinese government hopes that the formal promulgation and implementation of the Regulations shall not only enable the existing Chinese-foreign joint ventures to be run more successfully and have a greater development on the basis thereof, but also attract more foreign investors to cooperate with various departments concerned of [sic] our country to establish new joint ventures."[12]

The Implementing Regulations were designed to improve the investment environment not, primarily, by liberalizing it, but by clarifying it in a way that would give investors greater confidence and guide those who were negotiating joint ventures. In particular, these regulations provided greater detail about China's policy on the important issues of profit repatriation, technology transfer, and foreign exchange. By this time, moreover, investors also were growing more optimistic that the reformers would continue to dominate conservatives, at least in the area of economic policy. They could note with favor the efforts of reformers in 1984 to extend economic reform to the urban economy (particularly efforts to decentralize economic decisionmaking to provincial and local levels) and the promulgation of new patent and accounting laws that were to be announced in 1985. As a result of these changes in the views of both foreign investors and the Chinese government, many contracts that had been in the process of negotiation in prior years were concluded, and new negotiations were finalized much more quickly. The pace of investment flowing into equity joint ventures began to increase dramatically in the second phase. The growth rate of utilized and pledged investment in equity joint ventures in 1984 soared 257% and 463%, respectively, and, though not as dramatic as in 1984, remained high in 1985 (figure 3.2). The rate of growth in utilized and pledged direct investment in all forms also grew sharply in 1984 over 1983 (97% and 53%, respectively; figure 3.1).

But from 1985 to 1986 (that is, in the middle of the second phase), these growth rates slowed dramatically, and by some measures even declined. In 1986, the rate of growth of utilized investment in equity ventures plummeted by over two-thirds, to 39% from 132%. The rate of growth for utilized investments in all forms dropped to only 13%, from 32% the previous year. Even more striking were the losses in pledged investment, a leading indicator of investment. The rate of pledged investment in both equity ventures and all forms were even negative (-32% and -52%, respectively). Although drops in foreign investment can plausibly result from a number of factors, in this case the dramatic decline reflected not sudden changes in international investment trends or other exogenous factors but, rather, a growing wariness on the part of foreign investors about the problems in China's overall economy and the effect of these problems on joint ventures.[13] There was particular concern about the tremendous expansion in Chinese imports in 1985 and 1986 that caused the government to severely curtail domestic spending of foreign exchange. This curtailment affected joint ventures immediately, as fewer domestic buyers could pay for joint venture goods in foreign currency. Added to existing difficulties joint ventures were facing in exporting their products, the forced reduction of domestic sources of foreign exchange made it very difficult for them to earn the foreign exchange they needed to both import materials and, eventually, repatriate profits. (This crisis is discussed further in chapter 4.) These problems spurred lobbying efforts, and even vociferous complaints, by foreign business interests. The joint venture with the American Motors Company (AMC) to produce jeeps in Beijing became notorious for publicizing the problems that arose during this period, but other ventures were similarly affected. Their concerns were voiced through the major U.S. business association with interests in China, the U.S.-China Business Council. In meetings with Chinese officials involved in formulating investment policy, the Council members communicated explicitly that certain changes would be needed if China wished to induce more investment. The U.S. embassy in Beijing also circulated a memo to Chinese leaders during this period citing the major complaints of U.S. investors, and indicating that this environment was posing a strong obstacle to U.S. investment.[14] Adding to the external pressures on China was the fact that competition for investment within

Asia was growing throughout the 1980s; competitive liberalizations by Asian nations threatened to provide favorable alternative locations to some investors, particularly those seeking a source of low-wage labor.

During the second phase, the reformers also gave other indications that they were not satisfied with the flow of investment. The Seventh Five-Year Plan announced in September 1985 called for a significant increase over the previous five years of foreign investment absorbed during the 1986–1990 period to between $7 billion and $8 billion. That the reformers hoped for the conclusion of many more joint venture contracts was also suggested by the comments of some that China was far from reaching a point where foreign investment would threaten the values of self-reliance and independence; even before the 1986 decline, a key reform economist noted during the second phase that China could afford to have 5%, or 25,000, of its enterprises engage in joint ventures with foreign firms, a number that China was still far from reaching.[15] Other signs further signaled that the expectations of reformers for the level of investment were not being met. In Shanghai, for example, the goal stated in a plan approved by the State Council in 1985 was to absorb $4 billion in utilized investment by 1990, but this turned out to be unreachable without the unexpected inclusion of foreign loans.[16] Nor were expectations generated by the volume of pledged investment met; as tables 3-A and 3-B indicate, the portion of pledged investment that actually was utilized (in both equity ventures and all forms) was less than 50% in the first half of the decade.

By the middle of 1986, the reformers were well aware of the plummeting growth rates for foreign direct investment, of the complaints of foreigners, and of competition among developing countries for direct investment.[17] They sought ways to respond to foreign concerns and to satisfy their own goals. The government solicited foreign views on a draft of a new law, and in late 1986 announced the new law, which contained a number of clauses that had been lobbied for strenuously by the U.S.-China Business Council and by individual firms. In October, the State Council promulgated the "Provisions for the Encouragement of Foreign Investment" (the "1986 Provisions").[18] The 1986 Provisions marked the beginning of the third phase. They were followed in the next several months by a set of central regulations to implement them and by a flurry of municipal and provincial-level regulations. Like the 1983 Implementing Regulations, the Provisions clarified the legal environment for joint ventures. Yet they also went beyond clarification to liberalize substantially the investment environment in order to attract investors. The Provisions offered incentives explicitly designed to encourage investment in the very areas the government wanted to promote: advanced technology and export-capable sectors. They also attempted to further guarantee the autonomy of joint ventures from external bureaucratic interference, eliminate many local costs that foreigners had believed to be unfair, and provide alternative ways for joint ventures to balance foreign exchange—all problems about which investors had complained loudly. Many of the provincial and local versions of these regulations went even further than the central regulations to induce investment to meet the concerns of investors. New incentives, such as favorable tax and customs treatment, positioned China well in the competition with its Asian neighbors for investment. [19] The liberalizations continued throughout the third phase as well in an effort to attract still greater levels of investment. A sweeping policy announcement by Zhao Ziyang in early 1988 stressing the importance of developing the open coastal areas gave further signals that China was serious about the "open" policy.

In addition to the volatility and, after 1984–1985, the slowing of the growth rate of foreign direct investment, the reformers may have been reacting to evidence that the amount of capital coming into China was insufficient to meet the challenge, especially of transferring massive technology and management skills by the early twentieth century, and that foreign investment was playing less of a role in the economy than it had in other developing countries. The absolute amount of foreign capital that China had absorbed was not trivial; between 1980 and 1985, for example, China was the fifth largest recipient of foreign direct investment among all developing countries. [20] But when compared to the size of China's economy, the amount was relatively small. For example, the absolute value of U.S. investment in China by 1986, at $199 million, was still low compared to the $3.6 billion and $2.3 billion that U.S. companies had invested in Hong Kong and Singapore, respectively, by that time, although the latter economies had been open for a longer period. [21] Similarly, data on the contribution of foreign capital to China's own economy—an even better standard for judging the economic success of equity ventures—suggest that the contribution of foreign investment was relatively small. The foreign-invested sector accounted for only 1% of China's gross domestic product in 1985, for example, which was a fraction of the amount contributed by the foreign sector in 1979 to other large developing countries such as Indonesia (11%), Brazil (7%), and Mexico (5%). (The amount is comparable to India [2%], which like China is a continental economy and has a restrictive investment environment.) The value for China was also low compared to three of the East Asian "newly industrialized countries": Singapore (19%), Hong Kong (15%), and Taiwan (8%). (South Korea, also a highly restricted environment for foreign investment until the 1980s, had a figure comparable to China's [3%].) [22]

The effort to spur more rapid growth in foreign direct investment was relatively successful. Following the promulgation of the Provisions, the value of newly pledged investment in equity joint ventures in 1987 rose 41% (85% for utilized) and the value of newly pledged contracts signed in

1987 for all forms of investment rose 31% (23% for utilized). This level of growth was sustained across most measures in 1988, and the absolute value of equity joint venture contracts finally rose above the level reached in 1985. Another feature that appeared in the third phase was the increase in investment from Taiwan and, though to a lesser degree, South Korea. While restrictions by these governments formally prohibited Taiwan and South Korean investment, some had been channeled into China using Hong Kong "fronts." Beginning in 1988, though, this investment became more public, and began to rise; indeed, from January to September of 1989, Taiwan's pledged investment in China was $400 million, surpassing Japan's investment over the same period ($297 million), and putting Taiwan in third place among investors. The enthusiasm of Taiwanese businesses for investment in China just following the Tiananmen events is also notable.[23]

For most investors, however, the 1988 spurt of growth was halted in mid-1989 in the wake of the Tiananmen crackdown. Despite the fact that the government had embarked on a severe retrenchment program in the fall of 1988, growth of foreign investment remained strong in the first half of 1989: between January and June of 1989, utilized foreign direct investment (all forms) rose 21.5% over the same period in 1988. Pledged investment rose even more (44.2%). But for the whole year, utilized investment rose only 3.1% over 1988, and pledged only 5.6%. Both of these figures reflect a dramatic decline in investment after June, particularly after September.[24] The 1989 decline appears to have been particularly dramatic for Western and Japanese investors, as government figures showed that there was an absolute decline of investment in 1989 if Taiwan and Hong Kong investment were excluded.[25] Although a decline in foreign investment did not appear until after June 1989, investors were also cognizant of the effects of the broader economic retrenchment. Efforts to slow the economy, particularly by reining in *renminbi* credit, took a toll on existing joint ventures. The credit squeeze made it difficult for ventures to collect bills, which in turn stymied operations.

The government, in part out of recognition of the severity of the foreign—particularly Western and Japanese—reaction to the environment in late 1988 and 1989, went ahead with the passage of several amendments to the 1979 Joint Venture Law in the spring of 1990. These amendments neither introduced major new restrictions nor offered a major liberalization, yet they did codify several rules designed to encourage investment. Particularly important among the amendments were the agreements to eliminate the time limit applied to some ventures, and to allow foreigners to act as joint venture board chairs.[26]

Examination of the flow of investment over the 1980s, and even into early 1990, thus illustrates how this flow was tied to foreign views of the investment environment, and how in turn the reformers, desiring to increase the volume of investment and to allay the concerns of foreign investors, responded in ways that led to increases in the growth of foreign investment. Although liberalization did not occur across the board or, where it did occur, to the same extent for all controls, it was a significant trend for many controls. Chapters 4 and 5 examine precisely how the controls on specific issues that were established in the early years of the policy were changed in the second and third phases as a result of the various forces influencing the policy.

EQUITY JOINT VENTURES IN CHINA—
DESCRIPTIVE AND STATISTICAL DATA, 1979–1988

Having identified the factors fostering the changes in the government's controls over foreign direct investment and the pattern of such investment in China during the 1980s, it is necessary to establish precisely what constitutes the equity joint venture form of investment. This section defines this form of investment and places it in the context of other forms of direct investment. It also provides statistical data on the regional and sectoral trends apparent in investment in joint ventures, and on the characteristics of size of joint ventures and the origin and quantity of foreign capital involved. Finally, this part makes an early attempt to assess the contribution of equity ventures to China's overall economy and the success of joint venture operations. Much of the data contained in the tables that follow is calculated from large samples of equity joint ventures compiled by Nai-ruenn Chen (for 1979–1984) and by the Ministry of Foreign Economic Relations and Trade (MOFERT) (1985–1988).[27] The basic data from these two sources is presented in Appendix C.

The Context and Definition of Equity Joint Ventures

The Chinese government has attempted to attract foreign capital through a variety of formats: equity joint ventures, contractual joint ventures, joint offshore oil development projects, and wholly foreign-owned ventures. (Contractual joint ventures, joint oil projects, wholly foreign-owned ventures, and compensation trade are described in more detail in Appendix B.) Investment also has occurred through commercial credit channels, such as compensation trade, and processing and assembly agreements, though these are not considered direct investment. Government and private loans (which are technically distinct from foreign investment) have been another important source of foreign capital.

Tables 3-C and 3-D illustrate the pattern of investment during the 1980s for the various forms of foreign capital in China, excluding commercial credit. Direct investment made up a significant portion of all foreign

TABLE 3-C
Foreign Direct Investment and Foreign Loans (Pledged), 1979–1989

	1979–1984	1985	1986	1987	1988	1989	1979–1989
Loans							
Number	117	72	53	56	118	—	416[a]
Value ($billions)	15.96	3.53	8.41	7.82	9.81	—	45.53[a]
FDI							
Number	3248	3073	1498	2233	5945	5784	21,781
Value ($billions)	8.99	5.93	2.84	3.71	5.29	5.60	32.36

Sources: 1979–1988: MOFERT *Almanacs* for 1984, 1985, 1986, 1987, 1988, and 1989.
1989: FBIS-CHI-90-017 (25 January 1990), p. 29.
[a] Excludes 1989 in totals.

TABLE 3-D
Foreign Direct Investment (Pledged) by Type of Contract, 1979–1988

	1979–1984	1985	1986	1987	1988	1979–1988[a]
Equity JVs						
Number	931	1412	892	1395	3909	8539 (53%)
Value ($billions)	1.39	2.03	1.38	1.95	3.13	9.88 (37%)
Contractual JVs						
Number	2212	1611	582	789	1621	6815 (43%)
Value ($billions)	4.71	3.49	1.36	1.28	1.62	12.46 (46.5%)
Joint Oil Development						
Number	31	4	6	3	5	49 (.3%)
Value ($billions)	2.42	0.36	0.08	0.005	0.06	2.93 (11%)
100% Foreign Owned						
Number	74	46	18	46	410	594 (4%)
Value ($billions)	0.47	0.05	0.02	0.47	0.48	1.49 (5.5%)
All Forms						
Number	3248	3073	1498	2233	5945	15,997
Value ($billions)	8.99	5.93	2.84	3.71	5.29	26.76

Sources: MOFERT *Almanacs* for 1984, 1985, 1986, 1987, 1988, and 1989.
[a] Figure in parentheses is percentage of total for 1979–1988.

capital (including loans) that flowed into China by the end of 1989, reaching $32 billion, or 42% of the total. Within foreign direct investment, equity and contractual joint ventures constituted the most important sectors. As of the end of 1988, contracts for equity and contractual joint ventures accounted for the vast majority of the total number of direct investment contracts, 53% and 43%, respectively. Equity joint ventures and contractual ventures made up 37% and 46.5%, respectively, of the total dollar volume of direct investment. Although the volume of foreign capital invested in projects for oil development had been important in the early 1980s, this sector declined from one-quarter of the total volume of foreign direct investment at the end of 1984 to only 11% at the end of 1988. Conversely, wholly foreign-owned enterprises gained in importance in terms of numbers, although the share in volume of investment remained steady at approximately 5%.

Equity joint ventures thus played a central part in the government's strategy to attract foreign investment. Indeed, they were the government's preferred mechanism for introducing foreign direct investment into China during the 1980s. Largely because of this preference, the government made efforts to codify the legal status of equity ventures before they did so for any other form. The various nonequity forms of investment, especially contractual joint ventures, were subject to political, bureaucratic, economic, and (with some variation) legal environments very similar to equity ventures, and the provisions negotiated into contracts often resembled those found in equity joint ventures. Moreover, the changes that occurred in the investment environment for equity ventures extended in many ways to the other forms. Thus, although much of the analysis contained here and in the following chapters focuses on equity joint ventures, much of it can be generalized to the other forms of direct investment in China.

Equity joint ventures in China, as in other developing countries, were—and continue in the 1990s to be—characterized by several key features.[28] They are limited liability companies established by two or more partners that pool assets to create a separate legal entity for the purpose of undertaking a specific business (such as producing cars).[29] The objective is usually to extend or complement the business of the investors. Like other enterprises in China, a joint venture is a production "unit" (*danwei*). The partners to the venture own its assets (except that the Chinese government retains formal ownership rights to the land) and share in the profits, losses, and risks. The foreign partners routinely have been private foreign companies or individuals. Chinese partners have included state-owned enterprises, quasi-governmental investment "corporations," banks, or other government bureaus. Collective enterprises sometimes have entered into joint ventures.

By law, a foreign party to a joint venture in China may contribute between 25% and 99% of equity to an enterprise. The contribution of either side may be in the form of cash, material goods, equipment, buildings, know-how, or the right to use the venture site. The foreign contribution in most cases has been in cash and know-how, while the Chinese contribution has generally consisted of cash, the factory site, existing equipment, and site-use rights. The partners or the venture itself also may borrow capital from Chinese or foreign banks, although the permissible amount has varied depending on the size of the venture, and Chinese borrowers may need state approval.[30] With few exceptions, joint venture contracts have been limited to between ten and thirty years, although the precise duration is negotiable and the contract may be renewed. When a contract expires, all assets (including technology) are to revert to the Chinese, although the foreign partners are to be compensated.

Once established, joint ventures are to be run by a board of directors made up of representatives of both the Chinese and foreign partners. The Chinese partner is legally required to assign the board chairman, although contracts generally have provided that all major decisions must gain the tacit or explicit consent of all partners. On a day-to-day basis, most ventures have operated with the help of expatriate managers and/or technicians. The stated intention of both sides, however, has been that the Chinese managers should learn foreign management techniques so that foreign managers can be phased out. The Chinese government also has asserted that profit should not be the sole criterion of enterprise management (social welfare functions for workers and other socialist values are to be considered as well). Nonetheless, Chinese leaders have hoped for profitable sales in the international market. The government formally has guaranteed that foreign partners can earn and repatriate "legitimate" profits, which it has defined as the aftertax amount proportionate to the foreign partner's equity contribution. Moreover, the government has emphasized the goal of raising productivity and efficiency of the enterprise. Officials also have guaranteed that under "normal" circumstances, foreign holdings will not be nationalized, and that if nationalization does occur, the foreign owner will be "reasonably" compensated.[31]

The process by which joint ventures have been established also has followed international practice. As with equity joint ventures in many other countries, formal contracts for Sino-foreign joint ventures are negotiated between prospective partners, and must obtain the approval of the government before they can become operative. Initial contacts are made by either the Chinese or foreign partners, often with the help of a consultant who is familiar with the respective countries or sectors. The prospective Chinese partner to a joint venture (or a government bureaucracy interested in pursuing a joint venture) must in most cases obtain the permission of the State Planning Commission or its local branch to undertake formal negotiations with a prospective foreign partner. Once formal approval for the project proposal has been granted, but prior to signing a specific contract, the partners are to carry out a detailed feasibility study stating how the venture will be set up, what needs it will fill for China, how competitive the product will be internationally, projected costs, what materials it will require, which bureaucracy will allocate these materials, and how it will balance foreign exchange expenditures and receipts. The feasibility study also must be approved, usually by the local bureau of MOFERT or the planning commission. (The particular agency with jurisdiction depends on the size, proposed task, and location of the project.)

In the early years of the policy, joint venture contracts sometimes were negotiated quickly and lacked detail. During most of the 1980s, however, contract negotiations lasted several months or even years, and were more detailed. Government approvals routinely took several months, especially since many offices had to give their assent to the terms of the contract. Efforts were made to speed this process in the late 1980s. More generally, after the joint venture has been approved and the partners have signed the contract, they must register with the local government and obtain a business license. At this point, the partners to the new venture may become operative.

The Chinese government's preference for equity joint ventures over other investment forms arose from a number of factors related to these various characteristics. Leaders believed equity joint ventures would engender a greater commitment by the foreign side to the success of the project more than all other forms of direct investment, except wholly foreign-owned projects. As equity owners with some control over the operation of the venture, the government reasoned, the foreign partner would be more committed to transferring proprietary technology and management skills needed to make the venture succeed economically, particularly in export markets. Unlike wholly foreign-owned enterprises, moreover, equity ventures were seen to allow the government, as an active co-owner, a way to control more directly the activities of foreign investors. The symbolic value of being a co-owner also helped them preserve nationalist values. For these reasons, the Chinese government generally encouraged, and even pressured, investors to adopt the equity joint venture format during the 1980s.

The Regional Emphasis of the Foreign Investment Policy

China's foreign investment policy has had an important geographic dimension: the reformers targeted China's coastal areas as the leading regions for the country's economic development, and as the places from which the development process can spread to the rest of China. The Chinese government originally emphasized that foreign direct investment should flow primarily into only specially designated areas, hoping that by isolating foreign investment it could observe its activities and guard against any negative effects that might appear. In early 1979, the leadership formally created four SEZs in which foreign investment would actively be sought.[32] The four zones, each of which is a small area on China's southeast coast, are: Shenzhen, located opposite Hong Kong; Shantou, near Shenzhen; Zhuhai, across the border from Macao in Guangdong Province; and Xiamen (Amoy), on the coast of Fujian Province.

The SEZs originally were modeled after export processing zones (EPZs) found elsewhere in Asia. EPZs provide special production bases for export trade, a function that is central to the export-led development strategy of many Asian "newly industrialized countries." They also offer incentives in the form of reduced duties and taxes, flexible investment formats, relatively inexpensive unskilled labor, and streamlined administration. China's SEZs offered similar incentives, but quickly took on additional, more comprehensive functions than the EPZs: reformist leaders hoped not only that the SEZs, like the EPZs, would be a major source of export earnings, but also that they would become major centers of general economic reform. The SEZs were to emphasize modernization of a broader range of sectors than did the EPZs, including industry, agriculture, tourism, real estate, science, and education. (The exception was Shantou, which remained closer to the EPZ model.)[33]

The location of the four original zones in southern coastal areas had several benefits. They could take advantage of the proximity to overseas Chinese business communities in Hong Kong, Macao, and eventually, it was hoped, Taiwan. These overseas regions, with which southern China has strong cultural, familial, historical, and, in the case of Hong Kong, economic ties, served as convenient sources of capital and expertise, and offered additional links to other industrial nations. The SEZs also were isolated from major population centers of the PRC, thereby protecting the rest of the country from unforeseen negative results of their experimentation.[34] The reformers also hoped that, by exemplifying an official willingness to accept more market-oriented economies and by creating concrete ties with Hong Kong, Macao, and Taiwan, the zones would ease the eventual re-assimilation of these areas under PRC rule.

As the reformers intended, the four SEZs proved to be important locations for investment. They attracted $3.7 billion in foreign direct investment (all forms) by the end of 1986, or approximately 21% of all pledged foreign direct investment in China over that period. Shenzhen alone utilized $1.1 billion in investment (including loans) by the end of 1986. By the end of 1987, the SEZs had signed 3500 (35%) of the over 10,000 invest-

TABLE 3-E

Origin of Investors in EJVs in the SEZs, 1985–1988 (Sample)

	Origin of Investor					
Location of Investment	Hong Kong/ Macao	United States	Japan	Other Asia	W. Europe and Canada	Total
Shenzhen[a]	164	14	3	11	4	196 (62.0%)
Shantou	16	0	0	2	0	18 (5.7%)
Zhuhai	30	1	2	3	1	37 (11.7%)
Xiamen	40	5	3	14	3	65 (20.6%)
TOTAL ALL SEZs	250 (79.1%)	20 (6.3%)	8 (2.5%)	30 (9.5%)	8 (2.5%)	316[b]

Sources: MOFERT Almanac, 1986, 1987, 1988, and 1989 samples. Further data on this sample is presented in appendix C.

[a] Shenzhen figures exclude cases listed in the Almanac as located in Baoan County, which surrounds Shenzhen SEZ, and cases for which the origin of the investor was not identified.

[b] Of these, 56 were established in 1985, 129 in 1986, 98 in 1987, and 33 in 1988.

ment contracts, of which 1300 were operational.[35] The SEZs also housed a large number of equity joint ventures. They contained one-third of China's equity joint ventures at the end of 1984, and Shenzhen alone contained 23% of the total number of ventures in China.[36]

As table 3-E indicates, in the MOFERT sample nearly 80% of the ventures established in the four SEZs from 1985 to 1988 were from Hong Kong and Macao. The table also illustrates the extent to which Shenzhen dominated the other SEZs in attracting investment in equity joint ventures: 62% of the sample of ventures established in the four SEZs in this period were in Shenzhen.

Although Shenzhen housed a significant number of equity joint ventures, such ventures were less prevalent there than were other forms of investment. Shenzhen's location fifteen miles from Hong Kong, and its relatively inexpensive wage rates, held great appeal for highly competitive Hong Kong manufacturers. As noted in chapter 1, investments using Hong Kong capital consisted primarily of moving existing simple manufacturing or assembly operations across the border in order to garner even small cost savings. Rather than financing technologically sophisticated equity joint ventures, Hong Kong capital (which, again, dominated foreign direct investment in the SEZs) flowed primarily into low-technology processing and assembly plants and compensation trade arrangements, contractual joint ventures in tourism, or speculative construction or real estate deals.[37]

Despite their importance as locations for joint ventures, the unique role of the SEZs declined after the first phase of the investment policy. As the desire to absorb increasing amounts of foreign capital grew, and as the problems in the SEZs (discussed in chapter 4) became evident, the government tried new ways of absorbing foreign investment. Some economists argued that the SEZs should be de-emphasized in favor of China's northern areas because the zones had relatively little to offer investors. In the spring of 1984, the government granted much of the region along China's eastern and southern coasts a special "open" status.[38] The government designated fourteen major coastal cities as "open cities" and granted them many of the privileges it had earlier reserved for the SEZs. All of these cities were former Treaty Ports, and contained some of China's most advanced infrastructural and industrial facilities. Several inland cities, such as Wuhan, Chongqing, Harbin, and Shenyang, also were granted expanded authority to attract foreign investment in 1984. In February 1985, three other large coastal regions were declared Open Economic Zones (OEZs), and were given the task of focusing on export production and attracting foreign investment. (These new regions encompassed some of the SEZs and "open" cities.) The three regions were the Pearl River Delta OEZ (centered on Guangzhou, and including Shenzhen and Zhuhai SEZs), the Southern Fujian Delta OEZ (including Xiamen), and the Yangze River Delta OEZ (centered on Shanghai, and including Zhejiang and Jiangsu provinces). The total area and population encompassed in the SEZs, open cities, and OEZs was significant: by early 1988 the area covered 150,000 square kilometers and had a population of 90 million. In March 1988, Hainan Island, in the South China Sea, was declared a "super SEZ" and was given provincial status with greater authority to attract foreign business.[39] As a result of the expansion of the open regions, a much larger area thus faced the opportunities and risks of the foreign investment policy.

The central government granted a high degree of financial and administrative autonomy to the governments of the open areas, and most extensively to the Guangdong and Fujian provincial governments, in order that the localities might more easily make foreign business connections. Unlike most areas in China, the governments of the SEZs and several open cities (Shanghai, Tianjin, and Beijing) were given authority to approve projects with investment under a certain amount. Moreover, especially after 1986, the governments of the SEZs, open cities, and many provinces promulgated their own regulations offering incentives to investors to compete with other Asian countries and with each other. In granting substan-

TABLE 3-F
EJVs Established by Location, 1979–1988 (Sample)
(percentage)

Province or Municipality	Special Open Region[a]	1979– 1984	1985	1986	1987	1988	1979– 1988
Guangdong	Guangzhou, Beihai Zhanjiang, Shantou* Zhuhai*, Shenzhen*	40.3	26.6	35.7	28.1	16.4	31.1
Fujian	Fuzhou, Xiamen*	24.5	16.0	10.2	9.5	8.5	15.5
Beijing		4.6	6.8	3.3	7.8	5.0	5.3
Tianjin		3.4	6.6	5.0	5.0	4.8	4.7
Shanghai		3.5	5.7	4.8	6.1	8.7	5.4
Jiangsu	Lianyungang, Nantong	2.1	4.2	6.8	6.5	11.8	5.7
Liaoning	Dalian	3.1	3.3	3.9	4.3	6.6	4.1
Zhejiang	Ningbo, Wenzhou	2.8	1.8	4.1	6.3	6.4	4.0
Shandong	Yantai, Qingdao	1.4	3.5	3.7	4.5	7.0	3.6
Hebei	Qinhuangdao	1.3	3.3	2.2	3.2	5.8	2.9
Guangxi		2.4	2.6	1.7	1.3	0.6	1.8
Hunan		2.6	2.2	0.9	1.9	0.2	1.7
Jiangxi		1.4	2.9	1.3	1.9	2.5	1.9
All other provinces		6.4	14.5	16.3	13.6	15.7	12.2
TOTAL		99.8%	100%	99.9%	100%	100%	99.9%
(Number of EJVs)		(930)	(455)	(460)	(463)	(483)	(2791)

Sources: 1979–1984: N. R. Chen (1986), p. 18 (table 13); 1985–1988: MOFERT *Almanacs* (1986, 1987, 1988, and 1989). Further data on this sample is presented in appendix C.

[a] Localities noted in this column (plus Shanghai and Tianjin) are "open" cities, unless followed by (*), indicating an SEZ. Not all EJVs in a province (or municipality) with open coastal cities may be located in these cities or the SEZs in that region.

tial autonomy to the coastal regions, the government removed an unprecedented amount of formal authority over foreign transactions from direct control of central ministries.[40]

Still more efforts to expand the areas designated with the special "open" status were made in the mid-1980s. Zhao Ziyang, as premier, asserted in his speech to the Thirteenth National Party Congress in October 1987 that expansion should continue indefinitely, stating that it was necessary to consolidate the policy, "with the 'open' policy extending progressively from the SEZs to coastal cities, then to coastal economic regions, and finally to interior areas." In early 1988, Zhao further suggested that in the short term the privileges granted to the SEZs and "open" cities would be extended to the entire seaboard.[41] This would bring the number of people directly exposed to foreign investment on China's coasts to 200 million (approximately 18% of the population). With these extensions, the original experimental nature of the four SEZs to a large extent had been rendered moot.

The more developed coastal areas, especially the southern and southeastern provinces and the Beijing, Tianjin, and Shanghai metropolitan areas, were in fact the heavily favored recipients of equity joint ventures compared to inland areas, as illustrated in table 3-F. Consistent with the findings for the SEZs, the provinces of Guangdong and Fujian housed the majority of equity joint ventures at the end of 1984 (65%). According to the sample figures, the dominance of Guangdong and Fujian had weakened by the end of 1988 (to 47%). Yet equity joint ventures continued to be concentrated in the coastal regions; by the end of 1988, 77% of all ventures sampled were located in these or other coastal provinces that contain "open coastal cities" (Guangdong, Fujian, Jiangsu, Liaoning, Zhejiang, Shandong, and Hebei), or in the municipalities of Tianjin or Shanghai.

The Sectoral Emphasis of the Foreign Investment Policy

The Chinese government intended that joint ventures be set up in sectors it viewed as crucial to China's rapid modernization. Enterprises established in these sectors ideally were to provide advanced technology, foreign exchange, or export capability. In the early 1980s, energy, chemicals and metallurgy, building materials, machine manufacturing, instruments, electronics, computers, communications, and light industry were particularly encouraged, as was tourism. Table 3-G shows that the percent of foreign investment into industrial and tourism sectors was significant by 1985. After this time, the government began to discourage investment in tourism and real estate in favor of high technology and export-oriented manufacturing sectors, for while these investments did help generate foreign exchange earnings, they did not bring in advanced technology or industrial management skills. There was also much evidence of overexpansion in both industries. Although the effects of the new priorities were not immediately realized (by 1986 the amount of foreign investment in the service sectors reached nearly 60% of all foreign investment), by 1988, investment in tourism, real estate, and other services decreased dramatically, while investment in industry increased.

Data presented in table 3-H on a sample of 301 equity joint ventures established prior to 1985 (excluding any with Hong Kong and Macao partners) generally also show that the preponderance of foreign capital was invested in industry and property development (tourism and real estate). In terms of the numbers of equity joint venture contracts, the industrial sectors were the greatest beneficiaries; between 60% and 80% of the con-

TABLE 3-G
Value of Foreign Direct Investment (Pledged) by Sector, 1983–1988
(percentage)

Sector	1983	1984	1985	1986[a]	1987[a]	1988[a]
1. Tourism, real estate, utilities, and services	4.7[b]	32.7[b]	35.9	57.1	39.7	10.0[c]
2. Agriculture, forestry, husbandry, and fishing	2.0	2.7	2.0	2.2	3.4	3.9
3. Light and heavy industry	13.7	21.5	37.6	27.7	47.9	75.9
4. Geology and prospecting (coal, oil)	52.6	0.5	5.7	—[e]	—[e]	0.03
5. Building	2.6	2.7	2.1	1.9	1.5	2.2
6. Communications, post, and telecommunications	3.2	2.9	1.7	1.2	0.4	1.7
7. Commerce and catering	2.1[d]	3.8	8.3	3.5	0.8	1.2
8. Culture, education, social services, sports, and hygiene	0.2	0.1	0.9	2.0	0.7	0.9
9. Science, research, and technical services	—[e]	—[e]	0.1	0.01	0.02	0.1
10. Other[f]	18.9	33.1	5.8	4.5	5.7	3.8
TOTAL	100%	100%	100.1%	100.1%	100.1%	99.7%

Sources: Percentages calculated from figures in MOFERT *Almanacs*: 1984 (pp. 1100–01); 1985 (pp. 1075–76); 1986 (p. 1221); 1987 (p. 625); 1988 (p. 689); and 1989 (p. 617).

[a] MOFERT figures for 1986, 1987, and 1988 exclude compensation trade, processing/ assembly, and leasing. Figures for 1983 to 1985 include these activities.

[b] Category included only tourism in 1983 and 1984. It is possible that real estate and utilities are reflected in figures for "Other" in these years, but the data do not specify this.

[c] In 1988, this category excluded tourism, and no other category included it.

[d] Catering (which is mostly for the offshore oil industry) was included in category 3 in 1983. In the 1984 *Almanac* report of 1983 figures, category 7 was called "Commerce," and category 4 was called "Offshore oil development." Hence, it is likely that for that year catering ventures were included in category 4.

[e] MOFERT provided no separate category for this sector in this year. Figures are possibly reflected in "Other," or no investment was made in this sector.

[f] For 1985 and 1988 only, MOFERT included a separate "Finance and insurance" category. Here, this figure is included under "Other." "Finance and insurance" constituted 1% of the total in 1985, and 0.2% in 1988.

tracts concluded were for heavy and light industry projects. Although real estate and tourism sectors did not see as many contracts, they constituted a significant proportion of the value of investment prior to 1985. This discrepancy between number and volume reflects the fact that projects in these sectors were often very large, particularly those involving Japanese investors. There is also evidence that the preferred sector for investment

TABLE 3-H
Foreign Investment in EJVs by Sector and
Origin of Investor, 1979–1985 (Sample)[a]
(percentage)

	United States (n = 97) # / Value	Japan (86) # / Value	Other Western[b] (66) # / Value	Asia[c] (52) # / Value
Heavy industry (including electronics)	49.5 / 46.0	31.4 / 13.7	51.5 / 79.2	36.5 / 38.2
Light industry (consumer goods)	24.7 / 17.7	30.2 / 12.7	27.3 / 13.1	40.4 / 22.7
Property development (including tourism)	2.1 / 19.8	12.8 / 62.6	0.5 / 2.6	7.7 / 19.7
Services (including engineering, consulting)	8.3 / 2.3	14.0 / 5.2	12.0 / 2.3	3.9 / 0.7
Transportation	5.2 / 2.7	4.7 / 2.5	3.0 / 0.7	1.9 / 6.2
Medicine	2.1 / 9.5	0.0 / 0.0	3.0 / 2.0	0.0 / 0.0
Agriculture	3.1 / 1.7	7.0 / 1.4	1.5 / 0.0	9.6 / 12.5
TOTAL	95 / 99.7	100.1 / 98.1	98.8 / 99.9	100 / 100

Source: NCUSCT (1987), p. 131.

[a] Based on a sample of 301 EJVs established between 1979 and 1985. The sample excludes investment from Hong Kong and Macao. The source does not explain why some columns do not total 100%.

[b] Includes Europe, Australia, New Zealand, and Canada.

[c] Includes Singapore, Thailand, and Philippines only.

varied according to the origin of the investor: Japanese investors more often invested in property development, whereas U.S., Western European, and Asian investors (excluding those from Hong Kong and Macao) more often invested in heavy industry.

Additional Characteristics of Equity Joint Ventures

In addition to showing strong regional and sectoral patterns, the flow of foreign capital into equity ventures during the 1980s was characterized by distinct patterns in size, average value of foreign investment, percent foreign equity, and origin of investment.

The great majority of joint ventures established in the 1980s in China were quite small, with, again, the exceptions being mainly in real estate and tourism. The total investment from both Chinese and foreign partners together averaged about $4.7 million per project at the end of 1988. If the few largest joint ventures are excluded, the average total investment per

TABLE 3-I
Number of EJVs by Size of
Foreign Contribution, 1979–1988 (Sample)
(percentage)

FI ($millions)	1979–1984	1985	1986	1987	1988	Total
0–0.5	58.0	64.4	64.6	34.1	39.9	52.9
0.51–1.0	15.1	15.8	14.1	23.3	22.2	17.9
1.01–2.0	13.2	10.5	9.6	17.1	20.5	14.0
2.01–5.0	8.2	6.6	9.8	19.2	11.2	10.6
5.01–10.0	2.5	1.3	1.5	2.8	5.2	2.6
over 10.01	3.0	1.6	0.4	3.5	1.0	2.0
TOTAL	100.0	100.2	100.0	100.0	100.0	100.0
(n =)	(841)	(455)	(460)	(463)	(483)	(2702)

Sources: 1979–1984: N. R. Chen (1986), p. 16 (table 10); 1985–1988: MOF-ERT Almanacs for 1986, 1987, 1988, and 1989. Further data on the sample are presented in appendix C.

project during that period was only about $3 million.[42] The small size of these projects suited the objectives of both foreign firms and, in the early years, Chinese policymakers; Chinese reformers wished primarily to renovate small- and medium-sized enterprises whereas, by contributing relatively small amounts of equity, foreign firms aimed to minimize their financial risk while gaining a foothold in the domestic market. The average amount of capital contributed by foreign partners to equity joint ventures also was small. As is evident in table 3-I, 70% of equity joint ventures agreed to by the end of 1988 had $1 million or less in foreign capital and, of these, most had one-half million dollars or less of foreign capital. Very few equity joint ventures (4.6%) had a foreign capital contribution of more than $5 million. There was some change in this pattern over time: the ventures sampled in 1987 showed a trend toward larger amounts of foreign capital invested in each venture, with significant growth in the $0.51 million to $5 million range, coming at the expense of the lowest range. (Some reversal of this trend was evident in the 1988 sample.) Still, as of the end of 1988, the average amount of foreign capital per equity joint venture for all ventures was $1.25 million.[43]

Although the average size of joint ventures was small, their size varied substantially according to the origin of the foreign investor. As table 3-J indicates, the size of total investment in equity joint ventures ranged from "Other Asia" and "Other" categories at the low end (with an average of $3.4 million per venture) to Western European ventures at the high end (with an average of $8.7 million per venture). If the extremely large cases

TABLE 3-J
Average Size of Total Investment (TI) in EJVs by Origin, 1979–1988 (Sample)[a]
(millions of dollars)

Year	Hong Kong/ Macao	United States	Japan	Western Europe	Other Asia	Other	Un-known	All Origins
1979–1984	2.9	4.9	5.8	16.3	2.4[b]		N/A	3.8
1985	4.3[c]	2.8	6.4[d]	7.5	2.7	17.2	N/A	11.6
1986	1.7	4.5	2.4	3.2	1.8	6.4	N/A	2.2
1987	1.6	5.7	5.7[d]	8.4	1.6	2.7	N/A	2.6
1988	4.0	3.2	2.8	5.4	3.3	5.1	5.2	3.8
1979–1988	4.6[c]	4.1	4.6[d]	8.7	3.4[b]		5.2	4.7[e]

Sources: 1979–1984: N. R. Chen (1986), p. 17. 1985–1988: compiled from samples in MOFERT Almanacs (1986, 1987, 1988, and 1989). Data used to calculate this table are presented in appendix C.

TI = Total investment by both foreign and Chinese.

[a] Average is figured by dividing TI into number of ventures.

[b] Chen does not provide separate data for "Other Asia." 1979–1988 total combines "Other Asia" and "Other" categories.

[c] The sample includes an abnormally large EJV concluded in 1985 with a Hong Kong partner for a nuclear power plant worth $4 billion. If this case is excluded, the average TI for Hong Kong/Macao investors is figured as $4640 million divided by 1863 EJVs, or $2.5 million per EJV from 1979 to 1988.

[d] The sample includes two abnormally large EJVs with Japanese partners: one concluded in 1985 for a real estate investment project worth $150 million, and one concluded in 1987 for production of kinescopes worth $170 million. If these two cases are excluded, the average TI for Japanese investors is figured as $592 million divided by 198 EJVs, or $3 million per EJV from 1979 to 1988.

[e] If the three large cases noted in [c] and [d] are excluded, the total TI from all origins for 1979–1988 is $8244 million, and (divided by 2699 EJVs) the average TI is $3.1 million.

in the sample are excluded, joint ventures with Hong Kong/Macao firms are seen to have the lowest average total investment per venture ($2.5 million). Figures from the 1988 sample suggest an interesting trend: the average size of the investment increased significantly for ventures in the "Hong Kong/Macao" and "Other Asia" categories when compared with previous years.

Consistent with this data on the differentiation of total investment according to origin of investor is the substantial variation that appeared among countries in the amount of capital contributed by the foreign partner (see table 3-K). Western European countries contributed the largest amounts of capital, on average ($3.4 million per venture). Other countries fell in the $1.5 million to $2.1 million range. Once again, when the largest cases are eliminated (the cases of a $1 billion investment from Hong Kong,

TABLE 3-K

Foreign Contribution to Equity in EJVs by Investor Origin, 1979–1988 (Sample)

Origin	1979–1984 (%)[a]	1985 (%)	1986 (%)	1987 (%)	1988 (%)	1979–1988 (%)	Average Value of FI 1979–1988 ($millions)
Hong Kong/Macao	58.6	27.0[b]	39.1	33.9	37.1	36.4	1.7
United States	45.9	45.4	43.1	44.6	38.6	43.4	1.8
Japan	44.0	48.0[c]	41.7	48.1[d]	45.9	46.3	2.1
Western Europe	40.0	34.1	37.3	49.1	35.1	39.4	3.4
Other Asia[e]		45.8	44.6	47.5	34.5		
	46.6[g]					43.5	1.5
Other		60.4	31.0	40.0	44.6		
Unknown	—	—	—	—	42.3	42.3	2.2
All Countries	52.5	29.2[c]	40.5	41.4[d]	37.9	38.5[f]	1.8[f]

Sources: 1979–1984: N. R. Chen (1986), table 11. 1985–1988: compiled from samples in MOFERT Almanacs (1986, 1987, 1988, and 1989). Data used to calculate this table are presented in appendix C.

FI = Foreign investment; TI = Total investment

[a] Foreign investment as a percentage of total investment, combining all EJVs in each origin grouping.

[b] Includes a large case with a Hong Kong partner, with TI of $4 billion and FI of $1 billion. If this case is eliminated, the percentage of foreign investment for EJVs with Hong Kong firms for 1985 is 39%.

[c] Includes a large case with a Japanese partner, with TI of $150 million and FI of $75 million. If this case is eliminated, the percentage of FI for EJVs with Japanese firms in 1985 is 42%. If this case and the case noted in [b] are eliminated, the total FI for all countries in 1985 is $465 million, or 41% of a TI of $1.13 billion.

[d] Includes a large case with a Japanese partner, with a TI of $170 million and FI of $85 million. If this case is eliminated, the percentage of foreign investment for EJVs with Japanese firms for 1987 is 39%, and if eliminated for 1979–1988 (also excluding the 1985 case noted in [c]), it is 44%.

[e] Singapore, Philippines, Australia, New Zealand.

[f] If the three projects noted in [b], [c], and [d] are excluded, the total FI in the remaining 2699 EJVs for the 1979–1988 period is $3676 million, or an average of $1.4 million per venture. The total FI when these cases are excluded is 45% of the $8244 million TI.

[g] Chen does not provide separate data for "Other Asia." The 1979–1988 total combines "Other Asia" and "Other" categories.

and two investments—$75 million and $85 million—from Japan), the average foreign investment from Hong Kong and Japanese firms declined even further, to $1.2 million and $1.3 million, respectively.[44]

The percentage of foreign contribution to the total investment in equity joint ventures also varied somewhat according to the national origin of the investor, with investors from Hong Kong and Macao tending to contribute

TABLE 3-L
Frequency of Foreign Majority, Equal and
Minority Equity, 1985–1988 (Sample)

	% Foreign Equity			
	51–99	50	25–49	Other
1985	5.5	32.7	61.8	—
(n = 455)				
1986	11.3	26.3	62.4	—
(460)				
1987	13.8	25.1	60.4	0.4[a]
(460)				
1988	16.1	18.0	65.8	—
(483)				
Total	11.7	25.5	62.6	0.1
(1858)				

Sources: MOFERT Almanac, 1986, 1987, 1988, and
1989.

[a] Two EJVs in the 1987 sample were reported to have
23%–24%, which breaches the 1979 Joint Venture Law.

a smaller portion than other investors. Eliminating one very large case
from the sample of Hong Kong firms established in 1985 changes this
picture, however. Without this venture, with a total investment of $4
billion and foreign investment of $1 billion, Hong Kong firms in the sam-
ple contributed 46% of the foreign capital to joint ventures in the period
to 1988. This adjustment greatly reduces the difference among investors
of different origins, with all falling in the 40% to 50% range. As these
figures show, foreign capital makes up a significant portion of the equity
contribution (and thus ownership share) in all joint ventures. Table 3-K
indicates that foreign investors contributed almost 39% of the capital in
equity joint ventures established between 1979 and 1988, although that
figure rises to 45% if the three large outliers are eliminated from the
sample. The average for all countries, and for the individual countries,
was well above the 25% minimum required by the Chinese government,
but it also fell far short of the 99% foreign equity allowed under Chinese
law.

Consistent with these figures are data showing that a relatively small
number of equity joint ventures had over 50% foreign ownership (see
table 3-L). Of equity joint ventures concluded from 1985 to 1988, only
12% had greater than 50% foreign ownership. The majority (63%) had
foreign minority ownership, and the remainder had equal equity splits. As
will be shown in chapter 5, this pattern of ownership was generally satis-

TABLE 3-M
Origin of Foreign Investment in EJVs, 1979–1988 (Sample)
(percentage)

	Hong Kong/ Macao	United States	Japan	Western Europe	Other[a]	Un- known	All Coun- tries
Number of EJVS	69	11	7	4	8	0.2	99.2
FI value	65	11	9	8	7	0.2	100.2
FI value exclud- ing outlyers[b]	58	14	7	11	9	0.3	99.3

Sources: 1979–1984: N. R. Chen (1986), table 11. 1985–1988: compiled from samples in MOFERT *Almanacs* (1986, 1987, 1988, and 1989). Data used to calculate this table are presented in appendix C.

  [a] Includes both "Other Asia" and "Other" categories found in appendix C.

  [b] Sample includes three cases of extremely large ventures from the *Almanac*: a nuclear plant established with a Hong Kong partner in 1985 (TI of $4 billion, FI of $1 billion); a real estate project with a Japanese partner in 1985 (TI of $150 million, FI of $75 million); and a venture to produce kinescopes with a Japanese investor in 1987 (TI of $170 million, FI of $85 million). If these three cases are excluded, the total FI for 1979–1988 drops from $4836 million to $3676 million. This row shows the percentage of overall FI from each origin excluding these three cases.

factory to both the Chinese government and foreign investors, although the Chinese government began to press for a greater percent of foreign equity in the late 1980s. There was a slight trend in favor of foreign majority ownership during this time, with a concomitant decline in equal equity splits.

Among the various countries/regions of origin, Hong Kong and Macao investors contributed the greatest total volume of foreign capital in equity joint ventures across the country by the end of 1988: 65% of the total. The remaining amount was distributed fairly evenly over the other countries and regions (see table 3-M). The general pattern of Hong Kong/Macao dominance was accentuated in the number of equity joint ventures contracts, with these projects accounting for 69% of all contracts signed. (The smaller size of Hong Kong–backed projects accounts for the differential between value and number of contracts signed.) When compared to Japan's dominance in trade with and lending to China, the value (7%) and number (9%) of Sino-Japanese equity joint ventures was noticeably low. Japanese investors were much more cautious than Hong Kong or even U.S. investors about making the long-term investments in China required by the joint venture format, despite strong pressure from the Chinese government. As discussed in chapter 1, Japan's presence in China grew somewhat in the late 1980s as the revaluation of the Japanese *yen* began to encourage Japanese companies to move their manufacturing facilities off-shore, and as Japan formally agreed to raise investment in China. China became the second biggest Asian destination for Japanese manufacturing investment funds, after Thailand, and threatened to surpass the United States as the second largest source, after Hong Kong, of all foreign investment in China. Still, the amount invested by Japanese firms in China continued to be relatively low compared to Japanese investments elsewhere in Asia; in 1988, for example, Thailand approved investments from Japan worth ten times the amount approved for China.[45]

As with the value of foreign investment contributed, the level of technology transferred by foreign investors varied according to the origin of the foreign investor. In 1986, the government began to give special preferences to those equity joint ventures judged to be "technologically advanced." (Advanced technology in these ventures came almost exclusively from the foreign partner's contribution.) In general, the Chinese government cited U.S. and Western European investors for having transferred "advanced" technology. For example, 48% of Shanghai ventures that were officially designated as "technologically advanced" by the end of 1987 were from the United States, with no other single investor having over 8%. The predominance of the volume of foreign investment (45%) was contributed by West Germany ($128 million in three ventures) and the United States ($66 million, or 19% of the value of all such enterprises, in seventeen ventures). Hong Kong and especially Japanese investors contributed lower levels of technology according to this measure (10% and 2% of the total value in such enterprises, respectively). Japan's poor showing in this area perhaps reflected that country's reluctance to build up what might someday be a regional competitor. In the West, this consideration was outweighed by the desire to gain access to China's domestic market, access that the Japanese had acquired through exports.[46]

A final characteristic concerns employment in joint ventures. Chinese statistics on foreign sector employment vary widely, and they have not always clearly indicated to what their figures refer. For example, one set of figures, from 1985, claimed that in the previous five years, a half million people were employed in foreign-invested enterprises in Guangdong Province alone. Another set of Chinese government figures indicated that all "foreign-backed businesses" formed in China from 1981 to early 1985 (2100) employed about 160,000 workers, including 11,000 foreigners.[47] According to the latter figures, then, these businesses averaged 76.2 workers per enterprise, including 5.2 foreigners. Equity joint ventures generally employed more workers per agreement than other forms of foreign investment. In the sample of equity joint ventures interviewed for this study, the average number of workers per agreement was 739 workers, with a range of between one and four thousand.[48] This number is significantly larger not only than the average noted above, but also than figures compiled elsewhere on small and medium compensation trade projects (reported to have 177 workers per project) and processing/assembly projects (22 workers). Employment *creation* has not been either a major goal or a major result of the "open" policy. Although few statistics are available about the net number of jobs actually created by the formation of joint ventures, one estimate is that foreign investment was responsible for creating 598,000 jobs from late 1978 to 1981, or 2% of the 26 million jobs created by the government in China's urban sector over the same period.[49] Because most equity joint ventures were formed with existing enterprises and used workers from the original factory, they created a miniscule number of new jobs relative to those provided by domestic enterprises. (Many joint ventures actually cut the existing labor force, suggesting the possibility of a negative overall effect on job creation, at least in the short term.) Any positive employment effect of joint ventures was presumably in the coastal regions where joint ventures have been concentrated.

Performance of the Foreign Sector, 1979–1988

It is difficult to measure either the performance of the foreign investment sector or its contribution to the overall economy after only a decade of the "open" policy. The full results of efforts to use foreign investment to increase China's economic efficiency and international competitiveness, especially in industry, cannot be known until foreign projects have been fully operative for perhaps ten to fifteen years.[50] Moreover, few statistics are available to guide whatever assessment of the full economic impact of foreign direct investment is possible at this time. A preliminary assessment may be suggested at this stage, however.

As discussed previously, the foreign sector in China made up only a small portion of China's gross domestic product in absolute terms and relative to other developing countries: the foreign sector amounted to less than 1% of China's gross domestic product, and as a percentage of total investment in fixed assets, foreign investment (including loans) was only 2% in 1985. The value of direct investment as a percentage of total capital construction was also 2% from 1979 to 1984.[51] These figures indicate, generally, that the foreign sector, in its first decade, at least, was less important as an alternative source of capital accumulation than as a means of obtaining advanced technology and management skills. That the impact of foreign investment on China's economy was small in terms of these measures is not surprising, given the size of China's economy. This suggests that China has remained relatively independent from external sources of capital accumulation, thereby meeting an early concern of the leadership. These figures also suggest, however, that in order for foreign capital to make widespread contributions to China's economic development program, the government must make strong efforts to ensure that any benefits that flow to China's foreign sector are transferred to the domestic sector.

The performance of the foreign sector itself was more impressive in a number of ways. There is no doubt that this sector achieved high rates of growth. In 1987, for example, growth in this sector was approximately 100% over 1986, a level far above the state sector (10%), collective sector (25%), or even the small private sector (48%). The output value of the foreign sector grew by nearly the same amount in 1988 (97%).[52] Moreover, revenues from exports by foreign-invested enterprises showed significant growth; they doubled in 1987 to $1 billion, although this amount was still well less than the $1.5 billion earned through tourism in that year. More significantly, export revenues from foreign investment were insufficient to cover more than a small proportion of China's import bill which, in 1987, was $43 billion. Export performance had improved significantly by 1989, however, reaching $3.6 billion.[53]

Although China signed contracts for large absolute amounts of direct investment during the 1980s, it is important to recognize that not all of the contracts signed actually became operative in the year in which they were signed. As noted previously in tables 3-A and 3-B, only about half of the direct investment in all forms and in equity joint ventures pledged by the end of the 1980s was actually utilized. Some of the ventures contracted in any one year undoubtedly became operative in subsequent years; such time lags are not at all surprising. Moreover, the proportion of funds pledged for all forms of direct investment and for equity ventures that were actually utilized rose substantially in 1986 and 1987, a trend that (if the 1988 figure for all forms of direct investment was an exception) is favorable. However, many of these contracts and their pledged funds never materialized in operational ventures, as some approved contracts fail in the very early stages.

Little systematic, comparable data are available on the profitability of foreign-backed enterprises. This gap in data is attributable in large part to the hesitancy of such enterprises, whether successful or not, to release comparable financial data. What data do exist are contradictory. Reports released by individual joint ventures indicate that at least some firms made at least modest profits during the 1980s, but such reports were only sporadic. Some reports of joint venture profit earnings were highly favorable. Of those joint ventures sampled for this study for which data on profitability were available (17), only one reported that the joint venture had not made profits, and even this venture expected profits in 1988. This finding is supported generally by another study of manufacturing joint ventures, in which half of the fifty resident managers surveyed reported that the joint venture's return on investment "exceeded" or "greatly exceeded" the original expectation, and only three reported returns on investment that were below target. More broadly, MOFERT reported in 1986 that 90% of all equity ventures were earning a profit, while Xinhua reported in late 1989 that 85% of joint ventures were profitable. These signs were hence positive, although it appears that most successful joint ventures are not earning the 15%–30% return on investment the reformers considered favorable.[54]

Other data, particularly on foreign-backed enterprises of all types, suggest poorer performance. MOFERT reported that as of 1988 only one-third of the 4000 operating foreign investment projects were making a profit. Another Chinese analyst generally supported this, claiming that two-thirds of foreign enterprises in Guangdong, Fujian, and Beijing "reaped very little profit, and some even suffered losses." Moreover, the average profit rates (on sales) were also not as high as this analyst thought they should be: in 1985, the highest rate was 15% and the lowest 6.1%. The analyst attributed this performance not only to the newness of the enterprises, but also to a poor environment for investment and to poor management. A 1985 survey of 115 Japanese, U.S., and European companies in Beijing found that most firms were not satisfied with the financial returns they were projecting. It concluded that companies were probably making profits, but at a level below those they made in other markets.[55]

It would not be surprising if manufacturing joint ventures were not highly profitable in the 1980s. During that period, all joint ventures in China were still relatively young (under ten years old as of the late 1980s) and would not be expected to show profits. Moreover, foreign investors were not expecting major short-term financial rewards; their expected return on investment was often lower in China than for investment in developed countries.[56] Also, there were sufficient obstacles to profit generation (such as excessive fees levied at the local level) and to repatriation by foreign partners to warrant caution as to whether foreign direct investment in China would prove highly successful in these terms in the short-run. (See chapter 4 for further discussion of this latter issue.) Inefficiencies generated by the poor infrastructure and poor labor productivity, and problems spurred by the post-Mao reforms themselves (notably, cycles of inflation and government credit tightening), also produced tremendous problems in the structure of the Chinese economy. Such problems clearly raised the cost, and hindered the profitability, of running joint ventures in China.

Sporadic data have been reported on failures of foreign investment projects during the 1980s. It appears that the majority of ventures established during this time survived, despite the difficulties of the investment environment. In the previously cited survey of fifty resident managers at manufacturing joint ventures, 56% assessed their achievement of operational plans "satisfactory," whereas only 16% reported "great difficulties."[57] Moreover, although some had financial difficulties, only a few operative joint ventures are known to have failed. Most of these failures were related, not to problems specific to and controllable by China, but rather to economic problems besetting the international offshore oil industry and its ancillary servicing ventures (supply boats, platform construction, and so on).[58] Generally, *once operational*, most joint ventures were able to survive. Yet, as with profits, these positive signs must be taken in the context of two factors. First, it is certainly the case that disputes between partners have caused joint ventures to collapse after the contract was concluded but prior to operation (as reflected in the lower figures for actual utilization of foreign investment). Second, the difficulties that affected existing joint ventures—particularly the difficulties of balancing foreign exchange and of gaining access to the domestic market—indicate that operational success was hard won. These two factors temper somewhat the relatively positive assessment of the joint venture experience suggested by extant investors and by the relatively small number of outright failures.

Chapter Four

CONTROLS AT THE
NATIONAL AND REGIONAL LEVELS

IN LIGHT OF the views held by the Chinese leadership in the late 1970s and early 1980s about the risks and benefits of using foreign capital, the joint venture policy had to serve two purposes. It had to attract and keep foreign capital and at the same time meet the myriad concerns of both reformers and conservatives about possible negative effects of foreign investment. The need to control foreign direct investment thus was an integral, inseparable part of the original policy, and on a proximate footing with the goal of absorbing foreign investment. As one group of reformers stressed, "[W]e must maintain a sober attitude, have a full understanding, and cautiously handle [foreign investment], to prevent suffering losses [*chi kui*] and being duped [*shang dang*]. We must boldly, beneficially and according to law use foreign capital and technology, and place restrictions on the possible production of negative aspects."[1]

This chapter and chapter 5 draw on interviews as well as primary and secondary sources to discuss how the joint venture policy was originally designed to meet these goals, and the evolution of China's efforts to maintain controls over a broad range of issues during the 1980s. For each issue, chapters 4 and 5 show that the government attempted both to facilitate and, particularly in the first phase and the early part of the second phase, to restrict, or ameliorate the impact of, foreign investment. These chapters discuss where and why China's controls were effective and enduring. They also examine how the restrictions on foreign capital in China did not meet the original goals in two fundamental senses. First, controls intended to constrain foreign investment and protect the national culture were frequently diffused or distorted in the process of implementation. Problems in implementation were partly caused by obstacles in the domestic economy as well as by features that had long existed in Chinese politics: conflicts within the joint venture policy and between the joint venture policy and other policies, localism resulting from poor incentives for local officials and Chinese joint venture managers to implement all the controls, and unreliable monitoring of policy implementation.

Second, following the process described broadly in chapter 3, chapters 4 and 5 argue that the reformers deliberately weakened, or liberalized, many of the control mechanisms after the early years, especially in the third phase. At the same time that their commitment to absorbing foreign capital was increasing, reformers also recognized that controls, and the problematic Chinese economy, had made investors reluctant to invest at the level the reformers desired. These factors, and the decline of conservative opposition on issues of foreign economic policy, all facilitated their willingness to liberalize. Liberalization of a specific control is judged to have occurred when, as a result of new regulations, that control became less effective at meeting the original concern, and when changes were made to promote the absorption of foreign investment and its benefits at the expense of controls. Liberalization in the overall regulatory regime for foreign investment is judged to have occurred when there was loosening of a number of individual controls, but no concomitant strengthening of controls on other issues.

Poor implementation and deliberate liberalization resulting from both exogenous and endogenous factors were thus the chief inhibitors of the reformers' dual strategy. The controls discussed in chapters 4 and 5 also make apparent, however, that neither the problems in implementation nor the liberalization occurred to the same degree for all controls. Variations in interpretation and implementation of the policy occurred, sometimes in a regional pattern.[2] Moreover, despite some liberalization, the government continued throughout most of the decade to maintain relatively strict controls on some issues, while in contrast, liberalization in other areas was more thoroughgoing or faster. The reasons for the loosening of controls, where it has occurred, have varied. In some cases, it was a result of foreign pressure, but in other cases, the reformers liberalized controls in the absence of direct pressure from foreigners, as a by-product of reforms in the domestic economy or due to growing confidence in foreign methods. Over time, moreover, the reformers developed priorities among the controls, and carefully tailored their liberalizations to achieve their goals.

This chapter discusses the government's original controls, and the evolution of those controls at two levels of analysis, the national level and the regional level. The first part discusses those Chinese controls that defined and limited the status of foreign capital in China's economic, legal, and political structure. The set of national-level controls discussed in the second part consists of controls over five specific issues where foreign investment affected China's economy: domestic markets, foreign exchange, domestic content, profits and profit repatriation, and technology transfer. The third part examines the regional-level controls instituted uniquely for the "open" regions of China: the SEZs and, eventually, the "open coastal cities" and other coastal regions.

CONTROLS DEFINING AND LIMITING THE STATUS OF
JOINT VENTURES AT THE NATIONAL LEVEL

The reformist rationale for foreign direct investment made clear that investment was to have only a limited and clearly defined—albeit crucial—place in China's economy. In the early years, the government asserted a number of overarching, higher level controls defining and limiting the status of joint ventures. The government sought to make the joint venture policy consistent with the central principles of the regime. It also sought to subordinate joint ventures to Chinese law and procedures, Chinese modes of dispute resolution, the state plan, and the socialist sector of the economy. Finally, controls to guard against the emergence of unhealthy tendencies sought to protect certain elements of Chinese culture. This section discusses the establishment of these broadest of controls, and the ways in which they did and did not change over the course of the decade.

General Principles to Which Joint Ventures Must Adhere:
"Equality and Mutual Benefit" and Sovereignty

As discussed in chapter 2, the outlook of the post-Mao government repeatedly stressed that China's interactions with the outside world should proceed according to two central principles: "equality and mutual benefit" and respect for Chinese sovereignty. When the "open" policy was initiated in the late 1970s, the government formally applied these principles to equity joint ventures. Although exhortations to protect China's sovereignty and uphold "equality and mutual benefit" often appeared in Chinese foreign policy statements as abstract concepts, the Chinese government made a number of specific assertions about what the principles were to mean for joint ventures. Like many host governments, the Chinese government asserted that the joint venture format itself allows the absorption of foreign capital while also protecting equality and sovereignty. The joint ownership and management format of joint ventures was seen as a symbol of equality and as a way for the government to retain control over invested capital, as evident in Deng Xiaoping's statement in the early 1980s that "in joint ventures with foreigners, 50% still belongs to socialism."[3]

The Chinese government tried to uphold "equality and mutual benefit" in joint ventures in a number of ways. First, it repeatedly emphasized that all sides should bring to the negotiation and operation of joint ventures an *attitude* of "equality and mutual benefit"; even though the interests of the two sides can be expected to diverge on many issues, there should be mutual respect between partners and an effort to build an atmosphere in which mutual gain is possible. A commitment to work in this spirit was often stipulated in Chinese-foreign joint venture contracts. In addition to prescribing the proper attitude, "equality and mutual benefit" was codified in the major laws on joint ventures as contractual standards to which joint ventures were to adhere. The 1979 Joint Venture Law provided that rights, interests, and profits of both sides to an agreement are protected by Chinese law, while the 1983 Implementing Regulations stated further that applications for joint ventures are to be denied if the project involves "obvious inequity . . . impairing the rights and interests of one party."[4] Several more specific standards for promoting equality also were established, and were generally stipulated in joint venture contracts, if not in laws. Among these standards were provisions for the equitable sharing of profits and losses (with "equitable" defined as being divided according to the amount of equity contributed), comparable, though not identical, salaries for Chinese and foreign managers and directors, and unanimous decisionmaking through "equal consultations" (*pingdeng xieshang*) at the board and management levels.[5]

Although the effort to have the joint venture policy meet the principle of "equality and mutual benefit" was intended to protect a fundamental Chinese value, that it also was intended to protect rights of foreigners meant that the principle did not always further China's immediate interests. Indeed, Chinese leaders often pointed to these guarantees to claim that China was not seeking unilateral gain.[6] The guarantees of equality also helped allay the concerns of foreign investors about the legal protection of investments in China, and were used to justify to domestic interests why China should offer any incentives to foreign investors.

But guarantees of equality were, unsurprisingly, not as simple as these laws implied. The definition of equality had to account for the different bargaining powers of the Chinese state and foreign investors when formulating a contract: foreign investors had a relatively greater capacity to contribute managerial and technical skills, whereas the Chinese government had ultimate power to approve, regulate, and expropriate foreign capital. A mechanistic conception of equality that would dictate identical benefits and risks was unrealistic and at odds with the concept, increasingly legitimate in China, of comparative advantage. Even more important, the Chinese government still had to be concerned with protecting China's interests.

The government got around these problems in the way common to host countries (and elsewhere): they defined equality to mean that all parties to a joint venture would be equal before laws and procedures determined by China.[7] As this implies, although Chinese laws formally protected both Chinese and foreign interests, they were often operationalized in a manner that protected China. Along with assuaging foreign concerns, the most important function of "equality and mutual benefit" was to indicate that *Chinese* concerns must be protected and respected. Hence, foreigners involved in negotiations indicated that Chinese negotiators used exhortations to uphold "equality and mutual benefit" as a negotiating strategy designed to elicit concessions, and frequently charged foreigners who were showing little flexibility that their unwillingness to concede violated the spirit of "equality and mutual benefit."[8] Moreover, there is no evidence that those Chinese officials responsible for approving foreign investment contracts ever denied approval for a contract they deemed to favor Chinese over foreign interests. The very bargaining process through which contracts were reached also belied the notion that Chinese laws protected Chinese and foreign interests equally, for each side in fact was to maximize its own interests. Although the protection of foreign interests under "equality and mutual benefit" was important and was necessary to attract any foreign capital in the first place, then, upholding this principle was also crucial for protecting China's interests.

Protection of China's sovereign independence is a second major principle to which the joint venture policy was designed to adhere. The issue of whether absorption of foreign capital could threaten China's sovereignty by usurping the government's control over the economy was for both historical and ideological reasons highly sensitive and, as discussed in chapter 2, was addressed in the original rationale for the "open" policy. In that rationale, reformers made the central argument for why foreign direct investment would not threaten China's sovereignty: joint ventures would not impair China's sovereignty if they were subject to Chinese law. Unlike "old" China, "new" socialist China has the strength to enforce laws that protect the nation.[9] The government tried to ensure China's sovereignty by requiring that Chinese laws govern all aspects of joint ventures, that the state has authority to review and approve joint ventures, and that chairs of joint venture boards, who are the highest authority in ventures, must be appointed by the Chinese partner.[10] The 1983 Implementing Regulations asserted explicitly that the protection of China's sovereignty is a condition for approval of all joint venture projects, and that when disputes are to be settled in courts, proceedings must occur in Chinese and not foreign courts.[11] Officials also argued that China's sovereignty is protected insofar as foreigners or joint ventures are not permitted to own land in China, and insofar as the government will not approve joint ventures in defense or other strategic sectors.

It is interesting to note that China, unlike many other socialist and nonsocialist countries, did not try to preserve sovereignty through the maintenance of Chinese majority ownership of joint ventures. Indeed, other countries, especially during the 1970s, often limited foreign equity to 49% or less. Although in practice the Chinese government in the early years preferred Chinese majority ownership, it did not see this as vital to

China's sovereign interests. As one Chinese reformer asserted in the early years, "the proportion of the contribution of a party to a joint venture . . . has nothing to do with national sovereignty."[12] Rather, as discussed in chapter 5, China tried to neutralize the power that might be gained by foreigners via majority ownership through rules that divorce effective control over joint ventures from the division of equity.

With the exception of equity limits, however, the laws on joint ventures established in the first phase and clarified at the beginning of the second phase offered clear statements that protection of China's equal position and sovereignty was a priority of the government. (China's dominance of law-making and approval over joint ventures, discussed in the following sections, bear this out.) Moreover, the government's commitment to these principles remained throughout the decade. It is true that, in small ways, the Chinese reformers loosened a number of the specific provisions that they had originally designed to protect these values. Most notably, as is discussed subsequently, they liberalized efforts to enforce equal decisionmaking in joint ventures, and became somewhat more accepting of foreign arbitration of disputes. Yet these changes did not seriously threaten China's sovereignty or "equality and mutual benefit." Rather, the changes arose from the reformers' growing confidence that China's ability to protect these values was not threatened by the foreign investment policy. The deemphasis on these values and the liberalizations did not overturn the most fundamental features of China's laws protecting these basic principles.

Laws and Joint Venture Legal Status

The application of Chinese law to foreign investment projects was central to the joint venture policy not only because it was considered the central mechanism for protecting China's sovereignty, but also because it was the specific means for defining the legal status of joint ventures and for seeing that joint ventures met the myriad concerns of the leadership.[13] Because post-Mao China did not have a well-developed code of commercial law, a central task of the reformers was to develop such a code to govern foreign involvement in China's economy.[14]

The three major sets of laws (the 1979 Joint Venture Law, the 1983 Implementing Regulations, and the 1986 Provisions) introduced in chapter 3, and numerous sets of associated regulations that were promulgated during the 1980s, defined the legal status of equity joint ventures. This legal structure was intended to foster both of the major goals of the leadership's policy, attracting and controlling investment. To foster a stable and attractive investment environment, the early Joint Venture (JV) Law offered certain guarantees that the Chinese government would protect assets, "legitimate" profits, and other rights and interests of the foreign partner. The laws also carved out a degree of management autonomy for joint ventures within which outside authorities were not to interfere as long as the ventures adhered to the law. At the same time it offered these guarantees to foreign investors, the 1979 law stated that "all the activities of a joint venture shall be governed by the laws, decrees and pertinent rules and regulations of the People's Republic of China" (Article 2). This firmly implemented the general principle that Chinese laws would dominate joint venture activity.[15]

Nonetheless, in the early years foreign investors continued to press the issue of governing law in negotiations. For example, a 1980 draft contract between Schindler Holdings and the China Construction Machinery Corporation allowed that if a dispute could not be resolved by the joint venture's board of directors, it "shall be brought in principle before the ordinary court of the domicile of the actual defendant." The two applicable non-Chinese laws would have been British and Swiss. Yet the final agreement carried a Chinese governing law clause, and no other contracts with foreign governing law were approved. Furthermore, the Implementing Regulations, in an effort to close negotiations on this point, placed the legal status of joint ventures firmly in control of the Chinese state, stating that "the conclusion, validity, interpretation and implementation of joint venture contracts and the resolution of disputes thereunder shall be governed by Chinese law" (Article 15). The government argued that joint ventures were not "foreign enterprises"; rather, their nationality was determined by the country in which they were located. Joint ventures were deemed "Chinese legal persons" (*zhongguo faren*) and as such were to be subject to Chinese laws.[16]

But joint ventures were special "Chinese legal persons," for they also were to be subject to laws that did not apply to domestic enterprises. The government viewed separate laws for joint ventures as necessary to protect the socialist system. This differentiated China's treatment of joint ventures from the treatment of joint ventures in capitalist countries, where they are considered domestic enterprises.[17] The insistence of the Chinese government on Chinese governing law was in fact more strict than many other countries, including other socialist countries, where foreign joint venture partners could choose to have their contracts enforced according to laws other than those of the host government.[18] Once established as the arbiter of rules under which investment would occur, the government could of course go on to require specific controls on a wide range of issues. Moreover, although some early Chinese laws protected rights and a degree of autonomy for joint ventures, these same laws could be revised unilaterally to curtail the scope of these delegated authorities.

Over time, the Chinese government became somewhat flexible in its assertion of Chinese governing law. In some cases, it allowed the inclusion of provisions allowing foreign arbitrators to apply "commonly accepted international practices" when existing Chinese laws did not address the pertinent issue, although the international practice must be acceptable to the Chinese party. (This exception to Chinese governing law could be expected to narrow as the reformers completed their own company laws.) The reformers also increasingly accepted international laws, and adopted more and more international norms of business law, such as in the areas of contract law and protection of intellectual property.[19] Moreover, as discussed in the context of specific laws, the *content* of many laws changed, reflecting the leadership's adaptation to external and internal pressures, and the Chinese government was not always effective at enforcing its regulations. China's willingness, evident in the 1986 General Principles of Civil Law, to allow other types of foreign investments (though not equity joint ventures or oil exploration contracts) to designate the law of a third country as the governing law indicated that perhaps even greater flexibility in Chinese governing law would be possible in the future.[20] Yet despite changes in the content of laws, as with the principles of "equality and mutual benefit" and sovereignty, the crucial role of Chinese law remained largely intact during the 1980s as the Chinese government's primary tool for defining the status of foreign investment and for asserting Chinese control over foreign investment.

Two additional factors must be kept in mind when generalizing about the use of law as a control mechanism. First, internal (*neibu*) rules played an important if poorly understood role in guiding government officials and enterprise managers in their foreign economic activities. The internal rules were often an unknown element for investors; they were circulated to cadres who must implement and interpret the law, but were not intended for scrutiny by foreigners. The existence of authoritative rules that were not available for outside analysis meant that judgments about the Chinese leadership's efforts to regulate foreign investment must be based on an understanding of only a portion, although the most significant portion, of the regulatory structure.[21] Second, and relatedly, the existence of (or lack of) control mechanisms in the form of public laws did not preclude the existence of informal guard mechanisms in the negotiation or implementation process. For example, because the joint venture laws sanctioned "democratic consultation" as a first step in resolving problems between Chinese and foreign partners, many of the issues that might be formally stipulated in law were left instead to the realm of negotiation. Hence, while an understanding of the legal regime governing joint ventures is necessary to understanding the structure of control, an understanding of the informal dynamics of control is also crucial.

Chinese Authority to Approve Foreign Investment Projects

As in many developing countries, Chinese laws established in the early years required strict negotiation and approval procedures before a joint venture could be established.[22] These procedural controls allowed considerable state influence over foreign investment projects. Although many procedural rules for joint ventures were not actually codified until the 1983 regulations, procedural controls existed in practice in the early years. Before formal negotiations with a foreign party could begin, several steps were required. The *zhuguan bumen*, or "department in charge" (DIC) (the government bureau assigned to oversee the venture), and the formal ratifying authority had to approve the choice of project and the choice of the prospective foreign partner. The Chinese partner had to prepare a preliminary feasibility study, although this was not to be extremely detailed. More important, a proposed joint venture had to be included in the local annual plan.[23] Unsuitable foreign partners or projects in theory could not progress past this stage.

Next, the negotiating partners were to carry out a joint feasibility study that would reflect detailed study of major issues, such as the product to be made, its market and profit prospects, the technology to be used, and the value of the project to China. On the basis of information in the feasibility study, negotiations for a contract could proceed. In the early years there was little to guide negotiations. Beginning in the second phase, the basic Chinese position was clarified somewhat with the distribution at the end of 1984 of a "model contract" written by MOFERT, and negotiations frequently began with the presentation by the Chinese side of the model. It was not a complicated document, reflecting the Chinese practice of broadly worded and nonspecific contracts. However, foreign investors found it to be overly vague in certain areas and too partial to Chinese interests in others. Although MOFERT wrote the model contract with the intention of simplifying negotiations and guiding, though not dictating, the terms, local negotiators and officials frequently viewed it as establishing mandatory standards, and were very slow to deviate from the model. When foreigners would try to deviate, Chinese negotiators generally refused to accept the proposal without first clearing it with relevant government authorities.[24] Still, the language of the model contract did not become "boilerplate"; rather than either side being able to dictate or easily win its terms, negotiations were usually long and arduous, sometimes taking several years.

When negotiations between partners were concluded, the proposed contract, feasibility study, and several other documents were submitted for formal approval. Joint venture projects that received approval generally were to fit the broad guidelines set forth by the government; they were to support the state plan, adhere to Chinese laws on joint ventures, and uphold the principles of "equality and mutual benefit" and Chinese sovereignty. The government's standards in fact led to disapproval of some proposed joint ventures before they reached the stage of formal approval. For example, negotiations for automobile joint ventures with Japanese partners broke off because the Japanese side was unwilling to include sufficiently advanced technology.

Generally, the body with final approval authority in the early years was the Foreign Investment Administration of MOFERT. But because joint venture operations touched on matters of interest to many government organs, such as those with authority over customs and foreign exchange, proposed contracts were submitted to interested agencies and to the relevant state or provincial planning commission. For example, before it could approve a contract for a joint venture that required foreign exchange loans, MOFERT had to secure approval from the foreign exchange authorities. This added another dimension to joint venture approval: the standards of not just one but many bureaus had to be met. The bargaining and compromise that occurred had the capacity to delay approval significantly, rendering the approval process more strict and complicated than it appeared on the surface.[25] Thus, the procedural controls established in the early years allowed for rigorous state oversight of all projects with foreign investment.

The nature of this state approval changed somewhat in the second phase; while the 1983 Implementing Regulations were codifying the procedural controls that had been in practice in the early years, the reformers also applied the more general decentralization occurring in the domestic economy to the approval process. Specifically, the Implementing Regulations delegated authority for approval of small joint ventures—those with a total investment of $5 million or less—to municipal, provincial, or autonomous region governments, or to the relevant ministry branch, as long as these projects did not require allocation of raw materials from the center and did not influence the national balance of fuels, transport, and export quotas. Later in the second phase, they allowed several major municipalities in the eastern region (including Guangzhou, Beijing, and Dalian) and the provincial governments of Guangdong, Fujian, and Liaoning, to approve projects up to $10 million in total investment. The Shanghai and Tianjin governments were allowed to approve projects up to $30 million in total investment. All service joint ventures, regardless of size, required only local approval. In the third phase, municipal governments, such as in Beijing, decentralized approval for smaller ventures even further to local district governments, while in 1988 interior provinces and some central departments gained authority to approve foreign-backed enterprises worth up to $10 million.[26]

Decentralization of approval clearly affected state control over the joint venture approval process. It became possible, where local and central interests conflicted, for a project to be approved at the local level when it might have been rejected by the center. In one case, for example, local approval was crucial. Authorities from a central ministry opposed a venture because the ministry was involved in a similar venture elsewhere. Through various accounting and financing schemes, the venture's sponsors kept the amount of total investment low enough so that local authorities, who favored the project, would be authorized to approve it. More generally, the approval authority was used by localities in another way. Localities were under extreme pressure to show enthusiasm for and early results from the "open" policy. Although local officials were to apply the same controls as the central authorities, the major performance measure applied to localities was the gross quantity of foreign capital they absorbed. Shanghai, for example, was roundly criticized by central authorities in the second phase for absorbing too little investment. Localities thus felt pressure to approve large projects and large numbers of projects, even at the expense of other approval criteria. Two results were particularly notable. First, localities did not pay much attention to whether the projects they were approving were similar to projects under way elsewhere. This led to redundancy of projects across regions. Second, localities had incentives to approve service joint ventures, not only because these ventures were more often exempt from central approval, but also because they tended to be large, as noted in chapter 3. These incentives exacerbated the excessive investment in real estate and tourism projects in the open cities and the surfeit of low-technology assembly or service joint ventures in the SEZs.

It is important to note that the central government did not totally abdicate its authority to approve joint ventures. Despite the decentralization, MOFERT retained the right to review local approvals, and sometimes exercised this right. For example, the signing of a contract for a Shanghai electronics venture worth less than $30 million was delayed by central authorities, who argued that the project anticipated insufficient exports.[27] Nor was the center's decision to decentralize approval authority irreversible. The central authorities thus left themselves ultimate approval authority. Nonetheless, by the end of the decade the delegation of much central authority, in conjunction with the pressures felt by localities, resulted in patterns of investment that deviated from the original goals and that the government subsequently criticized.

Control over the Process of Dispute Resolution

Foreign and Chinese partners to joint ventures differed in their views as to the processes through which disputes should be resolved.[28] The Chinese favored informal consultation and conciliation between partners at the board level, reflecting a traditional preference that both parties to a dispute agree upon a solution rather than have an outside judge impose a settlement. The Chinese also preferred that the resolution of disputes take place within China and be handled by Chinese institutions. The foreign side often preferred to avoid both consultation/conciliation and litigation in Chinese courts in favor of third-party arbitration.

The Joint Venture Law was largely silent on the issue of dispute resolution, but during the early years a compromise between the two preferences arose in the context of individual negotiations. Part of this compromise was codified in the Implementing Regulations. On the issue of litigation versus conciliation, the Implementing Regulations strongly discouraged the use of *either* Chinese or international courts; they posited consultation and conciliation as first steps, followed by arbitration if early efforts failed. In practice, most disputes were settled internally through consultation and conciliation.[29] The Chinese government in the early years also preferred to "keep the initiative in our own hands" by encouraging arbitration within China when disputes could not be solved by discussion.[30] Although the Joint Venture Law (Article 14) made possible arbitration by a mutually agreed upon body outside of China, early joint venture contracts often disallowed this, particularly forbidding arbitration in the foreign partner's home country. Yet under pressure from foreign investors, in practice the Chinese increasingly approved contracts allowing arbitration in third countries such as Sweden and Switzerland, and in a few cases in the foreign investor's home country. The Implementing Regulations and later laws (notably the 1985 Foreign Economic Contract Law) allowed arbitration in the foreign partner's home country, and reiterated the validity of third-country arbitration.[31]

Even with the stronger sanctioning of third-country arbitration, most formal arbitration proceedings continued to be held in Beijing at the Foreign Economic Trade Arbitration Commission (FETAC). As of July 1989, only seven arbitration proceedings had been filed in Stockholm (the site of the most international arbitration proceedings). Most of these cases were eventually dropped or settled through conciliation within the arbitration institution. One arbitration proceeding was decided in favor of the Chinese party (in December 1988), presumably giving the Chinese government some degree of confidence that its interests could be met in such proceedings.[32]

The Chinese government from the early years hoped to prevent disputes from reaching Chinese courts, and saw no role for foreign courts in resolving disputes. Only one case of a joint venture dispute reaching a Chinese court was made public in the 1979–1988 period. The government limited Chinese courts to two roles: enforcing arbitration awards, and deciding disputes where no arbitration agreement is in effect. It also disallowed foreign courts a voice in the enforcement of arbitral awards within China. Chinese courts were further constrained to protect Chinese interests insofar as a Chinese court could agree to execute a foreign arbitral judgment only if it could show that "such a judgment or award does not violate the basic principles of the law of the PRC or the interests of [the Chinese] state and society." The court could refuse to accept such a case even if these criteria were met. These formal barriers to enforcement of arbitral awards were reflected in practice. In two notable cases, one of an award by FETAC and another by the Stockholm arbitral body, Chinese courts refused to enforce the awards made against a Chinese party.[33]

By maintaining domestic arbitration (in most cases), by reluctance to enforce foreign arbitral awards, and by the settlement of disputes that enter courts at all in *Chinese* courts, throughout the 1980s China retained much authority to resolve disputes in equity joint ventures. Although China's controls continued to dominate, that the government became somewhat more accepting of arbitration in third countries was an important sign of increased willingness to adopt international norms.

Control via the State Plan

Because the Chinese government intended for the foreign sector to supplement and complement the state-planned economy, it required that foreign capital be incorporated into China's system of planning, and hence into the socialist sector of the economy. Joint ventures were directed to operate "under the condition that the enterprise subjects itself to the guidance of the state plan. . . . "[34] The 1979 Joint Venture Law said little about how joint ventures would fit into the state plan, except for a basic statement that production and business programs of joint ventures "shall be filed with the authorities" and implemented through contracts (Article 9). But toward the end of the first phase, and in the 1983 Implementing Regulations that initiated the second phase, the government clarified the multifaceted role the state plan was to play in both the establishment and operation of joint ventures. At the broadest level, the total amount of and uses for foreign capital in all joint venture projects were designated in the national five-year plan; the government set targets for the amount of domestic and foreign capital to be absorbed into joint ventures in light of competing requirements for domestic capital. The Seventh Five-Year Plan (drawn up in 1985 for 1986–1990) established a target of $30 billion in foreign funds, with $7–$8 billion of this in direct investment. Moreover, as noted previously, a proposed project was first to be included in the annual plan before a Chinese enterprise could begin negotiations.[35]

Once operative, joint ventures were subject to the state plan primarily for procurement (including imports) and sales. In the early 1980s, many industrial supplies were allocated through a system of planned distribution. By law, joint ventures using materials that fell under planned distribution had to have their requirements included in the supply plan of their superior department. The prices paid for key materials, especially raw materials such as coal, could also be established by the state.[36] Sales activities were to be regulated in part by the state plan, though to a lesser degree than procurement. As with Chinese enterprises, if an item produced by the joint venture was subject to planned distribution, it was to be included in distribution plans of materials administration departments, which then sold the product to users according to the plan and distribution channels of that department. For example, joint ventures in the pharmaceutical sector sold mostly to local or national pharmaceutical supply bureaus, while some joint venture exports were sold overseas by China's foreign trade corporations.[37] The joint venture was allowed to sell directly to enterprises or departments only products in excess of those purchased by the state according to the plan. Moreover, the price of any joint venture products sold on domestic markets could be required to correspond with state-set prices for domestically produced goods of equivalent quality when the domestic products were also price-controlled (either set at a rigid price or allowed to float only within a specified range). When no equivalent domestic product existed, joint ventures could set their own prices. Items for export were generally controlled through licenses, although the licensing procedures were somewhat more flexible for joint ventures than for domestic enterprises.[38] Production in joint ventures was also subject to central direction and could be affected by changes in the plan. For example, the draft production plan of the Hitachi joint venture to produce televisions was routinely reviewed by both provincial and central organs after the board of directors had approved it. At one point in the first phase, central authorities unilaterally revised the plan to cut production volume by over half to reflect a new central directive to decrease national production of television sets.[39]

The ability of the government to use the state plan to control foreign investment was diluted during the mid-1980s in two ways. First, the strengths of the plan was diluted by the more general efforts of reformers to decrease the role of the plan in favor of the market, to separate government and economic functions, and to increase enterprise autonomy. These changes were at the center of the extensive urban reform program announced in October 1984. Although reformers did not completely repudiate the role of the plan, the urban reform program called for materials to increasingly circulate outside the plan. By 1986, the central government had reduced the number of major commodities distributed exclusively within the state commercial network to 20, from 256 in 1978.[40]

Second, the role of the plan was also affected by efforts to liberalize the foreign investment environment itself. Consistent with the 1984 urban reforms, the 1983 Implementing Regulations and the 1986 Provisions further liberalized the control function of the plan over joint ventures. While the Implementing Regulations formalized and clarified the application of the state plan to joint ventures, they also reflected the reformers' growing realization of the need to give ventures greater leeway in their operations if they were to operate successfully. Breaking with the norm for state-owned enterprises, the regulations formally allowed joint ventures greater autonomy to formulate their own production plans, which then would be approved by the board of directors.[41] The government did not always allow joint ventures to formulate production plans in practice; for example, as late as 1984, outside bureaucratic organs continued to determine the level of output of a machine-producing joint venture.[42] Nonetheless, government participation in setting production plans gradually declined. The 1986 Provisions formally guaranteed the autonomy of joint ventures to procure and sell goods according to their own judgments (Article 15). Complementing the broader drive to increase the export orientation of joint ventures, they also eased the requirement that venture exports be sold through China's foreign trade corporations (Article 12). Thus, the Implementing Regulations and the 1984 urban reforms generally in the second phase, and the 1986 Provisions in the third phase, weakened the state's ability to control joint venture activities through the plan. The plan continued to play a role—for example, the foreign sector still had to fit the national and local plans—but it was a blunter instrument of control than in the early years.

The move toward use of markets and greater enterprise autonomy had a variety of results for joint ventures. Localities (provinces and municipalities) and governmental departments were allowed to independently draw up their own lists of foreign investment projects they wished to pursue, and were allowed to actually pursue them. More important for the operation of joint ventures was that materials not allocated by the plan could be purchased directly from appropriate bureaucratic departments or on the domestic and international market. Although this release from the constraints of the plan for procurement moved joint ventures one step closer to autonomy from the state, it became immediately clear to joint venture managers that this was a two-edged sword. In an economy where shortages of materials are common and distribution channels are unestablished and unreliable, the relative security of being able to procure materials through the plan was for most joint ventures desirable. In this context, the function of the central and local plans was more facilitative than restrictive, as had been acknowledged earlier by a MOFERT official: "With the guarantee of the plan, investment projects will have a dependable foundation."[43] Chinese and foreign joint venture managers alike also realized their dependence upon government bureaus with authority to guarantee supplies. Many suffered operating dislocations from the need to rely on poorly developed markets. For example, one foreign manager who had 60% of his venture's inputs covered by the state plan complained in early 1985 that he had to "scrounge" for the remaining 40%. Another foreign manager emphasized that he could "hardly get supplies of even one ton of steel sheeting if it was not in the plans of our [state] supplier."[44] Although inclusion in a state plan did not necessarily guarantee the delivery of materials (for allocation by a planning bureaucracy was only formal authorization to buy from supply bureaus), it was nearly impossible for most joint ventures to get along completely outside of the plan during the mid-1980s.[45]

It was not only foreign and Chinese managers of joint ventures who recognized that release from the state plan bore some negative results. Although a number of the original planning mechanisms, such as the requirement that joint venture projects be included in the state plan, had been left intact even after promulgation of the 1986 Provisions, reformers began in 1987 to apply the plan more vigorously. (To some degree, this reflected the more general cyclical trend toward greater planning in the domestic economy.) They recognized the problems that decentralization had brought, such as the duplication of projects and poor coordination among agencies and levels. Reformers did not suggest extreme recentralization of control over foreign investment, but they did call for the use of state planning mechanisms to offer greater guidance and coordination to the various levels and agencies involved, and to balance foreign investment according to state interests. Some also called for the strengthening of foreign capital utilization and implementation plans to foster technology-intensive or export-oriented ventures.[46] This mild enhancement of the role of the state plan in the foreign sector was reinforced in the economic retrenchment of late 1988 and 1989 by conservatives who once again gained influence and re-asserted planning mechanisms over the economy as a whole. As in the early phases, inclusion in the state plan was still important for joint ventures, as procurement increasingly depended on incorporation in the plan, and enterprises outside of the plan found their sources of credit cut off.

The role of the state plan thus fluctuated during the 1980s, ranging from providing rather extensive control and coordination functions in the first phase (1979–1983), to partial (and not always helpful) loosening of these functions during the second phase and beginning of the third phase (especially 1984–1986), to efforts to strengthen them again in the third phase (especially 1987–1988). The liberalization of the middle years resulted to some degree from deliberate efforts of the reformers to improve the foreign investment environment. But direct pressure from foreign investors was not the driving force for liberalization; rather, the driving force was the efforts of the reformers to reform the urban economy generally. Similarly, the re-emphasis on the plan in the third phase resulted from internal factors: first from the reformers' realization that without the guidance of the plan, goals for the appropriate use of foreign investment were not being met, and later from the resurgence of conservatives in Chinese politics.

Examination of the role of the state plan is instructive not just because it illustrates the influence of domestic politics in determining the investment environment, but also because it illustrates how the Chinese state retained the ability to re-assert the tool of planning in light of problems of decentralization. This re-assertion of the plan, like the weakening of the plan, did not occur without costs and could not fully or easily solve the problems caused by decentralization. But it was significant that the Chinese reformers retained the will to call again on this tool, and that they, and conservatives, retained the capacity to do so after nearly a decade of the foreign investment policy.

Restrictions on the Scope of Joint Ventures

At the initiation of the "open" policy, the Chinese government asserted that it would restrict the number and value of projects, the sectors into which foreign capital would be allowed, and the duration of joint venture contracts. Such restrictions would keep foreign capital in a position subordinate to the socialist economy. The government was concerned that foreign-backed enterprises could grow too large and threaten the goals of independence and self-reliance. In practice, however, reformers recognized that this danger would most likely manifest itself over the long term, and hence it was less salient early on. Indeed, in the early years when the number and value of investments was small, no specific limits were specified for either the number or value of foreign direct investment. Even as the amount of foreign investments in China grew in the middle and late phase, however, the concerns for limits on the quantity of investment were expressed less and less frequently. The changing outlook of reformers, and particularly their belief that the amount of capital coming into China was insufficient to meet their targets for foreign investment, meant that limits continued to be of little relevance. Li Peng stated in 1984 that "at present, the question of putting a limit on foreign investment just doesn't arise," an idea that was reiterated frequently. This was consistent with the comment of the MOFERT official noted in chapter 3, who estimated in 1984 that even 25,000 joint ventures, constituting 5% of the total number of industrial enterprises, would still be subordinate to the socialist sector. By the end of 1988, China had approved 8530 equity ventures, or only about one-third of the 25,000 figure.[47] Investment therefore did not even approach the reformers' targets. Nor did it reach the level at which it was judged to threaten the country's self-reliance or independence.

The question of controls over the sectoral distribution of joint ventures was pursued more seriously. In the early 1980s, the Chinese government, like many host governments, adopted policies to restrict joint ventures from protected sectors and encourage them in other designated sectors. They intended to limit the number of joint ventures in any given industry to one or two, although this restriction was not widely publicized. In the early phase, the restriction was implemented successfully; with few exceptions the government approved only one joint venture in each industry.[48] Limits on the specific sectors in which joint ventures would be permitted were also in place in the early years, and were clarified in the Implementing Regulations. These regulations stipulated that joint ventures in China would be permitted in those sectors in which technology and management, natural resources, and export products were urgently needed. Officials also identified sectors from which joint ventures would be prohibited. As noted previously, joint ventures generally were *not* permitted in defense industries, where military security or other sovereign interests might be endangered.[49]

The definition of acceptable sectors evolved through the 1980s to meet changing goals. In the early 1980s, in addition to military industries, communications, aviation, and transportation industries were considered off limits, whereas tourism and services (which could earn foreign exchange) were encouraged and in fact were the recipients of much foreign investment (see table 3-G). After 1985, joint ventures were allowed in a number of the previously restricted sectors, including aviation and transportation, while new ventures in tourism and real estate were strongly discouraged. The fact that the joint venture of the American Motors Corporation (AMC) sold about half of its jeeps to the People's Liberation Army in the mid-1980s indicated that the general stand against foreign involvement in Chinese defense matters was interpreted less strictly, at least in one case, than China's traditional sensitivity to issues of sovereignty might have suggested.[50] The government thus adapted the designation of allowable sectors for foreign investment to meet its changing needs. Yet, although sectoral controls were adapted, the government was not always effective at enforcing them. By the second phase, it was clear that the limit of one joint venture per sector was not being enforced, as evidenced by the multiples of foreign investors in the automobile, pharmaceutical, and hotel industries. It also was evident in 1986 that efforts to discourage foreign investment in tourism and real estate and encourage it in technologically advanced or export-oriented industries were not quickly taking hold. One disappointed Chinese analyst contrasted China's experience with the newly industrialized countries of Asia, noting that in Hong Kong and Singapore almost 100%, and in Taiwan 77%, of foreign investment went into manufacturing.[51]

There were two reasons for these difficulties in implementing controls. First, with the broader decentralization of economic decisionmaking, localities with enhanced authority to seek and approve joint venture contracts autonomously did not need to take into consideration whether a project was repetitive of other similar projects in different locations. Indeed, competition between regional branches of ministries tended to ensure repetition.[52] Second, as discussed previously, tourism and real estate projects that brought in the largest amount of foreign capital were highly desirable from the viewpoint of local officials under pressure to show successes in absorbing foreign capital. In response, the government began in the third phase to pay more attention to the implementation of these controls. For example, in mid-1987, the construction of new luxury hotels and restaurants was banned in Guangzhou until 1990, and Shanghai specified more carefully the requirements for projects on foreign investment. As indicated in table 3-G, it appeared that by 1987 the effort to direct investment away from the service sectors, particularly tourism and real estate, had been relatively effective. Even so, efforts to direct the mix of investments continued throughout the third phase. In 1988, the government designated energy development, construction, chemicals, metallurgy, machine and equipment, process control, and electronics and computers as the priority sectors for foreign investment. In early 1989, the government further discouraged or required central approval (regardless of size) for investment in a long list of sectors, including taxi maintenance, automobiles, film development, cigarettes, cotton spinning and knitting, assembly of electronic goods and consumer goods (such as televisions, computers, washing machines, and bicycles).[53]

A third way to limit the scope of foreign investment was through requiring individual joint venture contracts to specify limits on the duration of the venture. In the early years, joint venture contracts usually were limited to from ten years to thirty years, although the exact period was negotiable. Only projects requiring large amounts of capital and low levels of profits could command a longer term contract, for this allowed both parties to reap what the Chinese judged to be legitimate profits over the life of the venture. In practice, most joint venture contracts were for less than twenty-five years. In the sample of equity joint ventures studied, 80% of the contracts were for between ten years and twenty years, with none below eight years or above twenty-five years.[54] The limited duration, in conjunction with the fact that all assets and know-how would revert to the Chinese side upon expiration, established in practice expropriation (with some compensation) as a condition of investment from the start.

Over time it became evident that while the relatively short duration of contracts was not always objectionable to foreign investors, it was increasingly contrary to the changing goals of reformers. One official complained, for example, that in 1984 only 17.5% of the joint venture contracts were for more than fifteen years. In January 1986, the government formally allowed contracts to be extended to a maximum duration of fifty years. There was no immediate jump in the duration of contracts, and most remained under twenty years. For example, none of the equity joint ventures in MOFERT's 1986 or 1988 samples, and only one of the ventures in the 1987 sample, took advantage of the possibility for a fifty-year duration. Some contract limits were lengthened in practice, however, as contracts were extended when their original terms expired. As part of its effort to stabilize the foreign investment environment in early 1990, the government further extended the possible duration of joint ventures. Despite some objections voiced in debate in the National People's Congress, it amended the Joint Venture Law to allow certain ventures to avoid specifying a term of operation. It was intended that ventures requiring large volumes of capital and technology, and with long payback periods, could set up joint ventures for an indefinite period, while others, especially in natural resource and service sectors, would need to specify limits.[55]

There is one area in which reformers from the start viewed it unnecessary to limit joint ventures: the duration of the foreign investment policy itself. Although individual joint venture contracts have limited terms, reformers stated that the policy as a whole would have no limit; China would pursue the joint venture policy for at least a century.[56] Following from the acceptance of comparative advantage as an "objective" economic law, reformers envisioned that cooperation with foreign investors would still be beneficial when it is time to make the transition to communism, for the scientific and technical benefits of foreign direct investment would remain significant. The view that absorption of foreign investment is a long-term policy was perhaps realistic and certainly necessary for enhancing the confidence of foreign investors. Yet this view clearly contradicted the idea that use of foreign capital would be merely an expedient tool for China's economic modernization.

Overall, then, the reformers were in some respects effective at maintaining the original controls over the scope of investment. The quantity of foreign investment was low enough to avoid infringement on China's sovereignty or independence. In the early years, moreover, the limits on contract durations were enforced. But not all controls remained strong. As the reformers became more oriented toward increasing the amount of foreign investment, they deliberately tried to extend contract durations. They also had difficulties implementing those controls they continued to desire; the decentralization of authority led to redundancy in the number of ventures set up in any sector, and to the excessive flow of foreign capital into the service sector at a time when the central government hoped to emphasize advanced technology in manufacturing. However, the reformers were eventually able to turn this trend around. As with the state plan, the experience with sectoral limits suggests that where the will to assert controls existed, the tools remained, albeit beset by implementation problems.

Prevention of Unhealthy Tendencies

A final type of control over the overall impact of foreign investment resided in mechanisms designed to prevent the "open" policy from bringing "unhealthy tendencies" ("spiritual pollution" or "bourgeois liberalization") into China. Controls over unhealthy tendencies drew on long-standing anti-imperialist and anti-foreign sentiments; they reflected the desire of both conservatives and reformers to protect from what they perceived to be harmful foreign influences "communist values" such as the spirit of collectivism, thrift, and self-sacrifice, and traditional Chinese values, including modesty, respect for authority, and conservative sexual mores.

Despite the acknowledgment by both conservatives and reformers that control of unhealthy tendencies was important, discussions of the precise causes and severity of the problem, and of possible solutions, were divisive, exceedingly murky, and colored by political factors. In particular, there was disagreement over whether to blame unhealthy tendencies on external causes, such as the foreign sector of the economy, or on internal causes, especially the domestic economic reforms.[57] Among conservatives, there appeared to be no consensus over whether unhealthy tendencies had external or internal causes. Some conservatives asserted that international class struggle between capitalist and proletarian classes was reflected in contradictions within China, including efforts of class enemies both at home and abroad to disrupt China's socialist system by attack with "sugarcoated bullets," to use one popular metaphor. Following this attribution of problems to external forces, in 1985 and 1986, party leaders from Heilongjiang and Liaoning provinces attacked the "open" policy (though not foreign investment *per se*) as a corrosive force that reflected class struggle. Other conservatives argued that new corrupt elements arose largely from domestic sources, such as the economic reforms or lax party discipline.[58]

Some prominent reformers, too, suggested that there were internal sources of corrosion. They argued that remnants of old exploiting classes (capitalist and national bourgeoisie, and feudal classes) and new exploiters (remnants of the "Gang of Four," those involved in corruption, smuggling, and so forth), along with their "exploitative" habits and ideologies, survived from the past and contaminated socialist ideology.[59] More commonly, reformers argued that economic crime in particular was not a product of the "open" policy but rather of "the poor development of commodity production, [of the] inadequacy of commodities, and [of] weak links in management systems." Another article stated that the main cause of negative social phenomena was the lack of "socialist ethics."[60]

Arguments made by Deng Xiaoping, on the other hand, focused on external rather than internal sources of unhealthy tendencies. Deng placed part of the responsibility for cadre corruption on acquisitiveness and "spiritual pollution" that he asserted must inevitably accompany exposure to capitalism. He also suggested that fears of China turning capitalist were "not without foundation," and asserted that China "cannot allow [its] young people to be corrupted by capitalist thinking." His statement that "the opening up of external relations will mean the infiltration of the corrupt things of capitalism . . . " also directly linked the "open" policy to unhealthy tendencies.[61] Another writer expressed concern that the "open" policy was allowing into China the "international bourgeoisie" and "bad elements" in Taiwan, Hong Kong, and Macao who engage in criminal activity.[62] According to still another, "[I]t is unavoidable that some filth and mire of capitalism will be brought in after the adoption of the open policy, and we must do our best to resist the inroads of these dirty things."[63]

The leadership's difficulty in defining the causes of and solutions to the problem of unhealthy tendencies to some degree may be attributed to the difficulty inherent in understanding a complex sociological phenomenon. But the lack of an underlying consensus also reflected the political constraints on engaging in frank debate, especially in the early years of the policy. Reformers in particular had good reason to be circumspect in their discussion of the problem. On the one hand, to tie the issue of unhealthy tendencies directly to the "open" policy or foreign investment might suggest the policy was illegitimate and that the door to China should be shut. And yet to blame internal "corrupt elements" would encourage criticism of the overall reform package or, worse, raise again the specter of domestic class struggle. Reformers such as Deng Xiaoping, as well as many conservatives, could be expected to find the latter unacceptable, not only because they wished to rid China of the Cultural Revolution legacy of class struggle, but also because those responsible for the post-Mao reforms would presumably be the first targets of struggle.

To lessen the danger of decisively blaming either internal or external causes, the explanation that was most frequently expressed vaguely conceded that there was a link between the "open" policy and unhealthy tendencies, but at the same time—and here the reformist justification for the

"open" policy was recalled—denied that the foreign influence must necessarily harm China if the proper controls were applied. From this position
the official line deflected blame from reformers to external forces (thereby
appealing to nationalist and anti-imperialist sentiment) and at the same
time argued against a return to a "closed" policy as a solution to the problems of unhealthy tendencies.[64] Even with this vague conclusion, however, the issue remained a political liability for the reformers, and hence
an issue about which they had to be very careful.

When the foreign investment policy was initiated, the government
drew on several long-standing tools to address the problem of unhealthy
tendencies: preceptoral methods to "inoculate" Chinese citizens against
corrosive influences; limits on contacts between Chinese and foreigners;
and suppression of the flow of tangible "unhealthy materials" from outside
China. The preceptoral controls of political exhortation and political study
were the most important part of the government's effort against unhealthy
tendencies. Preceptoral controls had long been used directly in work
units and in the mass media. They reflected the Maoist legacy of faith in
manipulation of individual consciousness as a means of social and economic change, as well as the Confucian value of education. Exhortation
and study were intended to teach the masses to interpret policy according
to official doctrine. As applied to the "open" policy specifically, preceptoral controls were not only used to communicate general party policy,
but also to teach people how to recognize and gird against unhealthy tendencies. Consistent with the reformist line, then, the thrust of the strategy to combat unhealthy tendencies was not to eliminate the alleged
source by reversing the "open" policy but, rather, to control its impact on
Chinese citizens. As a long-established method, preceptoral controls
were not controversial. Both supporters and critics of the "open" policy
stressed the importance of correct ideological work, although none suggested it should be applied as intensively as during the Cultural Revolution. For example, Deng Liqun, the conservative head of the CCP Propaganda Department in the early 1980s, and a critic of the "open" policy
precisely because of the danger of "spiritual pollution," stated in 1984
following the Campaign Against Spiritual Pollution (CASP) that "the more
we open up our external relations . . . the more we must insist on abiding
by the basic principles of Marxism and maintain the purity of communism." Similarly, at the Thirteenth National Party Congress in 1987, reformer Zhao Ziyang also emphasized the need for ideological work (although this statement was accompanied by the caveat that it should not
interfere with economic development or consist of empty jargon).[65]

But even with broad support at the top levels for traditional preceptoral
strategies of mass education and political study, the methods were not
effective enough at combating the problems in the eyes of conservatives

and older reformers. Indeed, they raised serious concerns about unhealthy tendencies repeatedly throughout the decade. As discussed in chapter 1, preceptoral controls had lost much of their impact by the late 1970s. Moreover, these preceptoral methods were closely associated with other political and ideological controls, notably mass campaigns and extreme workplace politicization, that the reformers and conservatives had tried to discredit. There was therefore dissonance between the continued reliance on certain preceptoral methods and at the same time repudiation of other methods to which the continuing controls had historically been linked. As a result, although mild preceptoral controls continued to be adhered to formally, they were used less and less over time—including in joint ventures.[66] The reasons for the ineffectiveness of preceptoral controls had little to do with declining conservative pressure at the elite level, for concern for unhealthy tendencies was the main area where conservatives remained influential. Nor was the failure of controls in this area due primarily to foreign pressures for liberalization, for foreigners expressed little interest in these issues. Rather, efforts to guard against unhealthy tendencies failed because they contradicted other policies being implemented at that time and, even more, because the specific methods employed against unhealthy tendencies were largely ineffective in the post–Cultural Revolution context.

The reformers also attempted to use tools other than preceptoral controls to fight unhealthy tendencies, but neither did these prove satisfactory. In response to lingering wariness of foreigners both within society as a whole and in the specific context of joint ventures, some effort was made to limit unfettered contact between foreigners and Chinese. This wariness was expressed in the belief that representatives of foreign business fall into two types. There were those who "sincerely hope to cooperate with us and use legitimate methods to do business" and those who "resort to dishonest means or even means in violation of China's sovereignty—such as swindle [sic], bribery, smuggling, infiltration, and espionage—to harm . . . the Chinese people and [to] corrupt Party members, cadres and other people."[67] To limit contacts between Chinese and foreigners, in the early years the government established various controls over expatriates, such as requiring them to carry identification cards and to live in foreigners-only hotels. Chinese were not allowed to meet alone with foreigners or accept gifts from them. Chinese who became too familiar with foreigners were harassed. In one rare case, a foreigner who had become intimate with several Chinese people was jailed. Several foreign managers cited instances prior to early 1985 in which Chinese managers or recruits to a joint venture "got into trouble" or were criticized because they were in close contact with foreigners at joint ventures. In another case, foreign managers were told by local officials not to discuss political matters with local people. The import of pornography and Western sexual mores by foreign business representatives was also highly sensitive; overseas Chinese managers in particular reported facing tough scrutiny from Chinese customs officials looking for pornographic materials. In addition, social visits by foreigners to Chinese homes had to be prearranged by local authorities. These controls, though widely reported by foreign managers, were not promulgated publicly. But either because they reflected well-entrenched policies or habits from the past, or were circulated widely enough in *neibu* documents, they were widely followed in the early years. Many expatriates also believed that Chinese employees reported on activities of or contacts between Chinese citizens and foreigners to a local party organization, although there was no independent verification of such surveillance.[68]

Control of contacts with foreigners or the activities of foreigners was not absolute, however, even in the early years. There was some effort to carve out a realm of legitimate contact essentially by differentiating personal contact—which could be corrosive—from necessary business contacts. The reformers exhorted Chinese people not to regard all business people from outside as "dangerous elements who have come to corrupt our people."[69] Even when anti-foreign sentiment was spreading during the 1983 CASP, although several foreign managers felt that personal relations between themselves and their Chinese counterparts cooled slightly, they did not note any effect on their business. The effort to establish a realm of legitimate contacts reflected the recognition that extensive restrictions on business-related contacts would be counterproductive to the goal of using foreign technical personnel and managers to train Chinese workers and managers.[70]

The government also tried to prevent unhealthy tendencies from entering China at all during the first half of the 1980s. It identified illegal drugs and pornography, for example, as undesirable and banned or closely monitored them. It initiated procedures to control international economic crimes by joining Interpol to "stop international criminals from taking advantage of China's decision to open up to the outside world," and by expanding its customs system.[71] The government also tried to suppress the spread of what it considered to be inappropriate consumption patterns by limiting advertising by foreign firms and by restricting sales for luxury products—foreign cigarettes, soft drinks, and liquor, for example—to stores and hotels that accepted only foreign exchange. Advertisements that were deemed "harmful to the dignity of China's various nationalities," labeled "reactionary, obscene, crude, or superstitious," carried "propaganda of a slanderous nature," or negatively affected the "political, moral, or social climate" of China were formally prohibited.[72]

As with preceptoral controls, efforts to limit contact with foreigners and to regulate customs and advertising weakened over the course of the 1980s. Personal contacts and friendships between Chinese and foreigners became more common and accepted, and many Western trends were imitated by the young. Contacts between foreigners and Chinese, especially in joint ventures, were less troubled by the sorts of controls found in the first half of the 1980s. This reflected a more relaxed attitude toward foreigners themselves and their "corrupt" habits.[73]

Yet it became clear that the issue was not dead in China when, in 1989, furor over "bourgeois liberalization" returned again. Conservatives and older reformers once again accused foreigners of suggesting the ideas behind—and providing support for—the student and worker protests in Beijing and in other major cities.[74] As before, post-Tiananmen leaders tried to use the same traditional controls, particularly intensive political study in factories, the monitoring of contacts between Chinese and foreigners, and customs control of Western materials (particularly political materials or media accounts of the student protests and government crackdown). As in the early years of the policy, the concern over unhealthy tendencies in 1989 did not lead to efforts to get rid of the alleged foreign source of unhealthy tendencies. The aim of the controls continued to be to inoculate Chinese citizens against the effect of "bourgeois liberalization" rather than eliminate the alleged source.

. . .

The seven overarching national-level controls discussed in this part—the establishment by China of general principles, law, procedures for approval and resolution of disputes, the state plan, controls on the scope of joint ventures, and controls over the the transmission to China of unhealthy tendencies—reflected the effort of the Chinese leadership to define the role that foreign investment would play in China's economy, politics, and culture. Several of these cases illustrate well where the strengths of the Chinese state in controlling foreign capital lay. Although perhaps obvious, it was nonetheless significant that the government did not abdicate or lose its ultimate sovereign authority to regulate joint ventures at any time during the 1980s; it maintained in particular the authority to assert Chinese governing law and the state plan. Even after decentralization weakened the role of the plan and the center's role in approving joint ventures, the government was able to re-assert these authorities.

Still, problems of implementation and liberalization were evident for these higher level controls. Liberalization was evident most often as a result of the evolving viewpoint of reformers toward foreign investment or as a by-product of broader reforms in the economy. As the desire to increase the amount of foreign investment deepened, concerns about the effect of such an increase on China's sovereignty diminished, and the willingness to adapt further to international laws and business norms increased. Similarly, as the "open" policy became more entrenched, controls over contact between Chinese and foreigners also weakened. Even more striking were the problems reformers encountered in the implementation of the controls, as was evident with attempts to guard against unhealthy tendencies. The patterns of liberalization and problems in implementation, though notable for this set of controls, came into even greater relief in the specific controls at the national level discussed in the following part.

REGULATION OF THE IMPACT OF JOINT VENTURES ON THE ECONOMY

The five sets of controls discussed in this part—controls over exports, domestic content, foreign exchange, profits, and technology transfer—all illustrate measures designed to regulate the economic impact of joint ventures, and hence to allow China to capture what the reformers believed was its legitimate share of investment benefits. While guided by many of the overarching controls defining the status of joint ventures discussed in the previous section, these issue areas also were the subject of explicit regulation.

Restrictions on Entrance to the Domestic Market

Governments in developing countries often restrict the sale of joint venture products in the domestic market. Export requirements became more common in many developing countries during the 1980s. For example, many Export Processing Zones (EPZs) required that export manufacturing operations represent 50% of the total output of the zones.[75] The major justification for such requirements was that, through exports, joint ventures would earn sufficient hard currency to pay for their import needs, and at the same time domestic markets would be protected from unfair foreign competition. In China, the major impetus behind exports was the concern to avoid foreign currency problems. But the desire to protect home markets cannot be ignored. Indeed, given the uncontrolled foreign penetration into Chinese markets between the mid-nineteenth and mid-twentieth centuries, it is not surprising that protection of the domestic market had been on China's economic agenda since 1949. Although reformers hoped that a degree of competition from foreign-backed projects would stimulate domestic enterprises, both they and conservatives viewed export requirements as legitimate to use in defense of domestic industries. (This, then, was a qualification on the reformers' acceptance of the principle of comparative advantage.)[76]

The Chinese government's effort to encourage exports conflicted directly with the interests many foreign investors had in gaining access to China's domestic market. As discussed in chapter 1, Western transnationals in particular entered joint ventures in China primarily because of the potential for increased access to the domestic market, rather than for short-term benefits anticipated from the joint venture itself. Domestic sales by joint ventures were sometimes more profitable than international sales, given China's pricing structure and, in some cases, the need for joint ventures to cut prices to compete internationally. Moreover, sales in the domestic market did not compete with the parent company's existing sales in Asia.[77] The depth of the conflict that could arise over the issue of domestic sales was exemplified by one case in the mid-1980s, in which conflict over whether the foreign partner could enter the protected market of the Chinese partner dominated the partners' interactions. Because the Chinese joint venture's Chinese parent monopolized the domestic industry, it believed it stood to lose much by allowing the joint venture to compete at home (even though it would still profit from the joint venture's sales). Although the foreign partner intended from the beginning to enter the domestic market, the joint venture contract envisioned only international marketing. The Chinese partner was successful at enforcing this term.

The government set up a number of controls to discourage domestic sales by joint ventures. From the earliest phase of the policy, the Joint Venture Law stated that each joint venture "is encouraged to market its products outside China" (Article 9). This clause did not appear particularly onerous, especially because it did not specify a quota of exports (in contrast to the EPZs). But it became clear in contracts signed in the early years that the law's mere encouragement to export had been given "teeth" in a variety of ways, both formal and informal. Formally, the government was able to use the state plan to pressure for exports. By including joint ventures in state marketing plans, the government was able to direct where joint ventures made sales, as described previously. It also could use its pricing authority to impose excessively higher prices for joint venture products than for the comparable local product, making domestic sales difficult. And the government in theory could use its Chinese managers within joint ventures to direct sales.[78] (The latter two means apparently were used infrequently.)

The most direct and most frequently employed means of encouraging joint venture exports was by formally negotiating contracts that set export targets, ranging from 20% to 100% (but often over 50%) of the joint venture product.[79] The Chinese government was fairly effective at obtaining commitments to export from joint ventures in the first half of the 1980s. In the sample of joint ventures conducted for this study, 81% had plans for export, and 59% of these had a goal of exporting half or more of the venture's product, or actually were exporting 50% or more.[80] In one case, the foreign partner's parent company agreed to purchase enough of the joint venture product to ensure sufficient foreign currency. A separate study found that contracts of seven of the eleven joint ventures it surveyed in 1983 required exports. Those joint ventures not stipulating exports were with foreign partners that had previously exported high-technology goods to China, and presumably were engaged in joint ventures using high technology.[81] Other foreign companies were pressured in negotiations to promise high levels of exports when, in calling for competitive bids from potential joint venture partners, Chinese negotiators required that proposals specify the level of exports foreigners were willing to meet.[82]

But by far the most effective restriction on domestic sales resulted from controls over foreign exchange; as discussed subsequently, because almost all joint ventures required foreign exchange income, and because domestic sales saddled joint ventures with nonconvertible domestic currency, most in practice had to export their products. Of the firms sampled that did not sign contracts calling for exports but exported nonetheless, virtually all were compelled to do so simply in order to earn foreign currency. (Unlike the previously noted survey of eleven firms, those firms sampled for the present study that did not export at all were engaged in construction or service activities that could earn foreign currency through domestic sales, generally ventures that serviced other joint ventures, such as offshore oil servicing companies.)

Exports were further encouraged through two informal means. In at least one case, the government on an *ad hoc* basis imposed export requirements that were more stringent than those that appeared in the contract. After Hitachi's joint venture to produce televisions in Fujian became operational, the export quotas agreed to in the contract were subsequently "revised" upward under pressure from central authorities. The venture's managers were directed by central ministerial authorities to raise the percentage of exports to 50% by the third year of operations, even though in the agreement exports were to fall under the jurisdiction of the Japanese partner and were to be increased more gradually.[83] In other instances, Chinese enterprises that faced competition (or potential competition) from a joint venture (or potential joint venture) moved to protect their burgeoning market positions. Such protectionism existed in China's service and consumer goods sectors, for example. Threatened industries acted either by influencing the government authorities to disallow the joint ventures or, in one case, by threatening customers that it would fail to honor their contracts if the customer patronized the joint venture. In still other cases, some Chinese trading organizations refused to buy joint venture goods or take joint venture bids for projects. For example, one bureau refused to invite joint venture bids for projects in order to protect the terms of an existing licensing agreement with a foreign firm.[84] Thus, protectionist interests reinforced the reformers' interest in inhibiting domestic sales by joint ventures. These barriers, and other restrictions on domestic sales, particularly in the form of contractual agreements to export and the practical need to earn foreign exchange, in many ways were quite onerous.

Yet the severity of these restrictions was mitigated by problems in implementation and by deliberate liberalization. Problems in implementing the controls arose from the fact that, despite export quotas stipulated in their contracts, many joint ventures, particularly those producing relatively sophisticated products, were unable to meet the export targets and were allowed to sell domestically. This was of course more true for those ventures (particularly those involving Western and Japanese partners) that produced relatively sophisticated products; ventures involved in simpler assembly and processing (often those with Hong Kong partners) were more successful at exporting.[85] Meeting export targets was difficult for a number of reasons. Poor export performance was largely a function of the Chinese economy. High costs such as for imported materials (despite an overvalued local currency) and local fees, low labor productivity, and the poor quality of local materials, meant that many joint venture products, especially in the early years, were not competitive in either price or quality on international markets. In some cases, moreover, the export targets provided in contracts were unreasonably high. Although the inability to export allowed joint ventures some inroads into the domestic market, and in this way served foreign interests, the technical problem of entering international markets, rather than deliberate obfuscation of Chinese controls, was primarily responsible.

The second, and related, factor weakening export performance was the formal actions taken by the government to respond to export difficulties. Understanding that the strict export quotas were a strong disincentive to foreign investors, the government began as early as the 1983 Implementing Regulations to formally grant access to the domestic market if the venture met certain conditions. Joint ventures that made products that reformers deemed China urgently needed or imported in large amounts were allowed to sell primarily on the domestic market.[86] This was the first time the government formally acknowledged that joint ventures could provide an import substitution function. It marked a major change from what the government had envisioned in the early years; indeed, a foreign lawyer who reviewed a 1980 draft of the Implementing Regulations reported that the draft contained no mention of the allowances for domestic sales eventually made in 1983. The reformers made still further concessions, in practice, in 1985 and then formally in February 1986, by allowing joint ventures to sell in China at international prices if they provided advanced technology or equipment, used large amounts of domestic materials or substituted for imports, or if their products were unique or of superior quality to those produced by local enterprises. Joint ventures also were allowed to sell goods meeting these standards for foreign exchange to domestic enterprises if the domestic enterprise had funds available to pay for them.[87] The preferential treatment for joint ventures that supplied advanced technology or equipment dovetailed with the new emphasis of the 1986 Provisions on attracting (largely through favorable incentives) "technologically advanced enterprises."

The concessions granted by the government in 1986 were significant, yet they were finely tuned to encourage investment where China very much needed it, especially in high-technology sectors. The concessions were tempered by the continuing *de facto* requirement that joint ventures earn the foreign exchange necessary to buy the imports they required primarily through exports. Moreover, the government began to engage in other activities designed to favor "export-oriented enterprises." Export-oriented enterprises (EOEs) were defined as "enterprises whose products are mainly for export, which have a foreign exchange surplus" after accounting for all foreign exchange expenditures (Article 2.1). Joint ventures designated as EOEs by local governments were eligible for special treatment on a variety of issues. Costs, such as land use fees, and certain subsidies to be paid to labor were lowered, as were both domestic taxes and taxes on profits remitted abroad. EOEs also were given priority in obtaining water, electricity, and other infrastructural services in short supply, as well as in receiving short-term bank loans. Several municipalities, including Beijing and Shanghai, quickly designated a number of joint ventures in this category. These were primarily joint ventures with Hong Kong or Macao partners, which tended to manufacture light industrial products with existing export markets, and had invested to take advantage of lower labor costs in China.[88] The granting of ever greater concessions for joint ventures capable of exports was designed to help meet the government's foreign exchange concerns. While they did not prohibit domestic sales, they did suggest that, except for the few ventures allowed to market domestically, the government continued to encourage exports at the expense of domestic sales.

Even with these concessions, investors continued to feel that the restrictions on access to the domestic market were severe. Some selective further liberalization occurred in the late 1980s. Import substitution regulations issued in October 1987 reiterated the central government's commitment to, and further clarified, the import substitution option.[89] Importantly, the government was to encourage domestic enterprises to buy joint venture products that served an import substitution function. Several key joint ventures, including Shanghai Bell, Volkswagen, and American Motors Corporation (AMC), were beneficiaries of the plan.[90] A greater number of joint ventures were granted import substitution status; for example, twenty-three were designated as such in Guangdong Province alone. Moreover, although the leaders had clearly envisioned that the greater allowance for domestic sales would not extend to consumer goods products, for which China presumably possessed the production wherewithal, in 1988 the government approved a number of large joint ventures to produce consumer goods for the Chinese market. These included ventures to produce crackers, shampoo, contact lenses, bandages, and household insecticides.[91] Although this change in policy came in practice, and was not codified, the approval of these contracts, many of which had been in negotiation for years, reflected some recognition among reformers that China needed mid-level technologies (such as aerosol technology, in the case of pesticides) as well as sophisticated technologies, and that providers of such mid-level technologies—many of them large TNCs—were interested in investing only when allowed to make domestic sales.

That Chinese controls over access to the domestic market continued to be relatively strict throughout the 1980s reflected the strength of concern about this issue. Yet problems in the domestic economy that thwarted the ability of joint ventures to fill export quotas made the effort to maintain controls problematic. The relaxation of some of the original constraints, moreover, showed not only the pressure foreign investors brought to bear, but also the reformers' willingness to trade off domestic controls for the benefits of foreign investment to which they had become most committed. It also suggested that a set of priorities was emerging from among the myriad original concerns, and that the desire to attract advanced technology was very high on the list. The attempt to use the incentive of domestic sales to attract advanced and, at least in some cases, mid-level technology illustrated the growing sophistication of reformers in tailoring regulatory means to meet their priorities.

Domestic Content

Multinational investors in developing countries are frequently criticized for failure to create backward (supply) linkages with local enterprises. Critics assert that an absence of linkages lessens the contribution of foreign direct investment to local development, for it isolates the benefits of foreign investment to the foreign sector rather than stimulating changes in the rest of the economy. The Chinese reformers agreed that in order to minimize the level of imports and foreign currency expenditures by joint ventures and to provide a competitive stimulus to domestic producers to raise the technical level of their inputs, it was important to foster linkages between joint ventures and the domestic economy.[92] Even without the Chinese government's requirement for local content, the ventures themselves had strong financial incentives to source locally; domestic materials were often less expensive than imports, keeping their costs competitive, and saving valuable foreign currency. Domestic sourcing also helped protect the joint venture against devaluation of the purchasing currency, usually the dollar or the *yuan*, which could make imports more expensive.[93]

The Joint Venture Law and Implementing Regulations strongly encouraged joint ventures to give priority to local supplies, although they also allowed ventures to import.[94] To strengthen the legal aims, in the first and second phase Chinese negotiators often insisted on domestic content clauses in contracts. Indeed, in light of the push to reverse foreign exchange drains, domestic content clauses became non-negotiable for the Chinese by the mid-1980s. Several joint venture agreements with Japanese partners faltered over the Chinese insistence on local sourcing.[95] Although no complete figures are available, joint venture contracts commonly specified that between 30% and 80% of inputs were to be from domestic sources, with specifications at the higher end of the range more prevalent. Absent specific targets for domestic content, other contracts called for local sourcing "to the extent possible." Moreover, many contracts, such as for electronic and automobile joint ventures, called for an increasing percentage of domestic supplies over the life of the venture under the assumption that the quantity and quality of domestic materials would increase. For example, the Hitachi joint venture contract specified that within three years of becoming operational (by 1983), domestic parts were to account for 50% of the inputs. By the fourth year (1984), the number was 90% for black-and-white televisions, and 60% to 80% for color sets. The Volkswagen automobile joint venture in Shanghai foresaw 80% domestic content after five years. Half of the ventures sampled for this study for which information was available reported that their contracts contained set targets for domestic content or that their partners or government officials encouraged it verbally. Although joint venture agreements have sometimes omitted domestic content clauses, the government has criticized this practice.[96]

But domestic content goals stipulated in contracts frequently were not met. The AMC venture in Beijing, for example, continued importing a large percentage of its products longer than the partners originally anticipated. As discussed with regard to the state plan and exports, investors often had difficulty obtaining supplies of a quality high enough to allow their goods to be exported, or of the proper quality and specification to be compatible with foreign processes and technologies. In the mid-1980s, the Chinese government reacted to these difficulties with increased pressure on joint ventures to improve domestic sourcing (particularly in order to solve their foreign currency problems), and sometimes gave ventures concrete help. Hence, whether because of contract stipulations or foreign exchange constraints, all joint venture interviewees who discussed this problem reported that they were moving rapidly to develop local supplies, including major industrial and high-technology ventures. The AMC venture in Beijing, for example, agreed to speed up domestic sourcing in exchange for short-term foreign exchange concessions from the government. (Even so, by the end of the 1980s, when the venture was to be sourcing 80% of the value of its materials locally, it was in fact only sourcing 35% locally.) Several firms also took significant steps to establish reliable supply sources within China, thereby phasing in their contractual commitments for domestic content. The joint ventures involving AMC, E. K. Chor, and Hitachi, for example, all tried to organize local suppliers, providing them with training and financial incentives as well as with the prestige of being linked with a joint venture. Hitachi's venture, which suffered steep rises in costs of imported kits due to the strengthening of the yen, got the Chinese government to finance local kit-makers. This was a major factor in helping the venture localize content to 85% from 40%.[97] More broadly, following the broad mandate in late 1986 to improve the investment environment, the materials departments of several municipalities established special companies to procure supplies for foreign-backed enterprises. By mid-1987, fifteen such companies had been set up in cities such as Beijing, Guangzhou, Shanghai, and Tianjin.[98] But this effort to ensure supplies, though helpful, was limited insofar as it did not address quality problems, and did not establish direct ties between suppliers and the joint venture. Indeed, there were strong limits on what such efforts could achieve in the short term. In the case of domestic content, then, the government's original goals of localizing production were hindered less by foreign pressure or a change in the reformist goals themselves than by structural difficulties inherent in the Chinese economy.

Restrictions on Foreign Exchange

Since 1949, China's economic policy has reflected strong concerns that national foreign exchange shortages be avoided. During the 1970s and early 1980s, foreign exchange was tightly regulated by central agencies in accordance with a national foreign exchange plan. The goal of this national-level regulation was to ensure that reserves were available to pay for imports China would need in its development program. As in Eastern

European joint ventures, throughout the 1980s Chinese leaders hoped that the foreign sector would earn foreign currency for China through exports, and regulated foreign-backed enterprises toward that end.[99] Yet given the small size of the foreign sector compared to all sources of foreign currency, the potential contribution of joint ventures to currency reserves was relatively small. Incentives routinely granted to foreign investors, such as the ability to repatriate profits, and the provision of tax holidays, also counteracted the accumulation of foreign exchange.[100] The requirement that joint ventures meet their own foreign exchange needs thus served more to prevent a drain on currency reserves than to encourage significant contributions to them.

Foreign exchange was also an important issue for joint venture operations. Joint ventures required a source of foreign exchange to pay charges denominated in foreign currency: imported supplies and machinery; return on equity to the foreign partner; principal and interest on borrowed funds; expatriate salaries; royalties; and purchase of the foreign partner's equity upon termination of the venture. But because *renminbi* was (and still is) not convertible, joint ventures required means other than free conversion of domestic currency (*renminbi*) earnings to obtain needed foreign currency.

The Chinese government established regulations governing joint ventures foreign currency accounts during the first phase, and clarified these controls somewhat during the second period. The Joint Venture Law itself was not detailed on this issue; it merely required ventures to adhere to the regulations of the State Administration for Exchange Control (SAEC). The SAEC's Foreign Exchange Regulations did strictly regulate foreign currency, however. They did this first and foremost by requiring joint ventures to balance their foreign exchange income and expenditures, a requirement that was reiterated in the 1983 Implementing Regulations.[101] In addition, the balancing requirement was sometimes written into specific joint venture contracts, either directly or through export quotas, as described previously.[102] To monitor this balance, several bureaucratic organs with overlapping functions were to have authority for foreign exchange control, but primary responsibility lay with the SAEC. In 1983, regulations on foreign exchange clarified the process of central oversight. Joint ventures were required to deposit all foreign exchange receipts in, and make all such payments from, an account with the Bank of China (BOC) or another approved Chinese bank. They also were required to periodically submit to the SAEC their balance sheets, profit and loss statements, statements of foreign exchange earnings and disbursements, an auditor's report, and any further information about foreign exchange activities that were requested.[103] Moreover, to gain access to the foreign currency they had on deposit, ventures often had to follow complex procedures. One possible procedure by which foreign exchange could be released was described by a Chinese official in 1985: a joint venture could submit a statement of need to the provincial-level government organ that supervised foreign investment, for which the venture would receive a document granting it authority to withdraw its foreign exchange. The venture would then need to send a copy of this document to the SAEC, which in turn would refer it to the BOC, which would then release the foreign currency. Two joint ventures (located in different cities) reported that the SAEC and the BOC frequently required in-depth negotiations and approvals in order to get foreign exchange released from joint venture accounts for legitimate purposes. The situation of another joint venture, located in Guangdong Province, indicated that implementation could vary, however. The foreign manager asserted that his venture had faced no abnormal interference from the Bank of China because, at the venture's inception, they had held a banquet for the relevant officials, and had made a concerted effort to remain on good terms.[104]

In the first phase, given the foreign exchange balancing rules, a joint venture realistically could attempt to earn the hard currency it needed in only one way: it could export goods produced by the joint venture. Yet the difficulty of producing goods of appropriate quality and competitive prices for export, as discussed previously, made foreign exchange balancing quite problematic, while forced exports conflicted with the desire of many foreign partners for access to the domestic market, and the desire not to undercut exports from other production bases in Asia.

The Chinese government began even in 1983 to search for ways to ameliorate foreign concerns, and made several changes to liberalize the rules. The first move was related to the allowance that permission for domestic sales might be granted if the product substituted for imports. Whereas the 1980 Foreign Exchange Regulations had required that all sales permitted on the domestic market be transacted in *renminbi*, 1983 Foreign Exchange Implementing Regulations permitted some joint ventures to sell to Chinese firms that could pay in foreign exchange.[105] The Joint Venture Implementing Regulations further provided that if a joint venture received permission under import substitution provisions to sell its products primarily on the domestic market for partial payment in *renminbi*, a municipal-, provincial-, or national-level agency should compensate for any resulting imbalance from their own foreign exchange reserves.[106] The Implementing Regulations also allowed the BOC or foreign banks to lend foreign exchange to joint ventures. After that time, the BOC policy was to give priority for foreign currency loans to joint ventures.[107]

Although these solutions were offered in good faith, their actual implementation was problematic. Foreign exchange loans were of course subject to repayment with interest, and hence were not a long-term solution to a joint venture's deficits. Moreover, not all joint ventures could take advantage of a number of the other concessions. Provisions both for government agencies to help joint ventures within their official jurisdictions meet foreign exchange needs and for domestic enterprises to purchase joint venture goods with foreign exchange were available only to a few firms that could gain the designation as import substitution ventures. In practice, such a designation was very difficult to obtain; the legislation was vague about which ventures could qualify, and the government was very reluctant to apply the designation. In most cases where sales to domestic firms for foreign currency were allowed, foreign trade authorities had to agree that the transaction provided an import substitution function.[108] Arrangements whereby local governments would compensate for joint venture shortfalls also had to be negotiated with the appropriate agency through the Chinese partner's parent department. Successful negotiations in fact proved extremely rare for investors because, since there was no formal obligation for any one department to part with foreign exchange and the department was unlikely to have a concrete interest in the project, they lacked any incentive to help. Interviews conducted for this study revealed only one successful case, in which a joint venture had negotiated with a provincial-level foreign trade corporation in the same sector to cover the venture's hard currency deficit.[109]

Several of these solutions also required that a broad range of institutions below the central level actually had foreign exchange to pay or contribute to joint ventures. This in turn required a good currency reserve situation. Foreign exchange reserves were at an all-time high between October 1984 and mid-1985. Tight control on foreign currency spending, together with increased exports, had contributed to a rise in reserves from $1 billion in the late 1970s to a high of $17 billion in July 1984. The urban reforms in October 1984 granted greater autonomy to municipal governments and enterprises, allowing them to retain and spend a portion of locally earned foreign currency. At that point, it seemed as though the government's provision of foreign exchange aid would be helpful. But the situation changed when the government loosened foreign exchange controls and relaxed credit, and strong demand for shortage import items appeared. These changes, compounded by a drop in the international price of oil and a rise in the value of the yen (Japan was China's leading trade partner), precipitated a drain on foreign currency reserves; by February 1985, reserves had fallen to $12.3 billion. In mid-1985 and again in 1987, the government severely curbed local authority to spend foreign exchange in order to rebuild reserves.[110] The national foreign exchange crisis and related recentralization of authority over foreign currency thus further decreased the likelihood that local, provincial, or central agencies would make such arrangements after mid-1985. The chance of finding domestic enterprises with surplus foreign exchange to whom a joint venture might sell, and the availability of foreign exchange loans, also decreased after the 1985 recentralization of authority. When firms did have foreign exchange, they often preferred—both because of the prestige associated with imports and distortions in tariff structures—to purchase goods from abroad rather than those produced domestically, even by joint ventures. In the meantime, many joint ventures continued to encounter major obstacles to domestic sourcing, and therefore often needed to import more inputs than they had anticipated during negotiations.

The 1984–1985 foreign exchange crisis had severe consequences for a number of joint ventures. Some smaller ventures were forced to close as their Chinese partners were suddenly faced with new government-imposed restrictions. The most extreme case of a foreign exchange problem was the decision by foreign managers at the jeep-producing joint venture of AMC to halt production due to foreign exchange difficulties. After the 1985 restrictions were imposed, the purchasers of the venture's jeeps (mostly government bureaus and the People's Liberation Army) did not have the foreign currency to cover the cost of the imported kits of components, payments for which comprised about two-thirds of the sale price. Nor could the joint venture arrange licenses to import, or letters of credit from the Bank of China, to pay for new kits.[111] The problems AMC encountered led not only to a halt in operations but also to general threats by the foreign partner to withdraw from the venture. AMC also convinced the U.S. treasury secretary to speak on its behalf in his meetings with Premier Zhao Ziyang.

Other firms also continued to face problems with their foreign exchange balances during the second phase. Most managers interviewed for this study viewed foreign exchange controls imposed by the Chinese government as extremely stringent, and 75% reported having problems balancing foreign exchange. Of those that did not have problems, half were joint ventures for light industry products with ready export markets, for example, those producing specifically for the foreign parent, and half, including tourism ventures, sold their services to foreigners in China for foreign exchange. Those that did have problems balancing their foreign exchange were in many cases ventures that required large equipment imports in the first years of operation. These findings are supported by other studies of joint ventures. In one study, over half of fifty joint venture managers surveyed in 1986 claimed that hard currency issues presented a major operating challenge, while in another study, most manufacturing joint ventures (but not hotels and other service ventures) faced serious foreign exchange problems. Chinese figures also reflected a problem: foreign trade officials estimated in early 1986 that, although tourism ventures were earning sufficient foreign exchange, half of the joint ventures in industrial sectors had a deficit in hard currency.[112]

By the latter half of 1985, the government realized that it had to make further efforts to mollify investors. In February 1986, the government codified in regulations certain concessions that China had begun to make in practice over the previous several months. These regulations allowed foreign firms involved in more than one joint venture to use a surplus in one to cover a deficit in another. A foreign partner could also invest any *renminbi* earnings in another joint venture (such as a hotel) that had greater potential to earn foreign exchange. The most significant concession of the February regulations was the stepped-up commitment for ventures producing import substitution goods. According to these rules, such ventures could sell on the domestic market for *renminbi*, and then convert the earnings to foreign exchange through the Bank of China. Unlike the earlier import substitution provision in the Implementing Regulations, this regulation gave the *central* government the primary responsibility to aid firms facing foreign exchange problems. The government at this time also seemed more serious about putting this concession into practice. For example, it used the import substitution provision to help the joint ventures involving Foxboro and Volkswagen. At the behest of Zhao Ziyang, the government also made special arrangements to resolve the crisis at the AMC jeep venture, agreeing to provide $120 million in foreign exchange to allow the venture to continue importing jeep kits. In return, AMC executives agreed to speed localization of supplies, as noted previously.[113]

Under the 1986 Provisions announced that fall, joint ventures were granted yet another means of easing the requirement to balance foreign exchange: they could, under government supervision, negotiate with other joint ventures to adjust their surpluses and deficits among themselves (Article 14). Shanghai and Shenzhen immediately provided specific locations for joint ventures to arrange currency "swaps," and by the end of 1988, thirty-nine such adjustment centers had been established. In these centers, an official would arrange a trade between two parties at the prevailing rate, but the parties were not allowed to meet each other. The swap system handled a significant volume of currency. In 1989, these centers handled $8.6 billion worth of foreign currency conversions (a 39% rise over 1988); foreign-backed enterprises traded 18% of this. The U.S. Foreign Commercial Service in Beijing estimated in 1988 that 130 of the 220 foreign invested enterprises in Shanghai engaged in swaps. The cost of currency trading was high, however; while the official exchange rate was 3.7 *yuan* to the dollar in 1988, special centers charged between 6 *yuan* and 6.5 *yuan* per dollar.[114] Nonetheless, the system worked reasonably well, and many joint venture managers reported that it had helped them allay foreign currency problems. The use of swaps was illustrative of a broader change in how the reformers were viewing the issue of foreign exchange balances. Increasingly, they appeared to believe that it was more reasonable to require the foreign sector as a whole, rather than individual joint ventures, to balance foreign currency. The legitimation of swaps was thus an innovative step, for it applied quasi-market methods to help ease the foreign exchange problem for joint ventures but without state subsidies and without relaxing the overall goal of having a balance-neutral foreign investment policy.[115]

As in the second phase, a number of important restrictions became evident in the reiteration and clarification of the import substitution option. This option was to be a *temporary* remedy, that is, to be used solely in the early phases of a joint venture's operation, when it had the most difficulty exporting. Domestic sales were not to constitute the only source of foreign exchange. Import substitution status still had to be negotiated and approved by foreign exchange authorities, and the terms set forth in the new regulations were strict: import substitution products had to be competitive with imports in terms of price, quality, delivery, and servicing, and moreover were required to use some domestic materials. But because many joint venture products could not meet these criteria, few ventures were in a position to receive approval even if China would otherwise import similar products. Several obstacles remained even after an official designation was obtained. Approval by the government still did not guarantee sales, for the government did not force domestic enterprises to buy joint venture goods. The higher price of joint venture products, and general prejudice in favor of imports, also continued to be potent disincentives to domestic purchasers. Finally, if a domestic buyer agreed to purchase from a joint venture, it could only pay part of the sales price in foreign currency, a proportion that had to be negotiated. (This had the effect of actually saving China some of the foreign currency it would otherwise spend on imports.)

During the third phase, one additional mechanism for remedying the foreign exchange problems of joint ventures was formalized. The government began to allow joint ventures to purchase, with *renminbi*, goods produced domestically that were unrelated to its own operations, and then export them. The government thereby overcame some of its earlier reluctance to keep joint ventures operating within the boundaries defined in their contract. Specifically, the 1987 "Domestic Product Export Measures" allowed joint ventures with foreign exchange deficits to seek permission of local trade authorities (local MOFERT branches) to purchase and export local products.[116] Although some foreign partners found little appeal in the prospect of becoming exporters, others saw such exports as a viable solution. Once again, however, there were restrictions and prob-

140   CHAPTER FOUR

lems associated with this solution. Not only did joint ventures have to renew permission to export domestic products annually, but the amount of hard currency a venture earned from exports could be no more than what was required for the venture's operating expenses and profit remission. More important, it was difficult for joint ventures to find goods to export. A number of the most exportable commodities (such as tobacco and tea) were subject to central export via the government's trading corporations, for example. It was also difficult to guarantee supplies, both because of structural difficulties of the Chinese economy, and because of the difficulties convincing domestic enterprises with exportable products to sell to joint ventures in exchange for *renminbi* when they themselves could be earning foreign currency by exporting.

In addition to the problems joint ventures faced in taking advantage of these concessions, the overall regulatory regime for foreign exchange remained tight. The growing emphasis on EOEs signaled that the government still wished to avoid aiding foreign exchange balances in all but those ventures that provided desired technology, or import substitution or other urgently needed goods. The government also added some new restrictions in the third phase: for example, in February 1987, the People's Bank of China restricted the providers and amount of foreign exchange loan guarantees required to secure loans (particularly from foreign lenders). Hence, in early 1989, foreign investors continued to view the foreign exchange regulations as strict, naming foreign exchange balancing concerns as a major, and often their biggest, problem.[117] But the record of controls over foreign investment makes clear that, over time, the reformers responded to pressures from foreign businesses to improve the investment environment, and to their own concerns about a downturn in foreign investment. At the same time that some of the solutions were innovative and were tailored to aid the kinds of projects the reformers most wanted to attract, the steps they took were significant and unanticipated.

It is interesting to note that in late 1988 and 1989, the problem of access to foreign currency became, for some ventures, secondary to gaining access to *renminbi*. Following restrictions imposed by the government in late 1988 to curtail credit expansion and inflation to slow the overheated economy, joint ventures like domestic enterprises often had problems collecting on bills denominated in *renminbi*. To the extent that they relied upon *renminbi* earnings to exchange at swap centers, the foreign currency position of ventures was hurt. Although the shift in demand to *renminbi* did drive down the relative price of foreign currency at swap centers somewhat, the downswing was halted by the tremendous drop in tourism revenues after the spring of 1989, which drained the coffers of those who had supplied the bulk of foreign exchange for sale at the centers: joint venture hotels.[118]

NATIONAL AND REGIONAL CONTROLS

Restrictions on Profits and Profit Repatriation

The Chinese government expressed two concerns related to joint venture profits in the early years of the foreign investment policy. The first concern of both conservatives and reformers was that the sole pursuit of profit for profit's own sake, a key element of capitalism, not be a practice that China should adopt. There was also a lingering distaste for and suspicion of adopting foreign financial practices wholesale. But reformers broke with conservatives by arguing that *some* application of profit criteria would foster increases in productivity.[119] A second concern was a legacy of Chinese views of the country's historical experiences and of anti-imperialist ideology: foreigners should not be allowed to extract "excessive" profits from China. Reformers and conservatives both argued that China should avoid yielding more profits than absolutely necessary to foreign firms. But reformers also viewed foreign firms as the key agent for teaching Chinese firms to be profitable. Reformist leaders not only recognized that foreign investors must be allowed to earn and repatriate "legitimate" profits in exchange for investment, they and Chinese joint venture managers also often attributed to foreign investors an almost magical ability to produce large profits.[120] On both issues—the use of profit criteria and the earning of profits by foreigners in China—the reformist combination of concerns about and limited acceptance of foreign requirements prevailed in the official policy. It should be noted that the issue of control over profits differed from other control issues in an important way. Because during much of the 1980s most joint ventures were still young, and not yet seriously confronting decisions about declaring and repatriating dividends, control over profits was not highly sensitive for foreign investors. Nonetheless, some liberalization of controls did occur, and not always as a result of foreign pressures.

The joint venture policy, reflecting the reformist view, encouraged ventures to seek profits. Although no law stipulated a proper or target rate of return on investment, reform economists generally considered a rate of between 15% and 30% (after tax) to be appropriate. Some joint venture contracts explicitly set targets of 15%–20% (after tax).[121] To help ensure that the joint ventures they approved would indeed be profitable, the government required that feasibility studies, which it subsequently approved, document how and at what level joint ventures would earn profits.

But concern about over-reliance on foreign methods and on profit criteria led to several further controls. Organizations external to joint ventures were authorized to monitor their financial activities. Chinese rules of accountancy for joint ventures, laid out in the Implementing Regulations and clarified in the 1985 Joint Venture Accounting Regulations, required that the Chinese partner's parent organization (the "department in charge"), the financial office at the parent firm's level, and local tax authorities review quarterly and annual fiscal reports of the joint venture to certify that profits declared were appropriate and correct. Chinese accountants were also to perform an annual audit.[122] The government also influenced what happened to profits that the joint venture itself earned. They attached certain claims to profits before they could be paid out as dividends. As would be expected, earnings of joint ventures were made taxable. A 1980 law set the combined local and national tax rate on income from joint ventures at 15% in the SEZs and other specially designated cities, and 33% elsewhere, although a venture that was to be established for ten years or more was exempted from the full income tax the first year and was given a 50% exemption in the subsequent two years. Moreover, although the board of directors of a venture was granted formal authority to decide when dividends would be declared, it was forbidden from distributing profits if losses remained from previous years.[123] The Joint Venture Law and the Implementing Regulations specified a number of additional uses for joint venture earnings. Before distributing profits between partners, a joint venture board of directors was required to make allocations to expansion funds, reserve funds (used to cover any future losses), and bonus and welfare funds for staff and workers. The combined amount for the three funds was usually fixed—often 10%–15% of aftertax profits— and was to be set either in the contract or by the board of directors. Distributions to these funds were to ensure that social welfare goals—worker welfare and enterprise viability—were met.[124] Higher charges for labor and services in joint ventures compared to state enterprises also were sometimes used for social welfare ends. Individual workers did not receive a large portion of the wage bill; rather, the department in charge or the Chinese partner retained much of the wage bill (often over 50%). As with the bonus and welfare funds, these funds also were to be used for purposes related to worker welfare, such as medical and retirement insurance, housing, education, and subsidies for fuel and cooking oil.[125] Most foreign partners did not object to the payment of welfare subsidies, for they viewed them as positive incentives for worker productivity.

The government also employed several controls to meet its concerns that foreigners not take "excessive" profits. In particular, the policy defined how China would distribute between partners profits generated by joint ventures. "Due" profits to be guaranteed foreigners was defined as the amount of (net) profit that is proportionate to the foreign side's equity contribution. This definition, which was typical of joint venture laws in developing countries and in the socialist countries of Eastern Europe, placed an upper limit on the portion of profits earned by a joint venture that the foreign side could claim. As Deng Xiaoping noted with favor, distribution of profits according to equity, in conjunction with a norm for Chinese majority equity positions, meant that a majority of profits would remain in the hands of Chinese state enterprises.[126]

A wide variety of constraints on the actual remission of profits overseas also existed. When joint ventures declared dividends, especially during the first half of the decade, foreign partners were encouraged both by laws and by their Chinese partners to reinvest profits or place distributed dividends in the Bank of China rather than remit them abroad. Contracts frequently carried pledges from both sides to reinvest early profits. A majority of the firms sampled for this project that reported any profits (ten out of fifteen, or 63%) also reported that they had reinvested most of those profits. Another venture that expected profits shortly planned to reinvest earnings for "several years." Although many foreign partners agreed that reinvestment made good business sense, for it allowed them to expand production, others felt pressure to do so against their will.[127] Moreover, although dividends could be declared in either domestic currency or foreign exchange, the nonconvertibility of *renminbi* meant that in practice only dividends declared in foreign currency could be repatriated. In most joint ventures in which dividends were declared (something that did not occur with any regularity until the middle part of the decade), they were denominated in *renminbi*, effectively preventing repatriation. Some foreign investors overcame this obstacle by negotiating contracts that guaranteed that repatriation of the foreign partner's profits was a priority for foreign exchange earnings, but even this strategy could do little good when there was a lack of foreign exchange.[128] In the first instance where a joint venture declared dividends in foreign exchange, the foreign partner (from Hong Kong) had to negotiate hard before the Chinese partner would agree. The difficulty of finding foreign currency, imposed more by foreign currency balancing requirements, the foreign currency shortage, and the fact of nonconvertibility than by explicit government intention to limit profits, was the biggest obstacle to repatriation for many joint ventures during the 1980s.

The Chinese government further reduced the amount of profits taken out of China by foreigners through taxation of remitted profits and expatriate salaries. In addition to the 33% joint venture income tax, a tax of 10% was levied on the repatriated earnings of foreign partners.[129] Foreign partners also could expect bureaucratic problems in the process of preparing repatriation itself. Formal procedures for profit repatriation existed, but information about who was authorized to approve remittances before the BOC would actually release the funds was poorly disseminated. Neither the joint venture nor the Chinese organizations that handled remittances were clear about the procedures in the early and middle years and, as with other foreign exchange transactions, much paperwork was involved in obtaining release of the funds from a venture's Bank of China account.[130]

Finally, audits by Chinese accountants would help the government detect transfer pricing. Although the joint venture and foreign contract laws did not explicitly provide for monitoring transfer pricing, and joint ventures themselves had formal authority to set export prices, export prices were to be filed with the departments in charge and price control bureaus, and imports required import licenses. The requirement that Chinese law govern joint venture contracts with foreign firms (including the foreign partner's parent corporation) offered another means for regulating transfer pricing.[131]

It is instructive to note that even in the early years, the reformers avoided controls that sometimes, though not always, have been used in other developing countries, especially in Latin America in the 1960s and 1970s. Other countries sometimes set an annual maximum limit on the percentage of capital that could be remitted overseas. Although the limits were often reasonable (14%–20%), and often were adjusted upward in the case of export-oriented companies, they nevertheless established an explicit definition of legitimate profits. Some countries also explicitly required government authorization of remittances.[132] That China did not impose such requirements indicates that at the start the reformers did not exert as much control as they might have.

Some liberalization did occur over time in the controls over joint venture earnings and profit repatriation, although the direct evidence of such liberalization was less than appeared for other controls. (Again, this was in part because the issue took longer to mature.) The efforts to ease foreign exchange restrictions indirectly and yet significantly eased the outlook for profit repatriation. Reforms were in part a reaction to growing foreign worries that, as the time came to declare profits, the nonconvertibility of *renminbi* would prevent the remission of profits.[133] Some direct liberalization also occurred. Following the AMC crisis of early 1986, Chinese officials converted profits the venture earned from *renminbi* sales to foreign currency in order that these profits might be repatriated. More broadly, there was an evolution in the reformers' view of profit, and use of the profit criterion. Over time, the profit criterion became an increasingly important indicator of performance. Although conservative exhortations to retain socially minded goals continued to surface occasionally after the mid-1980s, and emphasis on other values (particularly efforts to maintain social welfare standards in joint ventures) did not disappear completely, the message of the reformers increasingly was that profit was the primary indicator of success. This message was communicated both in statements and in reforms of the reward structure (that allowed greater retention of profits by enterprises, for example). In tandem with this change in outlook, the reformers showed a willingness to adopt international norms for accounting and to use indirect tax levers rather than directives. The Implementing Regulations and, with more specificity, the 1985 Joint Venture Accounting Regulations, drew on many international standards for accounting, and thereby led to a number of changes in China's extant accounting practices.[134]

Rules promulgated subsequent to the original 1980 Income Tax Law also contained liberalizing incentives. Tax holidays were extended first in 1983.[135] The 1986 Provisions offered further significant tax incentives to some ventures, exempting remitted profits of EOEs and "technologically advanced enterprises" (TAEs) from the 10% remission tax, extending the 50% tax holiday for new TAEs an additional three years, and cutting income taxes for EOEs. Exports from all joint ventures, as well as equipment and material imports needed for fulfilling export contracts, were exempted (implicitly in the case of imports) from the turnover tax and all customs duty. In addition to these national changes, from the mid-1980s onward many localities offered their own tax incentives for investors.[136] These incentives were designed to encourage more foreign investment, especially in light of the problems the government was having attracting investment in the first half of 1986. In the SEZs in particular, this liberalization was an effort to keep China competitive with other Asian countries. To meet its goals, the government moved increasingly toward the use of indirect levers such as tax incentives and away from directives, and tailored many of these incentives specifically to favor those enterprises the reformers most wanted.

Thus, the regulations the government established to control the earnings and distribution of profits from joint ventures were extensive. In many respects they remained strong throughout the decade, and were implemented effectively. Some areas of liberalization were evident, however, both as a by-product of foreign exchange reforms and as part of the effort to attract TAEs and EOEs. A mix of pressures were active in fostering these liberalizations; both external pressures—in the form of direct complaints and the need to compete with other countries for investment—and the reformers' own desire to increase the level of foreign direct investment, were evident.

Transfer of Foreign Technology

A primary goal of the joint venture policy was to provide China with foreign technology to which it might not otherwise have access. Joint ventures generally are a good means of attracting technology since, because foreign firms have a long-term desire to make joint ventures successful, they will have an incentive to successfully transfer technology to them. At the same time, a foreign firm may be more willing to transfer technology to a joint venture because it can retain some control over that technology.[137] In China during the 1980s, technology was usually transferred as part of the foreign side's capital contribution, or through licensing agreements attached to the contract.

As noted in chapter 2, at the beginning of the "open" policy the Chinese government had significant concerns about technology transfer. In many ways these concerns were reminiscent of the ambiguous view toward foreign technology captured in the *ti-yung* dichotomy: foreign technology should be used, but only as a complement to indigenous technology. The leadership's suspicions were enhanced by China's post-1949 experience with absorbing foreign technology; the transfer of large, complete sets of Soviet equipment in the 1950s had been fraught with both political tensions and problems with assimilation. Technology imports were greatly reduced in the 1960s, as dictated by the drive for national self-reliance, but those imports of foreign equipment that did occur often were poorly absorbed. In the 1970s and 1980s, cases where foreign (mostly Hong Kong) firms sold obsolete machinery and equipment continued to foster the belief that foreigners would try to dupe the Chinese into accepting inferior and "inappropriate" technology. The experiences also motivated the various controls over the introduction of foreign technology, and calls for China to continue developing indigenous technologies.[138]

Although in the early years foreign companies were often more willing to transfer technology through joint ventures than through other formats, they had an interest in refraining from providing technology and proprietary information that would not be appropriate for the joint venture. They also worried that their trade secrets might not be protected sufficiently in the Chinese environment, particularly because there was little codified protection of intellectual property. Finally, they had good reason to be concerned that the Chinese economic environment could not effectively assimilate their most sophisticated technology—technology that might require specialized inputs or management that would take many years to develop in China. This reluctance on the part of foreigners made negotiations over technology transfer particularly divisive.[139]

In its overall effort to attract foreign technology, the government made some effort to learn from past mistakes. The trend toward importation of know-how (*zhuanyou jishu*) rather than complete plants in particular was intended to enhance the capacity for dissemination of technology. To further enhance the chances for successful absorption of foreign technology, the government introduced strict controls over foreign participation in the transfer and assimilation process. In the first phase and at the beginning of the second phase, national laws (including the 1983 Implementing Regulations) and laws on transfer to Guangdong's SEZs were designed to guard against the dumping of obsolete or overpriced technology, and to make sure the government maintained control over transfer of technology at all stages.[140] Many of the controls were implemented effectively, although this was not uniformly so.

The Joint Venture Law set the standard that any technology contributed as investment to joint ventures "shall be truly advanced and appropriate to China's needs" (Article 5). Despite the law's emphasis on technology that was both "advanced" and "appropriate," in practice the government and Chinese negotiators in the early years often pressed for the most advanced technology. Chinese engineers in particular tended to be aware of international standards for given technologies. Because foreign firms preferred not to transfer "state-of-the-art" technology, they often tried to convince Chinese negotiators of the value of less sophisticated, but more appropriate, technology than the Chinese originally had envisioned. Chinese negotiators were frequently successful at getting around this pressure. To attain the technology they wanted, they sometimes compared the technologies being offered by competing firms, and chose their partners in part on the basis of the technology offered by the foreign firm. When Japanese companies, such as in the elevator and auto industries, were slow to conclude joint ventures because they were unwilling to transfer the type and level of technology that was desired by the Chinese, the Chinese often concluded deals with Western firms offering similar (though not always as advanced) technology. In order to be chosen over competitors, a European firm allowed prospective Chinese partners to examine usually secret research and development plans for both current and future technology, and supplied information on how the company intended to remain in the technological forefront of its industry. The Chinese manager pressed successfully in another negotiation for change in an original technology agreement to a higher level of technology.[141]

The Chinese government was extremely conscious of the possibility of overpricing of technology. The valuation of technology contributed as part of the foreign partner's investment was decided initially through negotiation or by an agreed upon third party, but ultimately had to be approved by Chinese authorities outside the venture. Moreover, technology contributed by the foreign side generally was not allowed to be valued at more than 20% of the value of the foreign side's equity contribution.[142] If technology was to be supplied under license, the royalties paid by the venture had to be "fair and reasonable," and not higher than the international rate (if one existed). Moreover, the Chinese side often preferred to tie the royalty rate to the joint venture's net profits or actual sales—that is, to performance—rather than to set a minimum fee.[143] The valuation of technology and level of royalties were contentious issues between potential partners, and many foreign (particularly Japanese) partners believed that the prices to which they eventually agreed were too low, although Chinese partners at times complained that royalty payments were too high.[144]

The Chinese also tried to negotiate technology transfer agreements that granted broad use rights to the Chinese partner. They frequently obtained agreements requiring training of Chinese personnel at the foreign firm's home or branch office; virtually all of the joint ventures sampled for this study provided technical training for Chinese personnel, either inside or outside of China. Moreover, the Implementing Regulations required "relevant documentation" (drawings, research reports, operation and maintenance guides) from the transferring party, and a "mutual exchange of information on the improvement of technology by both parties of the technology transfer agreement." The latter provision primarily benefited the Chinese side by requiring access to research and development in the parent office.[145] In fact, Chinese investors frequently were able to negotiate for the foreign side to provide wide-ranging technical documentation identical to that which the foreign parent firm used, as illustrated by the experiences of three joint ventures concluded in the first half of the 1980s. In one venture, the Chinese side negotiated a provision stipulating that the foreign parent would transfer to the joint venture all technology known to the parent within one year of startup, and that throughout the venture's twenty-year life, results of all new research and development conducted by the foreign parent company would be transferred. The contract for a pharmaceutical joint venture required that the foreign parent must transfer to the joint venture, without immediate compensation, its knowledge of U.S. Food and Drug Administration rules and standards for the design and manufacture of plants, and the company's patents and formulas to manufacture according to U.S. government standards. A third joint venture to produce machine parts agreed to transfer technology without patent protection, and to update continually the joint venture on relevant technology.[146] In the first two cases, the foreign companies were in industries characterized by international oligopoly, and in which competition to pre-empt competitors from new markets was fierce. All three cases involved Western firms.

The Implementing Regulations also prohibited the foreign partner from restricting the quantity and price of products manufactured with the transferred technology, and the area to which a venture could export. To prevent gouging by the foreign parent, the regulations prohibited tie-in clauses requiring the venture to purchase parts or raw materials needed for the technology from the original supplier.[147] To minimize the length of joint ventures' financial obligations, transfer agreements were limited to ten years (except in Guangdong Province's SEZs, where the limit was five years), after which the recipient was to have the right to continue using the technology. The combination of a short agreement duration and devolution of use rights to the recipient meant in effect that the foreign partner transferred the technology for free once the agreement had expired.[148]

Chinese negotiators sometimes succeeded in the early years at obtaining strict performance requirements that in effect relieved Chinese partners from the responsibility of having to judge technology about which they knew little prior to purchase. The performance standard contained in the 1979 law stipulated that the Chinese government had the right to demand compensation "in cases of losses caused by deception through the intentional provision of outdated equipment or technology." The Implementing Regulations extended the performance requirements somewhat by stating that technology acquired by a joint venture must enable it to compete internationally or show significant improvements in products sold domestically. The 1984 SEZ Technology Regulations further required the foreign transfer agent to guarantee that the Chinese side would "master the entire technology and method of operation," and to guarantee "the legal effectiveness of the anticipated results of the introduced technology."[149]

Government approval and supervision provided further institutional checks on technology transfer in joint ventures. The feasibility study assessed the contents, standards, performance, scope, and type of the technology proposed and compared it with other possible technologies; approval was to be denied for agreements that did not meet the government's criteria. In the Otis Elevator joint venture, for example, plans for technology transfer were carefully scrutinized by and analyzed against the standards of the Chinese customs agency, which required the foreign partner to provide a highly detailed list of all technology it would import according to the transfer agreement. The Technical Bureau reviewed the transfer agreement to see that valuation of foreign technology was reasonable, and asked the venture for details of the proposals for factory renovations.[150]

The government intended to oversee the implementation of approved technology transfer agreements. Although formal authority for oversight by agencies outside the joint venture was unclear, certain agencies apparently were designated to take action if an agreement was not proceeding as anticipated.[151] Foreign managers reported two instances where outside authorities checked on the implementation of agreements. In one case, the Chinese manager to a joint venture was fired when central authorities concluded that he had not transferred technology quickly enough. In the second case, quality control authorities from a municipal agency attempted to check imported equipment, although the foreign managers speculated that this may have been in order to copy it rather than to test its quality. Chinese managers to this joint venture also closely checked the high-technology machinery when it first arrived and complained when they discovered some of it was secondhand.[152]

Finally, although more a disincentive to investment than an explicit control, the absence, in the early years of the "open" policy, of a strong means to protect intellectual property meant that the government was able to disseminate technology beyond the foreign sector. Scientific and technical innovations were viewed as social goods and social wealth, and hence should be available for general use in the pursuit of economic development. The protection of intellectual property such as patents, trademarks, and copyrights was generally viewed as anathema to socialism. This view fostered such practices as freely passing acquired technology to other enterprises, and rotating many managers through joint ventures to expose them to imported technology. In one case, for example, following their tour of a competing joint venture's factory, Chinese managers from another joint venture were provided with designs for their competitor's imported technology. Moreover, Chinese partners frequently did not adhere to their pledges of confidentiality.[153]

Thus, during the early years of the "open" policy, the environment for technology transfer was characterized by a broad range of strict controls and a lack of protection for intellectual property. Yet the controls were not always successful. China's capacity for diffusion of technology throughout the Chinese economy should not be overstated. The tendencies for compartmentalism and protectionism among units that obtained new technology were strong barriers to the diffusion of technology. The flow of information outside of a unit tended to be vertical, moving up and down the lines of a bureaucratic organization, rather than horizontally across structures, as would be expected in a market economy.[154] Moreover, the implementation of controls was not always thorough. For example, although many contracts contained strict technology transfer clauses, not all did. Hitachi's contract to produce televisions required the Japanese parent to transfer only "minor technological improvements," and relieved the parent firm of the obligation to transfer "major breakthroughs." The contract prohibited the venture from transfering Hitachi's technology to third parties until five years after the contract term of the joint venture expired.[155] Nor were tie-ins generally disallowed in practice; the norm in the first half of the 1980s was for the foreign parent company to supply most of the imported materials to their joint venture, a practice that was difficult to avoid when the technical equipment originally supplied by the foreign partner required unique components or other materials. One joint venture had a twenty-year transfer agreement covering the life of the venture. In the case of the ten-year transfer agreement signed by Otis, the partners agreed to negotiate for a ten-year renewal after six years, and again after sixteen years, helping ensure that the transfer agreement was in force over the thirty-year life of the venture.[156] The Otis venture was also able to convince the technical bureau to lower the amount of detailed information they had requested, arguing that prior to actually implementing the transfer agreement, those involved could not know in detail what the process would require. The bureaus eventually approved transfer plans with less detail than they had originally wanted.

Much of the difficulty in implementing these regulations arose from the decentralization of control over technology transfer. When, in the mid-1980s, the central government began to disperse authority over various issues related to foreign trade, they also dispersed somewhat the control of technology transfer. For example, at the central level the China National Technical Import Corporation (Techimport) lost its virtual monopoly, while the Shenzhen municipal government was granted authority to approve technology transfer agreements in 1984.[157] Yet, as with the decentralization of the state plan, it soon became clear to the government that diffusion of control over technology transfer was distorting its goals. Duplication of technology imports, due to unsupervised municipal decisions and competition among localities, was particularly severe. A former head of the Technology Import and Export Department of MOFERT publicly complained about the "planless, chaotic situation despite the supposed inclusion of technology imports in national and local plans," and further criticized compartmentalism and duplication in the transfer process.[158] Moreover, as noted previously, the proportion of foreign investment in industries that brought advanced technology to China was lower than the reformers wanted. Results from Shenzhen SEZ were particularly disappointing, for although it was designed as a technological "window" for the rest of the country, few of the operations established there involved technology or know-how that was new to China. (Shenzhen's performance in the area of technology transfer is discussed further in the next section.)

In response to many of these problems, the reformers during the second and third phases re-asserted controls over many aspects of technology transfer, and even enacted some new controls. In 1985, they recentralized much of the control over technology imports. Technology regulations promulgated in May 1985 reiterated that the foreign seller could not require the Chinese buyer to accept "unreasonable restrictive requirements," such as requirements that the buyer purchase unnecessary tie-ins, purchase exclusively from the seller, or refrain from developing the imported technology or obtaining similar or competitive technology from other sources. The regulations also stated, very generally, the kinds of technology for which approval would be granted, although it implied that not all technologies must meet all requirements.[159] More technology regulations issued in 1988 tried to strengthen Chinese controls over, and the effectiveness of, technology transfer, and thereby to help overcome some of the earlier problems in implementation. These regulations further asserted the right for China to be compensated when a technology license failed to perform up to the standard anticipated in the agreement, and reiterated the need to provide "relevant documentation." They also limited the term of confidentiality agreements not to exceed the term of the technology contract, further restricting the protection of foreign technology.[160]

Although the government continued to make new efforts to set restrictive terms of technology transfer, by the mid-1980s the reformers were not satisfied with the level and amount of technology flowing into China. Thus, they made significant efforts to mollify foreign concerns about technology transfer.[161] Most important, in 1985 the government brought into effect a major patent law to protect foreign technology, and anticipated promulgating a copyright law by the end of the decade.[162] The new patent law codified the reformist assertion that in a socialist economy intellectual achievements, like other goods, are commodities and thus may be priced. The patent law did contain a number of restrictions, notably a prohibition on patents for inventions that "run counter to social morality" and, more specifically, patents on pharmaceutical products. But from the point of view of foreign investors, the new law was a significant step toward meeting their needs. As a further means of preventing diffusion of proprietary technology, the government also began to actively discourage the rotation of managers through joint ventures.[163]

The reformers also came to de-emphasize "state-of-the-art" technology in favor of "appropriate" (*shiyong*) technology over the course of the decade. They increasingly argued that the absorption of "state-of-the-art" technology was not helping China but, rather, was inefficient in a country that suffered from shortages of qualified personnel and energy, and had other resource constraints. "Appropriate technology" was defined as "methods and techniques applicable to Chinese conditions, reliable and up-to-date by world standards. The technology should be capable of turning out low-cost goods, competitive in quantity and quality, with low consumption of raw materials and energy."[164]

The patent and trademark laws and increasing acceptance of "appropriate" technology were part of another trend in the regulation of technology transfer: the attempt over the course of the 1980s to fine-tune laws that would attract the kind and level of technology the reformers wanted. While the early laws offered some economic incentives, such as tax exemptions, for firms that brought in high technology (Article 7), the effort to bring in advanced technology intensified in the mid-1980s, with special access to the domestic market for joint ventures with advanced technology, as noted previously. The 1986 Provisions went the furthest to expand these incentives. They created the designation of "technologically advanced enterprise" (TAE). TAEs were defined as enterprises that possess "advanced technology supplied by foreign investors which are engaged in developing new products, and upgrading and replacing products in order to increase foreign exchange generated by exports or for import substitution." Joint ventures that received this designation from their local government were eligible for, in addition to tax incentives, lower land use fees and labor subsidies, and priority for electricity and other infrastructural and financial services. Several municipalities, including Beijing and Shanghai, quickly designated a number of joint ventures in this category. (In contrast to the designation of export-oriented enterprise, U.S. firms dominated over Hong Kong firms in number the group of joint ventures receiving "technologically advanced" status.)[165] As discussed in chapter 3, these incentives appear to have been successful at attracting new investment to higher technology manufacturing industries (such as electric and communications equipment and electronic instruments) and away from tourism, hotel, and foods.

Thus, during the 1980s, as foreign technology acquisition became an even stronger priority of the "open" policy, the reformers strengthened the already tight restrictions on technology transfer and tried to reduce the gaps in implementation. Yet at the same time they recognized that the environment for transfer of technology was not appealing to foreign investors. They tried to overcome this situation in two major ways. First, they took bold steps to accede to international norms sanctioning the protection and reward of intellectual property. Second, rather than loosening controls over technology transfer—and thereby harming their ability to achieve a central goal of the "open" policy—they increasingly offered positive incentives on *other* issues (such as taxation) to firms that transferred advanced technology. This tailoring of the regulatory environment to achieve priority goals reflected a growing sophistication in the use of policy tools, as well as a willingness to trade off less important goals.

. . .

By the end of the decade, China's experience with controls over the five economic aspects of the foreign investment policy, as with controls on the overall status of foreign investment discussed in the previous section, showed some areas in which the government was effective at establishing and maintaining controls. But more than with the higher level controls, many of these controls had significant implementation problems, problems that often resulted from the economic context in which they operated, and from the decentralization of authority to localities. Liberalization, too, was more evident than in the higher level controls; although the reformers did not weaken the *role* of Chinese law, they did weaken the *content* of specific laws. They did not, however, do so indiscriminately. Rather, they liberalized in order to attract those types of investment they had come to emphasize most: joint ventures that would bring in advanced (and yet appropriate) technology, and those that would enhance China's export capacity.

REGIONAL CONTROLS: THE SPECIAL ECONOMIC ZONES, OPEN COASTAL CITIES, AND OPEN ECONOMIC ZONES

The "open" policy had a strong regional component; as the figures provided in chapter 3 illustrate, during the early 1980s foreign capital was concentrated in the SEZs. Although many of the concerns about and controls over foreign capital discussed with regard to the national level were applicable to the SEZs, these areas were also the focus of unique concerns and were subject to a number of special controls. China's leaders expressed four main regional level concerns about the SEZs in the early years: the zones could absorb "decadent" capitalist and foreign influences; they could become modern-day treaty ports; they could generate significant economic inequality among regions; and they could fail to spread the benefits of foreign investment (particularly technology and management skills) to areas outside the zones.

Preventing the Entrance and Spread of "Decadent" Values

The government's original strategy of geographically concentrating foreign capital in the SEZs was seen as a means to experiment with foreign capital in a controlled manner, and to weed out what should not be absorbed into the rest of China from what should.[166] But both reformers and conservatives remained concerned at the initiation of the "open" policy that, along with the desirable elements of capitalism, unwanted elements they associated with foreigners—crime, "bourgeois" decadent values, and so on—would enter China via the SEZs. The government therefore tried to design the SEZs to prevent the absorption of the perceived negative influences, and the subsequent spread of these influences out of the zones. The deliberate location of the zones away from major Chinese urban areas was one means to prevent the transmission of negative characteristics. Shenzhen, the largest of the zones, was physically cordoned off from the rest of Guangdong Province by a fifty-three-mile long patrolled high fence, which constituted a second border to control the flow of people and materials between the SEZ and the rest of China. The government also relied on control of the Hong Kong border to prevent smuggling of electronic goods, pornographic materials, and other "corrosive materials" from Hong Kong, and to prevent Chinese citizens from leaving Shenzhen for Hong Kong. More generally, the government tried to suppress activities it considered immoral, criminal, or otherwise anti-socialist, such as gambling and prostitution.[167] Offenders were punished harshly to provide examples for others.

As at the national level, the government employed the traditional preceptoral controls to avoid negative influences. As the reformist Shenzhen mayor of the early 1980s asserted in 1984 (after the CASP), "[T]he SEZs . . . should not loosen control internally while opening to the outside world, and they should set strict demands on ideology and work style while making wide contacts with foreign countries. Meanwhile, we must conscientiously strengthen political and ideological work and wage a struggle between corruption and anti-corruption in the ideological sphere. We must build material civilization and spiritual civilization spontaneously."[168] Party cadres in the zones in particular were to be "inoculated" in order to promote a "correct" work style and ideology. Strengthening political and ideological work and party discipline was most often posed as the solution to the problem of unhealthy tendencies, for "if cadres don't have the strength to avoid disease it is easy to fall into the mudpond." As at the national level, preceptoral controls were applied especially during the CASP of 1983 and the CABL of 1986. Foreigners were not to be subject to these controls, however; particularly in Shenzhen, the officials asserted that China could not be "overly strict with respect to [foreigners'] lifestyle, habits, and reasonable demands."[169]

Also as at the national level, these controls over the entrance and spread of "decadent" values and goods were not especially effective. Most often, the zones were considered the worst offenders in absorbing unhealthy tendencies. The appearance in the first half of the 1980s, especially in Shenzhen, of black marketeers, currency speculators, beggars, and prostitutes—all of whom benefited from the open status of the zones—was severely criticized but never eradicated. Border controls were unable to keep out undesired goods. Moreover, although preceptoral controls remained in place, interviews revealed that some younger, local-level reformers openly viewed the problem of unhealthy tendencies as less important than did older cadres. Younger reformers (in their forties and fifties) stated privately that foreign influences had come to seem less threatening, and that their desire to control the flow of foreign ideas over the second border had ebbed somewhat. One Shenzhen official said that state control of the flow of ideas and other superstructural elements from outside China to Shenzhen (such as the transmission of commercial television programs from Hong Kong) was not important; the Chinese people would learn for themselves what is good and bad. He also asserted that Shenzhen people were not "turning bad" as a result of foreign influences but, rather, that "their discipline [was] better than inside China" because their material standard of living had been raised. This official concluded that it was more important to pay attention to China's economic development than to unhealthy tendencies.[170] The younger local officials' less serious attitude toward the problem of unhealthy tendencies could not have helped the effort of conservatives and older reformers to combat the problem in the zones.

The SEZ experiment thus failed to meet the concern for the spread of negative influences into China. Once this failure was evident, the government had a number of possible avenues to take. It could have, but did not, go to the extremes of either closing the zones or declaring that the influences once considered negative were harmless. More realistically, it could have, but did not, search for new zone controls until it found ones that could work. The reformers did try to strengthen existing controls somewhat. In 1985, they upgraded the staffing of the second border, and initiated audits of enterprise finances to detect smuggling.[171] Yet the significance of these renewed efforts was undermined by another major initiative of the reformers during the middle period: the expansion of foreign investment to other areas. In conjunction with their increasing desire to expand foreign investment generally, their recognition that foreign investors would find the urban coastal areas to be more desirable locations for investment, and their recognition of other problems mounting in the SEZs (discussed below), the reformers de-emphasized the SEZ experiment and ended the strategy to isolate foreign capital in the zones.[172] The expansion of foreign capital to the coastal cities, OEZs, and Hainan Island effectively eliminated two major mechanisms found in the SEZs for guarding against negative foreign influences: the second border and the distance from major population centers.

Prevention of Modern "Foreign Concessions" versus
Limited Autonomy and Decentralization

Although the political, military, and international status of post-1949 China clearly differed from that of the Treaty Port era, the reformers found it necessary in the early years of the "open" policy to explain how the government would retain firm control over the SEZs and prevent them from devolving to the modern equivalent of foreign concessions. Controls to prevent the SEZs and, later, the other open areas from becoming foreign concessions were aimed primarily at maintaining strong ties between the zones and the central and provincial governments. In the early and middle years of the policy, the government frequently reiterated that these areas were still the sovereign territory ("part of the socialist motherland") of the Chinese government, that the central government exercised ultimate authority over them, and that the SEZ and "open" city governments must follow the policy of the party center. Echoing the rationale for foreign investment in China generally, they also argued that foreign capital invested in the SEZs was subordinate and complementary to the socialist economy; the zones would operate at the discretion of and to serve the needs of the state.[173] Politically, the zones maintained a party and state system (including economic planning) that was similar to that of localities elsewhere in China, and hence subject to the same statist controls. They were governed by Chinese laws and, unlike the treaty ports, offered no immunity to foreigners operating within them. And because foreign-backed projects were to be subordinate to the socialist state, foreign investors would be unable to transform their limited economic power into political power.[174]

As predicted in the official rationale, the SEZs and open cities did not evolve into modern treaty ports insofar as they were neither run by foreigners nor out of the ultimate reach of the central government to close them down. Yet the stated commitment of the early years that the SEZs would remain under the close supervision of the central government was counteracted by the significant decentralization of authority to the SEZs. Although the decentralization was restricted primarily to economic matters and, even at its most extreme, did not threaten to turn the zones into concessions, the devolution of economic authority did have a negative impact on state control of the zone economies.

Decentralization was considered by the reformers as a way to give the zones the flexibility necessary to attract foreign investment. Pressures also emanated from the zones themselves for more autonomy.[175] Hence, the center allowed local officials to draw up regulations applying central laws to their areas. Guangdong was allowed to promulgate regulations for its three SEZs as early as 1980. The regulations of the various zones did not breach the controls on foreign investment stipulated by the center, and were centrally guided and approved; nor did they contemplate a legal regime for the zones that was separate from the national regulations. But they did offer more extensive incentives for foreign investment.[176] Gradually, the SEZs were granted greater authority to approve foreign investment projects, retain foreign exchange, and decide how to use funds to improve their infrastructure. At the same time, zone administrators and managers were under much pressure from the center to show signs of economic success, measured especially in the attraction of large amounts of foreign capital in a relatively short period of time. This pressure was especially acute as the zones came under attack for harboring unhealthy tendencies.

The combination of pressure for quick results and the incentives arising from decentralization of authority actually hindered the capability of the

SEZs to fulfill their original developmental goals. The problematic performance of the zones was evident according to a number of measures.
Though from the early years they attracted a significant portion of China's
foreign capital, investment in equity joint ventures, the form of investment most conducive to transfer of technology and management skills,
was less than the government wished. Most foreign direct investment was
in low-technology plants such as textile manufacturing, or in assembly,
real estate, retail, or tourist ventures. Indeed, Shenzhen officials estimated that only about 10% of the approximately 500 manufacturing operations in Shenzhen at the end of 1984 involved advanced technology. Another Chinese report concluded that only 7% of Shenzhen's imported
technology (including all forms of direct investment and processing/
assembly ventures) was of international standard. According to one self-
critical Shenzhen official, "If a [foreign] manufacturer made a product just
a bit better than we could, we considered it high technology." Public criticism of Shenzhen's performance by some central leaders became intensive in 1985.[177]

Chinese officials expressed disappointment at the fact that commercial
construction activities were so prominent in Shenzhen.[178] Furthermore,
as might have been predicted by the early experiences of many Asian
EPZs, China's SEZs contributed little to the nation's exports and foreign
exchange earnings, especially in the early years. Total exports from Shenzhen were only 20% of the zone's industrial output in 1984, and far short
of the government's target of 60% by 1980. Shenzhen's imports usually
outweighed exports by a substantial margin (by five to one in 1983, for
example). While the overall contributions of the SEZs to national foreign
currency reserves started out relatively small, they apparently became a
net drain on reserves in the mid-1980s, when foreign exchange deficits in
the zones ranged as high as $542 million.[179] For reasons discussed below,
the incentive structure that existed under decentralization fostered massive imports and insufficient exports. Moreover, although the $1.3 billion
in direct foreign investment in Shenzhen by 1986 was not insignificant, it
accounted for only two-thirds of the approximately two billion dollars that
the Chinese government had spent there by that time on infrastructural
development, and was less than officials had hoped.[180] Finally, as in the
rest of the country, lack of coordination among agencies led to needless
duplication of projects, and hence to wasted expenditures.

These problems did not go unnoticed by China's leaders, and efforts
were made to redress them, primarily through central exhortations to improve and by some degree of recentralization. By placing strict controls on
credit to the zones, the central government tried to curb spending, especially in construction. There was new emphasis on absorbing advanced
technology and promoting exports, and in 1986 Shenzhen promulgated its

own regulations to reach these ends. This effort appeared to yield some success. Chinese sources reported that export earnings from domestic and foreign-backed enterprises in the SEZs were up 114% in 1987 from 1986 (although half of the foreign exchange earned via exports in the first half of 1987 was from processing fees). The figures remained at around the 1987 levels in 1988 and 1989.[181]

Despite the problems with the four original SEZs, the reformers opened China's fifth SEZ (and as of 1988, the newest province), Hainan Island. Hainan was permitted to grant even more favorable terms to investors than the SEZs, and to engage in more economic experimentation, than anywhere else in China.[182] In a departure from norms of social ownership, some buying and selling of land was to be permitted. Foreign investors were to have great discretion in management and hiring and firing. There also were to be no restrictions on profit repatriation, and foreign exchange transactions would not be taxed. As an island in the remote southern part of the country, Hainan had the advantage of experimenting in relative isolation, reminiscent of the SEZs in the early 1980s.

The early experience of Hainan belied any optimism that Shenzhen's mistakes would not be repeated. Early signs of poor planning and coordination of investment and infrastructural development were reminiscent of Shenzhen. The island extensively promoted foreign-backed development of tourist resorts, for example. Mainland companies immediately made claim to land without payment, and real estate speculation grew rapidly. A new provincial government structure to monitor development was slow to develop. Although, as in the original SEZs, the central government could attempt to rectify many of these problems, that the problems were repeated at all illustrated the depth of difficulties in designing a program of decentralization that did not distort central goals.

Thus, the problems from decentralization did not lead China's SEZs or the coastal areas to a situation analogous to the nineteenth-century treaty ports. But the devolution of control over economic development to the zones—a result largely of domestic trends toward decentralization and local pressure for autonomy—led to a palpable loss of the state's capacity to meet other development goals.

Creation of Linkages between SEZs and the Inland Economy: Domestic Content and Neilian

The ability of the SEZs to transfer the benefits of foreign investment to the rest of the Chinese economy depended largely on their ties to other areas. In EPZs in other Asian developing countries, host governments have often tried to create domestic linkages through requirements for local sourcing and by encouraging zone enterprises to subcontract production to domestic firms. During the 1980s, the Chinese government also tried to create linkages using these basic strategies. The SEZ regulations encouraged the use of domestic content in joint venture production by granting preferential prices on domestic goods to joint venture purchasers. Individual contracts for joint ventures in the zones also sometimes set the amount of domestic content. Yet the efforts in the zones to use domestic content were beset by problems similar to those that appeared nationally: supply, transport, and bureaucratic bottlenecks all limited the ability to source domestically. Moreover, because joint enterprises were legally exempt from import duties on supplies, domestic suppliers had difficulty competing with imports.[183] The creation of backward linkages with the non-SEZ economy was thus limited by the nature of the Chinese economy and the incentives for procurement.

The Shenzhen government began in mid-1982 to encourage economic ties between SEZ joint ventures and enterprises in the rest of the country through a second strategy: the *neilian* (internal linkage) policy. A central goal of the *neilian* policy was to encourage enterprises from inland areas to set up joint ventures or other cooperative ventures with foreign firms in the zones. Through interactions with foreign firms, reformers reasoned, the domestic firms would digest technology and management methods, and transfer them back to the parent enterprises. The policy assumed that *neilian* enterprises would be more prone to use domestic inputs because the inland firm would already have ties to domestic suppliers. The policy also provided incentives for inland enterprises to participate in zone enterprises, including low land use fees, authority to transfer profits from the zone inland, and preferential tax rates.[184] A successful *neilian* policy, therefore, would spread the benefits of foreign investment inland, without the negative effects.

But the incentive structure for *neilian* enterprises also contained distortions that hindered their success. Rather than forming joint enterprises in which they were exposed to foreign technology and management, Chinese entrepreneurs from inland enterprises more typically used the opportunity to establish themselves in the zones in order to sell for foreign exchange the goods they produced at home to foreign bargain-seekers. The Chinese entrepreneurs then used the foreign exchange to speculate on the foreign currency black market or to buy imported consumer goods at low prices in the zones to sell for higher prices inland, where demand was acute. Thus, although sale of domestic goods in Shenzhen created some foreign markets for domestic products and led to high retail sales volumes in Shenzhen, little joint production or learning from foreigners occurred.[185]

Two additional factors hindered the creation of linkages between the zones and internal areas. First, regional jealousies and regional competition for foreign direct investment made recipients of foreign technology hesitant to transfer the benefits of investment inland. Enterprises that received advanced technology through cooperation with foreign firms were highly reluctant to transfer it inland or to central ministries in Beijing, with whom they competed for prestige and central funding. Because of these tendencies for localism or compartmentalism, some foreign investors came under strong pressure from their partners or local government officials not to make contacts or discuss future deals in other regions. Second, whereas in other EPZs, such as those in Taiwan, the diffusion of technology and managerial skills out of the zones has depended upon the mobility of labor and management to outside of the zones, this mechanism of diffusion was untenable given state-imposed restrictions on the mobility of China's labor force.[186]

Regional Inequality

Although the early effort to concentrate foreign investment in the SEZs protected other areas of China both from shocks from the international economy to which the zones became more vulnerable and from other perceived negative influences, such concentration also hampered the dissemination of wealth generated by foreign capital in these areas. Maoist efforts to address the historical problems of inequality between coastal and inland areas included relocating heavy industry and technical personnel inland. The reformers, and especially conservatives, continued during the 1980s to express some degree of worry that the coastal areas would benefit disproportionately from the concentration of investment there. Reflecting this concern, in 1987 one reformer asserted that if the gap between regions were to become too wide (a point left undefined), the state would actively redistribute income.[187]

Yet this concern was not a priority for the reformers in the mid-1980s. With the exception of the ineffective *neilian* policy, the leadership made few concrete efforts to redistribute any wealth created by zone joint ventures to nonzone areas. Moreover, the extension of the areas open to foreign capital to the coastal cities was a decision to concentrate further on industrial development in what were already China's most economically advanced areas.[188] The concentration of foreign capital on the coasts was part of a more general trend specified in the Seventh Five-Year Plan (1986–1990) to allow the eastern portion of the country to take the lead in developing new, technologically intensive industries and to receive the bulk of foreign investment. The decision also reflected assessments that foreigners were much more likely to invest in areas that already possessed an industrial infrastructure, and that foreign capital, technology, and management would be more easily assimilated in the advanced areas of China.

Vice Premier Tian Jiyun also told SEZ delegates at the National People's
Congress in March of 1989 that some inequality had to be tolerated, and
reiterated that the "open" policy should not be halted because of the
coastal-inland gap.[189] Thus, reformers made a clear trade-off between promoting regional equality and concentrating foreign investment where
they believed it would be most successful.

Conclusion: Regional Controls

The SEZs did not, as some leaders originally feared, devolve into modern
concession areas. But many of the mechanisms the government enacted to
guard against other concerns at the regional level were ineffective. Moreover, although the zones and the coastal areas absorbed a significant portion of China's overall investment, and despite statements of support for
the zone experiment, the low level of technology embodied in the foreign
capital, the emphasis on assembly, services, real estate (such as golf
courses and hotels), and construction, and the poor export record, were all
disappointments. As at the national level, the causes of these problems
were manifold. The preceptoral controls to guard against cultural problems in these areas with extensive foreign contacts were as stale—or more
so—as in the rest of the country. The drive to decentralize, which was
linked both to efforts to attract investment and to broader trends toward
regional decentralization in the domestic economy, created extensive
problems for controlling the nature of both Chinese and foreign investments and activities in the zones. Efforts to see that the zones spread the
benefits of investment to other areas were thwarted both by incentive
structures that were inadequate to induce the behavior the government
desired, and by problems in China's economic structure. The shift of attention of both the Chinese government and foreign investors away from
the zones and toward the coastlines effectively prevented the zones from
vindicating their early role as the models for the government's strategy to
absorb foreign capital.

## Chapter Five

CONTROLS AT THE ENTERPRISE LEVEL

A CENTRAL REASON of China's reformers for deciding to attract foreign direct investment was to learn foreign management skills and improve the capability of Chinese managers. But, at the same time, the Chinese government wished to avoid domination of foreign sector enterprises by foreign managers, as they perceived to have occurred during the 1950s when Chinese managers were to learn "advanced methods" from Soviet technicians.[1] Also, their knowledge of local conditions, domestic labor, and so on, gave Chinese managers a technical basis for substantial control in some realms.[2] At the start of the "open" policy, then, a major goal of the reformers was to guard against foreign domination within joint ventures, while simultaneously fostering an environment where the foreign partner would provide training for Chinese managers. From the viewpoint of foreign investors, a central concern about entering joint ventures in China, as in other developing countries, was the desire to maintain managerial influence. They generally believed that they could run joint enterprise operations more effectively, at least until they could train Chinese managers. The fact that the foreign side possessed technical and managerial skills the Chinese did not gave foreign investors a technical or experience basis for assuming control. The foreign partner's desire to control the use and avoid misuse of technology they provided to the venture gave it further impetus to control operations.

In order to meet its concerns at the enterprise level, the leadership established controls to ensure that foreign firms did not dominate decisionmaking within joint ventures, and that investors did not turn joint ventures against the goals the state held for them. Some controls were also designed to create a favorable environment for the transfer of foreign managerial skills. The leadership's strategy to achieve these goals during the early years combined three elements: establishment of a management and decisionmaking structure within joint ventures that was *formally* equal, but that also retained some elements of Chinese domination; reliance upon existing state authority structures—the state economic bureaucracy, and labor organization and the party—as channels for outside influence over joint ventures; and encouragement of a consultative decisionmaking style so that Chinese management and workers could learn from foreign investors. This chapter examines the controls used to pursue this strategy and assesses when they were effective and when they were not. The first part of the chapter assesses the formal controls designed to avoid foreign managerial dominance over Chinese managers. These included Chinese domination of equity positions and of personnel and social welfare decisions, and the establishment of formally equal management structures. The second part examines the informal dynamic that actually appeared in joint ventures despite the formal controls, a dynamic that undermined many of the formal controls. The third part examines the channels of external Chinese control by the party, the labor organization, and the economic bureaucracies. As at the national and regional levels, enterprise-level controls were not always well implemented, and they were often deliberately weakened by the reformers. Once again, the outcome reflected a complex interaction of external and internal factors influencing the foreign investment policy.

As a preface to the description of enterprise-level controls, it is important to note that there was a diversity of experiences among individual joint ventures and in the fate of controls. Variation in the original strength of controls, degree of liberalization, and pace of liberalization that was noted in chapter 4 was also evident at the enterprise level. Moreover, variance in such important elements of the authority structure as, for example, the number of foreign managers and the amount of authority exercised by them, and the strength of the party organization that may compete with the managerial decision structure, came into relief when examining the experiences of individual joint ventures. To some extent, the variations were associated with how soon after the start of the "open" policy a particular venture was established, reflecting change in the investment policy over time. The level of technology offered by the foreign firm, the urgency of the project from the government's point of view, or the foreign partner's resistance to Chinese authority also accounted for some differences. In still other cases, more idiosyncratic elements were at work, such as the personalities of foreign and Chinese partners. Although it is possible to generalize about the experiences of joint ventures despite these variations, the variations themselves should not go unrecognized.

FORMAL CONTROLS OVER JOINT VENTURE MANAGEMENT

Control over Ownership of Equity

In most joint ventures outside of China, control over decisionmaking is directly tied to the division of ownership between partners; the partner with majority ownership has the majority of votes on the board of directors. As noted previously, host governments in both planned and market economies commonly restrict the percent equity held by foreigners to 49% or less (particularly ventures in raw materials, utilities, and other strategic industries) as a means of retaining control over jointly owned companies. Host governments often face countervailing pressures on this issue from foreign investors, who frequently prefer majority ownership under the assumption that this will guarantee management control. Foreign opposition to taking a minority equity position can be particularly strong when the sector is highly competitive or the technology used is very new. Host governments sometimes respond to these foreign preferences when negotiating for projects they most desire.[3]

China's policy on joint ventures broke with this common host country preference for majority equity. The Joint Venture Law did not specify a maximum limit on foreign ownership, thereby offering the possibility of 99% foreign ownership of a joint venture. The law did require foreigners to hold a minimum of 25% equity.[4] The precise division of equity was to be left to negotiation. Yet although the reformers formally argued that Chinese majority equity was not necessary in order to protect China's sovereignty, the potential link between majority ownership and control remained a salient issue to the Chinese government in the early years. Even though the foreign partner in theory could hold 99% of the equity, Chinese officials were clear in their preference for Chinese majority or fifty-fifty ownership, for the "comfort of control" over management.[5] Reflecting this preference, Chinese majority or equal ownership were by far more common than foreign majority ownership for joint ventures formed in the early years; of the twenty-eight equity joint ventures sampled for the present study (all of which were established before 1985), only two had foreign majority ownership. Half of the joint ventures had fifty-fifty equity splits.[6]

Most foreign investors did not oppose having only minority or 50% ownership, and in some cases even preferred it. The lack of opposition from Western partners was due, in part, to the fact that the major incentive for investment was the chance to explore Chinese markets and maintain defensive positions against international competition. For example, one foreign investor interviewed noted a preference for a 30% share because that amount kept the firm's financial expenditure and managerial commitment to the joint venture to a minimum, while establishing a presence in China. Others preferred foreign minority positions so that the Chinese would have a greater stake in the outcome.[7] The lack of conflict on this issue also resulted from the fact, discussed subsequently, that equity control did not always translate into management control.

But despite a Chinese preference for the symbol of majority or equal control, and despite an absence of foreign opposition, large Chinese ownership positions were potentially contrary to another value: absorption of large quantities of foreign capital. The Chinese government dealt with this potential conflict in two ways. First, the Chinese side in many cases valued its own noncash contributions to equity such that they constituted a percentage of 50% or more when measured against the value of the foreign contribution. Valuation of noncash items—including the factory land-use fees, buildings, existing equipment, hookups to local utilities—was subject to manipulation because these items generally had no market price in China. Although occasionally the Chinese side allowed a foreign accountancy firm to value the Chinese contribution independently, more frequently in the early years the figure was decided by local Chinese officials and managers (although it was subject to negotiation). Foreign perceptions that the Chinese negotiators often overvalued Chinese assets led to foreign complaints and to pressures on the central government to curb the practice. In 1986, site fees for "technologically advanced" and "export-oriented" joint ventures were set nationally, making it more difficult to overvalue noncash assets. [8]

Second, the government showed some flexibility with regard to the equity division in order to promote absorption of foreign capital. Although Chinese insistence on majority or equal ownership was more the rule than the exception, in the early years of the policy Chinese approval authorities (especially those at the local level) relaxed the normal strictures in some cases. They sometimes allowed foreign partners to hold a majority share in several types of cases where the foreign investors typically have very strong preferences to do so: when the foreigners invested large amounts of capital in projects with low profits, or when the project involved advanced proprietary technology. Chinese majority or equal ownership tended to be adhered to more stringently in the north and especially in Beijing, where there was less experience with foreign capital and where the official preferences held greater sway, than in the coastal areas and SEZs, where local officials were allowed to and were more willing to engage in flexible terms of investment. Consistent with this regional differential, since the initial years of the policy, Hong Kong investors more frequently obtained majority equity. [9] In the mid-1980s, the government relaxed the preference for Chinese majority or 50% equity even more, and without significant foreign pressure; indeed, the Chinese government increasingly asked foreign investors to take majority ownership positions as a means of raising foreign capital contributions. In the MOFERT sample reported in chapter 3 (table 3-L), although the percentage of ventures with foreign majority ownership remained low, the figure rose nearly threefold from 1985 to 1988. [10] The Chinese thus were increasingly willing to trade-off the "comfort of control" in order to obtain more capital or attract projects they might not otherwise secure.

The flexibility evident in the early years and the decline over time in the preference for Chinese majority or equal equity were both facilitated by another feature of the foreign investment policy that could allow the

Chinese the same "comfort of control" regardless of equity split. Through-out the decade, the Chinese preferred structures and styles of decision-making that de-linked equity holdings from *effective* (rather than sym-bolic) control of the venture. By weighting the composition of the board of directors in the Chinese side's favor, and by fostering unanimous, rather than majority, decision rules, the significance of equity divisions for effec-tive control diminished. The following section discusses these means of separating ownership from effective control.

Structural Equality of Joint Venture Management

Both Chinese and foreign partners had means available to them other than majority ownership to try to assert effective control over joint ventures.[11] In particular, each could attempt to dominate joint venture management structures. In the first half of the decade, the Chinese government at-tempted to regulate the organizational structure of joint ventures at the levels of both the board of directors and day-to-day management. The Implementing Regulations designated the board of directors as the high-est authority in joint ventures.[12] (This stipulation set up a contrast with the traditional system in state-owned enterprises, in which a factory director acted under the leadership of a party committee.) The board was empow-ered to decide all major issues, such as termination or expansion of the venture, approval of the annual operating plan, and the timing and amount of profit distributions, wage payments, and bonuses.

Each party to a venture was unilaterally to select its own representa-tives to the board of directors in proportion to its equity position, and board members were supposed to represent the interests of the partner that designated them.[13] Legal provisions encouraging appointment of di-rectors with reference to equity were nonbinding, but nonetheless usually were followed. Of the joint ventures in the sample for which information was available, 84% (twenty-one) had board representation in proportion to the equity split. The division of board seats failed to comport with the equity split in only four cases. In two cases, the Chinese partners, on their own initiative, gave the foreign side with 50% equity a majority position on the board. In a third case, the Chinese side maintained a majority on the board despite an even equity split.[14] Because the division of board seats in practice usually reflected the division of equity, Chinese partners held a majority or equal position on most boards.

The Joint Venture Law required that the Chinese side appoint the board chair, a provision that reformers viewed explicitly as a means of protecting Chinese control and sovereignty; as one group of reformers stated, appointment of the board chair by the Chinese side "protects our country's leadership authority [*lingdaoquan*] in joint ventures, and we cannot lose control over the enterprise because the foreign investor's proportion of capital is very large. The historical tragedy of old China's economy suffering under foreign control cannot recur."[15] This rule was adhered to in all joint ventures studied. Although the appointment of a Chinese board chair clearly held symbolic value, its practical effectiveness was questionable, for the chair was designated no special powers (such as tie breaking or veto) that might give an edge to the Chinese side.

Parties to a joint venture were permitted to negotiate the specific voting rules the board would use, except for a few decisions that were to be made unanimously.[16] Yet despite this leeway in determining decision rules, the Chinese government further emphasized decisionmaking styles characterized by "unanimous consultation" (*xieshang yizhi*) and "equality and mutual benefit." They encouraged ventures "as much as possible to avoid a large number of decisions where one side compels (*qiangzhi*) the other to carry out" its opinion. Such an emphasis was consistent with the tradition in political and economic organizations of rule by committee, and avoidance of processes that designate clear-cut winners and losers.[17] Contractual provisions promoting unanimity and equal consultation were strikingly pervasive in practice; in 96% of the joint ventures sampled for this study, the decision rules that partners negotiated *in effect* required both sides to agree to all decisions. This was achieved most commonly by combining requirements for majority rule with a right of veto for the minority owner, or by requiring majority rule but stipulating a threshold for passage (such as two-thirds) that required more votes than either side held independently. Because each side was expected to, and in practice did, vote as a bloc, a minority veto or a high-threshold rule meant that board decisions required the assent of both sides. In addition to these formal means of encouraging unanimity, Chinese board members in practice eschewed voting on decisions in preference for each side convincing the other of its view until the partners reached an agreement.[18]

Chinese negotiators thus were effective at obtaining agreements with their preferred decision rules for the board level. This mode of operation did not change much, formally, over the course of the decade. Significantly, there was no foreign pressure to change these norms. There was little incentive for foreign partners to press for change, for their voices as minority owners were protected by the decision rules that allowed a minority veto. Moreover, as is discussed in the next section, the informal dynamic that developed at the board level took advantage of the absence of formal Chinese voting control.

At the level of joint venture operations, the desire of the reformers to promote the absorption of foreign management skills dovetailed with efforts to emphasize technically based management rather than "politics in command."[19] This goal did not, in the early years, eradicate the desire to avoid foreign domination of foreign sector enterprises, however. The reformist effort to reconcile these two goals echoed the effort of the board level. Not all joint ventures employed expatriate managers, for they were costly to maintain in China and, when the project was in a well-developed Chinese industry (such as textiles), they were sometimes viewed as unnecessary. In most cases, both sides hoped that, even before the contract expired, the foreign staff would be phased out. Yet most joint ventures employed several expatriates as managers or technical advisors. Of the ventures sampled, 89% employed expatriate managers (including managers from Hong Kong).[20]

As at the board level, the major joint venture laws said little about managerial structure.[21] Yet the early joint venture management structures reflected very strong preferences on the Chinese side. To ensure that foreigners did not run ventures unilaterally, the Chinese side most commonly negotiated into the contract management structures that divided responsibilities evenly between partners. Specifically, they negotiated a "shadow" (or deputy) management system, under which each Chinese or foreign head of a department (such as personnel, finance, and procurement) was matched with either a deputy in the same department or with an equally ranked counterpart in another department, who was in turn appointed by the partner. Proposals for equal structures usually were initiated by the Chinese side, but were not opposed by the foreign side.[22]

The shadow management systems agreed to in contracts were in fact instituted. In all cases sampled that employed expatriate managers, the positions of general manager and deputy general manager were split between the two partners. Shadow management systems frequently extended to lower management levels too; of the joint ventures sampled that employed expatriates (23), 61% maintained a rough shadow management system. For example, in one extensive deputy system, the "management committee" under the board of directors included four foreign managers (general, market development, factory, and production/quality control managers), and four Chinese managers (deputy general, personnel and finance managers, and company secretary). Half of those with shadow systems also had Chinese majority ownership, indicating that equal management was pursued even where the Chinese might have assumed management control based on their ownership control. Those ventures that did not establish a shadow system usually had a predominance of Chinese managers, although the general manager still was an expatriate. This situation in large part reflected the high cost of expatriate managers.[23]

Chinese negotiators also tried in other ways to foster Chinese influence within the shadow system. For example, they sometimes insisted upon contractual clauses stating that approval of *both* the foreign general manager and Chinese deputy general manager (or their equivalent in a specific department) were required on major decisions.[24] Moreover, as at the board level, Chinese partners strongly emphasized a consultative style of decisionmaking among managers. They hoped that, by encouraging discussion, the Chinese managers would learn foreign decisionmaking processes and techniques, and at the same time would actively participate in decisions.[25] Finally, the deputy system could be structured to allow the Chinese partner to maintain formal authority without losing foreign expertise. In one case, for example, a Chinese comptroller was appointed even though both sides acknowledged that the foreign deputy comptroller was the only one competent in the financial accounting method that was to be used. The shadow system allowed the foreign deputy to take the initiative in most of the decisions, thereby preserving the formally equal status and authority over financial matters of the Chinese partners, while not sacrificing operational goals of the venture.[26]

In addition to the shadow system, a system of comparable salaries for comparably ranked Chinese and foreign managers also promoted equality in the joint venture decision structure. Through comparable payment of foreign and Chinese counterparts, the Chinese side wished to avoid either the reality or the appearance that Chinese labor and management were being exploited, and to avoid the inequality in salaries that had been prevalent with Soviet advisors in the 1950s.[27] Although the laws did not mandate it, Chinese negotiators generally were adamant about obtaining some form of parity. Yet joint ventures, at least in the early years, felt they could not pay Chinese managers the same amount as was required to attract foreign managers; the $50,000 or more annually it took to attract an American manager in the early 1980s was over one hundred times as much as a Chinese manager was typically paid. Not only would the payment of equal salaries for Chinese and foreign managers be very expensive for young ventures, but it violated the norm of more compressed salary ranges among Chinese workers. (Even though some greater discrepancy within the wage scale was being encouraged, salaries did not reach the level that was relevant for Chinese-foreign joint ventures.) Hence, equal payments raised concerns about intra-Chinese equality. Interviewees cited three methods designed to foster relative equality in salaries while avoiding dislocations in financial and distributive goals. One method was for the foreign parent firm, rather than the joint venture, to pay the entire expatriate salary. A second method was to have the joint venture pay the standard Chinese managerial salary to managers from both sides, but to have the foreign parent firm subsidize the expatriate to the necessary level. These solutions were extremely expensive for the parent. A third method, which sometimes was combined with the second, was to agree on a certain "comparable" percentage of the salary of the foreign manager to be paid to Chinese managers, usually from 20% to 90%.[28] To prevent the negative distributive effects of the third method, and perhaps to generate an extra source of revenues, the government usually retained a substantial portion of the salary of Chinese managers and workers. For example, the deputy general manager in a northeastern industrial joint venture earned a salary judged comparable to the foreign managers, but forfeited 25% of it to the government to cover welfare needs.[29]

Although the shadow management structure appeared on paper to promote the dual goals of preventing foreign domination and promoting Chinese learning, in practice it was implemented rather flexibly, and eventually was liberalized. These trends were manifested in three ways. First, although the positions of general managers and deputy general managers were split between Chinese and foreigners, of those ventures sampled for this study in the mid-1980s, the top post of general manager was held disproportionately by the foreign partner. The sample also suggested that Chinese managers were less likely over time to be given the position of general manager; of those ventures with Chinese general managers, all were established in 1980.[30] Moreover, the foreign general managers were granted final authority on many key decisions, such as the setting of international prices.[31] Chinese partners agreed to the assignation of expatriates as general managers rather readily, as was evident in the lack of conflict over management structures. This slippage in the goal of relative equality reflected, on the part of the Chinese partner, the growing tendency to promote the economic success of joint ventures over other goals, and, on the part of both partners, the growing belief that foreign general managers had the expertise to make this happen. The trend also was consistent with the efforts of the 1984 urban reforms to re-orient enterprise management toward functional specialization, provide managerial autonomy from outside agents, and downgrade the role of the party cell within the enterprise.

Second, over the years Chinese partners in negotiations and in operations began to pressure the foreign partner to send increasing numbers of expatriates to China. In the third phase, the reformers made an explicit policy to rely more on foreigners at both the board and management levels, undermining the original goal of Chinese learning on the basis of equality. In Guangdong's SEZs, regulations put into effect in January 1987 provided that the foreign partner could appoint the board chair (and the Chinese the vice chair), if joint venture partners and the municipal government agreed. These regulations also expanded the powers of the board chair to take action independent from the rest of the board. This early willingness in the SEZs to give up even symbolic control over a joint venture's top management was extended to all areas in which joint ventures were set up in the April 1990 amendments to the 1979 law.[32]

Central officials also strengthened the call for foreign-backed enterprises to be run according to "international standards using scientific management methods" and stated that if reaching this standard meant heavy reliance on foreign managers, so be it. Zhao Ziyang stated that:

> In the past, there was the erroneous view that letting foreign business people run enterprises in China meant giving up China's sovereignty. This view must be corrected. Nowadays, hiring professional managers from abroad is a common practice in the world. . . . It is beneficial to both foreign and Chinese sides to let Chinese-foreign equity joint ventures and contractual joint ventures be directly run by foreign business people experienced in management or run by foreign professionals employed by these people. This has many advantages. First, it will help shake off the old structural constraints in China and harassment caused by consideration of "connections," thereby establishing strict management. Second, foreign managers tend to show more concern for product quality, technological advance, and the marketing of the products abroad. . . . Third, their financial success will attract more foreign business people to China. Fourth, they can help us bring up people with modern managerial expertise. And fifth, they can help train our workers, thus improving the quality of the labor force.[33]

In response, the governments of Xiamen and Fuzhou (both in Fujian Province) decided to exclude Chinese managers from holding the positions of either general or deputy general manager, and to leave foreign general managers with full responsibility for joint venture operations. MOFERT also stated that, in general, Chinese partners that were not capable of management responsibilities should assume the role of students and claimed that the "deputy" system of joint management was impractical. MOFERT also criticized interference by some Chinese joint venture managers in the foreign partners' authority, a practice said to be "adversely affecting the normal production and operation of the joint ventures concerned."[34] Although the joint ventures might become more profitable and competitive internationally under this system, the result was an increase in the role of the foreign manager at the expense of the longer term economic goal of transferring skills to Chinese managers and the political goal of formal managerial equality.

The third way in which problems in the formally equal management structure were evident was that, in practice, foreign managers often dominated joint ventures through informal means. This third manifestation of weakness in the original controls is discussed subsequently in this chapter.

Special Realms of Control by Chinese Management

In addition to the Chinese government's effort to promote symbolic management equality between Chinese and foreign partners, it was careful to try to maintain Chinese dominance in two areas of decisionmaking that were central to the protection of workers under socialism: personnel and social welfare. In personnel matters, although the Implementing Regulations formally gave joint ventures greater authority than other state enterprises both to set personnel standards and to hire and fire workers, the formal guarantee of autonomy was belied by the continuing role of the state in deciding labor issues.[35] In particular, because joint venture labor policies were required to conform with the myriad existing labor laws and practices, they were constrained from taking independent action. For example, until 1986 wages and benefits paid out in joint ventures were required to exceed (by between 120% and 150%) the wages paid in equivalent state-owned enterprises, and firing of workers was prohibited without proof of strong breach of discipline and evidence that re-training (either in attitude or skills) had been unsuccessful.[36]

The Chinese partner controlled personnel issues in a number of ways. The personnel manager uniformly came from the Chinese side. Chinese personnel managers and Chinese deputy general managers in most cases had final authority over disciplinary actions taken against workers. Foreign general managers who wanted to fire workers could only do so in consultation with the deputy general manager or personnel manager, and often only with the agreement of the board of directors. Indeed, many foreign managers reported strong and successful resistance from the Chinese partner or from local labor authorities to their efforts to fire workers. In contracts or other agreements, foreigners often agreed not to fire workers and to abide not only by Chinese labor laws but also by common Chinese labor practices. Moreover, in labor decisions that required negotiation between partners (such as increasing or decreasing wages), the Chinese deputy general manager sometimes claimed to represent the workers against management, thereby supplementing the body formally in charge of representing labor interests, the labor organization. The institutional mechanism for wage distributions also fell under Chinese control in some joint ventures: wages paid in joint ventures for Chinese workers did not go directly to the individual worker but, rather, were distributed through the local labor bureau, to the Chinese partner's *danwei*, or to the labor organization.[37]

Wage and personnel issues were not always highly contentious points of negotiations between partners, as the two sides often found common interests. For example, foreign partners often believed that the mandate of higher wages for their workers than in comparable state enterprises enhanced worker productivity. They also agreed that it made sense to appoint as personnel manager a Chinese person familiar with the complexities and nuances of the Chinese labor system. Foreign investors also benefited to some degree from existing Chinese labor practices, notably the lack of an independent labor movement and, perhaps, poor labor mobility.[38] Subordination of Chinese workers to traditional Chinese structures and Chinese managers was consistent with foreign interests in labor discipline. But many foreign investors disagreed with other of the personnel policies by which they were constrained, and often were frustrated about the amount of power the Chinese side exerted over this realm. This led them over time to try to assert some influence over labor matters, an effort that comported with reformist leaders' own increasing efforts in the mid-1980s to move foreign enterprises more toward a foreign personnel model. Chinese reformers grew to be more welcoming of the efforts of foreign managers to design examinations and other hiring standards for potential employees, as well as regulations for labor discipline and wage incentive programs. The growing view among reformers that a great cause of enterprise inefficiency in China was redundant labor also made them more accepting of foreign managers' refusal to take on additional workers or workers they could not first examine. Most significantly, reformers adopted the view that firing workers—or threatening to do so—would be beneficial, and gave somewhat more support to foreign managers in this regard. Although efforts to fire workers continued to meet resistance of local labor officials and, still to some degree, Chinese managers, the growing commitment of central reformers was beneficial for foreign managers, and the efforts of some foreign managers were successful.[39] The lifting in the 1986 Provisions of the cap on joint venture wages (formerly 150% of the state enterprise wage) also complemented the desire of many foreign managers to use wage differentials as production incentives. In all these ways, then, the evolving view of reformers toward labor management led them to liberalize in ways consistent with the views of foreign investors.

The second realm in which Chinese partners dominated joint venture decisionmaking in the early years was in the provision of social welfare benefits for joint venture workers. After 1949, Chinese state enterprises routinely provided housing, medical care, child care, labor insurance, and other social services to workers. The provision by the state of these functions was integral to the leadership's conception of socialism. The post-Mao government intended that joint ventures retain these functions. According to one Chinese writer, the insistence that joint ventures "convert, through economic and administrative means, the surplus value created by our workers into the financial revenues of the state, funds for expanded reproduction of enterprises and welfare expenses for the workers . . .

limit[s] the extent of exploitation by foreign capital." Besides, another official rationalized, if investors provide these functions "the workers will be happier, and that is better for production."[40]

Although joint ventures were to provide these basic services, they were subject to modifications the reformers were beginning to make in China's social welfare policy. As part of the 1984 urban reforms, the reformist leadership attempted to transfer responsibility for providing many welfare benefits from the state to the enterprise, and concurrently granted joint ventures some autonomy to make certain welfare decisions. For example, joint venture managers were allowed to decide the amount of the lunch subsidy they would provide to workers, whereas previously, in a state-run enterprise, such a decision would require approval from outside the enterprise.[41] Nevertheless, joint venture social welfare standards were rigorous in several ways. Chinese managers maintained a substantial degree of control over social welfare issues, mainly through controlling the trade union that oversaw allocation of many welfare funds. Although the precise terms of the benefits were subject to negotiation, Chinese negotiators were insistent that the benefits provided in joint ventures must be at least as good as those in comparable state enterprises. As might be expected, joint ventures were to adhere to work and vacation schedules, and worker safety and environmental protection laws, at a standard not below that found in state enterprises. All joint ventures studied for which information was available provided social welfare facilities that met the government's standards.[42]

Furthermore, the government very much limited the autonomy of joint venture managers by regulating not only the amount but also the composition of wages paid. As in state enterprises, the wage payment for a joint venture worker contained not only a basic wage but also a package of benefits that sometimes exceeded the basic wage. (Together, the basic wage and associated benefits constitute the "real" wage [*shide gongzi*].)[43] The local Labor Bureau, as well as the joint venture's department in charge, had to ratify the wage package before it could be put into effect. Although allocation of benefit funds among the various functions was negotiable, the real wage package in joint ventures generally covered the same *type* of benefits normally paid to state workers. In one venture, for example, 90 *yuan* (45%) of the 200 *yuan* monthly real wage supported lunch subsidies, an annuity system, day care, company housing, and "cultural institutions." Another typical venture might provide that, of a total monthly real wage of 358.5 *yuan*, 168 *yuan* (47%) went to the basic wage and bonus, and 190.5 *yuan* (53%) covered subsidies for costs such as medical insurance, retirement, housing, and education.[44]

As discussed with regard to the issue of joint venture profits, in addition to the benefits included in the wage package, each joint venture was required to establish a separate bonus and welfare fund for staff and workers, to be financed out of aftertax joint venture profits. Bonus and welfare funds could be used to provide performance-based bonuses or other collective welfare facilities to its employees, such as nurseries, rest areas, medical clinics, canteens, and in some cases dormitories. The figure for the annual contribution to a venture's welfare fund usually amounted to between 5% and 10% of aftertax profits.[45] Local officials sometimes have demanded still other payments for welfare services. In one venture, for example, local authorities on Hainan Island required large sums for "social security contributions" and "staff housing levies."[46] Because foreign partners complained that such demands for extra payments were extortionate, the central government tried to halt them. Specifically, the 1986 Provisions provided a path for appeals to local economic commissions or even the State Economic Commission for joint ventures that believed they had been gouged by local officials (Article 16).

Thus, through a number of means the reformers persuaded joint ventures to take on many of the welfare functions that the state itself traditionally provided, and at the same time held joint ventures to rigorous standards in fulfilling these functions. The welfare activities of joint ventures remained strong throughout the decade, moreover, despite some increased autonomy. This is at least in part because, with the exception of local demands for additional funds, foreign investors did not object to provision of welfare functions, even though they increased the venture's costs.

One threat to provision of the welfare function was realized in the late 1980s. The 1986 Provisions (Article 3) exempted TAEs and EOEs from any labor subsidies beyond labor insurance, welfare costs, and housing subsidies, thereby reducing labor costs by perhaps as much as 20%. By sanctioning a reduction in funds previously available for worker welfare, the reformers made yet another tradeoff between their desire to absorb certain types of foreign capital and the desire to make foreign investment serve other goals.

.   .   .

The formal structures of joint ventures, then, were designed in the early years to reflect and maintain the Chinese partner's equality in and, to some degree, control over the making of key decisions. At both board and management levels, joint venture policy guided partners to establish structures that were basically equal. The Chinese also imposed their preferred style of decisionmaking, which fostered unanimity and consultation. In addition, in those policy realms within joint ventures that traditionally were integral to socialism, labor and social welfare, the government attempted to maintain a dominant role for Chinese managers.

Chinese controls over social welfare issues remained strong throughout the decade, with the only liberalization coming as part of the finely tuned policy to favor TAEs and EOEs. Yet, over time, in both the formal management structure and the control of labor issues, the original controls were weakened significantly. Moreover, they were weakened not so much by pressures from foreigners but, rather, by changes in the reformists' own goals for the foreign investment policy.

In addition to some formal liberalization of the original policy promoting equality between Chinese and foreign managers, the policy also was undermined by a second phenomenon: the formally equal structures devolved in many cases to a lack of cooperation between partners, and effective foreign domination of key joint venture decisions. These problems in the implementation of enterprise controls is the subject of the following section.

THE INFORMAL DYNAMICS OF ENTERPRISE DECISIONMAKING

As discussed previously, both the formally equal management structure and the emphasis on unanimous decision rules and a consultative style of interaction were intended to foster an operational jointness between foreign and Chinese partners to a venture. Ideally, a joint style of decisionmaking would discourage unilateral control by one party. Chinese managers and officials, and foreign managers, often expressed that success of their ventures depended on the relationship between the two sides, particularly trust (*chengyi*) and cooperation (*peihe*), as well as shared interests. Reformers also hoped this organizational style would create an environment in which Chinese managers could learn foreign managerial skills.[47] The reformers thus hoped significant Chinese learning would occur by stationing expatriate managers in joint ventures.

But at the same time that Chinese reformers wished to promote a tutorial relationship (within a context of formal equality), they tried to limit it in the first half of the 1980s. They hoped foreign skills could be transferred within five years or less, after which Chinese personnel would be able to assume full responsibility. Chinese managers were exhorted not to accept uncritically all of what they were taught by foreigners, but instead to "digest" their learning and draw on what suited China's conditions. As one commentator asserted in 1979, "Only if the opinions the foreign investor raises regarding management are scientific, feasible, fit China's rules and regulations, and are beneficial for the development of joint ventures should the Chinese side listen to and endorse them."[48] In this, the policy was similar to the *ti-yung* formula adopted by the "self-strengtheners" in the late Qing period. Moreover, although the Joint Venture Law was silent on the goal of Chinese learning, and the Implementing Regulations

(Article 92) referred only briefly to the idea that joint ventures "shall make efforts to conduct professional and technical training of their staff and workers," most joint venture contracts provided for training by foreign managers and technicians.

Interviews revealed some cases where the managerial policy succeeded as originally intended, that is, where Chinese managers both learned foreign methods and participated in a significant way in decisionmaking. Interviewees from several enterprises indicated that as their ventures matured, the Chinese managers took on a more dynamic role.[49] Efforts contained in the October 1984 urban reforms to bolster the independent role of managers were helpful in giving Chinese managers a greater degree of confidence to innovate in newly learned ways. The most notable case of Chinese managerial innovation in the joint ventures sampled was a Chinese deputy general manager who made continuous efforts to support and act upon managerial techniques he learned from foreign partners, while at the same time participating fully in decisionmaking and using his knowledge of the Chinese market and bureaucracy to help the venture succeed. For example, in order to keep the amount of registered capital for the joint venture low enough that local (as opposed to central) approval was possible, the Chinese manager was instrumental in devising and securing a scheme to lease the Chinese partner's assets to the venture and to borrow substantial sums from the Bank of China so that the venture had access to much more capital than the amount actually "registered." While the leasing and borrowing scheme would not have been feasible without reforms in the banking sector, it required considerable innovation by the Chinese manager as well as the use of his prior connections.[50]

But the government's attempt to promote Chinese learning on the basis of equality and through a consultative style was in most ventures not especially effective. At one level, most joint ventures had difficulty creating the most basic feeling of jointness between partners; in half of the joint ventures sampled for which information was available, there was evidence of substantial strains between partners.[51] In the foreigners' perceptions, problems in cooperation took several forms: unwillingness of Chinese workers to heed foreign managers; overconfidence of Chinese managers that the venture could succeed without foreign managers; personality clashes; an atmosphere of continual negotiation rather than partnership; and either the lack of or a breakdown in faith or trust. They often attributed the lack of jointness to different pressures on or interests of each side, poorly defined goals at the outset of the venture, and a lack of concrete incentives for Chinese partners to cooperate. Embedded in these negative responses was evidence of difficulties in combining management styles, lack of clarity about who has authority over workers and management, and poor communication.[52]

There was also evidence that the process of Chinese learning was problematic. Although the Chinese managers in joint ventures were often among China's most well-trained managers, many lacked the basic skills needed to run an internationally competitive joint venture. In one venture, for example, the Chinese deputy general manager was an engineer with no management training while, in a second (noted previously), the Chinese finance manager lacked any accounting skills.[53] Often, Chinese managers in the Chinese partner's original enterprise were taken on as joint venture managers automatically, with little regard for merit. Most foreign managers felt that Chinese learning was at best extremely slow and at worst nonexistent. Foreign managers felt they had to continue to supervise workers and deputy managers in a direct fashion if their ventures were to produce quality goods efficiently, and that Chinese managers did not absorb the skills to operate ventures on their own. Others noted resistance to change by foreign managers. One foreign manager, for example, likened his counterparts to bamboo: able to bend with the wind, but when the wind pressure ceased, they returned to their former position. Another, in a service industry that catered to wealthy foreign consumers, noted the difficulty of getting his Chinese partners to fully accept the notion, which he considered necessary to the success of his venture, of providing better service to better-paying customers. Several other foreign managers complained that, even while expressing a desire to institute Western management methods, their Chinese partners resisted the foreign methods by applying old methods (of accounting, for example) when actually implementing their tasks. There was also evidence that those Chinese actually sent overseas were reluctant upon return to share their training, perhaps believing that they were more valuable if they continued to have unique skills. Some bureaucratic problems hindered the training effort, moreover, such as problems of acquiring proper papers to send personnel overseas.[54] Several foreign managers indicated that because of failed training efforts, their joint ventures would need to maintain an expatriate presence longer than originally expected.

In the absence of effective training and, for many ventures, a good working relationship between partners, the tutorial system devolved into an over-reliance on expatriates to run the ventures. Foreign dominance— unilateral or nearly unilateral foreign control over decisionmaking in key areas—was found at the levels of both the board of directors and operational management. Underlying the *de facto* unanimity rules at the board level was evidence of an informal dynamic, in which the foreign side took the lead in decisionmaking. A number of boards operated such that the foreign side, regardless of its majority or minority equity or voting position, took the initiative in decisionmaking and obtained the agreement of the Chinese partners. In these cases, foreign managers, who also were board directors, stated that they ran board meetings, often by routinely drafting the minutes for board meetings ahead of time (including statements that the decision was unanimously approved) and obtaining votes of both blocs in favor of the minutes prior to the board meeting.[55]

At the management level, foreign dominance was the norm in about four-fifths of the joint ventures studied in the mid-1980s that employed expatriate managers; 81% showed evidence that the foreign managers dominated in most economic decisions except for the special realms of personnel and social welfare. Moreover, a Chinese manager interviewed in 1990 estimated that 80% of the disputes between partners over the years of the venture's operation had been settled in favor of the foreign position. The operational areas in which foreign domination was most evident included finance, international marketing, quality control and engineering, and production.[56] It is notable that this dynamic sometimes occurred without the resistance of the Chinese managers involved. As one foreign manager stated, "Although it is not in the contract, the Chinese side will take a back seat to the Hong Kong [manager] where training and skill are key, such as in engineering and accounting."[57] Occasionally the Chinese side even requested either in written agreements or verbally that the foreign side take prime management responsibility for a given number of years.[58]

Foreign dominance was by no means total. For example, Chinese directors (usually important state or party figures) did not routinely rubber stamp documents produced by foreigners, and stalemates, such as over wage increases for foreign managers or Chinese staff and workers, were known to drag on for several months. Foreign dominance also was circumscribed by maintenance of Chinese authority in personnel and social welfare matters, and by resistance to foreign methods, as discussed previously.[59] Nor was Chinese learning a total failure, as evidenced by the cases where Chinese managers showed tremendous learning capacity. But these factors did not outweigh the preponderance of informal foreign dominance.

The reasons for the generally poor success during the 1980s of training Chinese managers, and the widespread foreign dominance, were complex. Besides idiosyncratic conditions, three types of (not mutually exclusive) explanations appeared to be salient. The first type of explanation for foreign dominance was structural: the upheaval of the education system during the Cultural Revolution disrupted the formal training of those individuals in the 35–50 age group who under different circumstances would have been prime candidates to take over as middle- and, increasingly, senior-level managers during the 1980s. China thus had an insufficient number of people with appropriate skills who could be trained further as joint venture managers. A related structural explanation concerned problems inherent in the Chinese economy in the 1980s: because of poor labor mobility in China and the difficulty of hiring skilled managers from other enterprises, state enterprises that identified talented managers were very often reluctant to permit them to transfer to a joint venture. This situation was exacerbated by the reformist pressure on state enterprises to be competitive. Chinese reformers came to recognize this problem in the latter part of the decade, when they called for the provision of outstanding Chinese managers to joint ventures.[60] Thus, the problematic supply of talented Chinese managers made it very difficult to fulfill the goal of training Chinese managers to a level that would allow joint ventures to be truly efficient and innovative, and independent from expatriate influence.

A second, and even more important, part of the explanation for the devolution to foreign dominance relates to Chinese attitudes toward the capabilities of foreign managers and the incentives for managerial behavior. The very strong government pressure on Chinese managers to show rapidly both exports and profits gave them an incentive to neglect the goal of learning to be innovative managers. Several additional factors also produced disincentives for Chinese managers, and incentives for foreign managers, to have a full voice in decisionmaking. Because innovative behavior of the sort the reformers hoped Chinese managers would learn from foreign managers was not clearly rewarded under the "open" policy, there were few incentives for Chinese managers to take an active role in joint venture decisionmaking. Chinese managers were more likely to behave according to the long-standing system, which did not foster and indeed punished individual action. Thus, although Chinese managers were anxious for their joint ventures to show profits, they were hesitant to take personal responsibility for the implementation of profit-generating methods of management. More generally, the relative instability of the overall reforms in the early years contributed to an atmosphere in which Chinese managers perceived active embrace of Western learning to be personally risky. As long as the line between legitimate use of profit criteria and illegitimate "capitalistic profit-seeking" continued to be vague and subject to political manipulation, Chinese managers had incentives to leave responsibility for the pursuit of profits in the hands of the foreign partners.[61] The incentives to let foreign managers try to produce quick results were supported by the previously noted attitude among some Chinese managers that joint ventures would be more successful if the foreign managers, whose business after all always had been to make profits, were left unhindered to apply their "magic touch."[62]

A third explanation for poor Chinese learning and foreign dominance concerns the motivations, beliefs, and incentives of foreign managers. Although foreign managers formally understood their obligation to train their partners, and did not often press for formal control, they tended to offer the whole package of "Western learning" for unqualified acceptance, and expected to produce Western-style, business-oriented managers. They did not often encourage an atmosphere for their counterparts to digest only what was appropriate for Chinese conditions. In one venture, for example, the foreign managers felt it necessary to halt what they described as the workers' habit of "tinkering" with precision quality control instruments on their own, lest the workers compromise the quality of production. In doing so, the foreign managers inadvertently may have choked off a process of experimentation, learning, and adaptation. Chinese managers who perceived that the whole package of Western learning was inappropriate could be expected to resist the foreign methods, or to bow out of the decisionmaking process. In another venture, the foreign managers felt their Chinese counterparts got too involved in matters that were not directly related to production, such as issues of workers' housing and family problems. Although such matters reflect the integral place of the enterprise in Chinese society, these foreign managers were frustrated by what they perceived as the inefficient use of management time.[63] Creation of an atmosphere conducive to learning was also hindered by the pessimism held by many foreign managers that their Chinese counterparts would or could learn what they wanted to teach. Finally, many foreign managers seemed to feel that the risk-averse behavior of their Chinese counterparts was too deeply ingrained to be amenable to much change. Others sympathized with the inability of Chinese managers ever to be wholly free from potential criticism or punishment. Some even argued that foreign managers *should* take a leading role, because it was easier for them than for Chinese managers to take blame for mistakes, real or perceived.

Thus, although the goals of having joint ventures serve a short-term, positive training function and at the same time maintain managerial equality were important for the long-term success of the "open" policy, neither of these goals was effectively implemented. Rather, structural problems in the Chinese economy, the lack of strong incentives for Chinese managers to learn and adopt innovative behavior, and the perception of both sides that foreign managers would be more successful at making the venture more profitable in the short run led to foreign domination of key economic decisions. The formal call by reformers in the third phase for foreigners to run joint ventures hence served to formalize the dynamic that had already arisen in practice. Although the absorption of foreign management skills remained a formal goal, there was little evidence that the reformers were meeting this goal.

Externally Based Structures of Authority in Joint Ventures

Perhaps the strongest potential tool that the Chinese leadership possessed for controlling decisionmaking in joint ventures in the early years was the use of external organizations to influence management. Historically, the party, the labor organization, and the economic bureaucracy had maintained a central role in guiding and directing enterprise management in China's socialist economy. How well these organs retained influence over foreign investment is examined in this section.

All three of these channels of external state authority over joint venture management were affected by the broader reforms being carried out in the Chinese economy. As early as the late 1970s, the reformers began to experiment with loosening the administrative, bureaucratic constraints upon economic enterprises and treating state enterprises more like semi-autonomous corporate entities. In these early enterprise reforms, managers were to be granted more leeway in planning, production, marketing, and labor management in particular, and were allowed to retain and dispose of a substantial portion of any profits they generated. Production needs, rather than political norms and struggles, were to guide enterprise activity.[64] Although the enterprise reforms had a relatively small effect in the early years, the push for enterprise autonomy intensified with the announcement of the urban reform programs in 1984. In those reforms, the government made further efforts to separate the political and economic structures both within enterprises and between government bureaus and enterprises. (This effort was given the slogan "break apart government and enterprise"—*Zheng-qi fenkai!*) Along with these general reforms came a growing commitment to joint venture autonomy. Although autonomy had been promised implicitly in the Joint Venture Law, it was the Implementing Regulations, the 1986 Provisions, and other regulations of the later phase that took more serious steps to prevent interference in joint venture management by outside organizations. These changes were particularly evident in the changing role of the party and bureaucracy.

The Labor Organization

As in state enterprises, the labor organization (*gong hui*, or trade union) in joint ventures was to formally represent the interests of joint venture workers. The Implementing Regulations provided that, in joint ventures outside of the SEZs, staff and workers had the right to establish a labor organization (LO) and to carry on union activities in accordance with

Chinese trade union laws. (The SEZ labor regulations made no provision for trade unions.) Each joint venture was required to contribute the equivalent of 2% of its total wage bill to support the union, and provide housing and facilities for the LO's office work, meetings, and other union activities.[65]

Consistent with the idea that Chinese managers should have the primary authority over personnel and labor matters, LOs remained under the control of the Chinese side and allowed no participation by foreign investors. LOs were not independent organizations for Chinese workers but, rather, as part of the national All-China Federation of Trade Unions, were branches of the party. As representatives of investors, Chinese managers were not formally permitted to join the union, although this prohibition was sometimes ignored. In the Fujian-Hitachi television joint venture, for example, the Chinese general manager was also a "leading member" of the trade union, as well as the First Party Secretary.[66]

The multifaceted authority of the LO in joint ventures was specified both in regulations specific to joint ventures (in the 1980 Joint Venture Labor Regulations and in the 1983 Implementing Regulations) and in conjunction with the 1950 Trade Union Law. As the representative of the workers' interests, the LO concluded with the board and oversaw implementation of, a labor contract. This contract was to cover issues such as wages, recruitment, firing, welfare benefits, insurance, and safety. In addition to its role in overseeing the welfare and bonus fund and in distributing wages to workers, as discussed previously, the LO could dispute "unreasonable" firings of workers.[67] Moreover, LO representatives were given the right to attend meetings of the board of directors to argue the interests of the workers when the board discussed issues such as production and development plans. Although in these meetings LO representatives were to be nonvoting members, they were to report to the board the "opinions and demands" of staff and workers. When the board considered issues of direct importance to workers (such as wages and bonuses, and welfare benefits), the board was to "heed the opinions of the trade union and win its cooperation." What it meant in practice for the board to "heed the opinions" of the LO was not clear, since the board was to have final authority to decide labor matters, yet these provisions gave a specific channel to the LO to try to influence labor-related decisions. If unhappy with the board's decision, the LO could take the matter to arbitration or, ultimately, to the local People's Court.[68]

Despite the importance of its formally stipulated role, in practice the function of the LO in many ways was not as onerous as the regulations suggested. In some cases foreigners were able to negotiate the omission of contractual provisions granting LO representatives the right to attend board meetings without permission of the board and forbidding the presence of LO representatives at votes on labor issues. Generally, unions were reported to be "sheep" in board meetings, and rarely if ever attended.[69] Moreover, in addition to its role as representative of the workers, the LO was to operate not as an adversary to management but, rather, as a supporter of the smooth operation of the enterprise itself. Indeed, LOs at times were crucial for gaining labor support for management initiatives. For example, in one joint venture, in which extremely stringent hygiene standards were required of Chinese workers, the Chinese managers suggested that the only chance for worker cooperation would be if the union was called upon to carry out the hygiene directives. A second role of the LO, in other words, was to foster support among workers for party policy toward joint ventures, and to enforce labor discipline. As one reformist analysis asserted in 1984, "the trade union has the responsibility to supervise, urge, and educate staff and workers to implement the labor contract, carry out the system of enterprise rules, and enthusiastically complete the enterprise's economic tasks."[70] LOs attempted to accomplish this second task through a variety of means, ranging from organized study of production issues specific to the venture itself and central reform documents, to the use of propaganda posters, to professional and technical training and retraining of workers, to the provision of cultural and recreational activities (such as basketball games).[71] The comments of various Chinese joint venture managers that the role of the labor organization was "to educate workers and support the joint venture" and to "protect the interests [liyi] of both the Chinese and foreign sides," and that the LO did not "cause trouble for the joint venture but, rather, help[ed] it to work," all illustrate the labor organization's role in encouraging labor discipline. Many foreign managers also noted that their partners described the LO as a helpful body, and the foreign side should want it there.[72] Thus, the potential for the LO to act as a counterweight to the influence of foreign managers in important respects was subordinated to its role in supporting the interests of the Chinese state and of foreign investors in the smooth operation of enterprises.

The LOs failed to fulfill their function as a control over foreign management in joint ventures in a second way: neither joint venture managers nor local trade union officials enforced the implementation of the LO's role. Although the Joint Venture Labor Regulations and the Implementing Regulations clearly intended that all joint ventures would have a labor organization, in practice their level of activity was highly variable. In nearly one-third (29%) of the joint ventures surveyed for which information was available, interviewees reported that no LO had been established and that workers carried out no union activities. In 14% of those with unions, they were not active at all or were active only in organizing sporting events.[73] Variation in the role of LOs among joint ventures can be highlighted by comparing individual joint ventures. In one joint venture, for example, study meetings were held regularly and with active participation of people from outside the venture (presumably from the municipal or national trade union federation). The LO in this venture also was active in influencing the management and even the board to consider certain proposals, as well as in urging workers to work harder. At the other extreme, in one venture, although a formal union organization existed, it consisted of a "union girl" who organized sports activities. In still another case, when Chinese board members asked the foreign general manager (also a board member) if they could appoint an LO leader from outside the joint venture, the general manager insisted that he would only allow an outside leader if that leader were elected by the workers. No outside leader was elected, and the Chinese partners did not raise the issue again. The weakness of existing LOs was apparent in still another way. Foreign managers were able to confine LO activity to after regular work hours. This meant that LO meetings were an additional burden on joint venture workers, who already were subject to more strenuous work rules than their counterparts in most state enterprises. [74]

Thus, although the joint venture policy in the early years established labor organizations as a channel of outside control over the treatment of workers by foreign investors, in practice the control function was much weaker than it formally appeared. The role of the LO was weakened by the capacity of foreign investors to restrict it, and by the increased efforts of reformers to guarantee joint venture autonomy from outside organizations.

The Party

After the mid-1950s, the Chinese Communist Party (CCP) maintained the premier decisionmaking role in Chinese enterprises, dominating the role of technical and operational management. Party leadership of enterprises not only facilitated the implementation of party policy, but also fostered the "mass line" in production matters and de-emphasized the role of technical professional managers. [75] In enterprises, as in society as a whole, the party became the arbiter of "correct" ideological dogma and policy. The party's role in the management of joint ventures was not mentioned in any of the various laws pertaining to joint ventures prior to 1987 and was virtually never raised by the Chinese side in negotiations even when party personnel participated (as representatives of the party) in negotiations. Nor was the role of the party addressed explicitly in joint venture contracts. The party function in joint ventures was discussed in internal (neibu) regulations, but these regulations were not readily available to foreign investors. [76] Silence about the role of the party in joint ventures reflected the fact that the party cell was formally outside of the joint venture organization. But it also reflected a decision not to concern investors with talk of communism and the party, or to contradict openly the idea that the foreign side was negotiating to form an independent "legal person."

Despite this silence, it was clear in the early years that the party was to play a role. The presence of a party organization within joint ventures was accorded great significance by some Chinese leaders, including reformers. They intended the party to act as a communist vanguard in enterprises that might otherwise be threatened by the negative influence of foreign capital. For example, one writer in the early period, who was generally supportive of the "open" policy, viewed the role of the party in society as a whole and within joint ventures as one of carrying out "the most tenacious struggle with capitalist relations, pointing out for the masses the practical road to socialism and setting examples of working selflessly in the effort to achieve socialism."[77] The party therefore was considered the "leading core" of joint enterprises, even though, during the early years, the role of the party in domestic enterprises was undergoing some revisions.[78]

Chinese officials and managers described in interviews the role the party was to take on in joint ventures. In addition to the functions it carried out through the labor organization, it was to maintain a separate identity. As in all Chinese units (*danwei*), in joint ventures that had three or more party members these members were to constitute a party cell, headed by a party secretary (*shuji*), that was outside the realm of joint control. As with the LO, foreign investors and managers were completely excluded from its activities. In one venture, for example, the party cell was isolated in the Chinese-run Protocol Department, and had its own meeting room, complete with shaded windows.[79] The party cell had several specific functions related to its own perpetuation and its guiding role. First, it was responsible for recruiting and promoting cadres. During joint venture negotiations and operations, moreover, the party organ also played a "supervisory" role to see that the joint venture policy was carried out correctly. The willingness to use such authority was indicated in the case of a contractual joint venture for a Shenzhen hotel, in which local party officials investigated Hong Kong managers for illegitimate expenses (such as serving Hong Kong relatives underpriced food) and an "incorrect work-style."[80]

In addition, the party organization was to lead the fight against unhealthy tendencies within joint ventures. A major task of the party cell was to lead political and ideological study among party cadres within the venture. Although political study was never formally written into contracts between the parties and never included expatriate managers, in a few of the ventures studied in the mid-1980s, half-day sessions were held once a week. Occasional longer sessions would take workers away from work for several days. In several ventures, regular sessions were held during formal work hours.[81] According to one Chinese manager interviewed, the aim of political study was to "raise ideological understanding" of the joint venture and, "if the cadres' thoughts are not high enough, to educate their thinking [*jiaoyu sixiang*]." Another Chinese manager explained that the study was aimed at preventing "unhealthy tendencies, particularly among cadres who were in daily contact with foreigners."[82]

The general contents of study meetings in joint ventures were not difficult to discern, although they were considered private affairs of the Chinese. Most sessions, which the party cell carried out according to "party articles" (*dang zhang*), consisted of reading and discussing important documents, news articles, and tracts of Mao, Marx, Lenin, and Deng Xiaoping that were supportive of the "open" policy. In addition to the standard exhortation to cadres to support party and country, the content of political study in joint ventures in the mid-1980s was essentially fourfold, according to Chinese managers. First, study sessions warned them to guard against "bourgeois decadence" and economic crime. Second, they promoted a "socialist spiritual civilization." Third, they urged staff and workers to work hard in support of the joint venture and the economic reforms as a whole. Finally, in a break with tradition, some foreign managers also were told that the study sessions would increasingly include technical training, and would de-emphasize ideological work.[83]

Even in the mid-1980s, there were joint ventures in which the party organization competed with the formal management structure in joint ventures. Party duties or assignments of cadres (such as attending special political study conferences) sometime were allowed priority over their managerial work, and took those Chinese managers who were at the same time party cadres away from their job. More significantly, because cadre-managers possessed a second basis of authority, they sometimes exercised their authority as ranking party members to influence joint venture matters. In one Beijing venture, for example, the Chinese general manager was second in the party hierarchy to the party secretary. Although the party secretary was formally subordinate to the general manager by several levels in the formal joint venture management structure, the general manager found that he could not direct the party secretary to do anything the latter did not wish to do, even in operational matters. (The interference from the competing party structure was unusually significant in this case.)[84]

Although the party was positioned to act as a source of control over joint venture operations and set up the mechanisms to do so in some joint ventures, it was thwarted in carrying out its original function. Indeed, despite Chinese managers' understanding of the formal tasks the party was to fulfill, the party often was inactive. Foreign managers could identify some party structure in less than half (47%) of the joint ventures for which information was available, and in less than one-third (32%) of the ventures was any party activity discernible.[85] Even where party organizations were relatively open, their impact was often minor. In the only two ventures where cadres held the sole position of party secretary, that person did no overt party work but, rather, spent work hours reading the newspaper or, in the words of one foreign investor, "twiddling his thumbs." More commonly, the party secretary and other ranking party cadres simultaneously held another high-level management position, such as deputy general manager or personnel manager.[86] Any work done by party cadres had to be done in addition to a full-time position, and generally after working hours.

The organizational strength of the party in joint ventures varied somewhat among regions, with the influence of the party secretary much stronger in the north and especially in Beijing, and weaker in Shanghai and the south (including the SEZs). The relative strength of the central party in Beijing made enterprise directors less likely to ignore the requirements for party cells there. The distance from the capital, as well as the greater experience with the West in Shanghai and Guangdong, served as counterweights to the influence of party structures there.[87] Even where party cells existed, the record of political education was uneven. Study sessions were often held in addition to regular work, and in at least one case, sessions were regularly canceled when production was too busy. One foreign manager noted that his Chinese counterparts who were party cadres would skip study sessions if they could find something better to do.[88] More surprisingly, this important tool was ignored completely in many joint ventures; study was not carried out at all in nearly one-half of the joint ventures for which information was available. Often, those joint ventures that ignored political study were located in Guangdong Province, consistent with the general Beijing-versus-south pattern in strength of party oversight.[89]

Direct pressure from foreigners was one cause for a weaker party role in practice. Although in many cases foreign managers were willing to let the party exist unhindered, both because they believed it posed no real threat and because, as one manager put it, "it is not my mandate to change the political system," in other ventures foreign managers successfully pressed for a reduced role for the party.[90] For example, when one foreign general manager objected to Chinese board members' request to hold political study, the Chinese side acquiesced. During negotiations for another venture, the Chinese retracted their request that the venture pay for a party secretary when the foreign side objected. Other foreign managers reported using their influence with high-level bureaucrats in Beijing to have their Chinese counterparts with strong party ties removed. In some cases the foreign side negotiated agreements stating that no person in "non-productive" positions would be paid by the joint venture, eliminating the possibility of a full-time party secretary.[91]

The party's control over operations was also undermined over time by the government's own efforts to promote economic decisionmaking according to "objective" laws, and to limit the function of the party to a guiding, yet nonoperational, role through the Factory Director Responsibility System introduced in 1984. Under the new system, the party was formally removed as the "leading core" of the enterprise and retained authority primarily for "external relations" between the enterprise and the outside political, social, and economic organs, and for political and ideological work. The manager was responsible for running the enterprise and making it profitable. These reforms were evident in joint ventures, as one Chinese joint venture personnel manager indicated: "[T]he factory manager has the right to decide things in operations without the need to ask the party secretary, as he would in a state-run enterprise. . . . The activities of CCP members have nothing to do with joint venture [activities], and they do not interfere with [bu ganshe] the joint venture."[92]

When political education was carried out, it served more to fight against obstacles to the venture by those within the enterprise who opposed the "open" policy than to fight foreign investors. This function was reflected in the statement of one Chinese official that "[t]he government is sure that it wants the 'open' policy, but others view it differently. If there are obstacles to carrying out the policy, then the CCP should help remove them. . . . If there is a role to be played by the party, it is to help, not to let the joint venture go astray."[93] It was apparent, then, that Chinese joint venture partners felt little pressure to have the party retain its original role. Rather, given the growing pressure from reformers for joint ventures to succeed economically, there was little incentive for Chinese joint venture managers or local officials to enforce extensive political study or employ full-time party workers, both of which might hurt the productivity of the venture.

Overall, then, the role of the party in joint ventures was quite mixed during the 1980s. On the one hand, party units were positioned to exert control over foreign capital, and remained as a latent source of party authority. In some cases they did play an active supervisory role. But, on the other hand, the party's role shifted dramatically, along with the overall domestic trends in enterprise management and, in some cases, as a result of foreign opposition. The party had virtually no formal organization in a significant portion of joint venture operations. Where it did exist, it served more as an ally to joint ventures than an arm of state control against possible unwanted influences.

Bureaucratic Constraints and Opportunities

A final instrument the Chinese government used to try to control foreign investment was the economic bureaucracy, that is, the state organs that were positioned to oversee the establishment and operation of foreign-backed enterprises. Bureaucratic supervision of joint venture activities was intended to "guarantee that only if it is consistent with our interests can foreign capital develop its activities."[94] One of the greatest constraints on the activities of foreign capital grew out of the web of bureaucracy. The bureaucratic environment surrounding joint ventures in the early years consisted not only of the few bureaus directly above them in the ministerial (or equivalent) hierarchy, but also of other governmental organs, such as the Bank of China, to which enterprises in China and their parent organizations also were responsible. Thus, as is clear from the discussion of controls in chapter 4, many joint venture functions could not be carried out without the approval or cooperation of the relevant bureaus.

The jurisdiction of these bureaucracies over joint ventures was not clearly defined in the Joint Venture Law, and this vagueness was enhanced by that law's implication of joint venture autonomy. The role of bureaucracies soon became clearer in practice, and was further codified in the 1983 Implementing Regulations. Two organizations had direct vertical lines of authority over a joint venture. Immediately superior was the "department in charge" (*zhuguan bumen*, or DIC). The DIC was usually the local or functional branch of the central ministry—such as the Second Light Industry Bureau or the First Machinery Bureau of a given municipality—of which the Chinese partner to the venture was originally a part. Above the DIC bureau was the local or central branch of the Ministry of Foreign Economics and Trade (MOFERT) (whichever branch had authority to approve and oversee the joint venture).[95] During negotiations, the DIC was to be responsible for intermediary approvals, such as for the feasibility study and technology transfer agreements. Once the venture was approved, the DIC retained "supervisory" functions that allowed it to "hear" export prices, to "receive" accounting statements and copies of the production plan, and supervise liquidation.[96] MOFERT had primary authority for screening projects and granting final approval for joint ventures. It often was actively involved behind the scenes in negotiations to ensure that the Chinese negotiators agreed to the proper terms. It could cause significant delays in the approval of a joint venture, as was evident in the complaints of Chinese negotiators that they were having difficulty persuading opposition factions in MOFERT to grant approvals needed to proceed.[97] Finally, the myriad agencies that were not vertically above joint ventures but had overlapping jurisdictions over resources and issues that involved the joint venture had to be consulted by MOFERT or the DIC. As might be expected, the interests of these agencies were not always aligned with those of the joint venture, the DIC, or MOFERT. Even when top, central-level bureaucrats of those interested agencies offered support for the joint venture policy, opposition often emanated from the thick layer of local and/or middle-level bureaucrats, particularly when they competed with joint ventures for scarce resources.[98]

The economic bureaucracies had a potent role not only in theory but also in practice. As discussed in chapter 4, the financial bureaucracies were particularly effective at controlling joint venture foreign exchange accounts. Joint ventures reported that centrally mandated laws were supplemented by myriad other bureaucratic pressures: the management denied the existence of external state pressure in only one joint venture studied. The vast majority of Chinese and foreign managers alike expressed strong frustration over bureaucratic interference. One Chinese manager, for example, claimed that the biggest problem joint ventures faced was that of "many mothers-in-law [*popo duo*]." Some Chinese managers in joint ventures expressed that their main struggle was not against the foreign partners but, rather, against their own rigid, centralized economic system.[99] External bureaucracies extended their influence through several channels. First, as discussed previously, in addition to MOFERT a number of bureaucracies could assert strong influence over the approval process for joint ventures. The sheer weight of the bureaucracy was perhaps best illustrated by the case of a contract that needed sixty different "chops" (official seals) before it could finally be approved.[100] Second, Chinese partners to a venture were subject to pressure from superior ministries. This was evident, for example, in several cases in which Chinese members of the board explained to their foreign partners that they could not concur on decisions with their partners, even if they preferred to do so, because of a "political problem," usually opposition of the parent government organs. The tendency to pass responsibility upward to superior ministries encouraged acquiescence to such pressure.[101]

Third, central and local bureaucracies could issue formal directives to joint ventures. Examples of direct bureaucratic interference were legion throughout the decade, particularly with regard to foreign exchange, technology, and personnel. Soon after one venture began operations, it found that representatives from various local government agencies kept dropping by to check on equipment (boilers and calibration instruments) and on the quality of the product. They were also directed by the municipal flood control committee to draw up a flood control plan and form a flood committee within the joint venture. Another manager complained that local financial bureaus frequently asked for substantial information beyond what was formally required. Several other interviewees told of how they had to enter extensive negotiations in order to get foreign exchange that they had earned through international sales released from local banks. Local officials investigated a textile joint venture in Shanghai that they considered to have an unduly low level of profits. A hotel that was oriented to foreign business representatives and tourists was directed without explanation by Beijing public security to shut down the foreigners-only discotheque. The provincial branch of the Parker-Hannifin joint venture's responsible ministry unilaterally removed the Chinese general manager and deputy general manager of the venture without informing the venture or explaining its action. This occurred despite guarantees in the Joint Venture Law that the appointment and removal of top management was to be done by the board of directors. Contrary to the terms of its contract, the Fujian-Hitachi television joint venture was directed by central ministries to cease selling televisions outside of Fujian because it was taking advantage of disparate regional prices, which the government considered "profiteering." As described previously, the same venture was also ordered to raise exports to 50% of production by the third operational year (even though the contract agreed exports would be in the jurisdiction of the Japanese partner) and to reduce the production volume by over half.[102]

The presence of outside bureaucratic actors thus was marked, especially in the early years. By the beginning of the second phase, the reformers' recognition of the importance of enterprise autonomy in creating a favorable environment for foreign firms comported with their view that the elephantine economic bureaucracy and its links with the party was dysfunctional for development. Because bureaucratic interference was a continuing concern of foreign investors, the Chinese government tried in various ways throughout the decade to respond to complaints of foreign and Chinese managers about "red tape." The Implementing Regulations guaranteed both noninterference in "production and operating plans of the joint venture," and stated that the board of directors was the "highest authority of a joint venture" and that joint ventures would have the "right to do business independently" within the scope of the law. Joint ventures were allowed greater autonomy in realms such as personnel, finance, supply, production, international marketing, and were given authority to enter into contracts with other enterprises.[103]

Moreover, echoing the roles of the LO and party, the Implementing Regulations indicated that the role of the DIC and MOFERT should shift, after a joint venture's approval, toward one of facilitator. Because a venture's requests for labor, raw materials, and fuel were incorporated into

DIC and municipal plans, the DIC in practice took on responsibility for helping procure needed materials in the shortage economy, and gave its venture priority in allocating supplies. As one Chinese deputy general manager stated, "[I]f the joint venture did not have the help of the department in charge, it would be hard to handle [*buhao ban*]." Chinese and foreign partners in joint ventures recognized the value of keeping these essential relations well-oiled, such as by entertaining relevant DIC functionaries.[104] MOFERT, too, after establishment of a venture, was to help it to function in a difficult environment. Indeed, one official noted that MOFERT was to keep other agencies from giving orders to the joint venture, as well as to get it out of trouble in other ways. Its post-approval supervisory role was weak and not clearly defined. Its role was stronger than that of the department in charge, however, in that it had authority to investigate implementation of the agreement and to make final approval over activities (such as technology transfer) that only were to be reported to the DIC.[105] Officials such as mayors and vice ministers, who had a political stake in the success of joint ventures, also could be counted on as facilitators. Li Ruihuan, who was elevated to the Politburo following Tiananmen, was often mentioned as a strong advocate of Tianjin's joint ventures when he was mayor there. Similar, though less strong, statements were made about Shanghai's party leader Jiang Zemin prior to his appointment as CCP party secretary.

The 1986 Provisions renewed the promise of autonomy by allowing joint ventures to formulate their own production and operating plans, raise and use funds, procure materials, sell products, and so on. The DICs were to ensure this autonomy, and bureaucracies were admonished to coordinate foreign investment approvals and to expedite other matters related to joint ventures. Following through on this admonition, in 1988, Fuzhou, Xiamen, and other locations introduced a "one window" service whereby one government office had authority to handle all necessary government business and services on behalf of foreign-backed firms.[106]

Thus, after the early years of the "open" policy, the DIC and MOFERT came to be facilitators of joint venture operations. They reserved "supervisory" powers, but their role was less one of supervision than of defenders of the interests of joint ventures as carved out in the laws. Even when the reformers intended for the state organs to continue to control joint ventures, however, this role was problematic. In depending upon the bureaucracy to carry out controls, the reformers could not avoid being subjected to the norms that governed bureaucratic life in China. Traditional patterns of policy implementation in China—bureaucratism, localism, and *guanxi*—all affected central implementation of joint venture controls. Many of the examples of bureaucratic interference in joint ventures noted previously illustrate how such interference furthered local or bureaucratic needs and interests, rather than the interests of the reformist policy. Local interests, in showing quick results in attracting foreign investment, often caused local officials to ignore some of the stricter rules. (Recall, for example, the efforts of the central government to limit investment in services and real estate.) Conversely, when the views of reformers evolved such that they believed that the bureaucracy needed to be reined in, bureaucracies with interests to protect continued to meddle, as occurred with the levying of local taxes on labor and infrastructural services.

The use of *guanxi* (personal relations) and of the "back door" (*hou men*) to obtain approvals and resources is a long-standing characteristic of economic and political life in China.[107] To use *guanxi* is to tap into pre-existing networks of personal loyalties, networks that may cut across formal organizational lines. *Guanxi* is an exchange relationship, rather than a coercive or hierarchical one; whether in the long term or short term, or whether broadly or narrowly, each side expects to gain from the interaction. When the use of *guanxi* involves bypassing official channels in favor of informal contacts, someone is said to have gone "through the back door." Although such "backdoorism" frequently has been the subject of official attack, it was not considered by the reformers during most of the decade to be a serious form of corruption. Despite the economic reforms, the continued salience of the plan and materials shortages meant that the importance of *guanxi* was not eliminated; rather, it remained vital to the smooth operation of joint ventures. The importance of *guanxi* was acknowledged in one foreign manager's statement that joint ventures could expect help from the local bureaucracy because "we're their showpiece, their pride and joy."[108] Or, in the unambiguous declaration of a Chinese joint venture manager, "*guanxi* is very important."[109]

Because of the joint venture's need for resources to which the bureaucracy had access, then, Chinese partners actively tried to cultivate ties of *guanxi* with important persons in relevant bureaucracies. They did this, first, through assigning key positions in the joint venture to people who simultaneously (or previously) held positions of influence in the bureaucracy or the party.[110] Those people with dual positions, or who formerly held bureaucratic posts, were used frequently by the Chinese partner during negotiations for joint ventures to guarantee that the various approving agencies would sign off. Similarly, joint ventures gained tremendous advantage by having Chinese board members who were also in the DIC, particularly when the venture proposed something unorthodox; a board chair who sat on the DIC or in the municipal government could actively lobby for the venture's position among his or her colleagues. In a Shanghai venture, for example, the board chair from a national industrial bureau, a general manager from the local branch of the same bureau, and a board member from the municipal government all used their ties to other agencies to solve many problems. A similar role was played in other joint ventures when one of the Chinese investors, and hence a board representative, was from CITIC. Wealthy overseas Chinese investors often were able to use their notoriety, their new status as "friend of socialist China," and their familial and personal ties from the past, to the advantage of the venture.[111]

Ventures also utilized less formal ties of Chinese board members or managers, and sometimes even of foreign partners. This type of connection was seen most often in the use by some joint ventures of their ties to mayoral offices to call off hostile or meddlesome bureaucrats. As noted previously, these relationships were cultivated in part by entertaining key officials. But the support of such offices did not always need to be cultivated actively; the success of joint ventures was usually sufficiently important to the prestige of the locality or bureaucracy, to its access to resources, or to its ability to show results from the reform policies, that local officials had strong incentives to come to the aid of joint ventures. Indicating how vital these relationships were, every one of the joint ventures sampled for which information was available drew on one or both types of ties.[112]

Although *guanxi* involved state actors in the affairs of the joint venture, it did not necessarily ensure that the interests of the central party elite were carried out. Because *guanxi* was an exchange relationship in which those in the bureaucracy who formally oversaw the joint venture could also become increasingly indebted to, and identified with, the interests of the foreign sector, the interests of bureaucratic authorities in individual localities or departments easily could come to differ with those of the central government, particularly in central efforts to constrain investors. (In this way the roles of localism, bureaucratism, and *guanxi* overlapped.) Ties of *guanxi* could only enhance the incentive of local authorities to help rather than hinder joint ventures. Thus, as suggested by the recognition of Chinese and foreign managers of the importance of *guanxi* to the success of joint ventures, the persistence of *guanxi* competed with the bureaucracy's ability to function as a mechanism to control foreign investment.

Thus, bureaucratic controls were less effective than reformers assumed in their original rationale. In part this was because the reformers themselves over time came increasingly to try to reduce (though not remove) the influence of economic bureaucracies as they moved China toward a mixed economy, and as they recognized the disincentive effect of bureaucratic interference on foreign investors. But as important was the fact that the post-Mao reformers could not eradicate long-standing behaviors of

China's bureaucracy that served to hinder the implementation of central policy. At its strongest, the economic bureaucracy added to the center's arsenal of controls. At its worst, the bureaucracy actively contravened the capacity of reformers to regulate the terms of foreign investment.

Conclusion: Enterprise-Level Controls

As at the national and regional levels, at the enterprise level the leadership followed through in the early years on its original commitment to establish extensive controls over foreign investment. It instituted mechanisms to ensure that foreign managers did not unilaterally control enterprise decisionmaking, and that well-established socialist channels of control over the economy were applied to foreign capital. In addition to the formal sharing of power that was inherent in the joint venture format itself, the government established an authority structure designed to guarantee Chinese managers a voice in joint venture management and to uphold the traditional value of consensual decisionmaking. They positioned the state—via the government economic bureaucracy and, in many ventures, labor organizations and the party secretary—to maintain channels into joint ventures. By keeping labor and welfare issues under the purview of Chinese managers, and retaining with joint ventures the responsibility to provide social welfare functions, the government tried to foster key elements of socialism. Some of these controls remained strong throughout the decade, particularly Chinese control over social welfare matters. Moreover, although substantially weakened, the potential for enhanced state control via the LO, party, and economic bureaucracy remained.

But problems underlay the quest to avoid foreign dominance and promote effective Chinese learning within joint ventures. Mimicking the troubles that appeared at the national and regional levels were problems in implementation and liberalization of controls. In part, difficulties in implementation grew out of a difficult policy. In addition to an almost inevitable tension between encouraging Chinese learning and equality, implementation of these goals was made even more difficult by an environment that emphasized quick economic success of the venture, and thereby provided strong incentives for the foreign partner to run the venture. The difficulty of combining formal equality with a learning environment, then, led in many ventures to a devolution toward foreign domination of key decisions. Similar incentives to focus on production, as well as foreign pressures, led to the uneven implementation of party and LO controls. Controls that were to be exercised by the bureaucracy were compromised by, in some instances, the ability of bureaucratic actors—often at the local level—to act in their own interests, interests that sometimes coincided with those of joint ventures but conflicted with central policy. And, as at the national and regional levels, the use of traditional, preceptoral controls to inoculate Chinese workers within joint ventures was paid little heed.

Both internal and external factors led to liberalization of some of the controls. The reformers believed that they must reduce bureaucratic interference if they were to relieve foreign complaints about "red tape." Even more, trends in the overall reform policy, especially after 1984, toward using profitability as a central criterion for enterprise success, greater decisionmaking autonomy for state enterprises, and greater emphasis on management by experts rather than management by party committee, all undermined the traditional authority of the state bureaucracy and party within joint ventures. By the end of the decade, the reformers had come to believe that extensive foreign control of joint ventures was necessary to successful production. By allowing those with more managerial experience to respond to domestic and especially international market signals, joint ventures were more likely to grow and profit. But the trade-offs clearly compromised several of the key values that had been espoused by the reformers when they originally formulated the "open" policy.

## Chapter Six

CONCLUSION: THE CONTROL
OF FOREIGN DIRECT INVESTMENT
UNDER SOCIALISM

AFTER A DECADE in effect, the results of China's efforts to simultaneously absorb and control foreign direct investment proved to be highly complex. And yet several patterns in how the policy was set and how it evolved over time have become evident. These patterns, albeit uniquely Chinese in some important ways, have arisen from an interplay of forces that can be found generally in other socialist states that attempt the dual strategy of control and absorption of foreign investment. This concluding chapter explores the patterns that have emerged from the foregoing examination of national, regional, and enterprise controls in China. It also assesses the lessons China's experience holds for other socialist countries, and the degree to which socialism has in fact allowed China—and can allow other socialist countries—to absorb and control foreign investment effectively.

THE COMPLEX INTERPLAY OF FORCES

Chapter 1 outlined a framework for understanding the establishment and evolution of China's policy toward foreign investment in the 1979–1988 period. It identified the four factors that were positioned to strongly influence the policy: the bargaining capacities of the Chinese state vis-à-vis foreign investors, domestic politics, the domestic economy, and the goals and motivations of foreign investors. Indeed, all four factors did in fact influence the foreign investment policy throughout the decade. The first factor, the bargaining strengths and weaknesses of the Chinese state and foreign investors, highlights the relative capabilities each side brought to the process of negotiation over the terms of investment. Hence, examination of the Chinese state's monopoly over foreign currency, for example, helped explain China's significant ability to control the foreign exchange activities of joint ventures, while understanding the capacity of potential foreign investors to withhold capital helped explain why the Chinese government was subject to foreign pressure to modify its controls.

The second and third elements of the framework constitute the two domestic factors influencing the investment process: domestic politics and the domestic economy. Analysis of Chinese politics, the most complex factor, brings to light the ways in which the beliefs of reformers and conservatives and the dynamic between them were crucial for the formulation of the "open" policy. Long-standing characteristics of Chinese political and ideological life were important. Deeply rooted concerns that extensive contact with the outside world could be harmful to China led to the agreement of both conservatives and reformers that any effort to attract foreign investment must be accompanied by controls across a wide range of issues. This belief, particularly insofar as it continued to be held by reformers, remained a central influence throughout the period, even as other changes occurred. Many of the statist tools that had been used in socialist China were to be used as mechanisms of control over foreign capital and its influences, particularly extensive regulation by the economic bureaucracy and use of preceptoral controls. Long-standing modes of political behavior—localism, bureaucratism, and *guanxi*—were also evident in the implementation of the joint venture policy. The traditional tendency for localism during periods of decentralization, for example, helped explain the failure of the Special Economic Zones to become effective windows for high-technology and export-oriented investment. But changes that occurred in post-Mao politics also were important, for they also shaped the evolution of the policy over time. Although the desire to control investment was not negated, it came to compete even more with the reformers' growing commitment to the benefits of investment. The changing relationship between reformers and conservatives—the weakening of conservatives as an opposition force in the realm of foreign economic policy—reduced the political risks reformers faced as they remolded the policy. Policy reforms in other realms, particularly efforts to decentralize or otherwise weaken the state's economic controls (such as the state plan and the party) rendered less effective those tools upon which the "open" policy originally relied.

The influence of the structure of China's economy was, in contrast, fairly constant throughout the decade. Large numbers of foreign-backed enterprises faced great difficulty trying to produce efficiently and provide goods for export. Deep-seeded economic structures also limited the ability of the government to improve the investment environment in the short term. The importance of China's economic structure was evident in the government's difficulty in enforcing requirements for domestic content, for example. What did change over the decade with regard to the problematic economic structure was the degree to which foreign investors recognized the difficulties; increasingly, foreign investors became much less sanguine about their ability to successfully wrestle with China's underdeveloped economy than they had been in the early years.

Finally, examination of the fourth factor, the goals and motivations of foreign investors, brings into focus those issues over which conflicts between foreign investors and the Chinese government, and hence foreign pressure to liberalize, were most intense. The importance of differences in Chinese and foreign goals was especially crucial for understanding the deep conflict between the efforts of foreign investors to gain access to the Chinese market and the Chinese desire to promote exports and maintain a foreign exchange balance.

However, understanding the influence of any one factor on any particular part of the policy was seldom sufficient. Rather, a full explanation of the "open" policy requires an understanding of the complex interplay of the various forces. The example of foreign exchange controls illustrates this complexity. Despite the strength of the SAEC monopoly throughout the 1980s, foreign exchange was identified as a major problem for investors, for it in effect required joint ventures to export their products. Foreign dissatisfaction over the fact that this requirement hindered their central goal, in addition to the operational difficulty of obtaining a balance (as illustrated by the case of the AMC jeep venture) led foreign investors to press hard for modifications in the foreign exchange regulatory regime. Although the economic environment, particularly nonconvertibility of the *renminbi*, limited the range of the government's plausible solutions (an immediate move toward convertibility itself not being a plausible solution), the growing desire of reformers to improve the investment environment committed them to finding some solutions that would move toward satisfying both sides. The evolution of joint venture foreign exchange regulations, then, cannot be understood without examining aspects of China's bargaining strengths, the goals of investors, the economic environment, and changes in domestic politics. Similarly, several factors came together to influence controls to prevent foreign domination of joint venture management. Pressure on Chinese joint venture managers from reformers to produce quick results, a lack of suitably trained Chinese managers, and the belief of many foreign managers that they needed to take a leading role, hindered the reformers' effort to promote Chinese managerial equality and the training of Chinese managers. Thus, a simple explanation of the policy can lead only to an incomplete explanation.

THREE THEMES

What, then, has been the result of this complex interplay of forces? Although the results of this interplay varied with each specific control, three broad themes emerge. First, China's government effectively established and maintained controls over foreign investment on a number of important concerns. Second, although in some cases the government was able to set up controls, often the controls were not well implemented. Third, despite the fact that the government maintained strong controls in some areas, there was a liberalization in the overall policy to control the terms of foreign investment over the course of the 1980s; the liberalization was uneven, and often careful and hesitant, but it was undeniable. This section elaborates these three themes.

The Government's Effectiveness at
Establishing and Maintaining Controls

Review of the foreign investment policy at the national, regional, and enterprise levels illustrates the expansive and diverse range of controls the government was able to establish; even considering the problems in the policy, there was significant range and depth of controls. The government was effective at establishing controls according to several measures.

At the initiation of the "open" policy, the government established a number of higher level mechanisms that gave the Chinese state ultimate control over the overall shape of the investment policy. They established that Chinese law would govern nearly all aspects of foreign investment, and set up the procedures to be followed for approval of joint ventures and the resolution of disputes. They established principles to which foreign investment was to adhere. While it is true that the principles were in fact interpreted flexibly, the content of many laws relaxed, and approval procedures decentralized, it is also true that these control mechanisms remained available to the Chinese government to utilize in their stronger forms, or to reactivate, if they so desired. Even the state plan and socialist organizational tools (the labor organization, the party, and the economic bureaucracy), despite the fact that their roles were greatly reduced during the 1980s, nonetheless were not completely dismantled by the reformers. They continued to exist as latent powers retained by the Chinese state. Moreover, although the tightening of these controls would have costs, for it would re-impose disincentives to foreign investors, if the government decided that it needed to use these controls to their fullest potential, the controls were still available. For example, the central government showed its capacity to resurrect latent powers when it recentralized controls over the sectoral distribution of ventures at the beginning of the third phase. That the Chinese state did not forfeit its ultimate sovereign authority to regulate foreign investment or to approve what ventures would be established was an important attribute of the foreign investment strategy.

The government also was effective at implementing a number of specific controls at the national level. It was especially effective at imposing financial controls, that is, controls over foreign exchange and the related issue of profit repatriation. The effectiveness of financial regulations was due largely to the fact that a central bureaucratic organization was in place when the foreign investment policy was initiated, and it had an effective monopoly over all foreign currency transactions. Even when the reformers loosened the restraints on foreign exchange, this organizational strength allowed them to do so in a controlled fashion and without the problems they encountered with the decentralization of controls in other areas. Chinese negotiators also frequently were effective at negotiating favorable terms for joint ventures on a case-by-case basis. The venture for which the Chinese partner gained access to all research and development information formulated in the transnational's home office for the twenty-year life of the venture was one case in point. The ability to achieve contractual promises for high levels of exports, and to retain control over social welfare matters, were other areas where controls were often effective on a case-by-case basis.

The fact that for many controls the government did achieve some of its desired results reflected the ability of Chinese negotiators to bring into play China's bargaining strengths. It also reflected that the reformers continued throughout the decade to see the basic goal of maintaining control over foreign investment as very important. Yet, in tandem with a recognition of the effectiveness of certain government controls, the fact that the reformers encountered substantial difficulties in carrying out the full panoply of controls and at the same time absorbing foreign capital at the levels they desired cannot be ignored. Problems in implementing the reforms and the gradual liberalization of controls therefore also emerged as important themes.[1]

Problems in Implementation

The strategy to simultaneously absorb and control foreign capital was not carried out without encountering a number of the difficulties typical of policy implementation in China, as introduced in chapter 1. At the most basic level, some of the specific tools the government intended to use to control the negative effects of foreign investment were simply ineffective in the post-Mao environment. This problem was most clearly evident in the effort to use traditional preceptoral methods to inoculate citizens against unhealthy tendencies the government associated with foreign investment—the major issue of the "open" policy on which conservatives continued to voice far-reaching opposition. Both because reformers were under pressure from conservatives to respond to the problem and because many of them were genuinely concerned about the "decadence" brought in from outside, they responded with traditional controls. Yet the overall reformist program at the same time was committed to other tenets that undermined preceptoral methods: it de-emphasized the injection of politics in the workplace and more generally discredited the Maoist style of campaign politics, of which political study had traditionally been a part (albeit a more moderate part). There was therefore some tension between the use of political study and media exhortation to guard against unhealthy tendencies and other reforms that called for a de-emphasis on more extreme preceptoral methods long associated with the milder forms. Moreover, following the Cultural Revolution it was clear that the populace also had become increasingly immune to the inoculation strategy itself and, as suggested by the desire of many Chinese joint venture managers to avoid political study, became more inclined to resist it. In contrast with the growing penchant for innovation they showed with certain economic policies such as foreign exchange, reformers failed to devise innovative means to check the problem of unhealthy tendencies.

As the case of preceptoral controls suggests, another major problem was that the strategy to absorb and control foreign capital contained many contradictory goals, and that those responsible for implementing the policy pursued some goals while ignoring others. This was especially evident in the behavior of Chinese joint venture managers and the departments in charge in the first and second phases of the policy. On the one hand, these managers were pressured, through exhortations and through the establishment of shadow management structures, to play an equal role with foreign managers and to learn from foreign managers only the appropriate skills. They also were aware, in the early years, that the party and LOs were to be maintained as important channels of Chinese authority. On the other hand, however, these same managers knew that they must show quick results from the foreign investment policy, results that they believed could be obtained most readily by acquiescing to foreign managerial control over production matters and by reduced party interference. Similarly, local officials were pressed to show rapid results at the same time that they were to monitor foreign investment and adhere to centrally dictated controls that hindered these economic results. Local officials also had a strong interest in showing quick results, for profitable projects would bring tax revenues and prestige to the municipality. Thus, the performance of both Chinese managers and local officials was measured more in terms of growth in profits and productivity (for managers) and the aggregate local inflow of capital (for local officials) than in terms of their effectiveness at meeting the original concerns. Performance indicators that measured learning of foreign skills or effectiveness at applying such skills to Chinese conditions were not for the most part used. Hence, those implementing the controls had much reason to pursue economic results at the expense of Chinese learning and other controls. They transformed their functions from overseeing joint ventures in order to guard against concerns to facilitating the operation of those ventures.

Another problem was that the tendency toward foreign managerial control of many joint ventures apparently was not identified by central agencies that might monitor such trends. Even in the early years, before the reformers stepped up efforts to guarantee autonomy for joint ventures and foster foreign management, a significant portion of the offices responsible for monitoring joint ventures either were too implicated in the need to have joint ventures succeed economically, or were not properly prepared to monitor joint venture management. The spotty activity, and even nonexistence, of labor organizations and party cells in joint ventures set up in the first half of the decade suggested how weak the monitoring, even by the party, could be. This was in sharp contrast to the effectiveness of foreign exchange and banking bureaucracies at monitoring in these areas.

The difficulty of ensuring that the policy was implemented well was compounded by the tendency for localism in Chinese politics. Localism may occur when policies are centrally designed and monitored, but it can increase under periods of decentralization. This was the case, for example, when during the mid-1980s localities and SEZs were granted authority to approve joint ventures worth under $10 million (or in some cases $30 million). Local officials approved ventures that were redundant of existing projects elsewhere. They also approved large hotel and real estate ventures, projects that bolstered the appearance that localities were obtaining quick results, but did not attract much investment involving advanced technology. This latter problem was especially evident in the SEZs. The center's goal of turning SEZs into export platforms and, through the *neilian* policy, of encouraging linkages between inland enterprises and the outside world, was undermined by local preferences to engage in the more profitable activity of selling imported goods inland. Although the central government was able to correct for some of these distortions by recentralizing control, the basic problem of localism would remain when the next decentralization effort was introduced.

Another traditional element of Chinese bureaucratic behavior, *guanxi*, also hindered effective central control. *Guanxi*, characterized by extensive personal networks that generally are not coterminous with official authority channels, undermined these official channels of control insofar as they provided ways for certain ventures to receive special treatment that greatly facilitated, or even was necessary to, successful operations. While ties of *guanxi* undoubtedly helped the economic performance of joint ventures, they competed with official bureaucratic channels.

Other control mechanisms were not implemented effectively because they required actions that could not be accommodated under the conditions of the Chinese economy. Although Chinese negotiators often obtained contracts stating that goods produced by joint ventures would be made up of as much as 80% of domestically produced inputs, the fulfillment of these quotas was hampered by the poor quality of domestic materials, especially for ventures that tried to export. Similarly, contractual obligations to export a percentage of goods were for many ventures impossible to fulfill because of the poor quality of the goods produced.

A final difficulty in effectively implementing the policy arose from foreign pressure on Chinese officials and managers to ignore controls. Such pressure occurred within the confines of negotiations for joint ventures, resulting in contracts that did not always fully adhere to the formally established controls. But because these contracts were approved by the central or local MOFERT offices, the government had final responsibility to disallow contracts that contradicted national policy. This was true, for example, of joint venture or technology transfer contracts that, contrary to law, allowed tie-in clauses for foreign technology, or breached formal limits on the duration of technology transfer agreements. Foreign pressure or resistance also thwarted implementation of contracts once a joint venture was operational, as when foreign managers strongly resisted the activities of labor or party organizations. It is important to note, however, that direct pressure by foreign partners or foreign managers was less often a cause of ineffective implementation of control policies than were problems internal to China—difficulties posed by choice of poor control mechanisms, conflicting goals, localism, and the economic structure. It is not so surprising that the government encountered problems in its own efforts to implement the policy; what would be surprising would be if a policy designed to simultaneously absorb and control foreign investment, and operating in the complex and rapidly changing policy environment found in China in the 1980s, did not stumble in significant ways in the process of implementation.

The Liberalization of Controls during the 1980s

The third major trend evident in China's effort to absorb and control foreign investment was a broad liberalization of controls over time. Two types of liberalization occurred: that which was a by-product of the broader post-Mao economic reforms, and that which was related to—grew out of considerations arising specifically from—the foreign investment policy itself.

LIBERALIZATION AS A BY-PRODUCT OF
ONGOING REFORMS OF THE DOMESTIC ECONOMY

Liberalization in controls that occurred as a by-product of broader reforms being carried out in the post-Mao era appeared primarily in the second phase of the joint venture policy as an outgrowth of the major urban reforms in the domestic economy that were introduced on a broad scale in October 1984. The effort of the urban reforms to separate the roles of party cells and economic managers within enterprises (*zheng-qi fenkai*), and to weaken the role of the former, meant that in addition to the other problems in bringing to bear the authority of the party, the reformers themselves were undermining this potentially very important control. The attempt of the reforms to decentralize planning to local levels, to increase enterprise autonomy from state planning, to increase enterprise responsibility for profits and losses, and generally to reduce bureaucratic interference, all weakened the authority of economic bureaucracies over joint ventures.

Similar to the problems in implementation, the liberalizations in controls over foreign investment that filtered through from broader domestic reforms were results of decisions made by the Chinese government itself; they were not responses to foreign pressures to improve the investment environment. Indeed, this liberalization could not be heralded completely by joint ventures, for while the reform tried to eliminate "red tape," it also quickly became apparent that freeing joint ventures from bureaucratic constraints removed them from the security and predictability formerly provided by their incorporation into the state plan and by their closer relationships with bureaucracies. This was particularly true with regard to procurement and marketing. From an operational standpoint, then, this liberalization was a two-edged sword for joint ventures.

The spillover effect of the urban reforms on the foreign investment policy also illuminates the interrelationship between the foreign and domestic sectors of the economy. It was clear that the foreign investment policy did not operate in isolation from the rest of the economy, and that the original foreign investment controls could be influenced by other policies simultaneously being promoted by the reformers in the domestic economy. That it is difficult to envision that China's "open" policy would have remained viable, politically or economically, in the absence of the simultaneous reforms in the domestic economy, moreover, suggests that from the beginning of the policy it was highly probable that the mechanisms of socialism upon which the government depended to control foreign investment would be eroded over time.

LIBERALIZATION ARISING FROM THE FOREIGN INVESTMENT POLICY

The groundwork for those aspects of the liberalization that grew specifically from the dynamics of the foreign investment policy had been prepared during the earliest years of the policy in the very ideological rationale for foreign investment. The leadership's justification, while couched in confidence that China's socialist state could maintain extensive controls, accepted that some bargaining over the terms of investment would be necessary, and recognized that China would have to accept less than complete control. The broadening of the definitions of self-reliance and independence to encompass a significant, though imprecisely defined, degree of engagement in the international economy, moreover, indicated that the reformers viewed these core values as somewhat flexible. The earliest formulation of the joint venture policy evidenced this flexibility and acceptance of the need for trade-offs in the formal protection of the rights and interests of foreign businesses operating in China, and the right to a greater degree of autonomy for joint ventures than was allowed state enterprises.

There was no indication in the early rationale that the reformers perceived the degree to which they would eventually loosen controls, however. And they did loosen them to a significant degree; after establishing a generally strict web of controls in the first phase of the policy (1979 to mid-1983) and to some degree at the beginning of the second phase (late 1983 to mid-1986), liberalization became a major trend over much of the second phase and particularly in the third phase (late 1986 through 1988). The liberalization did not occur across the board, and where it did occur it was not even across all areas of control; in some areas it was moderate, while in others it was extensive. Nonetheless, the general trend was evident.

Hence, although the 1983 Implementing Regulations in many ways clarified the regulatory environment, they contained the seeds of liberalization in several areas. For example, these regulations allowed joint ventures that produced urgently needed products or import substitution products to sell primarily on the domestic market and, in conjunction with specific regulations on foreign exchange, authorized either payment by domestic firms in foreign exchange or state aid to joint ventures to correct a foreign currency account imbalance that resulted from domestic sales for *renminbi*. The impact of these changes was moderate, for there were major obstacles to making these concessions work, the benefits were limited to a narrow spectrum of highly valued joint ventures, and the overall control regime for foreign exchange remained strong. Yet they provided some concrete aid and were important symbols of the willingness of reformers to trade off the strong desire for exports in order to attract certain types of projects. Very late in the second phase (February 1986), the reformers made additional, though still relatively moderate, concessions that strengthened the commitment to convert *renminbi* earnings of special import substitution ventures to foreign currency. The reformers took an even more dramatic step in the area of technology transfer during the second phase by promulgating a new patent law that sanctioned the protection of foreign intellectual property. In doing so they traded off the goal of unfettered and potentially (though never previously attained) rapid dissemination of foreign technology within China in an effort to overcome foreign hesitancy to transfer the technology in the first place.

The 1986 Provisions that initiated the third phase also brought liberalizations. Some of these applied to all ventures. In the area of foreign exchange, the reformers allowed swaps of *renminbi* and foreign currency among joint ventures (and sometimes domestic enterprises). Contracts for all types of joint ventures could be for longer durations. Most dramatically, reformers called for foreign managers to run joint ventures unilaterally. Extensive liberalizations were also applied to TAE and EOE ventures. These enterprises were given extensive infrastructure supports and preference in obtaining shortage materials, particularly energy. Such supports were significant given the difficulty of operating without them under ordinary circumstances. TAEs and EOEs were also granted additional incentives, such as lower taxes and land use fees, and freedom from the obligation to pay certain social welfare subsidies.

In an important sense, factors external to China fostered these liberalizations; overall, they reflected the pressure brought to bear by foreign investors, individually and in the aggregate, directly and indirectly. Foreign investors readily perceived that the extensive original controls created operational problems across a host of issues, ranging from bureaucratic interference to problems in profit repatriation. Controls also hindered foreign investors from achieving their primary goals. For Westerners and Japanese, the emphasis on exports and foreign exchange problems prevented them from establishing themselves in the domestic market. (Japanese manufacturing companies found that they were able to gain access to the domestic market from sales from Japan, and that, for the time being anyway, they did not need to depend on direct investment; hence, the relatively low number of manufacturing projects among Japanese joint ventures.) Dissatisfaction by Western investors in particular was expressed strongly and frequently, and particularly at the end of the second phase, as in the AMC jeep venture case, and the mid-1986 memo to Chinese leaders from the U.S. embassy in Beijing protesting the strict investment environment. Hong Kong investors, who disproportionately invested in labor-intensive operations in Guangdong and Fujian, found that although they were able to meet their goal of transferring production to lower wage areas, they complained that they were assessed numerous fees and indiscriminate taxes on wages and materials. Foreign investors also reacted to the broader economic environment they encountered once their operations were established. Excitement about the huge market was strongly tempered by the realization that China's economy presented serious obstacles, for example, to procuring inputs of sufficient quality and quantity, and operating at a reasonable level of productivity.

Direct pressure from foreign investors was not the only factor fostering liberalization, however, for reformers themselves actively pursued ways—primarily through legislation—to improve the investment environment. In choosing to liberalize controls on investment, reformers of course were reacting to foreign concerns about the investment environment, and to the ability of potential investors to withhold investment. But to understand the liberalization fully it has been necessary to examine closely the dynamics of domestic politics that made liberalization possible and, for the reformers, desirable. As noted previously, that conservatives, who had originally exhibited a much greater wariness of foreign investment, became less significant in formulating foreign investment policy and apparently less opposed to the policy after the first phase meant that one important impetus for controls was greatly eroded. In this changed political context, evolution in the views of reformers toward liberalization was less dangerous, politically. As reformers themselves became more aware of how much of a disincentive were controls posed as originally envisioned, their views did in fact evolve. They also recognized China's poorly developed economy to be an additional disincentive, despite the lure of the domestic market. And they became increasingly convinced of the benefits of direct investment, and wanted to obtain those benefits at a level much higher than that at which the benefits were flowing in during the mid-1980s. Consequently, their statements about the foreign investment policy during the second and third phases emphasized the need for increasing investment rather than for controls. Although they did not abandon the desire for many of the original controls, they did become more willing to trade off controls when they perceived that benefits would accrue. These convictions were bolstered by the fact that great disasters had not befallen China as a result of the "open" policy.

Several generalizations can be made about the nature of those liberalizations that arose specifically from the foreign investment policy. First, *liberalization occurred where reformers believed it would enhance their ability to obtain those benefits they had come to value most highly.* Beyond this simple pattern, however, lay more complex dynamics. Although the reformers wanted the benefits that would result from liberalization, they did not renounce wholesale, or for each case, the desire to meet the original concerns. Rather, when reformers desired both the benefits from liberalization and some degree of control, the result was very cautious liberalization, tailored carefully to meet both goals. This pattern was evident with two major controls. In the area of foreign exchange, most of the liberalization—and any that implied subsidies by the state—was tailored primarily to TAEs and import substitution ventures, two of the most valued types of foreign investment. The reformers did less for joint ventures that did not provide advanced technology or an import substitution function. The swap system they established for all ventures, while helpful, would continue to ensure the goal of a net hard currency balance for the whole joint venture sector. Careful liberalization was also evident in the encouragement of TAEs and EOEs in the 1986 Provisions; rather than loosening controls over technology transfer and exports per se, the regulations offered greater positive incentives, such as tax cuts, to induce the behavior reformers wanted in the valued areas. Alternatively, they loosened controls for the favored enterprises in other realms (such as, for TAEs, in foreign exchange and domestic sales).

The differential liberalization, and targeting of areas for liberalization to achieve certain ends, suggested that reformers were learning about more effective means to achieving their goals. It also suggested that priorities were emerging from among the goals. By making explicit priorities among their concerns, and becoming more willing to make trade-offs on issues of lesser priority, reformers were able to strengthen regulations in areas about which they were most concerned. The reformers clearly had gained a more sophisticated understanding that, whereas a *blitzkrieg* of regulations may not be sustainable, they could pick and choose a more limited number of areas in which to maintain controls. In the area of foreign investment policy, then, the leadership was overcoming the dominance of the "thumbs, no fingers" approach to policy implementation.[2] Thus, export capability, acquisition of technology, and—given the difficulties that continued to be posed by foreign exchange regulations— protection of foreign exchange reserves all emerged as high priorities. Chinese managerial equality or dominance and, given the willingness to pursue the "open" policy despite the inability to control unhealthy tendencies, the building of a "socialist spiritual civilization" emerged lower on the list of priorities.

Liberalization in cases where the reformers believed it would bring desired benefits did not only occur when foreign pressures were strong or where they were trying to induce certain behavior from foreign investors; it also occurred occasionally where reformers themselves, without direct pressure from foreign investors, came to question the very utility of the original controls. Reformers at the center became more convinced that foreign methods of personnel management, particularly enterprise autonomy to hire and fire workers and to institute complicated wage and bonus incentive systems, were beneficial, and relaxed somewhat the effort to maintain personnel policy as a realm controlled strictly by Chinese managers. (Such changes were still frequently resisted by local labor bureaus and personnel managers, however.) The decisions to encourage foreign majority ownership in the second phase and to allow foreign managers unilaterally to run joint ventures in the third phase also resulted from changes in the beliefs of reformers that economic success could be attained more easily in this manner, rather than as a result of strong foreign demands. (Although foreign managers often felt they could run joint ventures better and acceded to this change, the new policy was in fact inconsistent with the goal of reducing their expensive managerial presence.) These cases of dramatic liberalization in the absence of foreign pressure are further evidence that the reformers themselves had come to place a somewhat lower priority on a number of the original controls.

Two additional generalizations concern where liberalization did not occur. *Liberalization did not occur where reformers continued to value controls and at the same time where liberalization would be of little help in enhancing their priority goals.* In some cases, few benefits of liberalization would result because foreigners simply did not object significantly to the controls. For example, reformers did not abandon use of preceptoral controls—a control for which lack of serious foreign concern was striking. (The maintenance of these controls did not, of course, guarantee their effectiveness.) Similarly, reformers did not significantly lessen the requirement that joint ventures provide social welfare benefits required of state enterprises. The lack of foreign pressure on this matter, and the fact that there was strong pressure from conservatives and workers to retain these benefits in *state* enterprises, both discouraged liberalization. Yet even where there were foreign complaints, reformers also sometimes avoided or only partially weakened controls if such liberalization conflicted with major goals. Reformers did not loosen significantly the requirements to export or maintain foreign exchange balances for ventures that did not incorporate significant technology, despite foreign complaints. They made it easier for low-technology ventures to achieve foreign currency balances through swaps, but denied them the opportunity provided TAEs to convert *renminbi* earned domestically, an opportunity that, unlike swaps, required the state to sacrifice portions of its own foreign currency reserves. Hence, not all types of joint ventures were beneficiaries of liberalization, and the government did not respond to all foreign complaints. Moreover, as discussed previously, *China's reformers did not forgo ultimate authority to regulate joint ventures or to decide what ventures could enter China.* They did not liberalize significantly the higher level controls that claimed for China the right to regulate and approve joint ventures.

Thus, liberalization did not occur on every issue or, where it did occur, to the same degree. The fact that liberalization did not occur across the board suggests that the reformers had not completely abandoned their original commitment to guarding against perceived problems of foreign investment. Yet that they sometimes made significant liberalizations in the face of this remaining commitment also evidences the growing understanding by reformers of the complicated task of both absorbing and controlling foreign direct investment. Moreover, it is also clear that not one but all four factors identified in chapter 1 played important roles in the liberalization process. Indeed, what emerges clearly from analysis of this process is that to focus *solely* on one factor—and particularly to focus solely on direct pressure for liberalization by foreign investors—is misleading. Although the conflict between Chinese and foreign goals and the pressure from foreign investors that surfaced when their goals were thwarted were extremely important, to focus only on the degree of foreign pressure cannot fully explain the variability in degree of liberalization among different controls, or the care and hesitation with which the reformers approached liberalization on major issues. It is crucial to recognize the role domestic economic and, especially, political factors had in determining liberalization of the policy toward foreign investment.

Could the reformers have avoided the liberalizations? While this counterfactual question is impossible to answer directly, it is possible to make several observations. Had the reformers been contented with the (not insignificant) level of investment flowing into China prior to the major liberalizations, and had they been contented to allow foreign reactions, such as those that precipitated the sharp downturn in the level of investment that occurred in 1986, to continue unaddressed, they presumably could have resisted foreign pressure to loosen controls. Although such a course would have had costs—it would have disillusioned investors further, and perhaps had a spillover effect on the generally positive strategic relationship China had built with the West—it was not implausible. In an important sense, then, the reformers chose to liberalize controls. But it is unlikely that China could have maintained the full complement of original controls and absorbed the level of foreign capital they desired, given the ways that the reformist outlook evolved during the decade. The growing belief that their economic modernization program required them to absorb foreign capital at even greater levels put them on a course whereby they had to pay attention to foreign concerns, and more generally to ways they might be able to improve the investment environment. Under these conditions, the reformers had little choice but to liberalize. There were few indications that (except on issues such as change in the personnel system) liberalization was the preferred course of reformers. There was little indication that without pressure from foreign investors reformers would have liberalized unilaterally. Rather, although they came to believe that eroding certain controls was worth the ability to gain other benefits, the reformers for the most part continued to wish to pursue the strongest set of controls possible and at the same time absorb foreign capital.

. . . .

Thus, three broad patterns are evident in the analysis of China's dual-edged strategy to absorb and control foreign investment over the course of the 1980s: effectiveness at maintaining controls in some areas, liberalization in some areas, and problems of implementation. On the one hand, the strength of the regulations, which constituted the control element of the strategy, was striking. The reformers' attempt to establish and enforce an extensive web of controls indicates that they had not been paying mere lip service to the need for controls. Even at the end of the third phase, the web of controls was strong enough to allow foreign investors to continue to characterize China as a difficult destination for overseas investment. Moreover, even when the reformers were pressed, by external forces or by their own beliefs about the need to improve the investment environment, to liberalize some of the controls, they often did so with hesitation and caution, carefully trading off some less important controls in order to foster the most important values. In none of the liberalizations did the reformers concede their ultimate sources of authority, particularly the requirement that foreign investment adhere to Chinese laws. And though greatly weakened, the organizations that could oversee the establishment and operation of joint ventures remained latent tools of state control.

Yet this assessment of effectiveness must be tempered by recognition of the problems in the dual strategy. The reformers faced difficulties implementing the controls that echoed problems common in the implementation of other economic policies in postrevolutionary China, albeit with the addition of foreign resistance on some fronts. Indeed, reformers might well have anticipated these implementation problems. Reformers clearly did not anticipate the extent of the changes that they eventually would make over the course of the policy, particularly the extent to which they would draw on the flexibility implied in the acceptance of bargaining norms or in the original rationale. But these changes ultimately would become, in the reformers' view, the crucial factor in making their strategy work.

The Future of Foreign Investment in China

What can be expected for China's policy toward foreign investment in the future? Although the precise contours of the policy may well take a number of turns, the understanding of the major factors influencing the policy, and of the dominant trends that appeared in the first decade, make prediction of the overall direction of the policy a less uncertain task than it would be otherwise. The same four factors that influenced the Chinese policy toward foreign direct investment during the 1980s can be expected to remain salient in the near term. Two of these factors are unlikely to undergo dramatic changes during that period. There is no reason to suspect that the norm of bargaining over international investment will be replaced as the framework for interaction between states and foreign investors, particularly in light of the failure of international efforts to establish a New International Economic Order that would change fundamentally the bargaining relationship between industrialized and less developed countries. Moreover, the constraints posed by China's domestic economic structure can be expected to remain relatively constant; although specific economic policies will certainly change and key measures of economic performance will fluctuate, and although improvement can be expected in the long term, problems in China's economic infrastructure, the availability of energy and supplies, worker productivity, international competitiveness, and so on, are too deep and tenacious to expect immediate improvement. Indeed, the process of economic reform itself will in all likelihood continue to generate tremendous dislocations—inflation, unemployment, social unrest—that will themselves harm the investment environment.

The major goals and motivations of Western and Japanese investors can be expected to remain relatively constant in some ways, but perhaps to change in others. Western and Japanese investors can be expected to continue to hold the more realistic view of the China market that developed in the second half of the 1980s, but will retain the goal of gaining access to the China market. They can be expected to continue to invest in China, subject to the same influences they faced in the first decade. The behavior of Hong Kong companies, which accounted for a major portion of foreign investment during the 1980s, could change as reabsorption into the mainland in 1997 draws near, although the direction of that change is uncertain and largely dependent upon the evolution of the Chinese–Hong Kong relationship during the first part of the 1990s. If their businesses prosper in China, if wage rates continue to be competitive, and if the economic reforms proceed with some success, Hong Kong investors may choose to leave their funds in China. Yet political fragility in China such as occurred in the spring of 1989 and serious retrenchment of reform could lead Hong Kong investors gradually to reduce their exposure in China in favor of other investment sites in Asia and the West. This would have a serious negative impact on China's "open" policy, although given the nature of Hong Kong investment, the impact would be more on the volume of capital and export earnings than on the absorption of advanced technology.

Largely because of the expected FDI continuity in the international bargaining norm, in the obstacles posed by China's economic structure, and, to some degree, in the goals and behaviors of foreign investors, two of the major trends identified in the overall policy can be projected into the near future. There is no reason to expect dramatic changes in the Chinese government's *ability* to maintain controls over some areas of foreign investment, or in the willingness to do so. The government will undoubtedly retain the ultimate authority over regulation of foreign investment. It also can be expected to continue to move up the "learning curve" in its understanding of how to achieve its priorities. But, at the same time, many of the problems of *implementing* the controls will almost certainly remain important obstacles to carrying out a fully effective policy of controls. The long-standing problem of local distortion of central policies, and the difficulties posed by problems of the domestic economy, likely will be the most difficult to solve of the implementation problems.

Although in many respects the analysis of the first decade of China's "open" policy can be projected into the future, examination of domestic political factors injects elements of lesser certainty into predictions. China's domestic politics have in the past been characterized by great fluctuation and, at the end of the 1980s, remain so, despite efforts of reformers earlier in the decade to stabilize and routinize domestic politics. The tendency in postrevolutionary China for swings between reformers, conservatives, and "radicals" lends historical weight to the idea that a major shift away from the "open" policy is plausible, as have periodic retrenchments in the overall reform program, incidents of student protests about Japanese investment, and the serious consternation on the part of leaders (especially older leaders) about the threats posed by unhealthy tendencies from outside. The resurgence of more conservative leaders and the retrenchment of a number of the domestic economic reforms following the events at Tiananmen in the spring of 1989 illustrated dramatically that the source of such swings has not been eliminated. Moreover, it is certainly possible that problems in areas not specifically related to the "open" policy— inflation, the social upheaval caused by modernization, or growing intolerance over "bourgeois liberalization"—could spill over into the realm of foreign economic policy and provide an impetus to halt foreign investment. It is also important to recognize that those who were the beneficiaries of more extreme self-reliance, or who have not benefited from the "open" policy, form the seeds of political opposition to the policy. A possible source of opposition is from inland areas, which historically have had less experience with, and currently maintain fewer ties to, the outside world. Also important as potential agents of opposition are cadres associated with those industries, especially heavy industries that flourished under Soviet-style planning, that did not receive injections of foreign capital or technology.[3] Protectionist sentiments against foreign-backed enterprises can be expected to be exacerbated if these enterprises, especially in the consumer goods sector, are allowed increasingly to sell on the domestic market and compete with domestic industries.

Although swings are part of the fabric of Chinese political life, and although sources of potential opposition exist, it also is possible to point with caution to alternative signs that the foreign investment policy will remain in force. There have been no serious attempts to reverse the policy since the CASP in 1983. Those who in the early years were less comfortable, ideologically, with the policy over time appeared to adopt a "wait and see" stance, a stance that likely has been encouraged by the fact that foreign investment has not threatened the central values of independence and sovereignty. Those who have not benefited economically from the policy did not during the first decade mount campaigns for reversal. The actions of the post-Tiananmen leadership also support the idea that the "open" policy can endure substantial political instability within the context of the current terms of debate, and even that conservative leaders have themselves grown somewhat committed to foreign investment. Despite the intensive Campaign Against Bourgeois Liberalization that was mounted in 1989, the more conservative leadership repeatedly and firmly reiterated that China would remain open to the outside world.[4] The choice of Jiang Zemin to replace Zhao Ziyang as party secretary, and the ascension in the Politburo of Li Ruihuan, who in their previous posts as party chief of Shanghai and mayor of Tianjin, respectively, were known to be supporters of foreign investment, also suggested such a commitment. Believing that repression in the political realm need not dictate closing China's doors to the world economy, the post-Tiananmen leadership tried to isolate the "open" policy from political swings. An outright reversal of the "open" policy for political reasons also can be expected to become more remote in the long term, as the policy itself creates its own constituency. As the foreign sector becomes more entrenched and amasses its own resources (including capital, foreign exchange, technology), leaders, government cadres, technicians, and managers involved in carrying out the policy can be expected to have a greater interest in seeing the foreign sector remain strong.

There are also reasons to believe that the cautious, uneven liberalization that occurred in the first decade of the policy will continue toward some point at which China has sufficient control to achieve its ends and investors attain sufficient benefits to warrant their continuing presence. To the extent that the government continues to support the "open" policy, it will feel pressures from both potential and existing investors to provide an environment attractive to investors. The relative consensus of the post-Tiananmen government about the need to attract foreign investment and technology will encourage it to respond to these pressures. How far the liberalization will go, and whether a point of equilibrium between the Chinese government and foreign investors can actually be reached, is difficult to determine prospectively, of course. The prospect of reaching an accommodation is made tenuous, again, by uncertainties in Chinese politics: the point at which in the course of trade-offs conservatives (or a renewed group of "radicals") will blanch; the capability of opponents to intervene; the point at which reformers themselves, in an effort to protect basic concerns, will refuse to make further trade-offs; and whether at the point where the government's will to liberalize might stop, China can absorb satisfactory volumes of foreign capital. Nonetheless, the overall prospect in the near and medium term is for slow, cautious liberalization.

GENERALIZING FROM CHINA'S EXPERIENCE: DOES SOCIALISM MAKE A DIFFERENCE?

A major issue underlying this study has been to discover whether a socialist state can exert sufficient control over the terms of foreign investment to allow it to meet a range of concerns commonly held in developing countries. China's experience has provided a mixed answer: the reformers succeeded in establishing and sometimes in maintaining a web of controls. But they were not as effective at simultaneously maintaining controls and absorbing investment as they, or others who have adopted this strategy, originally envisioned; they encountered major difficulties in implementing the controls and, finding that controls at their original level conflicted with the increasing desire to gain the benefits of foreign investment, gradually liberalized the investment environment. Drawing on China's experience, two broader questions remain to be answered directly: To what extent is China's experience generalizable to other socialist countries embarking on a similar strategy? Have China's socialist characteristics made a difference in how well it has been able to fulfill this strategy?

In addressing the latter question, it must be noted that, to assess fully whether socialist countries are better able than nonsocialist countries to accomplish the goal of both absorbing and controlling foreign investment requires a comparative study that is beyond the scope of this book. Yet it is clear from the present study that China's socialism had some, though not complete, influence over the outcome of its strategy. Socialism clearly was a factor in China's effectiveness at controlling foreign investment. Foreign firms that invested in China encountered a well-developed bureaucracy that at times effectively used its monopoly to control which joint ventures would be allowed and which would be turned away. The effective monopoly in finance also allowed China to maintain extremely stringent control over the foreign currency and profit repatriation transactions of joint ventures. Despite some erosion, that China retained latent, ultimate channels of authority for the economic bureaucracy and party and labor organizations was a function of the entrenched socialist structure as well. Finally, there is no evidence that social forces outside the state—the equivalent to the local bourgeoisie in Nigeria and Mexico—were able during the first decade of the policy to dilute the goals of reformers to control foreign capital, although there was potential for such a group to grow strong in the future.

The extensive controls set forth by the socialist state had a disincentive effect, however. China's socialist economy as it existed in the 1980s was an additional source of serious problems for the effort to attract foreign capital; the lack of horizontal, or market, links between economic units and regions, the relatively low worker productivity, and, where it did not facilitate the operation of joint ventures, the cumbersome planning bureaucracy, were further disincentives for investment. Though the disincentives related to socialism often were no worse than (and sometimes were the same as) the disincentives found in any developing country—poorly developed markets, unskilled labor, and a problematic infrastructure—they did pose an obstacle to achieving the two-edged strategy.

A significant part of China's ability to both absorb and control investment at the level it did during the 1980s is attributable to strengths that were *not* related specifically to socialism. Some of China's control mechanisms, such as the creation of a detailed code of law and the development of procedures to enforce contracts, are universally available in the postcolonial world. China's increasing use of economic levers, such as taxation and other incentives for guiding investment to particular regions or sectors, also are far from specific to socialist regimes. Moreover, in some cases China's effectiveness in applying controls can be attributed to the lack of foreign opposition to them rather than to the strengths of socialism. This was true, for example, of foreign investors' lack of opposition to the requirement that joint ventures provide social welfare provisions. The most important source of China's effectiveness at maintaining controls was completely unrelated to China's socialist strengths: foreign perceptions of its huge domestic market. Indeed, the fact that most investors were willing to tolerate difficult investment conditions and poor access to domestic markets during the 1980s suggests the importance of their belief in the potential for a great payoff, if and when domestic market access could be realized. The need of many transnational corporations to pre-empt their competitors from capturing the China market first was another impetus for investors that was unconnected to China's socialism. The "carrot" of China's domestic market, therefore, undoubtedly was crucial to China's capacities to control foreign investment.

Thus, the answer to whether China's socialist structure made a difference is a mixed one. On the one hand, when assessing China's controls per se, it is clear that elements of socialism did influence foreign investment in China, and the net result of this influence was that China was better able to control the terms of investment. But the role of socialism also must be judged in light of the whole foreign investment strategy; both the control and absorption of foreign investment must be considered. Socialism was not the only factor responsible for the ways in which China was effective at attracting foreign investment, despite controls, for the lure of the domestic market played a crucial role in encouraging investment. Socialism also did not prevent China's difficulties in implementing the policy; as noted, some of these problems were related to socialism. Moreover, socialism did not allow China's reformers to avoid pressures to loosen the controls if they were to be able to attract investment at the level they believed necessary to achieve the Four Modernizations. Hence, although socialism bolstered China's controls, it was not sufficient to enhance—and in its own way hindered—the Chinese state's ability to carry out the goals of both absorbing and controlling foreign investment to the degree Chinese leaders and others who advocate socialism have asserted.

China's experience has important implications for other socialist countries. The Soviet Union, Vietnam, Laos, Tanzania, and even hyperisolationist North Korea during the last half of the 1980s took some steps toward a Chinese-style strategy to absorb and control foreign investment. Yugoslavia, Poland, and Hungary all revamped their foreign investment laws in efforts to attract foreign capital in the late 1980s. Although there are a number of possible points of departure for these countries from the Chinese experience, the Chinese case can guide our understanding of what is likely to happen elsewhere. China's experience is relevant insofar as the factors that influenced the establishment and evolution of China's foreign investment policy during the 1980s all can be expected to play roles in other socialist countries, and often in ways similar to China. Other socialist countries will be able to bring their bargaining strengths to negotiations over the terms of foreign direct investment, including those strengths related to socialism. But just as China has not been able to avoid the international norm for bargaining that gives play to the strengths of foreign investors, other socialist countries will be unable to control the outcome unilaterally. Foreigners investing in other socialist countries will have goals they wish to see fulfilled, often the desire to gain access to a previously closed domestic market. Socialist host states will be faced with the need to respond to those goals if they are to attract investment. Other socialist states therefore can be expected to face pressure to liberalize regulations or suffer the consequences of reduced investment—lower, perhaps, than they are likely to desire. Elements of the Chinese economy that have created a difficult investment environment there are in many ways characteristic of the economies of existing socialist countries, even the more industrialized Soviet Union.

Domestic political factors are perhaps the most variable factor and may be the major cause of differences that appear in the politics of socialist countries.[5] The choice to adapt (or not) to international pressure may carry a different set of risks and opportunities for leaders in different countries. For example, this choice may be easier in a country such as Hungary, where cultural and economic ties to Western Europe are extensive and the politics of international integration less divisive, than for a country such as North Korea, which has relatively few ties to the international economy and where the ideology of Kim Il-sung has long stressed the need for *juche*, or extreme national self-reliance. Reformers in the Soviet Union, as in China, may find it easier to remain confident that an "open" policy does not seriously threaten independence than might the smaller socialist countries of North Korea, Laos, Tanzania, and even Vietnam. The relative strength of reformers, conservatives, and other elite factions in these countries also varies; reformers such as Mikhail Gorbachev in the Soviet Union or Nguyen Van Linh in Vietnam may be less adept at silencing or winning over conservative leaders to the cause of foreign investment than China's reformers were during the 1980s.

Yet, despite important differences in the domestic political dynamics of socialist countries, some common threads run throughout the politics of socialist countries. The development debates that in China shaped the conservative-elite dynamic and the concerns over foreign investment are themselves long-standing debates of socialist development that are repeated in similar form throughout the socialist world. We can therefore anticipate the terms of the internal debate in other socialist countries to be familiar. Similarly, the trend in China during the 1980s toward the dominance of economic policymaking by "reformers" is evident elsewhere; historically, socialist countries have not allowed foreign investment outside of the advent of broader economic reform. The influence on the foreign investment policy that in China resulted from broader domestic reforms can be expected to some degree in other socialist countries embarking on an "open" policy. In China, moreover, the growing commitment of the reformers to increasing the absorption of foreign investment resulted in large part from their assessment of the results of the early years of the "open" policy. Seeing that the early years of the policy brought needed technology and management skills to China instead of economic destruction, they became convinced that the absorption of these benefits should proceed faster, and that controls were hindering absorption. We can expect that the forces that shaped this evolution in the outlook of China's reformers will be repeated in broad strokes elsewhere.

Although the factors that influenced China's "open" policy can help establish a framework for understanding other socialist countries, and can help anticipate the broad outcomes, it is unlikely that other socialist countries following policies identical to China's, with the possible exception of the Soviet Union, will fare even as well as China did during the 1980s. A minor reason is that, although China's relatively good strategic relationship with the West was not a major factor influencing the will or ability of Western companies to invest in China, neither did strategic considerations imposed by home governments present a major obstacle to most Western countries. This was true even after the Tiananmen events, for the restrictions of military sales imposed by many Western governments were relatively minor. Yet other socialist countries may face obstacles related to strategic politics. Although the strategic relationship with the USSR improved rapidly beginning in the 1980s, countries such as Vietnam and North Korea failed to have the degree of improvement in their strategic relationship that China formed with the West in the early 1970s. Nor did they have the advantage of being a "China card" in the U.S. competition with the Soviet Union. For China, this special position resulted in favorable treatment, relative to many other socialist countries, by the U.S. Commerce Department and by the multilateral Coordinating Committee for Multilateral Export Controls (COCOM).[6]

Second, smaller socialist countries such as Vietnam and North Korea, once they undertake a development strategy that calls for engagement with the international economy, will perhaps find it more difficult to limit their exposure to external forces. China and the Soviet Union are continental economies that have shown a relatively strong (albeit flawed) capacity for self-sustained growth and the development of indigenous technologies compared with smaller socialist countries. Moreover, almost any single investment in the large socialist economies will constitute a minor portion of the total investment in that sector, such that it is more difficult for foreign companies to dominate any sector. Smaller countries are more likely to find that use of foreign capital will make them more vulnerable to outside forces than larger countries; it will be difficult for these smaller countries to turn away investors, for the costs will be higher. Any investment of significant size also will tend to constitute a larger proportion of total investment in that sector.

Most socialist countries are in a less favorable position than China to carry out the strategy of simultaneously absorbing and controlling foreign investment for a third, and even more significant, reason: with the possible exception of the Soviet Union, they lack China's powerful lure of a huge domestic market. China's experience has been that the incentive of access to the domestic market was crucial for attracting Western and Japanese investors with the technology China most desires. Although foreign investors in China complained about poor access to the domestic market and pressured the Chinese government for liberalization, the goal of entering the market gave them more reason to tolerate controls than could be expected in a country where the future market prospects are not so compelling. The smaller socialist countries simply do not have this attribute to use as a "carrot" to lure investors. The attributes these smaller countries offer, such as low-wage labor or natural resources, are more likely to be found in other nonsocialist countries. (For example, Malaysia or Thailand provide feasible alternatives for investors seeking alternatives for their low-wage investments in Vietnam or North Korea.) The fact that other countries lack the lure of the domestic market as a strong bargaining chip further places them in a worse bargaining position than China held during the 1980s.

Thus, the outlook for other socialist countries is more pessimistic than for China. No other socialist country is, overall, better positioned than China was during the 1980s to achieve the dual strategy of attracting and controlling foreign direct investment; other socialist countries are unlikely to fare better than the mixed result achieved by China. Any expectations that socialism will be adequate to allow these countries to control substantially the terms of investment while absorbing satisfactory amounts of such investment are unlikely to be met.

Appendix A

METHODOLOGICAL ISSUES

ALTHOUGH THE RESEARCH in this study is applicable in many ways to other forms of foreign direct investment, this study focused on equity joint ventures for three reasons. First, equity ventures were clearly a major format for direct investment in China during the period studied. Second, because they allowed the Chinese government to retain influence through its ownership position, equity joint ventures were the form of foreign investment over which the Chinese state could, arguably, exert the greatest degree of control. As such, China's experience with equity joint ventures provides a good test for the issue of how well a socialist government is able to retain control over the negative effects of foreign capital. Third, because of the relatively large amount of attention that both the Chinese legal system and the Chinese media granted to equity joint ventures, and because these ventures were relatively well established compared to other investment forms, it was much easier to obtain comprehensive information about them.

Two sources of data provided the majority of information for this study: interviews with people directly involved in Chinese-foreign joint ventures; and published materials, including Chinese and foreign press and scholarly articles, and several longer Chinese and foreign studies of foreign investment.

INTERVIEWS

Interviews were the most important source of detailed information about how joint ventures in China actually were set up and operated, particularly during the first half of the 1980s. From August 1984 through March 1985, I conducted a total of eighty-nine interviews on equity joint ventures.[1] The interviews fell into four major groupings. Foreign managers of joint ventures and representatives of the foreign partner made up the first and most numerous group, with forty-six interviews. The second group consisted of seven interviews with Chinese managers in equity joint ventures.[2] Third, I interviewed nine Chinese officials from seven governmental or state-controlled organizations at both the national and local level.[3] The fourth group consisted of twenty-seven interviews with foreign "experts"—bankers, lawyers, consultants, and foreign government officials—

with direct knowledge of joint ventures through their roles as negotiators with, or partners or advisors to, foreign investors.

The interviews took place primarily in China and Hong Kong, except for several with foreign partner representatives that I conducted in the United States. Interviews averaged one hour and fifteen minutes, although in some instances I spent several hours over several separate interviews with one person. Interviews conducted in Chinese were carried out without a translator. In the course of interviews, I asked open-ended questions. Because I used this method rather than a set, closed-ended method, different interviewees did not always answer every question, or answer with the same degrees of thoroughness. This method encouraged the interviewees to pursue issues they considered important, and that I might not otherwise have pursued. Thus, for some issues, I obtained responses for less than the full sample. The questioning generally focused on the major issues discussed throughout the book, for example, foreign exchange controls, domestic sales, "unhealthy tendencies," and management structures.

There were twenty-four equity joint ventures for which interviews yielded full and comparable information. Interviews supplemented by printed sources provided sufficient information on four additional ventures. These twenty-eight cases constitute my sample of firms.[4] In addition to reporting results of interviews from the sample, throughout the analysis I have drawn on results of interviews with foreign experts or with several managers of contractual ventures or wholly foreign-owned enterprises.

The sample of twenty-eight is reasonably representative of the universe of equity joint ventures that existed during the 1980s, although it contains certain biases. The sample consists primarily of a variety of manufacturing concerns, ranging from heavy industry to high-technology instruments to consumer goods. I have included two cases of service ventures and one agricultural venture. Foreign investment in extractive industries is excluded, for investment by foreign oil companies in offshore drilling or mining were primarily in nonequity forms (contractual joint ventures and joint oil development). The sample also covers a variety of national origins. Ten (38%) of the foreign partners in my sample were from the United States and Hong Kong, five (18%) were from Western Europe, one (3.5%) was from Japan, and two (7%) were from Thailand. When compared to the universe, however, the sample under-represents Hong Kong investors and and over-represents American and West European firms (see table 3-M). The bias toward U.S. and European firms resulted from the relative difficulty of gaining information about and permission to interview representatives of Hong Kong companies. Whereas U.S. and European firms were usually willing to disclose information about their joint ventures, the extremely competitive environment of Hong Kong made many of its firms hesitant to discuss their projects in China, or even to identify their investment activities. Japanese firms, to which access was similarly difficult, were represented proportionally in the sample.

The average size of joint ventures in the sample, measured in terms of total capital initially invested by all partners, was about $9 million, approximately two times the size of the average equity joint venture. The larger-than-average size of the ventures sampled reflects the preponderance of U.S. and West European firms. The effect of the sample's bias toward the large U.S. and European investments is difficult to assess. On the one hand, U.S. and European ventures may have been subject to stricter regulations over domestic sales, foreign exchange, and so on, not only because they were "showcases" for advanced management and technology, but also because their larger size meant their potential impact (both positive and negative) was greater. On the other hand, these ventures may have been less subject to certain controls because of the Chinese government's desire to keep the showcase ventures running, and because problems in these ventures more easily drew negative media attention outside China. The latter factor appears to have been more significant.

The primary motivation of many U.S., West European, and Japanese firms for entering joint ventures was to gain eventual access to the Chinese domestic market and to pre-empt competitors, while for Hong Kong firms (and to some degree for Japanese firms) the major motive tended to be to shift the base of manufacturing to a less expensive location. To some extent, the difference in motives could be expected to influence what conflicts were most likely to arise between partners. The sample's focus on larger Western firms tended to highlight concerns about gaining market share, at the expense of concerns over wages and other production costs (although evidence of these latter issues did come to light).

All but three ventures in the sample were located in coastal cities or Beijing, or in Guangdong and Fujian provinces. The sample is therefore representative of the concentration of foreign investment in the more developed eastern cities and coastal areas. The predominance in the sample of non–Hong Kong investors, however, led to some under-representation of joint ventures located in Guangdong and Fujian provinces, including the Special Economic Zones. The sample over-represents joint ventures located in the other coastal areas and Beijing.[5] Because of this, the analysis also highlights the areas with more stringent controls over foreign capital (such as Beijing) and under-represents the more liberal Special Economic Zones. Finally, virtually all ventures in the sample contained 50% foreign equity or less. This is consistent with figures from the broader sample presented in table 3-L.

During the general process of interviewing, I conducted in-depth case studies of two equity joint ventures. These studies turned out to be extremely useful means of making general propositions more concrete. Both of the case studies in industrial cities in northeast China were of ventures with large American companies. Both projects involved the manufacture of products where quality and technology are important. The Chinese hoped that both would export a significant portion of products, although access to domestic markets was the prime motivating factor behind each firm's investment decision. The first venture, located in one of the fourteen "open coastal cities," produced heavy machinery under a twenty-year contract. The initial capital investment paid in by the partners exceeded substantially the 1979–1984 average project size of $3.8 million. The foreign partner was the minority shareholder, and the majority share was split between the former factory and CITIC. At the time of my study, it employed five expatriates (one of whom was the general manager) and several thousand Chinese staff and workers, most of whom had worked in the Chinese partner's previous factory. Although the proceedings for operation had been going on for several years, the venture was not operating at full scale at the time of my visit and had not recorded any profits. The second venture produced consumer products for both domestic and overseas sales, also under a twenty-year contract. It was significantly smaller than the first case, with investment of less than the project average of $3.8 million. The Chinese and foreign partners each contributed 50% of the equity. A formally equal management structure, in which key positions were divided between each side, reflected the equal ownership position. There were four expatriate managers, and about eighty Chinese staff and workers. The number of Chinese workers employed in the venture was significantly less than the over two hundred workers in the existing Chinese factory of the Chinese partner. This venture, which began production in 1983, recorded profits after one year. At the time of study, however, the foreign parent had not repatriated any of the profits.

I spent several days at each venture site interviewing a number of Chinese and foreign managers. In the first case I also interviewed several local political officials who had extensive involvement with and responsibility for the venture. While on site, I also had the opportunity for informal observation of operations and meetings, as well as for conversation with managers outside of a formal interview setting. I also interviewed other managers of the ventures during their visits to Hong Kong, as well as executives of the foreign parent offices who were responsible for setting up the projects.

For all twenty-eight cases in the sample, discussions revealed that each of the four categories of interviewees had different outlooks. I have tried to take these differences into account when drawing conclusions from interview data. With few exceptions, representatives of foreign businesses involved in joint ventures tended to be more optimistic about the prospects for their ventures and about the ability to overcome difficulties posed by the bureaucracy, regulations, personality conflicts, and so on, than did foreign "experts." They did express serious discontent with the investment environment, however. Foreign experts, many of whom had broad exposure to joint ventures, were significantly more pessimistic and even cynical. This is perhaps not surprising, since the "experts" were most often at the forefront of the adversarial and unusually trying negotiation process, and had little immediate financial stake in the actual success or failure of ventures. It is, of course, important to treat statements by foreigners involved in joint ventures with some caution, for interviewees may have some interest in emphasizing some points at the expense of others—either downplaying problems for reasons of privacy, or overplaying problems as a bargaining tool. However, the statements made by foreign investors during interviews can be judged to be representative of their views for two reasons. First, because foreign investors were guaranteed anonymity in interviews, the incentive that might arise in attributed interviews to color their remarks was removed. Second, the comments of foreign investors were consistent with my more independent observations of joint ventures, especially those impressions I formed in the two case studies noted previously.

Although Chinese officials and managers often provided information about various aspects of the joint venture policy not discussed in the Chinese press, their statements were generally consistent with the official line and were, with some exceptions, noncontroversial. The generally optimistic support by Chinese officials and managers for joint ventures reflected their strong stake in the "open" policy and perhaps the fact that they were speaking to a foreigner.

Published Materials

An important source of written information used in the study was books published in China and the Chinese press (both in Chinese and in translation). Books published in China for a Chinese readership were wide-ranging, noncontroversial explanations of various aspects of the "open" policy, and were generally supportive of the policy. Where they delved into theory, they followed the trends set forth in the government's rationale.[6] I surveyed various Chinese daily newspapers and economic journals during the period 1978 to the end of 1988.[7] Press and journal articles provided information about official policy and the justifications for it. Official publications that focused on economic aspects of the policy often did not contain useful statistics or objective analysis of individual joint ventures or the policy as a whole. Although some articles contained evidence of leadership debate over issues such as the dangers and causes of "unhealthy tendencies," newspapers and journals, like published books, primarily supported the "open" policy and followed the official rationale.[8] As expected, then, Chinese press and journal articles reflected less opposition to and problems with negative effects of foreign investment than in fact may have existed. On the other hand, the concerns they did express were probably not especially controversial, or at a minimum were issues to which leaders had to respond. Statistical sources published by two Chinese government agencies, the State Statistical Bureau and MOFERT, provided increasingly reliable and usable summary statistics over the course of the decade.[9] I have drawn on these primarily in chapter 3 in the discussion of joint venture trends from 1979 to 1987. Several non-Chinese journals and newspapers offered up-to-date coverage of particular Chinese equity joint ventures and of statistics and trends in the general policy.[10]

In addition to readings in the relevant academic literatures that I discussed in the first chapter, I examined several English-language studies of foreign investment in China. Foreign investment by private firms in China is a phenomenon of the late 1970s and 1980s, and academics outside of China have written relatively little about the issue directly (although much popular literature has been published). Several scholarly works on the first years of the "open" policy provided an initial guide to how foreign investment operated, and have important descriptive value.[11] Most of these early works did not, however, analyze how the policy reflected broader political, ideological, and historical trends in pre- and postrevolutionary China, or how the policy evolved over time. Writings that have analyzed the broader theoretical or historical significance of the policy generally have assumed that, for better or worse, China's turn away from the self-reliance model reflected the embrace of capitalism, but have not sought to explain in an in-depth manner why this is so. Writings reflecting Western business interests have celebrated China's newfound "pragmatism," while those who had previously praised Chinese-style self-reliance have reflected dismay about China's turn down a "revisionist" road.[12]

Two 1987 studies of equity joint ventures went a long way toward redressing this gap. One was carried out by the U.S.-China Business Council (formerly the National Council for U.S.-China Trade, NCUSCT), a nonprofit organization that aims to facilitate commercial relations between the United States and China. The second is a commercially available study by the consulting firm of A. T. Kearney, in partnership with the International Trade Research Institute of MOFERT.[13] While these studies do not pursue the same goal as does the present study, they present valuable supplementary information. They each have compiled data on a number of firms investing in equity joint ventures in China, most of which are not contained in my own sample. In the analysis in the text I have frequently reported findings of these studies to expand the data in my own sample. Unfortunately, both the NCUSCT and the A. T. Kearney studies tend to reinforce several of the biases of my own sample. The NCUSCT study used data almost solely from U.S. investors, and the A. T. Kearney study did not report on the Hong Kong ventures it originally studied. The A. T. Kearney sample focused solely on manufacturing joint ventures. The NCUSCT study did included other sectors, thus providing some variety in the data base. Although both studies provide a fairly representative sample in terms of average size of the joint ventures included (in both cases, a large portion of firms surveyed had a foreign contribution of under $2 million) they contain a larger proportion of joint ventures with over $5 million in foreign contribution than found in the universe of data.

NONEQUITY FORMS OF
FOREIGN DIRECT INVESTMENT

SEVERAL FORMS of direct investment other than equity joint ventures were allowed in China during the 1980s.[1] Of these other forms, contractual joint ventures (*qiyueshi heying qiye*) were the most prevalent. As of the end of 1988, contractual joint ventures accounted for the largest percentage of the value of all foreign investment projects, with contracts totaling nearly 47% of China's pledged foreign investment (see table 3-D). The overwhelming majority of contractual ventures were formed with Hong Kong firms, and were located in Guangdong Province. Unlike equity ventures, contractual ventures are similar to partnerships in which no separate "legal person" is formed. A legal framework for contractual joint ventures was established only in March 1988. Although previously they had been guided by equity joint venture laws, contractual ventures remained much more nebulous in form and content. Contractual joint ventures also have some strong similarities to equity joint ventures. According to most contracts, partners to contractual ventures contribute capital, in a variety of forms (such as cash, buildings, equipment, know-how), toward a project that runs for a specified number of years. Partners also accept rights (primarily to profits) and obligations as negotiated, and usually manage them jointly.

Although, in terms of numbers, the fifty-one offshore oil joint development projects (*hezuo kaifa*) that existed at the end of 1988 initially appear insignificant (constituting 0.3% of all projects), the total amount of foreign capital invested was significant (11%). Joint oil projects are governed by a special set of laws. For the first round of bidding, these laws required the foreign firm to bear the whole expense and risk of the project until oil was discovered. Once oil was discovered by the foreign party, however (and like contractual ventures), Chinese and foreign partners were to distribute risk and profit according to a negotiated formula.[2] The drop in oil prices in the 1980s, and the poor results of early exploration projects, forced the Chinese to grant better terms to investors in the second round of bidding for exploration projects.

Wholly foreign-owned ventures (*duzi jingying qiye*) were small both in number and in overall value, although they became increasingly important in the late 1980s as the Chinese government tried harder to attract them. Most of the 594 wholly foreign-owned enterprises set up by December 1988 had been set up in 1988 (table 3-D). Most were owned by investors from Hong Kong or Macao and were located in the SEZs. As sole owner, the foreign investor bears all the risks and formally has rights to management and all (aftertax) profits. Few separate laws existed to govern these projects in the 1980s, but they had to pass through approval and operational procedures similar to those applied to equity ventures.

Compensation trade (*buchang maoyi*) and processing and assembly arrangements (*lailiao jiagong* and *laijian zhuangbei*) both absorbed significant amounts of foreign capital. As with contractual joint ventures and wholly foreign-owned firms, agreements of these types were signed during the 1980s primarily with Hong Kong investors and were located mostly in Guangdong Province. Many involved textiles, toys, foodstuffs, electronic goods, and other light industries. Under compensation trade arrangements, Chinese enterprises paid (in part or in full) for the cost of and interest on equipment they purchased from abroad with products they produced with the new equipment. The foreign partner then sold overseas the goods it received in payment (sometimes including products not directly made with the imported equipment). Through compensation trade agreements, Chinese enterprises could obtain the advanced equipment or raw materials they desired without spending foreign currency. They also introduced Chinese goods to international markets, and introduced the skills (including packaging and quality control) needed to break into those markets. Processing and assembly arrangements boomed earlier than other investment forms, reaching 16,000 in number by the end of 1982 by one estimate.[3] As of the end of 1986, foreign investment in this form was approximately $2.2 billion. These arrangements earned valuable foreign exchange in processing fees, but generally used unsophisticated technology.[4] Beginning in the mid-1980s, the government de-emphasized them in favor of more technology-intensive forms of investment.

SUMMARY OF SAMPLE DATA
PRESENTED IN THE TEXT

Number, Total Investment, and Foreign Investment
in EJVs, 1979–1988 (Sample)[a]

Country of Origin	1979–1984	1985	1986	1987	1988	1979–1988
Hong Kong/Macao						
#	663	323	306	309	263	1864
TI	1942	4639[c]	519	490	1050	8640
FI	1138	1251	203	166	390	3148
United States						
#	59	39	53	56	80	287
TI	266	108	239	320	254	1187
FI	122	49	103	143	98	515
Japan						
#	48	34	35	36	47	200
TI	279	219[d]	84	206[e]	133	921
FI	123	104	35	99	61	422
Western Europe						
#	33	19	19	14	34	119
TI	537	143	48	118	185	1031
FI	215	49	19	58	65	406
Other Asia						
#	f	35	42	37	43	f
TI	f	96	74	59	142	f
FI	f	44	33	28	49	f
Other						
#	38[f]	5	5	11	11	227[f]
TI	193[b,f]	86	32	30	56	768[f]
FI	90[f]	43	10	12	25	334
Unknown						
#					5	5
TI					26	26
FI					11	11
Total						
#	841	455	460	463	483	2702
Sample % of total[g]	90%	32%	52%	33%	12%	32%
TI	3217	5282	996	1223	1846	12,564
FI	1688	1540	403	506	699	4836

Sources: 1979–1984: N. R. Chen (1986), p 17. 1985, 1986, 1987, and 1988: compiled from samples in MOFERT *Almanacs* for 1986 (pp. 1222–1317), 1987 (pp. 626–79), 1988 (pp. 690–743), and 1989 (pp. 619–65).

Key: # = number of EJVs; TI = total investment by all partners; FI = foreign investment. FI and TI are calculated in millions of dollars.

[a] Table presents a sample of 2702 EJVs, of a total of 8539 EJVs concluded during the 1979–1988 period.

[b] Figure as it appears in Chen is apparently an error. (It appears as $90 million in Chen, but $193 million is consistent with other data.) The corrected figure is provided here and is used to calculate tables in the text.

[c] The sample includes an abnormally large EJV concluded in 1985 with a Hong Kong partner for a nuclear power plant with a TI of $4 billion and FI of $1 billion.

[d] The sample includes an abnormally large EJV concluded in 1985 with a Japanese partner for a real estate investment project with a TI of $150 million and FI of $75 million.

[e] The sample includes an abnormally large EJV concluded in 1987 with a Japanese partner for an EJV to produce kinescopes with a TI of $170 million and FI of $85 million.

[f] The data source for 1979–1984 (Chen 1986) does not provide separate data for "Other Asia." Thus, investment by countries included in the "Other Asia" category in the MOFERT *Almanacs* for 1985–1988 are presumably included under "Other" in the Chen data for 1979–1984, and are included under "Other" in the 1979–1988 total given here.

[g] Sample size as a percent of total number of EJVs contracted (pledged) in that period.

NOTES

NOTE: "C," "E," and "F," followed by a number, identifies those interviewed in the course of research for this study. The letter "C" signifies Chinese officials. "E" signifies foreign "experts," such as lawyers and consultants. "F" signifies foreign representatives of joint ventures or their parent corporations or, where noted, Chinese managers in joint ventures. The number following a letter identifies a specific joint venture. Letters following the number identify different interviewees at ventures where more than one representative was interviewed. For more on the sample of interviewees, see appendix A.

INTRODUCTION AND OVERVIEW

1. This phrasing is from Liu Peng (1985), p. 128.

2. In this study, I consider socialism to be characterized by the dominance of public or collective ownership of capital; the absence of a private class of owners of capital; extensive mechanisms for and use of state control over the economy (most often planning), although this control does not have to be exercised exclusively at the central level and can include some use of price mechanisms; an ideology that supports state rather than private control over domestic production and foreign trade; and a state that pursues these goals. I consider capitalist states to be characterized primarily by the dominance of private ownership, a private entrepreneurial class, and an ideology and state that supports private ownership. Markets are possible in either capitalist or socialist countries.

3. Several of these studies are discussed in chapter 1.

CHAPTER ONE
THE POLITICAL ECONOMY OF FOREIGN INVESTMENT IN CHINA

1. This debate focuses on whether involvement of capitalist firms in developing economies fosters "modernization," "stagnation," or "dependency." A concise review of the literature on this debate appears in the first chapter of Gereffi (1983).

2. Proponents of liberal foreign investment regimes argue that host country benefits include a net inflow or balance of capital transfers, transfer of technology and managerial knowledge, access for host exports to international markets, increased tax revenue for the host government, creation of linkages to the local economy, more efficient use of local resources, better quality products and greater choice for local consumers, a positive demonstration effect for local businesses and consumers, and a competitive stimulus to local enterprise. While many proponents of liberal investment regimes acknowledge that certain negative results may occur, they argue that these results are not necessarily a result of foreign direct investment (FDI) per se and that the *net* result is beneficial. An excellent sum-

mary and analysis of the view of both proponents and opponents of uncontrolled foreign direct investment is found in Biersteker (1981).

3. Many early postwar Latin American critics of foreign investment (*dependentistas*) believed that the path of a developing host country's development would be conditioned solely by its place in the international economy and that extensive foreign control of the economy would lead to stagnation. (See for example Dos Santos [1970], pp. 231–36.) More sophisticated, later studies judged the net effect of FDI to be negative, but allowed for the possibility of economic development (albeit distorted) and emphasized the very complex interaction between exogenous and indigenous factors of development. See Cardoso and Faletto (1978) and Evans (1979). For a review of works in both these categories, see Palma (1978), pp. 881–921 and Biersteker (1987). More orthodox Marxist views, of course, have a bifurcated view: foreign investment harms host countries, yet, as part of the spread of capitalism worldwide, is part of the progressive march toward the next historical stage of socialism.

4. In Biersteker's (1987) sixfold categorization of opinions on foreign direct investment (FDI), "structuralists" (exemplified by UN agencies concerned with FDI, Dudley Seers, Raul Prebisch) and, to a lesser degree, "sophisticated *dependentistas*" (Evans, Cardoso and Faletto) see more room for host countries to effect change through indigenization policies (including mandatory joint venture programs) than do "orthodox Marxists" (Anthony Brewer, Colin Leys) or "vulgar *dependentistas*" (Andre Gundar Frank, Theotonio Dos Santos, Samir Amin). The latter two schools and the "world systems" school (see note 5 below) take the deterministic view that change in the terms of foreign investment comes only with progressive development of the means of production and associated changes in class relations. Among those who believe FDI is beneficial for development, "liberal internationalists" (many U.S. government officials and American academics) see more room for host controls than do "conservative neo-classical realists" (managers of TNCs).

5. Those who take a "world systems" view also believe that most socialist states are constrained by an uneven global distribution of productive forces and hence cannot avoid entering the world capitalist system. A world system perspective is exemplified by Wallerstein (1974) and many of the essays in Chase-Dunn (1982a). China (from 1966 to 1972), Albania, and Tanzania, for example, each tried versions of national "self-reliance" that bordered on autarky. The Andean Pact countries in Latin America have attempted regional integration.

6. This alternative view was popular in Latin America in the 1960s and 1970s, although the emphasis was more on controlling for negative results than capturing benefits (Gereffi [1983], pp. 23–24). The United Nations Conference on Trade and Development (UNCTAD), the United Nations Centre on Transnational Corporations (UNCTC), and the United Nations Industrial Development Organization (UNIDO) played key roles in formulating guidelines for host country controls. For example, UNIDO in the late 1960s drafted the prototype "free trade zone," the contents of which (incentives and investment codes) have been copied in many developing countries.

7. For a succinct review and critique of the standard bargaining literature, see Bennett and Sharpe (1985), chap. 4, and Gereffi (1983), pp. 69–73.

8. The pervasiveness of the Western view of bargaining for joint ventures as a

non-zero-sum game is noted by Harrigan (1985), p. 73. This view, of course, assumes that each side will understand and bargain in its own interest. The freedom to opt out of negotiations is a point of disagreement between standard bargaining models and many world systems analyses. The latter argue that developing countries have no freedom *not* to interact with capitalist nations (see Chase-Dunn [1982], p. 39).

9. The notion that there are "rules of the game" that govern bargaining is consistent with, though not explicit in, Caporaso's notion of "structural power," or the power to shape the very norms or rules that govern bargaining. Caporaso argues that freedom of action by either party is constrained by international norms that govern interactions (1978, p. 4).

10. I have found the following studies of foreign investment in developing countries most useful for this discussion of host controls: Bennett and Sharpe (1985), Biersteker (1987), Cardoso and Faletto (1978), Evans (1979), Gereffi (1983), Moran (1974), and Stepan (1978). These studies range in their view of state interests in capitalist societies from a Marxian structural dependency perspective, in which the state is the instrument of dominant classes in society and of historically determined structures that preserve capitalism (Evans, Cardoso and Faletto, Gereffi), to a more conventional "liberal" perspective, in which the state is a pluralist arena in which different interests seek to assert their goals (Moran). Some mixture of these perspectives is also represented (such as Bennett and Sharpe, who also incorporate a Weberian view, Biersteker, and Stepan). An early view of the potential for a positive state role in economic development is the classic Gerschenkron (1962).

11. The list of regulatory mechanisms is suggestive rather than exhaustive. These possible forms of regulation are also available to developed countries.

12. Bennett and Sharpe (1985), p. 264; Biersteker (1987). Evans, in his study of Brazil, also found some successes in efforts of the Brazilian state to enhance control over TNCs, yet argues that this did not change the basic domination of foreign capital (1978, p. 28).

13. The definition of "effective" controls varies according to the goal of what the controls should achieve. Analysts of foreign investment from a wide spectrum of views agree that attempts at host control in nonsocialist states are ineffective, but for a number of different reasons: (1) host control drives out foreign capital; (2) programs have been poorly designed and implemented; (3) despite some limited effect, host attempts to control foreign investment do little to change the dominance of foreign capital. There are two exceptions to this general pessimism about the effectiveness of controls: (4) some who write from what Biersteker terms a "liberal internationalist" perspective see controls as working, but as negative nonetheless because they erect barriers to free trade; and (5) as noted previously, orthodox Marxists see indigenization and similar policies as effective in furthering the progressive spread of capitalism to developing countries. (See Biersteker [1987], chap. 1, for a fuller explication of these views.)

14. Biersteker (1987), chap. 1. TNCs also mounted counter-strategies to indigenization in India. See Encarnation and Vachani (1985), p. 152.

15. On Nigeria's two indigenization decrees (1972 and 1977), see Biersteker (1987), chaps. 5 and 7. Bennett and Sharpe (1985, p. 47) fault the Mexican state's

orientation toward capital and the influences of the national capitalist class, and the state's lack of organizational ability in explaining the poor implementation of controls. It is also possible to analyze problems of interference from societal forces in terms of Poulantzas' theory of the relative autonomy of the state. See Stepan (1978). A state-capital alliance is suggested in a study of foreign investment in export processing zones worldwide by Froebel, Heinrichs, and Kreye (1980). Cardoso and Faletto suggest that compradors may facilitate alliances between state and foreign interests (1978, p. 202).

16. For Mexico, Bennett and Sharpe (1985), pp. 143–45 and 267–69. Mexico's two state-owned firms in the auto sector could not effectively pursue these goals alone. The Latin American writers Cardoso and Faletto have prescribed socialism. Except for a preference for democratic rather than "bureaucratic" socialism, however, they do not elaborate on what they mean by "socialism" (1978, pp. 213–14). Others writing from a dependency perspective also suggest socialism, but less as a way of controlling foreign investment than breaking the ties with the capitalist world economy (Biersteker 1987, p. 29). Finally, even if there is no explicit call for socialism, strong state control—a key component of socialism—is often the goal of critics of FDI, for example, Evans (1979), p. 278.

17. That prospects of entry to China's domestic market have long enticed Westerners is reflected in McCormick (1967). On the importance of industry structure see Newfarmer (1984) and Bennett and Sharpe (1985). As discussed in the fourth part of this chapter, the lure of the domestic market was stronger for Western and Japanese firms than for Hong Kong firms.

18. Stoever argues that if a country tries to extract too many benefits from foreign investors (given what it can offer to investors), the result will be to discourage investors. Thus, a country must be sure its demands do not outstrip the resources underlying its bargaining power. Stoever (1985), p. 9.

19. As I argue subsequently, however, control over investments in manufacturing (the dominant form of foreign investment in China) tends to shift toward the investor *once investments are made*, thereby counteracting to some degree this potential bargaining weakness.

20. I draw here on the argument that host countries do not face competitive markets for capital and technology but, rather, that a few TNCs monopolize (or "oligopolize") these goods. Hymer (1976). This is truer for some industries than others, as I discuss further below.

21. These problems are laid out in Lampton (1987).

22. The importance of standardization of technology and industry structure are suggested by theories of, respectively, international product-life cycle (Vernon [1977]) and international industrial organization (Newfarmer [1984], Moran [1973], and Kindleberger [1969]). An interesting project for future research would be to analyze China's relative bargaining strength by industry of the investors. Bennett and Sharpe (1985) demonstrate how industry structure drove the automobile TNCs' interests in Mexico.

23. On shifting bargaining power in the extractive sector, see Stepan (1978), p. 242, and Moran (1974). On bargaining in manufacturing industries, see Bennett and Sharpe (1985), p. 262, and Gereffi (1983), pp. 48, 157–58. On countervailing

TNC strategies, see Biersteker (1987), chap. 7. There is some disagreement about the shift in bargaining power over time for manufacturing sectors: "liberal internationalists" (such as Bergsten, Horst, and Moran [1978], p. 374) are more optimistic about a shift in bargaining power to the local partner.

24. As will be seen, it was also true that changes in China's bargaining strength as reflected in national laws and policies frequently followed changes in bargaining at the firm level; the government in a number of cases approved contracts containing concessions to individual investors prior to codifying such concessions in national laws. This division between firm- and national-level bargaining is distinct from the discussions of national-, regional-, and enterprise-level controls in chapters 4 and 5, which consider the type of controls imposed rather than the actors involved in bargaining.

25. The literature on Chinese politics generally differentiates between the terms "factions" and "tendencies" by associating the former term with divisions that arise over pure power struggles (Nathan [1973]) and the latter with divisions based more on ideology. (The classic text on tendency analysis was developed for the Soviet Union. Skilling and Griffiths [1971].) The analysis of divisions here is closer to the tendency analysis model, although it can accommodate some elements of factional analysis. A third model of politics, the bureaucratic model, also is often applied to the policy formulation process. The present tendency analysis does not exclude or refute bureaucratic analysis; indeed, tendency groups may be coterminous with or situated within bureaucracies (as suggested in the analysis of Shirk [1985]). However, tendency analysis that is informed by bureaucratic and factional models appears to more fully explain the dynamic of conflict and reconciliation over the original formulation of the foreign investment policy than do pure bureaucratic or factional models.

26. Divisions among three leadership groups are discussed for a range of domestic and foreign policies in, for example, Solinger (1984), Friedman (1983), Cumings (1984), MacDougall (1982, p. 150), and Sutter (1982). Although leadership divisions were seldom discussed explicitly in China during the 1980s, they were reflected in actions, such as the removal of reformist Party Chairman Hu Yaobang (in January 1987) and Zhao Ziyang (in June 1989), and in articles in the Chinese press calling for an end both to party factionalism remaining from the Cultural Revolution and to foot-dragging in implementation of the reforms. See Li Qiming (1985). The classic statement on policy cycles between the three groups is by Skinner and Winckler (1969), who draw on Etzioni's categorization of organizations according to their use of physical, material, or symbolic rewards to achieve compliance. Skinner and Winckler find that leadership groupings and policies can be identified in accordance with Etzioni's compliance means as, respectively, "conservative," "liberal," and "radical" or (as characterized by Solinger [1984] for economic policy) "bureaucrat," "marketeer," and "radical."

27. The group of "radicals" included former Cultural Revolution leaders such as ideologist Chen Boda and Mao's wife Jiang Qing, Red Guards and others who entered the party during the Cultural Revolution, and PLA leaders who adhered to the Maoist view of guerrilla warfare and self-reliance. Their views were articulated in the clandestine press in the early 1980s. (See for example the broadcast by

Radio October Storm (1984). This analysis does not deal further with "radicals" in the Chinese elite, except insofar as they influenced some of the original concerns about the results of absorbing foreign capital, as discussed in chapter 2.

28. The description of these groups and their eras of dominance is meant to be general, not exhaustive. Moreover, it is difficult, given the closed nature of politics in China, to fully identify these groups or to place specific individuals in different groups. On the basis of views expressed about economic development, however, it is generally agreed by foreign scholars that the group of conservatives have included Li Xiannian, Peng Zhen (former mayor of Beijing), Deng Liqun (the party's Propaganda Department director until mid-1985), and PLA Marshall Ye Jianying. Reformers have included Deng Xiaoping, Zhao Ziyang, Hu Yaobang, and many younger cadres elevated by Deng. Economist Chen Yun was an early advocate of *limited* decentralization and use of market forces, and along with Li Peng showed some reformist leanings, but both were more conservative than Hu, Zhao, or Deng Xiaoping. Chen and Li also appeared to ally with conservatives after the spring of 1989. This analysis assumes that the shifts that occurred in the foreign investment policy during the 1980s reflected to a large degree shifts in influence between the two groups that are conventionally labeled "reformers" and "conservatives," although it is not always possible in practice to tie the specific changes to specific people within these groups.

29. For example, tendency or factional models alone do not offer satisfactory explanations for similarities in statements made by both reformer Deng Xiaoping and conservative Deng Liqun indicating concerns about negative results of using foreign capital and the need to control foreign investment. Conservative statements by Deng Xiaoping are quoted, for example, in *South China Morning Post* (hereafter *SCMP*), 12 March 1985, p. 7, and *Boston Globe*, 5 July 1985. One scholar associated with the bureaucratic perspective also acknowledges the importance of recognizing consensus in his finding that in 1982 "while the economic vice premiers had distinctive responsibilities, they also shared in and had to concur in many decisions. In a very real sense, many of the most important policies were collective decisions, requiring a high degree of consensus." Oksenberg (1982), p. 177. Finally, the likelihood that most of the prominent, older leaders in all factions were similarly influenced by the negative lessons of past foreign aggression, common participation in the 1949 revolution (and sometimes the Long March), and a general acceptance of the Leninist view of imperialism, support a more consensual scenario and undermine the idea that reformists were merely "paying lip-service" to the concerns of others. It should be noted that the range of consensus posited here between reformers and conservatives tended to encompass primarily the older generation of reformers who were especially influential in the late 1970s and early 1980s. Younger reformers, especially those with extensive exposure to the outside world, over time came to take the concerns of their elders less seriously.

30. The scenario developed here shares many features of Solinger's (1984) model of policy disputes over domestic commerce, in which she posits the existence of a core of shared values among radicals, marketeers, and bureaucrats in the area of domestic commerce. In her view, leaders dealing with the commercial sector would, in their ideal, pursue equality, efficiency, and order simultaneously. When trade-offs are apparent among values, each group presses for policies to

maximize the value it cares about most: radicals maximize equality, reformers maximize efficiency, and bureaucrats maximize order. But compromise or alliances between groups often occur. This view is further developed in the findings of Lieberthal and Oksenberg (1988, pp. 227–28) about the 1979 decision to allow foreign equity holdings in offshore oil projects. Through the means of risk contracts (which provide that only if foreign companies fund and discover viable reservoirs can they take a previously contracted percentage of the oil that is eventually pumped), those who favored foreign participation in offshore oil exploration assuaged the fears of those concerned about China's sovereignty and possible foreign exploitation.

31. A pure consensus scenario would posit the existence of a leadership unified in its view of foreign investment. Consensual models for communist politics have their roots in the model of the monolithic totalitarian party that was formulated in the West during the Cold War to explain Soviet politics. See Friedrich and Brzezinski (1956).

32. Chinese interviewees provided evidence of a divergent leadership dynamic underlying the "open" policy: C1, for example, noted wariness among conservative leaders who "think the openness is the same as the Opium War." Division was also evident in justifications of the policy in published articles directed at "some comrades . . . " who were said to oppose the policy. Such a statement appears in Li Yanshi (1980), p. 34.

33. On Deng's efforts, see Hong Yung Lee (1986), pp. 81–85. Lee terms this new elite cadre corps "bureaucratic technocrats." Lockett and Littler discuss Chinese efforts to upgrade enterprise management (1983, pp. 691–93).

34. In an interview in late April 1989, an economist from the Chinese Academy of Social Sciences confirmed this view, stating that there was no longer significant disagreement between reformers and conservatives on the need for FDI and foreign technology.

35. The 1983 CASP, which originally had support of reformers, began as a drive against humanist ideas such as "alienation" that were being espoused in literary circles. When conservatives such as Deng Liqun began to extend criticism to economic crime and the "open" policy generally, the campaign was quickly halted by reformers.

36. On socialist China's control mechanisms, see Tsou (1983), White (1983), and Schurmann (1968). Studies of policy cycles in China's economic policy indicate that within these broad elements that characterized the 1949–1978 period there were shifts in emphasis between radical, conservative (bureaucrats), and reform (marketeer) approaches to control. See especially Solinger (1984).

37. The party was still in the position to "discover" the truth that emanated from fact, but to seek truth from concrete practice (an idea originally advocated by Mao) allowed greater room for input by experts. On the evolution in control mechanisms, see Tsou (1983).

38. Lindblom (1977) suggests that market inducements are forms of control.

39. On the concept of *guanxi*, see Schurmann (1968), pp. 223, 259. See Walder (1983) for a study of *guanxi* in enterprises in the 1980s. On traditional elements in socialist bureaucracy and the contrast with the Weberian system, see Kraus (1983), pp. 140–47.

40. A theory of bureaucratic bargaining in policymaking in China is found in Lieberthal and Oksenberg (1988). Their discussion of the 1979 policy decision to allow foreign equity participation in offshore drilling shows that although bureaucratic and local politics did not strongly shape the broad decision (which was made instead primarily by those actors at the pinnacle of power), these factors did come into play in the process of formulating the precise policies to be used to carry out the broader decision (1988, chap. 5). In the present study, bureaucratism and localism were found to affect the implementation more than the formulation of either broad or specific policies toward foreign investment. The classic statement on localism, or the "cellular" model of China's economy, is Donnithorne (1972). Other examples of how localism has affected various aspects of the post-Mao reforms are found in Perry and Wong (1985) and Lampton (1987).

41. The tandem occurrence of economic reform and allowance of foreign investment is unsurprising since both are based on economic theories favoring the market, comparative advantage, and so on.

42. The discussion in this section is based primarily on World Bank (1985), Lippit (1987), and Riskin (1987).

43. Efficiency may even have declined in industry before 1978. Measuring the rise in the amount of investment required per marginal unit of output, Riskin (1987, pp. 264, 371) concludes tentatively that the rate of growth in long-term productivity may have fallen between 1957 and 1978, although the rate of labor productivity grew somewhat compared with output per unit of capital. He finds no significant change in the productivity rate between 1978 and 1985. Real industrial growth was maintained despite the decline in efficiency between the mid-1950s and late 1970s because of the continual increase in capital inputs. See also World Bank (1985), pp. 110–11.

44. National Council for U.S.-China Trade (hereafter NCUSCT) (1987), pp. 163–64.

45. This was less true for light industries, and particularly textiles, but was salient for most Western investment projects, which more frequently manufactured industrial products or used advanced technology. NCUSCT (1987), p. 154.

46. In the 1980–1985 period, 86% of the flows of foreign direct investment to developing countries was spread over eighteen countries, of which China was one. UNCTC (1988), pp. 74, 80 (note 4), and 370.

47. Loosening of tight controls has occurred, for example, in Indonesia (*Far Eastern Economic Review* [hereafter *FEER*] 22 May 1986, p. 62), and in a host of other countries including India, Mexico, Nicaragua, Egypt, and Guinea (*NYT*, 11 May 1985, p. 1), and Angola (*NYT*, 20 February 1989). On competitive liberalization in East Asia, see Haggard and Cheng (1987), p. 1. As noted subsequently, China has competed with Thailand for Japanese investment following the strengthening of the yen in the 1980s. This trend is predicted in Stoever (1985) and in Tomlinson (1970), pp. 28, 37.

48. Companies generally engage in direct investment abroad for a combination of the following positive and negative/defensive reasons: to maintain profit margins; to maintain or expand markets; to forestall pre-emptive entrance to new markets by competitors; to avoid protectionist barriers to imports; to gain access to

new or cheaper materials, labor, or transportation routes; and to respond to host country incentives. The precise mix of these reasons depends upon factors idiosyncratic to the specific company, to the sector, and to the host market. Critics of foreign investment find the root motivation as imperialism, the classic statement of which is Lenin (1966). See also Hymer (1972). Proponents of foreign investment focus on reasons related to oligopolistic rivalry and the "product-life cycle" theory of the firm, as discussed previously.

49. Most Western investors believed that, although wholesale pre-emption of other firms was impossible, an early entrance into China's market might secure them a substantial market share, and would prevent others from freezing them out. Access to Chinese markets and market pre-emption, and not access to resources, were found to be the prime motive for U.S. firms in surveys by Daniels, Krug, and Nigh (1985), pp. 48–49, and A. T. Kearney and International Trade Research Institute of the PRC (hereafter A. T. Kearney) (1987), p. 27. The 170 foreign banks with representative offices in China (as of early 1986) also followed the defensive, "foot-in-the-door" strategy, and did not profit. FEER, 8 May 1986, p. 74. For an excellent description of the strong desire of one firm to position itself for a time when the China market might open, see Mann's (1989) description of the Beijing Jeep JV.

50. Several foreign managers indicated in interviews that immediate profits were not their first objective. On the notion of "old friends," see Pye (1982), pp. 20–32.

51. In a 1985 survey of foreign firms in Beijing, 76% of all Japanese firms questioned cited China's legal framework as inadequate. FEER, 14 August 1986, p. 103. Japanese firms also preferred investment contracts about twice as long as the ten- to fifteen-year contracts the Chinese wanted. AWSJ, 29 January 1985, p. 5. MITI's attitude toward joint ventures was officially "neutral." This decidedly negative label warned that Japanese investors became involved in China at their own risk. The Japanese attitude was undoubtedly shaped by the well-publicized difficulties faced by Hitachi's joint venture. On Japanese firms' interest in thwarting long-term competition, and on their preferences for Thailand, see Westendorff (1989), p. 12.

52. One survey shows that Hong Kong firms were motivated to invest in China for these reasons, while opening new markets was fifth in a ranking of motives. Edward K. Y. Chen (1983), pp. 96–97. On an informal survey confirming these motives, see FEER, 29 May 1986, p. 88. Costs for low-skill Chinese labor in southern China were at least one-third below those in Hong Kong in the mid-1980s. On export-oriented investors located in Jiangsu, see Pomfret (1989).

53. There are several reasons why, in any country, foreign firms enter equity joint ventures per se: to gain access to new markets, cheap labor, raw materials, and transportation links; to share costs and risks; to obtain financing to supplement a firm's debt capacity; to share output of large plants or create minimum efficient scale plants; to pioneer development of new industries; to form coalitions; and to take advantage of other "synergies." In a negative sense, foreign investors may form joint ventures when forced by indigenization policies designed to increase host control over existing wholly foreign-owned investments, and to avoid granting simple licensing agreements for their technology. Most of these explanations

pertain to investments in countries that, unlike China, previously housed wholly foreign-owned subsidiaries. Tomlinson (1970) argues that much of the bargaining literature wrongly implies that foreign firms enter into joint ventures only under negative circumstances.

54. Daniels, Krug, and Nigh (1985). The standard sequence is predicted by product life-cycle theories.

55. The value of "critical cases" for verifying and falsifying hypotheses is discussed in Eckstein (1975). Gereffi's study of multinationals in the developing world also employs this method (1983, pp. 62–65).

CHAPTER TWO
THE CHINESE OUTLOOK AT THE
OUTSET OF THE FOREIGN INVESTMENT POLICY

1. The history of nineteenth- and twentieth-century foreign aggression in China is recounted in a vast literature, summarized only briefly here. The following account draws primarily on Rodzinski (1984, chaps. 8–11); Spence (1981); Liao (1984); Wang Yihe, Xu E, and Zhou Jianping (1984, pp. 77–84); and Feuerwerker (1976).

2. Anti-foreign sentiment was certainly not new to China in the nineteenth century. Yet it had never before been manifested in widespread activity against Westerners, as the threat from the West was new.

3. When they perceived it to be in their interests to do so, however, foreign powers supported the Qing government militarily. For example, the French and others aided the government during the Taiping Rebellion (1841–1864).

4. The Nanjing Treaty had granted Britain "most favored nation" status as well as power of consent over tariff increases. Rodzinski (1984), p. 183.

5. For example, Germany's sphere of influence contained Shandong Province, and Russia's included Outer and Inner Mongolia and Xinjiang. The settlement of the Second Opium War (the Treaties of Peking) also opened Beijing to foreign envoys; allowed Catholic missionaries to preach, practice, and hold land in China; required payment of further indemnities; and ceded portions of the Kowloon Peninsula.

6. The Russians came to occupy Lushun (Port Arthur) and Dalian (1897–1898), the Germans occupied Qingdao (1897–1898), the British controlled Weihaiwei, and the French occupied Guangzhou. More significant, perhaps, the 1901 Boxer Protocol/Treaty of Tianjin concluded between the Qing and eleven foreign governments following foreign-aided suppression of the Boxer Rebellion (1898–1901) forced payment of further indemnities, allowed foreign troops to be stationed in Beijing Legations and along the Beijing-Tianjin railway, and obliged the Qing to suppress anti-foreign rebellions.

7. This was followed in 1915 by Japan's "Twenty-One Demands" to Yuan Shikai to take over control of Manchuria and the lower Yangze Valley, and in 1919 by attempts at the Versaille peace conference to transfer to Japan German rights in Shandong Province. (The latter was the immediate cause of the May Fourth Movement.)

8. Although they were only in Manchuria until the spring of 1946, the Soviets looted much of the region's industrial equipment. The Soviets retained control of the warm-water port of Dalian (Dairen) until 1950, and of its base in Lushan (Port Arthur) until 1955.

9. Figures are from Wang Yihe, et al. (1984), pp. 77–80, and N. R. Chen (1986), p. 3.

10. The debate on the impact of foreign investment in China in many ways mimics the liberal-dependency debate discussed in chapter 1. The central question in this historical debate concerns the net impact of foreign investment on China's economy, and whether China would have been better off absent the foreign pressures. Feuerwerker (1976), Hou (1965), Dernberger (1975), and Rawski (1989, pp. 3–12) all make the counterfactual argument that, though painful, foreign economic activity left China better off than it would have been otherwise. These scholars also argue that, although the impact of the foreign presence outside of the small modern sector was minor, in some cases, such as the development of railroads, the Chinese benefited greatly from the foreign presence. Hou (1965, pp. 214–15), for example, argues that the volume of foreign investment in China was low, with the bulk of British investment, for example, flowing to recently settled, low-population areas such as the United States, Australia, Canada, and Argentina. But he also states that foreign investment helped bring about whatever "modernization" there was in China before 1937 because it introduced modern technology and funded a large share of the modern sector. Mao Zedong (1967) and Chiang Kai-shek (1947), in contrast, asserted that the foreign economic activity was decidedly negative. It is their view that has generally been accepted by the Chinese since 1949. The early 1980s saw some re-evaluation among Chinese historians of the dominant Chinese stance on these issues. While these re-evaluations did *not* generally argue that foreign aggression did not occur, they also found some of the results of foreign economic and cultural (missionary) activity to be positive. Luo Rongqu and Jiang Xiangze (1983). On foreign investment in this whole period, also see Remer (1968) and Liao (1984).

11. The discussion here should not suggest that Chinese perceptions were invalid. Indeed, most scholars acknowledge that the experience was a painful and in some respects a harmful one. The following discussion focuses on those negative results as perceived in China.

12. For example, the 1895 settlement with the Japanese required payment of the huge sum of 230 million taels. Because annual Qing revenue amounted to only 75–80 million taels, the regime was forced to borrow 370 million taels between 1895 and 1899, with the result that in the following years most of the regime's revenue was put to servicing the loans. A sum twice that required in the Treaty had to be borrowed from foreign banks. Rodzinski (1984), p. 229.

13. Wang Yihe, et al. cite specific cases, particularly during the Japanese occupation of Manchuria, where foreign investors, using investment capital extorted from Chinese citizens, formed foreign-owned and controlled enterprises (1984, p. 83). Liao (1984, p. 61) notes that foreigners gained mining rights through "political intrigue" tied with the expansion of spheres of influence.

14. Wang Yihe, et al. (1984), p. 80.

15. On the abolition of restrictions on foreign control, Liao (1984), p. 61. An example of foreign government intervention is the 1925 revisions of the China Trade Act of 1922. Wang Yihe, et al. (1984), p. 83.

16. This figure includes interest payments and profit remittances abroad (Hou 1965, p. 214). Wang Yihe, et al. assert that the $2 billion in remitted profits obtained on $1 billion investment between 1902 and 1937 was not found in any other country using FDI at the time. They do not provide information on the pace or timing of investment that might (using Western standards) either support or refute the claim (1984, p. 84).

17. Hsiao (1977), pp. 123–24; Swindler (1984), p. 1012; and Wang Yihe, et al. (1984), pp. 86–87. The government asserted that foreigners left because China had abrogated "imperialist privilege," and because the U.S. embargo had cut off supplies to these firms. Hsiao (1977), p. 76.

18. Thompson (1979), especially chap. 5. China did offer to loosen the terms on British firms in exchange for Britain's break with the U.S.-led policy to isolate China. Although "hostage capitalism" ended for the most part by 1954, the last British firm left in 1957.

19. The *ti-yung* rationale was not explicitly applied in this instance, not in the least because as a remnant of the Qing legacy it was discredited politically. On the period of Soviet advisement, see Schurmann (1968), pp. 239–53. On investment by Soviet and East European governments, see Klenner and Wiesegart (1980), p. 87; Wang Yihe, et al. (1984), pp. 86–87; and Swindler (1984), p. 1012.

20. China during this period was limited as to sources of imported technology, and when it did occur it also was not always successful. In the 1950s, China was under a Western trade embargo imposed by the United States. Although China imported some technological goods (particularly machinery and equipment) in the 1960s, such imports were greatly de-emphasized under the extreme self-reliance model. In the late 1970s, the import of expensive German and Japanese equipment worth $500 million by a Wuhan steel mill proved disastrous, as the technology could not be operated due to lack of skills and poor compatibility and planning. Dernberger (1977). According to one author, Chinese explanations for the low volume of technology purchases focus on external factors (such as the 1950s U.S. embargo), reluctance to take on debt, and adherence to self-reliance. Westerners point more to China's limited ability to absorb technology due to a shortage of infrastructural requirements and skilled personnel. Reynolds (1984), p. 89. On post-1949 technology transfer generally, see also Lubman (1984), pp. 84–86.

21. On Chinese leaders' negative view of Sino-Soviet projects, see Lubman (1984), pp. 84–5, and Ray (1975).

22. Liao (1984) argues that anti-foreignism in China has been a reaction to failed modernization and foreign aggression usually manifested in mass demonstrations or literature and propaganda, rather than a cultural trait. His argument contrasts with Pye's (1968) explanation that anti-foreignism is an inexorable cultural trait. Wakeman (1966) cites the first anti-foreign mass movement as an 1841 reaction of peasants in Guangdong against the British during the Opium Wars.

23. In general, however, the gentry was not as hostile to foreigners as was the case with previous anti-foreign movements or with other, more radical groups.

Also, the movement to recover mining rights stopped short of demanding abrogation of the unequal treaties. Liao (1984), pp. 60–64. Workers joined the protest on a major basis only after 1925.

24. Unlike Lenin, Sun viewed imperialism as primarily a political force. Moreover, the Nationalists often relied on foreign aid, leaving both Sun and Chiang vulnerable to CCP criticism. Chiang (1947). On the Nationalist policy toward JVs during the Republican period, see Kirby (1990).

25. Mao (1967) drew from Lenin's *Imperialism*, which argued that the monopoly phase of capitalism is characterized by the export of capital to countries with cheap labor, rent, and raw materials in order to gain higher returns on investment. By gaining control over the means of production in developing countries, capital exporters accelerate the development of capitalism in those countries. The continuing salience of Lenin's analysis for the "open" policy of the 1980s was expressed in Wang Yihe, et al. (1984, pp. 24, 41), although these authors do not engage in an in-depth discussion of Lenin. See also Liao (1984), p. 109.

26. The self-strengthening movement started with conservative reformers of the Tongzhi Restoration (1862–1874). It ended in 1894 with the Sino-Japanese War, in which China was roundly defeated despite the extensive self-strengthening efforts. Generally, see Rodzinski (1984), pp. 211, 234; Liao (1984), pp. 29–36; Spence (1981), pp. 6–12; and Spence (1980).

27. Mao (1974) stated this in his 1956 speech, "On the 10 Great Relationships." Even some of Mao's most ardent statements made later in favor of self-reliance embody the idea of learning from the outside those things helpful to China.

28. Tan Sitong (1954).

29. The quote is from Wang Yihe, et al. (1984), p. 82. Hu's statement is noted in *NYT*, 11 December 1985, p. 2. A similar sentiment is found in Editorial Department of *Hongqi* (1982), p. 379.

30. For a thorough discussion of the concept of self-reliance during the Cultural Revolution and under the post-Mao regime as it applies to foreign economic policy, see Wu (1981).

31. Ma Hong (1985), p. 5; Juan Wenqi, et al. (1980), p. 26; and Wu (1981), p. 465. On the need to develop indigenous technology, see Shen Yurui (1980), p. 37.

32. Quote is translated in *SWB*, FE 7614-BII: 5–6, 10 April 1984. C1 also linked these principles with historical experience, and noted sovereign dignity. The term "equality and mutual benefit" was used as early as 1955 in the "principles of peaceful coexistence" worked out with India. Deng Xiaoping in a 1974 speech at the United Nations, at a time when he was advocating rejection of the Maoist self-reliance model, noted the guiding principles of respect for state sovereignty and "equality and mutual benefit" when engaging in international exchanges. In the 1980s, these principles were used in economic contexts that ranged from joint venture contracts to nuclear energy cooperation pacts.

33. Sun Ru (1983), p. 14. Deng's slogan, "socialism with Chinese characteristics," was legitimated with Mao's 1938 call to apply Marxism-Leninism to the concrete Chinese situation "so that its every manifestation has an indubitably Chinese character" (Report to the 6th Plenum of the 6th Central Committee, quoted in *FEER*, 21 March 1985, p. 88).

34. Quoted in Ma Hong (1985), p. 2. A similar analysis, including the commitment to the transition to communism, is found in Editorial Department of *Red Flag* (1987), p. 1.

35. Editorial Department of *Red Flag* (1984), pp. 3, 9.

36. Su Xing (1984), pp. 65–66.

37. See, for example, Zhao Ziyang (1987), pp. 10, 12, 13, and 47; Editorial Department of *Red Flag* (1984), pp. 12–14, and Xiang Nan (1984), p. 37. Ideological articles usually label the values "socialist" or "communist," although many are consonant with both Chinese tradition and communism. See, for example, Deng Liqun (1984), p. K5.

38. Su Xing (1984), p. 72. See also Editorial Department of *Hongqi* (1982a) and Xu Daohe (1982).

39. Editorial Department of *Hongqi* (1982a), pp. 1–2. The party ideologues did not claim that China had approached a communist economy; indeed, one of the theoretical innovations was that a commodity economy still existed in China. For a brief but able summary of this view, see *FEER*, 21 March 1985, p. 91. On the link between morality and production, see Xiang Nan (1983), p. 4.

40. Editorial Department of *Red Flag* (1984), p. 12.

41. A third issue was the visit to a World War II memorial by Prime Minister Nakasone. *FEER*, 9 January 1986, p. 86, and *FEER*, 24 October 1985. On the decline in anti-foreign sentiment and demonstrations in the post-Mao period, see Liao (1984), pp. 211–33. The continuing existence of anti-imperialist sentiment did not translate into Chinese support for drastic change in the global economic system, however. Reynolds (1984), p. 95.

42. Quote is from Xu Xuehan, Mao Rongfang, and Wu Jian (1982), p. K16. For other examples of Chinese analyses of imperialism at this time, see Fan Kang and Wang Huaining (1984), Li Cong (1982), and Juan Wenqi, et al. (1980).

43. Chu Baotai (1984), p. 115. See also Wang Yihe, et al. (1984), pp. 24–40. These are two of the few Chinese sources I have seen that view joint ventures per se as transmitters of global imperialism.

44. Quote is from Hu Yaobang when he was party secretary, in a speech to the 12th Party Congress, *New York Times Magazine*, 3 April 1983, p. 31.

45. See also Xi Wen (1982), p. 69.

46. Oksenberg and Lieberthal put the date of the original decision to attract foreign investment at September 1978 (1986, p. 201). The first evidence that the Chinese were considering utilizing foreign direct investment (FDI) came from French leaders and was reported in Agence France Presse. Foreign Broadcast Information Service (hereafter FBIS), No. 231, 17 November 1978. The new economic reform program was clarified in December 1978 at the Third Plenum of the Eleventh Central Committee. For an overview of this period, see Dernberger (1982), pp. 36–43.

47. As noted previously, there was not a total absence of foreign participation in China's economy. A modest degree of imports and exports was usually encouraged, although trade policy vacillated over the years, and during the 1950s some joint ventures were established.

48. *Peking Review*, No. 9, 25 February 1977, p. 18. This quote appeared prior to the second rehabilitation of Deng Xiaoping in July 1977, when radical influence

was still felt. It is probable that the editors reaffirmed the previous line *because* of behind-the-scenes discussions of foreign investment. The party had seriously considered a similar package of reforms in the early 1970s and, to a lesser extent, in the early 1960s, but these discussions were dropped as the fortunes of their major supporters, Deng and Liu Xiaoqi, suffered.

49. On theory following practice for the establishment of Shenzhen, see Chan, Chen, and Chin (1986). On the oil industry, see Lieberthal and Oksenberg (1988).

50. See World Bank (1985, pp. 110–11), and Riskin (1987). It should be noted that some studies have disputed this, however.

51. The reformers in the late 1970s initiated the "Four Modernizations" to put China on the level of the economies of the advanced industrialized nations within several decades. On the reforms in general, see Harding (1987), Feuchtwang and Hussain (1983), and essays in Perry and Wong (1985).

52. One discussion of the efficiency of Western (nonsocialist) capital in capital construction that exemplifies the reformist view of benefits from cooperation with the West is Zhou Shude (1984), p. 19. The economic goals of the Chinese government are stated in Wang Yihe, et al. (1984), chap. 1 and p. 45.

53. Indeed, contemporary Chinese historians criticized the self-strengthening movement as reactionary because the leaders wished to preserve feudal rule. Huang Yifeng and Jiang Duo (1984).

54. China reportedly looked at the experiences of Yugoslavia, South Korea, Singapore, and Hong Kong. See FBIS, No. 231, 17 November 1978. Taiwan's experience is used as a model by Wang Muheng and Chen Yongshan (1981). Halpern (1985) argues that although China's reformist leadership observed the experiences of Eastern Europe, it is far from clear that it took a critical eye to their socialist counterparts in the Soviet bloc. Rather, it seems to have used Eastern European examples to bolster decisions already made.

55. He Xinhao (1980), p. 1. This article cites the experiences of the United States, Western Europe, Japan, and (briefly) Singapore, Mexico, and Brazil. Another article citing the positive role of TNCs in other countries is Teng Weizao and Jiang Zhei (1981).

56. Lo Yaoqiu (1978). Lo does not explicitly state that China should allow FDI, but asserts that Sun's views can be applied to modern China.

57. From 1922 to 1925, 10 joint ventures and over 200 other cooperative enterprises were set up in the USSR. Stalin canceled the contracts in 1930. Wang Yihe, et al. (1984), pp. 25–26. Chan, Chen, and Chin (1986, p. 92) note that provincial-level officials first set forth the rationale based on NEP for the Shenzhen SEZ. For other discussions of Lenin's plan by Chinese writers, see Qi Mingchen (1978); Jiang Yiguo, Wang Zumin, and Jiang Baoqi (1978); Fang Zhuofen (1981), p. 56; and Editorial Department of *Hongqi* (1982). On Stalin, see Juan Wenqi, et al. (1980). Quote is from Juan Wenqi, et al. (1980), p. 19.

58. Zhao Ziyang quoted in Reynolds (1984), p. 90. Deng has stated that joint ventures enhance self-reliance in the long term. *China Daily*, 13 October 1984, p. 1.

59. See Mao's speech, "On the Ten Great Relationships," which was delivered in 1956 and often quoted in Beijing in 1977 (Mao 1974).

60. The foreign policy corollary of this tempered view of the capitalist world was

Mao's "theory of the three worlds" (presented by Deng Xiaoping at the UN in 1974), in which the Soviet Union, rather than the United States and other non-superpower capitalist nations, poses the greatest threat to China.

61. That China should inherit the "fruits of civilization" was argued in Sun Ru (1980, 1982). This idea was also reflected in Zhao Ziyang's speech at the 13th Party Congress in October 1987. That science and technology are not products of a particular class but, rather, of mankind is also noted in Liu Peng (1985), p. 126. These ideas also echoed the view that "late" industrial developers have the advantage of access to the product of others before them, and hence can gain from the uneven development of productive forces.

62. Although the most obvious application of these "laws" was to trade, they also underlay the rationale for allowing international capital to flow to where it is most productive. Clear statements of the reformist view are found in Dong Fureng (1980), Juan Wenqi, et al. (1980), and Liu Xiangdong (1985).

63. Sun Ru (1980), p. 53.

64. Liu Peng (1985), p. 126. This idea is also expressed in Chu Baotai (1984), p. 115.

65. Juan Wenqi, et al. critique Ricardian comparative advantage for not exposing the exploitative forces of free trade, while praising its progressive and scientific nature (1980, pp. 10–11).

66. Sun Ru (1980), p. 53. Another reformer expressed the same sentiment: "Letting the capitalists have something to gain is equivalent to paying 'tribute and taxes' to them. But in so doing, we will have exchanged for ourselves the most urgent capital, advanced technology, and scientific management methods, and won time to raise more quickly the economic and technical standards of our country. For [the Four Modernizations] it is necessary and worthwhile to pay a small price" (Liu Peng [1985], p. 127). See also He Xinhao (1980), p. 3. Wang Yihe, et al. also note the antagonistic goals of China and foreign partners (1984, p. 25). On similar ideas as expressed in Eastern Europe, McMillan and St. Charles (1973), p. 21.

67. Juan Wenqi, et al. (1980), p. 12. A separate article argued that while participating in the international division of labor was an objective necessity, using it was a subjective capability with two preconditions: possession of sovereignty and possession of economic strength. Editor of GMW (1983), p. 5.

68. These arguments are suggested by Chu Baotai (1984), pp. 110–13. Wang Yihe, et al. also discuss these special tools of the socialist state, especially that joint ventures fit the state plan and are subordinate to the socialist economy (1984, pp. 45–46).

69. Chu Baotai (1984), p. 111.

70. A small number of "democratizers" outside the party in the early 1980s did argue that by re-entering the international economy, China would become a "capitalist state without capitalists" and the party would necessarily become even more entrenched as a power above society. See Friedman (1983), pp. 157, 160.

71. Several foreign representatives interviewed in joint ventures were from families of "wealthy capitalists" who left China around 1949 (F12, F16). Some former capitalists who remained in China, notably CITIC president Rong Yiren, were assigned prominent posts in the state foreign economic sector.

72. He Xinhao (1980), p. 2. For similar arguments, see Wang Yihe, et al. (1984), p. 87; Wang Zhaozheng (1982), pp. 25–28; Sun Ru (1982); and Wu Shuqing (1982).

73. Liu Peng (1985), p. 128. Another statement on the role of the socialist state is from Sun Ru: "As long as we keep our minds sober, as long as we firmly maintain the political and economic sovereignty in the hands of the socialist state and as long as we restrict the economic support we draw from foreign capital within certain limits, there will be no risk of the degeneration of socialist society" (1982, p. P2).

74. The argument about Chinese concerns in this part is construed from a wide array of press and interview sources. The levels refer to major points of impact of FDI, not of articulation of concerns. Because debate about issues of control and threats to socialism could act as a disincentive to investors, it is highly possible that the leadership was even more sensitive to the form and content that expressions of hesitation over foreign investment took in written materials available to foreigners. Publicly circulated press materials may have presented these fears in a more moderate tone than was actually felt.

75. Zhong Douyang and Yin Youguo (1984), p. 4; Chu Baotai (1984), pp. 112–14; Juan Wenqi, et al. (1980), p. 21; Wang Yihe, et al. (1984), p. 117; and Li Cong (1982), p. 81. Li discusses this with reference to other developing countries.

76. C6; F28; Wang Yihe, et al. (1984), pp. 69–71, 92; Zhong Douyang and Yin Youguo (1984), p. 4; Wang Yaotian (1982); and Editorial Department of *Renmin Ribao* (1982). In at least two industries—cosmetics and insurance—there was concern that JVs posed threats to Chinese monopolies (F1 and F28). However, the tobacco industry was apparently willing to allow some competition from JVs (F21-A). Wang Yihe, et al. (1984) also note the counter-argument that JVs could provide a positive competitive stimulus to domestic industries.

77. F14-C; C6; Wang Yihe, et al. (1984), pp. 69, 71. The latter note that the profit rate in 1977 for U.S. firms investing in developed countries was 11.4%, whereas it was 24.9% in developing countries. While acknowledging a difference in investment conditions, they imply that the difference rendered the latter rate "excessive." On international conceptions of "excessive" profits, see Biersteker (1981), p. 92.

78. F14-B; F27; C6.

79. On concerns over technology transfer in negotiations and operations: F8, F9-C, F9-D, F14-B, F14-C (Chinese manager), F21-A, F24-A; Wang Yihe, et al. (1984), pp. 71, 92, 108; and Wang Chiwei and Liu Mindong (1982), p. 3.

80. Wang Yihe, et al. (1984), p. 91.

81. F14-E (Chinese manager) notes that there are those who worry foreign businesses will "cheat us" (*pian women*). See also Li Yanshi (1980), p. 35; Wang Yihe, et al. (1984), pp. 69–71, 91; and Wang Lin (1983). The latter notes the prevalence of this view among middle-level bureaucrats.

82. In one case, machinery had been built in the 1920s and was sold at what were considered excessively high rates. Chai (1983), p. 125. C6 also noted the special sensitivity toward profits and technology, and Wang Yihe, et al. (1984, p. 108) note sensitivity to being tricked in technology transfer deals.

83. F14-A, C1, and Xu Xuehan, et al. (1982), p. K16.

84. Editorial Department of *Hongqi* (1982), p. 4.

85. A reformist statement of concern on this issue is Rong Yiren (chairman of

CITIC and former Shanghai capitalist) (1984), p. 73. Hu Yaobang, in a speech reprinted in *RMRB* in early April 1985, stated that China had not negated the idea of fighting against "spiritual pollution."

86. See his speech to the Central Committee in October 1983, and cited in *NYT*, 20 December 1983, p. 2. Deng made similar criticisms in 1985. See *NYT*, 24 September 1985. Assertions of foreign capital as transmission mechanisms for negative influences are similar to arguments that FDI promotes "inappropriate consumption patterns" and cultural imperialism. Biersteker summarizes this argument (1981, pp. 14–17).

87. Director of the Institute of Marxism-Leninism and Mao Zedong Thought, quoted in *NYT*, 17 December 1984, p. A1.

88. On working for personal gain: Editorial Department of *Jingji Ribao* (1983), p. K5. The quote is from Guangzhou Provincial Service Commentator (1982), p. P1. See also Xin Ren (1982), p. 35.

89. See *JJYJ*, No. 8, 1982, pp. 54–58; De Min (1982), p. K1; and Ren Zhongyi (Guangdong Province First Party Secretary) (1982a). These statements were made prior to the launching of the CASP. That these problems are not found exclusively in capitalist or even Western societies was not discussed.

90. Criminals were to be treated more seriously than those who had erred due to influences of "spiritual pollution," however. FBIS-CHI-83-218, 9 November 1983, p. K5.

91. On bribery, see "Guangzhou Municipal Party Takes Lead in Rectifying Devious Wind . . . " (1979), p. 66.

92. Quote is from senior CCP official Bo Yibo, quoted in *NYT*, 1 July 1985, p. A5. See also Ji Si (1984), pp. 76–78. Ji argued that the causes were complex and could not simply be regarded as a result of the "open" policy. On accounting fraud, see *International Herald Tribune*, 14 March 1985, p. 1. Ren Zhongyi (1982) noted problems with ideological corruption within the party. Deng Xiaoping suggested similar reasoning. *International Herald Tribune*, 14 March 1985, p. 1.

93. "*Shenzhen Tequ Jingshen Wenming Jianshe de jige Wenti*" ["Some Problems in the Construction of Shenzhen Special Zone's Spiritual Civilization"] (1984), p. 4.

94. Zhang Hanqing (1982), p. P2. See also Lo Ping (1984), p. 5.

95. Editorial Department of *Hongqi* (1982), p. 6; see also Ma Hong (1985), p. 3. According to another *Red Flag* editorial, "[W]hen most places in China got developed, the government will be able to devote more help to the poorer regions. Regions which have become rich before others can help the poorer areas develop their resources and commodity production by channelling their capital and technology into them." [*sic*] Editorial Department of *Red Flag* (1987), p. 3.

96. For evidence that "some comrades" believed the prospect of "modern foreign concessions," see Ren Zhongyi (1982), p. W4; Xu Xuehan, et al. (1982), p. K16; Liu Peng (1985), p. 127; Zhang Hanqing (1982), p. P2; and Lo Ping (1984), p. 5. On concern from inland areas that the coastal regions not become politically and economically advantaged, see Shirk (1985), pp. 206–7.

97. Chen Yun and Hu Qili are the leaders mentioned, although Chen Yun also evidenced reformist tendencies, as discussed in chapter 1. *SCMP*, 21 September 1984. On the spread of "contamination" to other regions, C4 (Shenzhen official);

NYT, 25 April 1982, p. 17. Wariness by conservatives is also reported in Chi Shi-ching (1982), p. W1, and *NYT*, 31 March 1983. Several delegates at an early 1985 session of the National People's Congress also expressed wariness. *NYT*, 15 April 1985, p. A12.

98. One prominent case in 1982 involved two influential party officials in Shenzhen who were arrested for smuggling consumer items and avoiding taxes, the total cost of which was estimated to be $US 35 million. *The Economist*, 27 November 1982, p. 8. On corruption and consumerism, see "Guangzhou Munici-pal Party Takes Lead in Rectifying Devious Wind . . . " (1979), p. 66.

99. Negotiations were obviously a prime locus for expression of concerns. The pattern of negotiations is discussed by Pye (1982), p. 70, and E5. My interviews supported his argument that Chinese negotiators had incentives not to make inde-pendent decisions or to risk challenge by higher officials for being "soft on foreign-ers." Chinese negotiators did not refrain from discussing issues about which the Chinese side was concerned. On the other hand, the continual emphasis on build-ing a positive and trusting relationship between the two sides could have mitigated the Chinese negotiators' voicing of concerns somewhat. (Virtually all the foreign business representatives and lawyers noted this latter behavior, for example, E6, F4-A, F21, and F14-E [Chinese manager]). A caveat: one often hears the old saw that the Chinese are "hard bargainers." Some may interpret Chinese negotiators' expressions of concern over technology transfer, and so on, as mere rhetoric that cloaked the desire to obtain concessions from the foreigners. However, that con-cerns expressed in negotiations were more than bargaining ploys is supported by other data, such as Chinese press articles written for a domestic audience.

Interviewees noted that Chinese negotiators did not repeatedly show concern about a number of national-level negative effects (such as threats to sovereignty, control of the economy), although they did speak of the need to protect "China's interests" (for example, F14, F7-A). Concerns were more often expressed with regard to the enterprise level. Concerns expressed in negotiations and operations were for the most part mutually consistent, moreover, although once operations were under way, the Chinese partners came under great pressure to make the venture profitable, and thus had an incentive to suppress concerns, especially if expressing them were to risk causing major financial or managerial troubles to the venture.

100. Wang Yihe, et al. (1984), pp. 92, 153. Zhong Douyang and Yin Youguo note this concern in the context of discussing the experiences of other countries (1984, p. 4).

101. See, for example, F14-F (Chinese manager) on the need to protect the joint venture labor organization. This concern was seldom—and in the case of the CCP organization within JVs, virtually never—broached by the Chinese either in publications or negotiations, probably lest it deter foreign investors (E15, F28). The existence of concern about threats to these "socialist" functions must be in-ferred from controls to guarantee them, as discussed in chapter 4.

102. E7, E14, C6.

103. C1, F7, E7. Sensitivity was evident in the negotiations for Occidental Pe-troleum's contractual joint venture in Shaanxi Province, as the Chinese side re-portedly insisted for months that Chinese workers be paid the equivalent of U.S. union wages ($14 per hour). *NYT*, 3 July 1985, p. D5.

CHAPTER THREE
THE PATTERN OF FOREIGN DIRECT INVESTMENT
IN CHINA: 1979–1988

1. Deng Xiaoping (1987) pp. 9–10. See also Xie Min (1987), Wang Luwen (1987), and Wang Yihe (1987). Documents released at the 13th National Party Congress (October 1987) also made explicit the leadership's commitment to open wider to the outside world. JPRS-CAR-88-4, p. 51.

2. Kim (1989), pp. 160–62. Kim believes that theories of interdependence wholly replaced self-reliance in Chinese analyses of the world economy. I argue, in contrast, that self-reliance remained in its reformulated version, as discussed in chapter 2, although it was emphasized less.

3. See Chan, Chen, and Chin (1986) on the de-emphasis on Lenin's NEP. Zhao Ziyang's theory was enunciated in his speech, "Advance Along the Road of Socialism with Chinese Characteristics," delivered at the 13th National Congress of the Communist Party of China, 25 October 1987. Zhao stated that it will take one hundred years from the 1950s (the official date of the "socialist transformation") to the time when socialist modernization will be complete, thereby implicitly extending the period in which foreign investment would be used.

4. The decline of concerns on specific issues is discussed in detail in chapters 4 and 5.

5. In the continuation of Deng Xiaoping's speech noted above (Deng Xiaoping [1987], p. 10), Deng's solution to the risks of foreign investment was the use of proper laws and education of Chinese people. Another essay, on bourgeois liberalization, asserted that any risks caused by the "open" policy were much smaller than the benefits, and could be overcome through a strengthening of socialist ethics. Editorial Department of *Red Flag* (1987), pp. 4–5.

6. For example, in 1986 reformist Vice Premier Tian Jiyun asserted that "[t]he main purpose of our policy of opening to the world is to import advanced foreign technologies and managerial expertise and attract foreign funds. In doing so, our ultimate aim is to improve the quality of our own products, *to increase our capacity for self-reliance* and to speed up China's modernization" (emphasis added). (Quoted in Uehara [1987], p. 14.) *Red Flag* editors argued further in 1987 that "The policy of opening to the outside world . . . is not only aimed at developing our socialist economy, but also guided by the two principles of always taking the economy of public ownership as the mainstay and achieving common prosperity. . . . Learning from advanced technologies and management skills of other countries serves as a useful and necessary supplement to the development of our socialist economy. . . . *The state apparatus of our socialist country is strong and powerful, which is able and has the means to protect the socialist economic system and able to guarantee the mainstay status of public ownership in the whole economy. Once the development of the economy departs from its socialist course or the mainstay position of public ownership in the economy is threatened, the state apparatus would intervene and correct them* with recourse to policies, legislation as well as administrative and economic measures." (Editorial Department of *Red Flag* [1987], pp. 1, 4. Emphasis added.) This ideological journal was one of few places

in which this sort of theoretical argument was made in support of the "open" policy.

7. On the general need for controls, see for example Li Boxi (1987). On the danger of unhealthy tendencies see, for example, Deng Xiaoping's 1987 comment: "We are now devoting our efforts to the promotion of the cultural and ideological advance of our socialist society while furthering its material progress. . . . While we pursue the open policy, *something evil is bound to come about, affecting our people*. If there are risks involved, this is the greatest risk" (1987, p. 10. Emphasis added).

8. In the early 1980s, China surpassed the $2.7 billion peak figure, reached in 1936, for FDI prior to 1949. N. R. Chen (1986), p. 3.

9. Several points should be noted about this categorization of phases. First, while the delineation of phases holds generally, for some specific issues changes came slightly earlier or later than the start of a new phase. In some cases, changes of rules in practice preceded formal legal codification. Second, the beginning of the second phase, in late 1983, was a transitional time. The Implementing Regulations, with which I mark the start of the phase, clarified many strict controls alluded to in the JV Law, and even added some new strict terms. But it also began the process of liberalization. The dual character of the Implementing Regulations should be borne in mind when considering the analysis in chapters 4 and 5. Third, the changes in the formal regulatory environment for equity joint ventures (EJVs) affected the flow of investment in *all* forms. This was because, in the absence of laws on other forms, the laws drafted for EJVs were either applied directly to, or used to guide investment in, other forms. Fourth, although the third phase ended at the end of 1988, some data that was available for early 1989 and the post-Tiananmen period at the time of writing is included in the analysis. Fifth, this delineation of phases is suggested by the pattern of investment that actually occurred, rather than by any analysis on the part of the Chinese government.

10. The formal title of this law is "The Law of the People's Republic of China on Joint Ventures Using Chinese and Foreign Investment" (*Zhonghua Renmin Gongheguo Zhong Wai Hezi Jingying Qiye Fa*), but is referred to herein as the "Joint Venture Law." It was adopted at the Second Session of the Fifth National People's Conference on 1 July 1979. For an English translation, see Chu, Moser, and Nee (1982).

11. For a list of laws published primarily in the first phase of investment that are relevant to foreign investment, see Moser (1984), pp. 331–35.

12. The regulations referred to herein as "Implementing Regulations," are formally titled "The Implementing Act for the Law of the People's Republic of China on Joint Ventures Using Chinese and Foreign Investment" (*Zhonghua Renmin Gongheguo Zhong Wai Hezi Jingying Qiye Fa Shishi Tiaoli*). Translated in *Beijing Review*, No. 41, 10 October 1983, pp. 1–16. Quote is from Yuan Mu (State Council spokesman) (1983). Foreigners recognized the improvement of these regulations over the original Joint Venture Law. See Cohen (1984), p. 10.

13. The decline in *value* of contracts in 1986 was influenced somewhat by the fact that a number of very large projects had come on line in 1985. However, this factor did not affect change in the *number* of projects concluded, which showed

the same trends: the number of projects for EJVs and for all FDI declined 37% and 51%, respectively, between 1985 and 1986.

14. *WSJ*, 6 June 1986, p. 28.

15. On the 7th Five-Year Plan, see N. R. Chen (1986), p. 30. On the 25,000 JV limit, Chu Baotai (1984), p. 113.

16. Westendorff (1989), p. 15. Westendorff also suggests that Shanghai leaders had raised their expectations for FDI, hoping to absorb $10 billion–$20 billion by the year 2000, or in eleven years to absorb five times the amount Shanghai absorbed in the first nine years of the policy ($1.8 billion), and that Shanghai's promulgation of an additional set of favorable investment regulations in November 1988 was intended to help spur further investment after stagnation of the growth of FDI during that year. Lardy also notes that some Chinese were disappointed with the capital flows (1987, p. 36).

17. Cohen and Chang (1987), p 11.

18. The 1986 Provisions are reprinted in *CBR*, Vol. 14, No. 1 (January–February 1987), pp. 14–15. On soliciting foreign views for the 1986 Provisions, see U.S. Congress, Office of Technology Assessment (hereafter OTA) (1987), p. 33 (note 31). For general statements indicating commitment to increasing foreign direct investment, see, for example, Xie Min (1987) and Suo Qian (1987).

19. For example, tax holidays outside of the SEZs set China in the middle of the range among Asian countries during the third phase. China's 33% effective tax rate on profits for joint ventures located outside the SEZs was higher than the rate on ventures in Hong Kong and South Korea, and than EJVs in Taiwan's advanced-technology sector, but less than or comparable to the rate applied to most ventures in Thailand, in Taiwan's low-technology sector, and to all Malaysian and Philippine ventures. The SEZs offered incentive packages that were more competitive with similar zones in Asia, although competitive liberalization by other Asian countries lessened the effectiveness of China's own liberalization. Details of tax incentives and comparisons with other Asian countries are in *CBR*, Vol. 15, No. 2 (March–April 1988), pp. 50–51; Ho and Huenemann (1984), pp. 81–83, and chap. 7; NCUSCT (1987), pp. 21–46; and, on SEZs, Moser (1984a). On competition in Asia, see Haggard and Cheng (1987).

20. China (with 5.8% of the total) followed Brazil, Mexico, Singapore, and Malaysia. *CBR*, Vol. 15, No. 2 (March–April 1988), p. 49; and U.N. Centre on Transnational Corporations (UNCTC) (1988), p. 85.

21. *CBR*, Vol. 15, No. 2 (March–April 1988), p. 49.

22. Comparative figures on contribution of foreign capital to gross domestic product are from World Bank (1988), p. 243. This figure for China is for utilized investment ($2.4 billion). The World Bank study indicates that the figure for Brazil, which has an economy about two-thirds the size of China's, may be as high as 12%, as official reports may underestimate the figure (p. 252). This figure for China in 1987 also was 1%. CIA (1988), p. 4, figure 3.

23. Unclassified Department of Commerce Memorandum from the U.S. embassy in Beijing, April 1990, p. 3. See also *NYT*, 14 April 1990, and *FEER*, 16 November 1989, p. 68. Most Taiwan investment was concentrated in Fujian Province (especially in Xiamen SEZ), across the strait from Taiwan. Taiwan investors

committed $520 million to 435 projects in the first 11 months of 1988. *China News-letter* No. 84 (January–February 1990), p. 17. It was also reported that Taiwan investors were the first to return after the Tiananmen killings. *FEER*, 16 November 1989, p. 68.

24. These figures, which are consistent with (but more detailed than) MOFERT figures in table 3-A, are from Unclassified Department of Commerce Memorandum from the U.S. embassy in Beijing, April 1990, p. 3, using data from the State Statistical Bureau (SSB) and MOFERT. Somewhat surprisingly, the SSB figures showed growth continuing at a relatively strong rate (32.5% for utilized FDI) from July to September, immediately after the crackdown. Negative growth (− 17.4% for utilized) was shown only in the fourth quarter (September to December). The *number* of approved contracts did decline 14% in the third quarter (July to September). The strong third quarter figures may be a result of lags in the reporting of projects to the SSB, or of a larger size in the contracts approved.

25. For example, in July and August of 1989, the pledged value of U.S. FDI declined 29% from the same period in 1988, and Japanese investment declined 34%. Moreover, it appeared that Taiwanese investment did not decline at all. (Unclassified Department of Commerce Memorandum from the U.S. Embassy in Beijing, April 1990.)

26. These amendments first appeared in *Renmin Ribao* on 8 April 1990, having been passed at the 7th National People's Congress. They were translated in *China Daily* on 9 April 1990. The specific provisions are discussed in chapters 4 and 5.

27. A number of the tables in the third section utilize data tabulated from large samples of pledged equity venture projects that MOFERT has published in its annual *Almanac of China's Foreign Economic Relations and Trade* (hereafter "*Almanac*") for 1985, 1986, 1987, and 1988. The samples contain for each year over 450 cases of EJVs, and provide data on names and nationality of partners, business objectives, equity split, foreign investment, total investment, and registered capital. Chen (1986) provides much data that is compared to the MOFERT samples for the 1979 to 1984 period based on his sample of 841 EJVs concluded during those years. MOFERT does not indicate how it compiled samples. Chen used information available from China at the time of his writing.

28. Most of the characteristics noted here are established in the 1979 JV Law or the 1983 Implementing Regulations. Other descriptions of EJVs in China appear in Ho and Huenemann (1984), chap. 4; N. T. Wang (1984); and Moser (1984a). The basic format of EJVs is the same in China as elsewhere. The specific terms of investment can vary widely, however. On EJVs in other countries, see, for example, McMillan and St. Charles (1973), Friedmann and Beguin (1971), Tomlinson (1970), and Walmsley (1982).

29. The JV Law (Article 4) and Implementing Regulations (Article 19) state that each side's liability is "limited to the amount of the capital subscribed by each" and that each shares risks and losses in proportion to equity share. The exact meaning of "limited liability" in the Chinese legal context was not clear during much of the 1980s, for China had no company law. Limited liability companies (which exist in most civil law jurisdictions except the United States) are corporations "which sue and can be sued, and generally have two owners, no share certificates, and are not

subject to the same statutory formalities that govern the civil law corporations on shares." Swindler (1984), p. 1020, note 84.

30. The terms for JV borrowing fluctuated. In January 1989, in the face of rising concerns about foreign debt, the State Council limited foreign borrowing by the Chinese partner by requiring prior (and increasingly difficult to obtain) approval by the State Administration for Exchange Control (SAEC). Also restricted was the Chinese partner's ability to guarantee foreign commercial loans without SAEC approval. Foreign partners were still able to borrow from abroad, but the absence of guarantees from Chinese partners made this kind of lending less appealing to international banks. Haley (1989), pp. 30–31.

31. On nationalization, see Ho and Heunemann (1984), p. 80. Originally, these guarantees were made only verbally. The 1990 amendments to the JV Law added this guarantee against nationalization to the written code.

32. For the genesis of this decision, see Crane (1986), pp. 198–206, and Chen, Chan, and Chin (1986).

33. A comparison of China's SEZs and Asian EPZs, and a discussion of incentives offered by China, are found in Wong and Chu (1984), and Chan, Chen, and Chin (1986), pp. 90–91.

34. Ma Hong (1985), p. 5.

35. The figure of 21% is derived by taking $3.7 billion invested in the SEZs as a percentage of the cumulative 1979–1986 pledged FDI figure ($17.7 billion). Percentages of the $3 billion held by the SEZs are Shenzhen and Shekou, 60%; Zhuhai, 11%; Shantou, 4%; and Xiamen, 25%. The figure of 35% is derived by taking 3500 as a percentage of the total number of contracts signed during the 1979–1987 period, 10,052. For figures for all foreign investment, see table 3-A. The figure for total cumulative investment in the SEZs and Shenzhen likely includes processing and assembly/compensation trade. *FEER*, 1 October 1987, pp. 102, 105. On the number of contracts through 1987, see *China Daily*, 26 March 1988.

36. As of the end of 1984, 34% of all EJVs were located in the four SEZs. (23% of all EJVs were in Shenzhen, 3.7% in Zhuhai, 1.2% in Shantou, and 5.9% in Xiamen.) Across the four EJVs, 68.4% were in Shenzhen, 10.7% were in Zhuhai, 3.5% were in Shantou, and 17.4% were in Zhuhai. These figures are directly from or derived from N. R. Chen (1986), p. 19 (table 14). Sample data compiled by MOFERT for the years 1985–1987 are consistent with figures from earlier years, indicating that the SEZs housed 281 (20%) of the 1378 EJVs tabulated in the 1985–1987 MOFERT samples. The figure falls to 11% when the 1988 MOFERT sample data are included, however (table 3-E).

37. One Chinese newspaper reported in the mid-1980s that only 7% of Shenzhen's imported technology (within and outside of joint ventures) was of international standard. Reported in *FEER*, 1 October 1987, p. 104. Shenzhen's performance is analyzed further in chapter 4.

38. On the reform economists' view, see Pepper (1988), pp. 15–16. On the opening of the 14 "open" cities, *Shenzhen Tequ Bao* (*Shenzhen Special Zone Herald*, hereafter *SSZH*), 18 January 1985, p. 1. The fourteen "open" coastal cities were Guangzhou, Tianjin, Shanghai, Dalian, Qinhuangdao, Yantai, Qingdao, Lianyungang, Nantong, Ningbo, Wenzhou, Fuzhou, Zhanjiang, and Beihai. Al-

though the designation of "open city" was withdrawn from ten of the cities in mid-1985 (Tianjin, Shanghai, Dalian, and Guangzhou were the four exceptions), the designation was later quietly restored.

39. On the OEZs, A. T. Kearney (1987), pp. 8–9, and *China's Foreign Trade*, November 1987 (No. 11), pp. 20–22. The figure for area and population in the SEZs, OEZs, and fourteen cities is from *China Daily*, 9 March 1988. On Hainan, *CBR* Vol. 16, No. 1 (January–February 1989), pp. 20–34. Aside from the common purpose of attracting foreign investment, these areas were to have slightly different emphases. The SEZs were to emphasize developing advanced technical industries, the "open" cities should stress machinery and electronic exports and upgrading existing enterprises, and the OEZs should emphasize agricultural exports and the development of township enterprises. *China Daily*, 9 March 1988, p. 2.

40. The Shekou Industrial Zone (located in Shenzhen SEZ), run by the China Merchant Steam Navigation Company, was granted the greatest degree of formal autonomy. The precise degree of autonomy for all open areas fluctuated throughout the 1980s along with more general decentralization and recentralization cycles.

41. Quote is from Zhao Ziyang (1987), p. 22. Zhao's plan to open the entire seaboard is reported in *The Economist*, 12 March 1988, pp. 61–62.

42. Both figures are calculated from sample figures presented in table 3-J, with the latter figure excluding the three very large EJVs presented in 3-J.

43. This figure is calculated from the figures in table 3-B and is generally consistent with the figures presented in table 3-K for the sample of EJVs if the three largest projects are excluded (table 3-K, note f). Also using the figures from table 3-B, it is evident that the average foreign investment per EJV is somewhat smaller than the average foreign contribution in all FDI projects ($1.67 million).

44. Firms in the Hong Kong/Macao category are overwhelmingly from Hong Kong. These figures are broadly consistent with the previously reported study of 301 EJVs established by industrialized countries by the end of 1986, which indicates that U.S. investors tended to contribute the smallest amounts (with average commitments of $1.9 million/venture), reflecting a preference for CJVs for their larger projects. Japan's EJVs were the next smallest among the industrialized countries, with a $2.7 million average commitment. Investors from Western Europe, Canada, Australia, and New Zealand averaged $4.5 million. The figure for Asian countries of Singapore, the Philippines, and Thailand was $1.7 million. NCUSCT (1987), p. 125.

45. *FEER*, 10 March 1988, p. 63, and Westendorff (1989), p. 12.

46. Westendorff (1989), pp. 11–12. The Volkswagen JV was responsible for West Germany's strong percentage in value of FDI in technologically advanced enterprises (TAEs). Shanghai was well represented by firms from Hong Kong and Japan, so the U.S. and European domination of TAEs was not a result of their domination in the number of EJVs. Also see chapter 4 on TAEs.

47. The figures for Guangdong Province are from papers presented at a 1985 conference. Chu Baotai (1987), p. 37. The second set of Chinese government figures are cited in *Boston Globe*, 12 May 1985, p. 87. "Foreign-backed businesses" was not defined in the article but probably referred to all forms of foreign investment. *China Economic News* (9 September 1985, p. 6) reported that to the end of

1984, foreign-backed enterprises employed 211,255 workers and staff, with 15,331 of these being foreigners.

48. Information was available for 22 EJVs in the sample. Taking the product of the average stated in the sample (739) and the number of EJVs in operation by the end of 1985 (766) gives a figure of 566,074 workers employed. Because the sample is weighted toward U.S. and European firms (which tend to be larger), the true figure is probably less.

49. Chai (1983), pp. 128–29. The forms of investment used to calculate this estimate included processing and assembly plants, and small and medium compensation trade projects (neither of which are direct investment), as well as equity joint ventures.

50. As a point of reference, it took the Japanese and South Korean auto industries ten to fifteen years to become internationally competitive and to have exports that provided a significant share of total production. World Bank (1988), p. 54.

51. In 1985, total value of investment in fixed assets was 254 billion *yuan*. Of this, value of foreign investment was 5 billion *yuan*, or approximately 2%. The 1985 figures are from State Statistical Bureau (1985), p. 366. The 1979–1984 capital construction figure is from Chu Baotai (1987), p. 23.

52. These 1987 growth figures are approximate. On 1987 figures, CIA (1988), p. 4, figure 3. The 1988 figures are from SSB, "Communique on the Statistics of 1988 Economic and Social Development," in FBIS, 2 March 1989, p. E15.

53. Figures on export earnings for 1987 are from CIA (1988), p. 9, and for 1989, from FBIS-CHI-90-017, p. 29. On foreign exchange earnings from tourism, *China Sources*, January 1988, p. 92. Import figure is from *CBR*, Vol. 16, No. 3 (May–June 1989), p. 44. Imports rose 28% in 1988 to $55.3 billion.

54. Some data on firms in the sample are from sources published after the original interviews were conducted. The other sample reported is A. T. Kearney (1987), p. 28. The 1986 figure was reported in *China Daily*, 30 January 1986, p. 2, and the 1989 figure in *NYT*, 25 November 1989. Other apparently favorable data on the profitability of selected ventures is presented in Chu Baotai (1987), pp. 35–36.

55. MOFERT figure is reported in *FEER*, 24 March 1988, p. 78. The Chinese analyst cited is Suo Qian (1987), p. 11. The British survey, which included trading companies and banks, as well as manufacturing projects, is Campbell (1986), pp. 11–13. On average, Japanese companies surveyed were least satisfied, and U.S. companies most satisfied. Poor profit performance was also suggested by E11, E16, and F9-C.

56. This more positive view of lower returns was taken by many investors, at least publicly, and was reflected in the commercial study by A. T. Kearney (1987), p. 28.

57. 28% responded that it was "too early to tell." A. T. Kearney (1987), p. 29.

58. NCUSCT (1987), p. 123. *China Daily* reported in 1986 that only four EJVs had failed, and less than ten had experienced serious financial problems. (30 January 1986, p. 2.) Chinese analysts did become worried that the high ratio of debt to total assets of foreign enterprises (as high as 80%) might precipitate some failures. This concern led in early 1989 to borrowing restrictions on joint ventures. Suo Qian (1987), p. 72.

CHAPTER FOUR
CONTROLS AT THE NATIONAL AND REGIONAL LEVELS

1. Wang Yihe, et al. (1984), p. 91.

2. Although this study does not focus on regional variations, I have noted where foreign interviewees indicated differences in operational constraints between regions. As a whole, interviewees characterized Beijing as much more rigid than either Shanghai or Guangzhou. Regional differences were considered to be a result of closeness to the central government in Beijing, and business acumen and desire to make money in Shanghai and Guangzhou (F4, F24-A, and F16-A). Variability in interpretation by regions is noted generally in N. T. Wang (1984), p. 95, and *AWSJ*, 10 November 1984. The central government attempted to respond to foreign complaints about local variations in the interpretation of tax laws, which local governments sometimes applied more strictly than intended by central authorities, by distributing clearer guidelines.

3. Deng Xiaoping was quoted in Ma Hong (1985), p. 6. On the Chinese view of JVs as inherently offering host country control, Wang Yihe, et al. (1984), pp. 45, 51, and 87.

4. On JV contracts encouraging "mutual benefit," F14, C1, C1-A. "Mutual benefit" and protection of foreign resources, profits, and lawful interests were codified in the Joint Venture Law, Articles 1 and 2. "Obvious iniquity" was prohibited in Article 5 of the Implementing Regulations. See also Wang Yihe, et al. (1984), pp. 56, 104. On the Chinese view that "mutual benefit" was the standard behind much law on JVs, see Economic Information Agency (HK) (1982), p. 25. Mutual interests are also supposed to guide the negotiation and operation of joint ventures in Eastern Europe. Szasz (1982), p. 100.

5. Article 4 of the JV Law defines "equitable divisions" of profits and losses. Because joint ventures are limited liability companies, partners share losses according to their equity contribution, and losses cannot exceed the total value of either partner's contribution. Cohen (1984). Standards of equality in contracts generally were noted by C1; C3; F12-A; *JJDB*, 15 July 1981, p. 6; and Economic Information Agency, p. 25. Chinese negotiators were responsible for seeing that these guarantees of equality and mutual benefit appeared in the contracts, according to a Chinese official (C1). This official also noted that even though the board of directors (BOD) chair and general manager have final authority, the spirit of equality and mutual benefit, and consensual discussions, should nonetheless prevail. On comparable salaries, and equality in decisionmaking structures, see chapter 5.

6. Claims for protection for foreigners were made in Wang Yihe, et al. (1984), p. 117; *JJDB*, 18 April 1983, p. 18; *SSZH*, 11 January 1985, p. 1; and Li Yanshi (1980), p. 34. On the desire for friendship as well as economic benefit, C1, and Wang Yihe, et al. (1984), p. 28.

7. The guarantee of equality before Chinese law was asserted by Wei Yuming (1982), p. W3, and Economic Information Agency (1982), p. 25. To the extent that arbitration and mediation were favored over Chinese court procedures, this guarantee of legal equality could be undermined.

8. Many foreign interviewees did note sincerity of the Chinese side's desire to uphold "equality and mutual benefit" (F21, F24, F16-A, F18, F14, F7-A, E7, E5, E6, E8, E17, F26, F9-D). In contrast, Moser (1984a, pp. 121–22) commented on using this principle as a negotiating tactic. Pye's interviews with traders confirm the latter view. His explanation is that, while it is the Chinese negotiating style to "hold up for praise ideals of mutual interest," negotiators are nevertheless wary of being cheated by foreigners and wish to be seen as hard-nosed by their superiors to avoid criticism (1982), pp. 70, 77.

9. As one Chinese joint venture manager put it, "Protection [for China's sovereignty] comes from China's laws and regulations. If joint ventures follow the laws, then sovereignty will be protected." This manager also conceded that it is difficult to be more specific on how laws are protective of Chinese sovereignty (F9-E). See also Rong Yiren (1979), p. 77. Chinese who write on FDI repeatedly emphasize the importance of laws. Shenzhen mayor Liang Xiang noted that "[i]n order to safeguard our country's sovereignty and interests . . . in recent years the state has proclaimed a series of laws and regulations" (1984), p. 14. Wang Yihe, et al. note with admiration that the defense of national sovereignty is a primary goal of Mexico's foreign investment law (1984, p. 30).

10. Wang Yihe, et al. (1984), pp. 104–5. Host country governing law is often seen as a way of protecting the sovereign rights of host countries.

11. Dispute resolution provisions in the early years, which allowed for arbitration in a third country if "friendly consultation" and mediation within China failed, took a more flexible approach to sovereignty, although in practice the government generally disallowed this until the mid-1980s. Cohen and Horsley (1983), p. 47. Laws setting maintenance of Chinese sovereignty as a condition of JV approval are Implementing Regulations, Article 5 and "Provisions of the Shenzhen Special Economic Zone on Economic Contracts Involving Foreign Interests," Article 6 (promulgated February 1984), translated in CBR, September–October 1984, p. 19. A Chinese trade official did note that when reviewing a contract, MOFERT would make a judgment as to whether the contract was detrimental to China's sovereignty (C3).

12. Rong Yiren (1979), p. 77. See also Chu Baotai (1984), pp. 110–11. The JV Law, Article 4, stipulates only that foreign ownership must exceed 25%. In the socialist CMEA countries of Poland, Romania, Yugoslavia, and (for production ventures) Hungary, foreign shares in joint ventures are limited to 49%. Countries such as Bulgaria, Zaire, Indonesia, Pakistan, and Australia do not make across-the-board restrictions on foreign majority ownership, although they may ban FDI from designated strategic sectors. On CMEA countries, see Szasz (1982), p. 104. On other countries, see UNCTC (1983).

13. This section on investment laws discusses, with a few exceptions, the use of law as a regulatory mechanism rather than the contents of specific laws. The latter are discussed in the context of the issues to which they are relevant. For example, the content of foreign exchange laws are discussed under general foreign exchange controls.

14. Although a legalist tradition in imperial China emphasized rule by written law, the more dominant Confucian tradition emphasized correct behavior rather than written law. Moreover, the socialist economy since 1949 had been directed

more by plans that were continually revised, not by commercial law codes. On reformists' recognition of the importance of law in controlling FDI, Juan Wenqi, et al. (1980), p. 25; Rong Yiren (1979), p. 77; and F14-E (Chinese manager).

15. On the rights and authority of foreigners, see Wang Yihe, et al. (1984), pp. 113–14.

16. A copy of the draft Schindler agreement was reprinted in *China Economic News* in the spring of 1980. On early disputes over Chinese governing law, see also Moser (1987), p. 105. On JVs' status as "Chinese legal persons" and their subjection to Chinese law, see Wang Yihe, et al. (1984), p. 107, and Chu Baotai (1984), p. 111.

17. Wang Yihe, et al. discuss this distinction (1984, pp. 52–54). For models from other socialist countries, they cite Yugoslavia, Poland, Hungary, and Romania.

18. Although the use of a host country governing law clause was not unusual, especially among developing countries, in Poland, Hungary, Romania, Czechoslovakia, Bulgaria, East Germany, North Korea, and the Soviet Union, for example, the parties to foreign economic contracts could choose a nonhost country governing law. Polish law was more restrictive on this issue than were others in Eastern Europe (Szasz [1982], p. 101).

19. On acceptance of foreign arbitrators, Moser (1987), p. 105. On the acceptance of international business standards, see Cohen (1985), p. 52.

20. Chang and Olofsson (1989), p. 18.

21. *Neibu* rules did not always pose a problem, for they apparently often contained rules that eventually were to be publicly promulgated.

22. Article 3 of the JV Law required Chinese governmental approval of contracts, a requirement reiterated in Article 8 of the Implementing Regulations. On central approval of JVs in CMEA countries, see Scriven (1982), p. 109. On approval of JVs in other developing countries, see UNCTC (1983).

23. On various pre-negotiation approvals, see Implementing Regulations, Article 9, and Moser (1984a), pp. 107, 119. On the choice of a particular partner, Zhou Douyang and Yin Youguo (1984), p. 4. Authorization from the ministries of foreign trade and finance to negotiate was also required in Hungary. Lorinczi (1982), p. 114.

24. See the JV model contract in Moser (1987), pp. 142–56, and commentary in Ta-kuang Chang (1987), p. 9. If Chinese partners *did* accept a proposal prior to government authorization, and the government approval agency disagreed, the proposal was subject to re-negotiation. Interviewees (for example, E7) noted this, confirming Pye's (1982) finding that negotiators are hesitant to make independent decisions lest they be penalized later. See also Zhang Shangtang (1984), p. 363, and Moser (1984a), p. 107.

25. Cohen (1984), p. 12, and Moser (1984a), p. 107. See Lieberthal and Oksenberg (1988) for an illustration of this in the offshore oil industry. Multiple approvals were also needed for joint ventures in Romania and Hungary. Business International (1983), p. 80, and Lorinczi (1982), p. 114.

26. Implementing Regulations, Article 8, allowed for delegation of approval authority for small ventures when the noted conditions were met. The ceiling was also high for the SEZs, as long as raw materials and energy were supplied locally

and products were primarily for exports. Even these guidelines were not rigidly applied, however. On these decentralizations to localities in the second phase, see Moser (1987), pp. 92–93. On further delegation by cities in the third phase, see Liu Lei (1988), pp. 48–49. On interior provinces and central departments (including, for example, the State Bureau of Building Materials, the State Pharmaceutical Administration, the National Tourism Administration), JPRS-CEA-88-050 (25 August 1988), pp. 42–43.

27. On ultimate MOFERT review, Ta-kuang Chang (1987), p. 10, and Moser (1987), p. 93. The case noted is F14-B. The Implementing Regulations (Article 8) also state that JVs with local approval must still be sent to MOFERT "for the record."

28. Information in this section is based primarily on Cohen (1987) (for a discussion on current laws); Kam C. Wong (1984); Wang Yihe, et al. (1984), chap. 14; *Wo Guo Liyong Zhongcai Jiejue Dui Wai Jingji Jiufen* [China Uses Arbitration to Solve Foreign Economic Disputes] (1984), p. 1; and Peele and Cohan (1988).

29. The findings of this study are supported by NCUSCT (1987), p. 171. Even when disputes reached arbitral bodies, the Chinese government preferred to settle them with conciliation rather than formal arbitration. Cohen (1987), p. 510.

30. The major Chinese arbitral body was the Foreign Economic and Trade Arbitration Commission (FETAC) under the China Council for the Promotion of International Trade (CCPIT). The law in Eastern Europe allowed joint ventures the option of submitting to arbitration in a foreign country. Hungarian JVs also used foreign courts, at the choice of the partners. Szasz (1982), p. 103.

31. Implementing Regulations, chap. 15. On the July 1985 Foreign Economic Contract Law (formally entitled the "Law of the PRC on Economic Contracts Involving Foreign Interests"), see Cohen (1987), pp. 512–13.

32. Chang and Olofsson (1989), p. 18.

33. Quote is from the Civil Procedure Law, Article 204, in Cohen (1984a), pp. 21–22. On the two cases, Peele and Cohan (1988), p. 47.

34. Quote is from MOFERT vice minister Wei Yuming (1982), p. W4. See also Wei Yuming (1983), p. 20, and Qian Zongqi (1983), pp. 18–19. The state plan had long governed foreign trade. The First Five-Year Plan (1953–1957), for example, had at its core massive imports of complete plants from the Soviet Union (Dernberger [1977]). Romanian joint ventures had to draw up annual and five-year economic plans that fit within the parameters of the national plan. Scriven (1982), p. 109.

35. On inclusion of FDI in the five-year plans, Chu Baotai (1984), p. 112, and Zhou Shude (1984), p. 20. On the Seventh Five-Year Plan targets, see *AWSJ*, 16–17 October 1984, p. 17. Moser (1987, pp. 90–91) gives an overview of how JVs fit the plan as of 1983. One function of the feasibility study was to assess how the project under consideration would fit the state plan. Other countries, such as Tanzania, also screen foreign projects for fit with the national plan. UNCTNC (1983), p. 23.

36. As of the early 1980s, more than two-thirds of the nation's industrial output was produced by state-owned enterprises, all of which was subject to planned supply and production by state planning agencies. Reynolds (1984), p. 78. On pricing according to the plan, Implementing Regulations, Article 65. On supply of materi-

als both subject and not subject to planning, see Implementing Regulations, Article 58. Although not explicitly stated, the price for these materials was sometimes negotiable. Imports, however, were to be negotiated in the joint venture contract, and were subject to the state licensing scheme. Imports exceeding the scope of the contract required further licenses. Implementing Regulations, Article 63.

37. On planned sales see Implementing Regulations, Article 64.1, and Moser (1984a), p. 130. The situation of the pharmaceutical and export industry is noted in NCUSCT (1987), p. 152. Government distribution organizations were often not particularly good at or interested in marketing JV products, so that the JV still had to work to promote goods sold via government channels. In general, goods handled by materials (and commercial) departments were to be sold under contract by the joint venture to the departments (Article 64.2).

38. Implementing Regulations, Articles 63, 64, and 66. At least one EJV contract stated this pricing standard explicitly (E7). Prices for domestic sales were to be filed with the department in charge (DIC) and price control departments. The exception to state setting of prices was for items designated by the price control department for "valuation with reference to the international market." See also NCUSCT (1987), p. 153; Moser (1984a), p. 131; and Cohen and Horsley (1983), p. 46.

39. Fujian-Hitachi's plan was approved first by the Fujian provincial government, then by MOFERT (in consultation with the Ministry of Electronics Industry), and finally by the State Planning Commission. Imai (1984), p. 17. On the central orders to cut production, see Fujimura (1982).

40. FEER, 16 July 1987, p. 70. These urban reforms were formalized in the "Decision of the Central Committee of the Communist Party of China on Reform of the Economic Structure," adopted at the Third Plenum of the Twelfth Central Committee on 20 October 1984.

41. Article 56. The DIC was not to direct JV production; the plan was merely "to be filed" with the DIC (C1).

42. F14-A. A Chinese official suggested that this may have been the result of the venture's contractual provision to cover original production obligations of the Chinese partner under the state plan (C1).

43. Wei Yuming (1983), p. 20. See also Wei Yuming (1982), p. W5 (C1).

44. The first example is from F14-B. The Chinese deputy general manager in this venture also emphasized the importance of the plan for guaranteeing supplies (F14-E). The second example is from a Shanghai-Foxboro manager, quoted in Imai (1984), p. 19. See also Fujimura (1982).

45. Several producers, all with formal allocations, might have to compete for short supplies. The government increasingly tried to give priority in supply allocations to joint ventures. NCUSCT (1987), p. 147–48.

46. Calls for greater use of plans were made in Li Boxi (1987), p. 51; Yang Aiqun (1987), p. 17; and Kong Xiangyi (1987), pp. 790–91.

47. Li Peng's statement was reported in China Daily, 11 September 1984, p. 1. The MOFERT official is Chu Baotai (1984, p. 113). Chu also wrote in 1985 that China had one million enterprises, and that if enterprises using foreign funds (all types) equaled 5% (or 50,000) of the total, "they would be . . . a beneficial complement" to the national economy. By 1988, China had 15,500 foreign-backed enter-

prises of all types, also approximately one-third of Chu's 5% figure. Chu (1987), p. 22. The view that China was far from reaching a maximum goal was echoed in a 1987 statement (written in 1986) by the Editorial Department of *Red Flag* (1987, p. 3), and informally in an interview with a scholar from the Chinese Academy of Social Sciences in April 1989.

48. Kawai (1984), p. 13.

49. Specific industries in which joint ventures were encouraged were stipulated in Article 3 of the Implementing Regulations. These industries are similar to those open to FDI in Bulgaria and Romania. In Yugoslavia, JVs were not allowed in most service sectors in the early 1970s. In Hungary they were allowed only in foreign and domestic commerce and in service activities but were not allowed to engage directly in production. McMillan and St. Charles (1973), pp. 23–24. In the 1980s, sectoral restrictions on FDI were loosened in many developing countries, especially where the host government hoped to gain foreign technology (as, for example, in India, Mexico, Venezuela, Singapore). This was not true across the board, however. UNCTC (1988), p. 269.

50. On sectors that previously were considered off limits, see Zhong Douyang and Ying Youguo (1984), p. 4; Chu Baotai (1984), p. 113; Wang Yihe, et al. (1984), p. 152; and He Xinhao (1980), p. 2. On AMC, Uehara (1987), p. 16. A visit by U.S. military industrialists to China in late 1985 suggested that joint ventures even in military technology fields were possible. *Boston Globe*, 5 November 1985, p. 39.

51. Criticism of the sectoral composition of foreign investment was expressed in Wang Yihe (1987), p. 48.

52. Such competition between Dalian and Shanghai over cooperation with foreigners in agriculture and food processing is well described in Grow (1989).

53. On 1988 "favored" sectors, *China Economic News*, 4 January 1988, p. 3. On Guangzhou, see *Xinhua*, 9 May 1987, in JPRS-CAR-87-013, p. 63. On Shanghai, see *China Daily*, 4 June 1987, p. 2, and "Vice Minister Addresses Foreigners on Investment Climate" (1987), p. 70. The 1989 limits were reported in *FEER*, 2 March 1989, p. 59.

54. Of 24 EJVs sampled for this study, 4% (1) were for 0–9 years, 46% (11) were for 10–15 years, 33% (8) were for 16–20 years, 17% (4) were for 21–25 years, and none were for 26–30 years. One exception to the general limit was a banking joint venture in Xiamen SEZ agreed to in mid-1985 that reportedly had not fixed an expiration. *FEER*, 4 July 1985. Some involved claimed that this privilege grew out of special circumstances between investors and approving authorities. The contract limitation of 30 years was longer than in Poland and Bulgaria (a maximum of 15 years, with the possibility of extension), but was shorter than possible in Hungary and Romania, where the governments allowed both fixed and indefinite term ventures. Scriven (1982), p. 109.

55. *China Daily*, 9 April 1990. According to this article, those on the Congress' Standing Committee who opposed dropping the requirement for a fixed term "argued that China lacked the relevant laws and regulations for deciding how and under what circumstances joint venture contracts could be terminated."

56. See, for example, Chu Baotai (1984), p. 114–15. Chu's estimation that JVs would be around for "at least 100 years" was supported by repeated leadership assertions that the joint venture policy would not change. Chu also reiterated the idea that China must control the negative effects of FDI.

57. The difficulty of assigning the source of this problem is illustrated by the 1985 case of Hainan Island. In order to meet strong central pressure to develop quickly, Hainan officials were allowed to—and did—import luxury goods (particularly Japanese cars) under their preferential customs scheme. They then resold the goods at higher "market" prices to inland regions. Local officials argued they were not acting corruptly because they were actually helping their island and meeting inland demand and did not pocket the profits. They were subject to central government rebuke nonetheless. On this case, see *NYT*, 27 September 1985, p. D2, and 13 December 1985, p. 2.

58. Reflection of class struggle was not considered to be the same as class struggle itself. This distinction was important for analytically distancing post-Mao China from the Cultural Revolution when the "Gang of Four" was blamed for promoting class struggle everywhere. For articles applying class analysis, see Fan Juyi (1982); Editorial Department of *Hongqi* (1982a), pp. 1–8; and Xin Ren (1982), pp. 35–36. On the 1985–1986 debate in the northeast, Sullivan (1988), p. 201. On domestic sources of corruption, see Zhu Shenqing (1982), pp. 48–49, and Commentator, *Hongqi* (1982), p. 44.

59. See, for example, comments by CITIC head and former Shanghai capitalist Rong Yiren (1982), p. 73. Rong had a personal and professional incentive to deflect such criticisms from himself, of course.

60. Chen Yun, who appeared to support the "open" policy despite some conservative leanings, cited poor party discipline as a cause of the problem. *FEER*, 5 December 1985, p. 15. The solution for these reformers was further reform of the economic system. Commentator, *Hongqi* (1982), p. 41.

61. Deng's speech is cited in *SCMP*, 12 March 1985, p. 7. A trade official expressed similar concerns regarding the "open" policy: "The adoption of the open economic policies will definitely bring the ideology of capitalist societies, and the bourgeois way of life and customs will inevitably pound at our society." Sun Ru (1982a), p. K5. See also Deng quoted from *Selected Works of Deng Xiaoping*, p. 364, in Deng Liqun (1984), p. K5.

62. Xi Wen (1982), pp. 69–71.

63. Feng Sheng (1984), p. K16.

64. Chen Yun stated this view. See "Build a Great Wall Ideologically" (1982), and "Deng Xiaoping Is Concerned About Guangdong and Fujian" (1982), p. W1. This general line was reiterated in September 1986 in the "Resolution of the Central Committee of the Communist Party of China on the Guiding Principles for Building a Socialist Society with an Advanced Culture and Ideology" (1986), pp. 2–3.

65. See Deng Liqun (1984), p. K5, and Zhao Ziyang (1987), p. 47. Many other statements in the press reflected the emphasis on political and ideological work, such as Editorial Department of *Hongqi* (1982b), p. K5; Zhu Dingzhen (1984); and Xiao An (1984), p. 4. See also Sullivan (1988). For a brief discussion of the traditional role of political study, see White (1983), p. 45.

66. Wang Daming, head of the Beijing party propaganda office, acknowledged that as a result of its poor post–Cultural Revolution stature the party should soften the old way of sloganizing and replace political jargon with reason and sympathy. *SCMP*, 27 January 1985, p. 6. Deng Xiaoping also expressed the need to replace political movements and mass criticism with milder forms of persuasion and educa-

tion. *FEER*, 3 October 1985, p. 12. Discussion of political study in EJVs is discussed further in chapter 5.

67. Editorial Department of *Hongqi* (1982), p. 380.

68. Controls on foreigners were mentioned by F4, F5 (CJV), F9-F, F14-A, F22 (CJV), F28, C1 (Chinese official), E11. On identification cards for foreigners, *JJDB*, 18 July 1983, p. 8.

69. *NYT*, 25 April 1982, p. 17.

70. Most Chinese JV partners preferred to have many more expatriates than the foreign side—because of the expense and difficulty of employing them—often was willing to send (F6, F9, F12-A, F27). During the CASP, some expatriates noted Chinese managers' coolness (F7-A and F28); one expatriate noted greater difficulty in carrying videotapes for private use across the border (F14-C), and another noted that its commercials could not be shown on television (F28). Yet only one foreign manager felt hostility directed at "capitalism" from his Chinese partners (F-9A).

71. On pornography: C1; F4; FBIS-CHI-82-069, 9 April 1982, p. P1. During the CASP, one EJV expatriate saw two Chinese tied up by police in a marketplace for selling contraband tapes of popular Taiwanese singers (F14-C). On Interpol, *China Daily*, 9 September 1984, p. 1.

72. See especially Article 8 of the "Provisional Articles on Control of Advertising," promulgated by the State Council on 17 February 1982 (published in *East Asian Executive Reports*, May 1982, pp. 24–25).

73. Chinese officials (C1, C4) noted the official relaxation toward foreign habits.

74. Deng Xiaoping's first major speech following the June 1989 events blamed foreign sources for "bourgeois liberalization."

75. UNCTC (1988), pp. 272–74. For example, the Indian government encouraged exports by restricting the foreign side in a JV to minority ownership unless the venture exported a "significant proportion" of output or operated in priority industries using "sophisticated" technology. If a company exported all of its products, 100% foreign equity could be permitted. Although JVs in Romania could sell their goods on the domestic market, they had to operate in convertible currency, thereby emphasizing exports and isolating JVs from the domestic market. Generally, conflicts between host governments and multinationals over domestic sales by joint ventures also existed in CMEA countries. Scriven (1982), pp. 108–10.

76. China routinely protected domestic industries after 1949. The 1949 Common Program (Article 37) stated that "control shall be exercised over foreign trade and the policy of protecting trade shall be adopted." Wang Yihe, et al. (1984), pp. 92–93. The principle of comparative costs as the basis for trade was criticized at a 1983 conference of Chinese foreign trade specialists for not reflecting the fact that protectionism historically has been a part of international trade. A report on the conference implied that protectionism is still a legitimate tool. *GMW* Special Reporter (1983), p. 5. Protectionism was also supported in Wang Shouchun and Li Kanghua (1981), p. 40. Both the benefit of competition and protection of infant industries were favored by reformist Zhang Xinda (1987), p. 98, and Wei Yuming (vice minister of MOFERT) (1982), p. W2. Joint ventures may even be the beneficiaries of protectionism, as the government has restricted imports of, for example, cars from Japan. *NYT*, 5 November 1985, p. D27.

77. F16 noted that his JV's domestic sales were relatively more profitable, and were not subject to import quotas.

78. These possibilities were suggested in Chu Baotai (1984), p. 114.

79. The model contract drafted by MOFERT to guide joint venture negotiations stipulated that quotas for exports should be set, and which parties—the JV, a foreign trade corporation, or a third party—should handle what percentage of the exports. Moser (1987), pp. 147–48.

80. Twenty-two ventures sampled planned to export. Of these, thirteen were exporting or planned to export 50% or more, and seven (32%) exported or planned to export less than 50%. (One would not specify the target level, and one was involved in two ventures, one of which exported more than, and one less than, 50%.) Five ventures in the sample (19%) did not have contractual commitments to export.

81. The authors of the second study imply that these firms' previous status as exporters *to* China gave them an advantage in terms of negotiating export requirements *from* China for their prospective joint ventures. The more probable reason for these JVs' exemptions is that they produced goods that China continued to urgently need. Daniels, Krug, and Nigh (1985), p. 50.

82. For example, F24-A.

83. Fujimura (1982).

84. On refusal to take JV bids, NCUSCT (1987), p. 156. The other examples are from F14, F28, F22 (CJV).

85. F28 and F18 (CJV). These findings are supported by Mann (1989); Pomfret (1989); NCUSCT (1987), pp. 150 and 154; and A. T. Kearney (1987), p. 77. The latter survey of 54 EJVs found that "very few JVs have been able to meet the export targets set in their JV contract."

86. Implementing Regulations, Articles 61 and 64. The SEZs offered some concessions on domestic market access for firms bringing in advanced technology as early as 1982. Crane (1986), p. 321.

87. *FEER*, 6 February 1986, p. 70, and Imai (1984), p. 16. The rules, entitled "Regulations on Foreign Currency Balance of Equity Joint Ventures," became effective 1 February 1986, but had in fact been operative for several months.

88. NCUSCT (1987), p. 139, Of fifty-five JVs designated as "export-oriented" in Beijing and Shanghai, twenty-eight (51%) were with Hong Kong or Macao partners, whereas only eight (14.5%) were with partners from the United States.

89. These regulations are the "Measures Concerning the Substitution of Imports with Products Manufactured by Chinese-Foreign Joint Ventures." They were written by the State Planning Commission and cover most products. The State Economic Commission wrote its own set of regulations to cover machine and electronic products. Frisbie (1988).

90. See *FEER*, 6 February 1986, p. 70, and 12 June 1986; Frisbie (1988), p. 26; and A. T. Kearney (1987), p. 84.

91. Zhang (1987, pp. 97–102) remarked on the desire to favor technologically advanced enterprises at the expense of consumer goods and JVs with existing technology, as did a senior official of the Chinese Council for the Promotion of International Trade (CCPIT). *Los Angeles Times*, 9 August 1984, and *FEER*, 20 March 1986, p. 88. On the 1988 consumer goods ventures, *Business Week*, 8 August

1988. Foreigners complained that domestic market access was still too restricted, even after the February 1986 concessions. See *WSJ*, 6 June 1986, and *FEER*, 12 June 1986. Interviews conducted at JVs in Beijing and Shanghai in mid-1990, moreover, suggested that MOFERT was becoming even firmer in its insistence that export quotas be included in new JV contracts, and that it was pressuring existing JVs with contractual obligations to export to do so.

92. On historical failures of foreign business to create linkages in China, see Feuerwerker (1976), p. 86. At the start of an FDI project, use of domestic supplies was generally low, especially when local producers were unknown. For a brief description of this issue in developing countries generally, see Biersteker (1981), pp. 5, 38, and 51.

93. Both the dollar and the *yuan* were devalued during the 1980s. Hitachi's JV, which imported many components from the parent corporation in Japan, was hit hard after 1985 by the sharp revaluation of the yen against the dollar.

94. Article 9 of the Joint Venture Law states that "in purchase of raw and semi-processed materials, fuels, auxiliary equipment, etc., a JV should give first priority to Chinese sources but also may acquire directly from the world market . . ." Article 57 of the Implementing Regulations applies the less stringent condition that "a JV has the right to decide whether it buys [inputs] in China or from abroad. However, where conditions are the same it should give first priority to purchase in China." Although less strict than the JV Law, the actions of China's negotiators kept the requirements strict during the second phase. The "Regulations of the PRC on Special Economic Zones in Guangdong Province" (adopted 26 August 1980, hereafter "SEZ Regulations") (Article 17) also encouraged use of Chinese-made machinery and raw materials in the SEZs by offering JVs lower prices on these goods.

95. The level of domestic content requested by the Chinese in the Japanese JVs was 70%. *FEER*, 22 August 1985, p. 100.

96. One EJV contract in the sample specified preference for Chinese products, with payment at the prevailing domestic price (E7). Two joint ventures did not have such requirements, and one consumer goods joint venture imported 95% of its raw materials in order to guarantee quality. These findings on domestic content are supported by other accounts. On Hitachi, Sun Guanhua and Wang Yuan (1984), p. 41. On Volkswagen, *FEER*, 23 May 1985, p. 75. The Peugeot auto JV contract (concluded in early 1985) foresaw a gradual increase in domestic components from 20% to first 70% and then 95%, although the latter was considered "years away." *SCMP*, 17 March 1985, p. 29. Rikio's JV (to produce cotton shoes) was to use 60% local materials. Imai (1984), p. 17. Contracts for oil exploration frequently required use of local materials and contractors (F17). On government criticism that the lack of domestic content requirements was an "unhealthy tendency," see *FEER*, 23 May 1985, p. 75.

97. On Hitachi, *China's Foreign Trade*, March 1985, and Whiting (1989). The AMC JV in late 1986 set up the "Community on Localization of Beijing Jeep," involving thirty-five research institutions and parts manufacturers from eleven provinces. *China Daily*, 7 January 1987. On AMC's difficulty in localization, see also Mann (1989), p. 230. E. K. Chor's JV to produce motorcycles had 100 local

parts and components suppliers under contract. *China Economic News*, 21 September 1987.

98. They were not to produce supplies themselves but, rather, helped JVs procure goods through both state (central and local) and market channels. *China Daily* (Business Weekly Supplement), 8 June 1987, p. 1.

99. On the national foreign exchange plan, see Chu (1984), p. 253. Romania, Hungary, and Yugoslavia required that JVs export enough to be self-financing in foreign currency. Romania required JVs to conduct all operations in convertible currency. Sources of foreign exchange for CMEA JVs were to be clarified in the joint venture agreement. See McMillan and St. Charles (1973), p. 2; Scriven (1982), p. 108; and Lorinczi (1982).

100. One analyst estimated that contributions from joint ventures (measured using the foreign share of total investment as a proxy) together with the sum of processing and assembly fees earned, and the value of machinery and equipment imported under compensation trade agreements, totaled US$1.172 billion in 1980, or only 5% of China's gross foreign exchange earnings at a maximum. Chai (1983), p. 127.

101. The JV Law (Article 8) referred to the SAEC's "Provisional Regulations on Foreign Exchange Control of the PRC" (promulgated December 1980; hereafter "Foreign Exchange Regulations"). These are translated in Chu, Moser, and Nee (1982), pp. 21–25. Guangdong's SEZs had a separate set of foreign exchange regulations for its SEZs, but were still subject to the national regulations. Moser (1984b), p. 150. The Implementing Regulations, Article 75, reiterated the requirement for foreign exchange balances.

102. The Parker-Hannifin, Squibb, and Gillette joint venture contracts, for example, included provisions guaranteeing a balance. See Cao Zhi (1984) and *China's Foreign Trade*, November 1986, p. 12. A fourth EJV's contract specified only that the venture was to abide by the foreign exchange laws (F14), while a fifth set some foreign exchange targets that the JV should try to maintain. Some contracts also guaranteed priority uses, such as for expatriate salaries or dividends, for earned foreign exchange. In one JV, the top three foreign exchange priorities were, in order, wages for foreign personnel, payment for imports, and payment of the foreign partner's dividends. The contract also stipulated that, if foreign exchange was insufficient to pay dividends, then the dividends were to accrue until there was enough foreign exchange to pay them out (E7).

103. Regulations noted here are from Articles 7 and 9 of "Detailed Rules for Foreign Exchange Control for Enterprises with Overseas Chinese Capital, Enterprises with Foreign Capital and Chinese-Foreign Joint Venture Enterprises" (promulgated August 1983; hereafter "Foreign Exchange Implementation Rules"). Technically, according to Article 4 of the 1980 Foreign Exchange Regulations, "All Chinese and foreign organizations and individuals residing in the PRC must, unless otherwise stipulated . . . sell their foreign exchange proceeds to the Bank of China. Any foreign exchange required is to be sold to them by the Bank of China in accordance with the quota approved by the State or with relevant regulations." Quoted in Chu (1984), p. 255. As other institutions gained authority to deal in foreign currency, however, they could also handle JV accounts, as codified in

the 1990 amendments to the JV Law. Chu (pp. 253–57) also notes the role of monitoring agencies.

104. The two JVs with problems were F28 and F26. The JV without problems was F8. C3 described the procedure for release of foreign exchange.

105. Foreign Exchange Implementing Rules, Article 12. See Chu (1984), pp. 257–58. Domestic sales for foreign exchange were made by F14-A.

106. If the imbalance could not be solved by the provincial or municipal government, it was to be solved through inclusion into the plan after the examination and approval by MOFERT together with the State Planning Commission. Implementing Regulations, Article 75.

107. Implementing Regulations, Article 78, authorized foreign currency loans. Interest rates for BOC loans were set by the bank. By November 1988, the BOC had lent $1.32 billion to 2904 Sino-foreign joint ventures. Valerie Chang (1989), p. 21. JVs did not need permission to take out loans, but had to report them to the SAEC.

108. See Chu (1984), pp. 257–58. Detailed rules on import substitution were not promulgated until 1986, however. See the discussion below.

109. E23-A noted the need to negotiate such arrangements, and the one case where this sort of deal was negotiated.

110. See *FEER*, 27 June 1985, p. 110, for the 1984 and 1985 foreign exchange figures. By the end of 1987, the $15.2 billion in reserves was sufficient to cover more than four months of imports. CIA (1988), pp. 5–6.

111. AMC's case is well documented in Mann (1989), chaps. 13 and 17. See also *WSJ*, 20 April 1986, and *FEER*, 12 June 1986, p. 133. On the closing of smaller JVs, *FEER*, 12 June 1986, p. 133.

112. Many respondents in my sample felt this was the single most difficult issue for joint ventures. The sample of fifty JVs cited is from A. T. Kearney (1987), p. 30. Interviews for the A. T. Kearney studies were done in 1986, at the end of the second phase. Lags in the implementation of new foreign exchange rules from February 1986 (discussed below) can be expected to have occurred. The Chinese estimate of the foreign exchange situation of individual JVs is from MOFERT's deputy director of foreign investment, Chu Baotai. *FEER*, 20 March 1986, p. 88. See also NCUSCT (1987), p. 136.

113. The "Provisional Measures Guiding the Provision of Foreign Exchange Guarantees by Domestic Organizations" of February 1986 are discussed in Nee and Jones (1987), pp. 54–56, and in Yowell (1988), p. 12. See also *FEER*, 6 February 1986, p. 70. The regulations also codified the practices, noted above, of sales to domestic producers for foreign exchange. On Bank of China regulations, *Boston Globe*, 10 August 1986. On AMC's resolution in May 1986, Mann (1989), chap. 17. The government also conceded to purchase a higher number of kits than it originally wished.

114. There is some evidence that the Chinese government tried to limit exchange at rates above six *yuan* to the dollar, although the rate had drifted up to 7: 1 by 1988. Foxboro's JV swapped currency with a hotel JV at a 37% premium. (*China's Foreign Trade*, October 1987.) This may have been a preferential rate allowed to certain ventures. Domestic enterprises also were allowed to participate in swaps, using the foreign exchange they were allowed to retain (12.5% of what

they earned in the mid-1980s). Yowell (1988). For rates, and swaps in Shanghai, see Frisbie (1988), and Woetzel (1989), p. 113. On volumes traded, *China Daily*, 13 February 1990. At first, foreign-backed enterprises could arrange to exchange hard currency and *renminbi* among themselves. Eventually, however, the government required such exchanges to take place within the officially established centers.

115. The idea that the aggregate of foreign enterprises, rather than individual enterprises, should balance foreign exchange was suggested indirectly in Kong Xiangyi (1987), p. 792. In interviews conducted in mid-1990, some JV managers indicated that, while the swap system had been helpful, it was not an acceptable long-term solution—it was simply too expensive. Some began to pressure the government for foreign exchange subsidies. MOFERT officials, too, were beginning to assert that swaps were only a temporary remedy; they stepped up pressure on a number of JVs that had been relying on swaps for foreign exchange to import.

116. Formal codification was included in MOFERT's "Measures on the Purchase and Export of Domestic Products by Foreign Investment Enterprises to Balance Foreign Exchange Account," promulgated 20 January 1987, and in the January 1986 Foreign Exchange Balancing Regulations. The former regulations are translated in MOFERT, *1988 Almanac*, pp. 131–32. See also Barale (1988) and Frisbie (1988). For example, Pepsi Cola was also involved in a JV that earned it foreign currency by exporting toys, and in a project exporting spices to its Pizza Hut subsidiary. *Fortune*, 27 February 1989, p. 98. Joint venture export of unrelated domestic goods had been allowed to a limited extent in practice prior to 1986. For example, Volkswagen's automobile joint venture in Shanghai exported dyes and other related products. *FEER*, 23 May 1985, p. 75.

117. On new foreign exchange restrictions, see Nee and Jones (1987), pp. 54–56. Views of foreign firms were reported in *CBR*, Vol. 16, No. 4 (May–June 1989), p. 12.

118. See *FEER*, 4 May 1989, p. 19, and *CBR*, Vol. 16, No. 5 (September–October 1989), p. 5.

119. See reformers Zhong Douyang and Yin Youguo (1984), p. 4. Two interviewees also found this to be the case (F14). A Chinese official criticized foreign investors for not realizing China's goals other than profit.

120. Several foreign managers noted that Chinese joint venture partners often overestimated the potential for profits from a joint venture. F26, E6, and Imai (1989), p. 15. Conservatives retained the traditional and Marxian disdain for profit-taking. The distinction between "legitimate" and "illegitimate" profits was also used domestically in the 1950s. Solinger (1984), pp. 12–13, and p. 136.

121. One foreign expert noted several contracts that specified 15% (E5). Cohen noted a 20% (pre-tax) standard (1982, p. 27). Another foreign expert noted a 20% to 30% range, and that the desirable return for a domestic Chinese enterprise was 30% (E7). Another standard, used by the Schindler Elevator EJV in Shanghai, specified a 15% profit rate (after tax) on total turnover as a target to be used when pricing JV products to be sold in China, but not a guaranteed return on investment.

122. On accountancy controls, C5 and chap. 11 of the Implementing Regulations. "The Accounting Regulations for Joint Ventures Using Chinese and Foreign

Investment" (hereafter "JV Accounting Regulations") were promulgated by the Ministry of Finance in March 1985. See Tam and Cheung (1988). All formal reviews were required to be conducted by Chinese accountancy offices. Accountancy offices—such as the "Tianjin Certified Public Accountants"—were increasingly set up at the local level.

123. The 1980 law was "The Income Tax Law of the PRC Concerning Joint Ventures Using Chinese and Foreign Investment" (hereafter "JV Income Tax Law" or "JVITL," promulgated 10 September 1980, and translated in Chu, Moser, and Nee [1982], part 14). Another early tax law was the "Detailed Rules and Regulations for the Implementation of the Income Tax Law of the PRC Concerning Joint Ventures Using Chinese and Foreign Investment" (promulgated 14 December 1980, translated in Chu, Moser, and Nee [1982], part 5). For a discussion of these laws and other taxes, see Gelatt and Pomp (1987) and Moser (1984a), pp. 132–33. See the 1980 SEZ Regulations, Article 14, on SEZ tax rates, and JV Income Tax Law, Article 3, on rates elsewhere. The "Provisional Tax Regulations for 14 Open Cities, SEZs and Hainan Island" (promulgated 1 December 1984) stated that in taxation the 14 cities and Hainan were to be treated the same as the SEZs. (Translated in *China Economic News*, No. 46, 3 December 1984, pp. 1–3.) The 30% rate outside of the SEZs was somewhat lower than rates on JVs in Eastern Europe. In the early 1970s, the rate was 40%–60% in Hungary, 35% in Yugoslavia, and 30% (plus 10% if profits were repatriated) in Romania. McMillan and St. Charles (1973), pp. 63, 48, and 29. JVs in Romania were granted similar tax holidays as in China. Business International (1973), p. 85. On restrictions on profit distribution where losses exist, Implementing Regulations, Articles 87 and 88. JVs were not required to distribute profits annually. Cohen and Horsley (1983), p. 48.

124. See JV Law, Article 7, and Implementing Regulations, Article 87. On these funds, Moser (1984a), p. 134. Cohen notes the figure for the combined amount of funds, and states that the highest total percentage he had seen for JVs was 20% (1982, p. 30). Both Romania and Hungary required reserve funds, and Hungary required payment into a bonus ("profit-sharing") fund for personnel. McMillan and St. Charles (1973), pp. 63, 80. The social welfare function in Chinese JVs was justified by He Xinhao: "Under the condition of assuring foreign capital the opportunity to obtain legitimate profits, we also convert, through economic and administrative means, the surplus value created by our workers into the financial revenues of the state, funds for expanded reproduction of enterprises, and welfare expenses for the workers. This serves to limit the extent of exploitation by foreign capital" (1980, p. 2).

125. According to early policy, wages in joint ventures could be 120%–150% higher than in comparable domestic enterprises (Article 8, "Regulations on Labor Management in Joint Ventures Using Chinese and Foreign Investment," promulgated 26 July 1980). In 1986, this restriction was abolished, however. The SEZ Labor Regulations were more flexible from the start, stating only that wages would be negotiated (Article 7). Both laws are translated in Chu, Moser, and Nee (1982), part 9 and part 14. In negotiations for the Occidental strip mine CJV in Shaanxi, the Chinese requested that 50 times the local wage rate ($14 per hour) be paid to Chinese workers, with the effect that the department in charge would reap an additional $45 million per year, according to one estimate. This arrangement was

not eventually incorporated in the contract. *NYT*, 3 July 1985, p. D5. See also NCUSCT (1987), pp. 162–63.

126. The rule is in the Joint Venture Law, Article 7. ("Net profit" is gross profit minus income tax and money set aside for the reserve, bonus and welfare, and expansion funds, as required by law. See below. Also see Cohen [1982], p. 30.) On division of profits according to equity, and the right to remit profits abroad in Yugoslavia, Romania, and Hungary, see McMillan and St. Charles (1973), pp. 29, 35, 47, 63, and 80–81. Deng Xiaoping is quoted in Ma Hong (1985), p. 6.

127. In some cases, the Chinese side pressured the foreign side to reinvest any profits (E23-A, E18, C2-A). Foreigners were often willing to reinvest dividends in the joint venture in the initial years of a JV, only paying dividends after five to seven years (E1). The parties to the Schindler Elevator JV contract, for example, agreed to reinvest 100% of net profits for the first three years, and 50% for the next three. Cohen (1982), p. 30. In another JV contract, the foreign partner reserved the right to remit profits abroad in the amount equal to its initial cash investment through the receipt of dividends, but was also encouraged to reinvest a portion of the annual dividends (E7). Reinvestment was also induced through tax policy, as in the JVITL, Article 6. Gelatt and Pomp (1984), pp. 44–45. This also occurred in Yugoslavia, Romania, and Hungary. McMillan and St. Charles (1973), p. 25. In 1989, the pressure by the Chinese partner to reinvest was reported to have eased, at least in Guangdong. During a period of severe shortages of *renminbi* credit, which resulted from central policies to slow economic growth and inflation, Chinese JV partners (mostly state or municipal agencies) preferred to pay out dividends to both partners rather than invest them. *FEER*, 4 May 1989, p. 69. Presumably they could earn more money by loaning out dividend funds, or needed funds elsewhere.

128. C6 and F16-A.

129. JV Law, Article 7; JVITL, Part 5; and SEZ Regulations, Article 16. JV Law, Article 10, encouraged the deposit of distributed dividends in the Bank of China. Gelatt and Pomp (1984), p. 45.

130. E1, E16, E18. Wang Yihe, et al. note that JV partners who wished to remit foreign exchange profits abroad could "apply to withdraw and transfer [the funds] from the enterprise's foreign exchange savings account," but did not elaborate on this procedure (1984, p. 110). One foreign expert asserted that foreign partners were unable to get the Chinese side to guarantee outright that foreign currency profits could be repatriated (E6). Profits apparently could be remitted out of the SEZs more easily than elsewhere (F4).

131. Transfer pricing is the overpricing of imports (including technology) and/or underpricing of exports in intrafirm transactions, when compared to the international market price. It can be a means of transferring profits out of a country without paying taxes. Chinese analysts explicitly noted the need to monitor tax and finance matters to prevent transfer pricing. Zhong Douyang and Ying Youguo (1984), p. 4, and Wang Yihe, et al. (1984), p. 71. Suo Qian (1987, p. 72) asserted that "some foreign businessmen are making use of their multinational corporations and the means of transferring prices to seek exorbitant prices . . . " but offered no evidence. The Implementing Regulations stated authority to set and review export prices (Article 66) and grant import licenses (Article 63). Chinese legal jurisdiction

over contracts between joint ventures and foreign companies was stipulated in the Foreign Economic Contract Law, Article 5.

132. UNCTC (1988), pp. 270–71. Although some countries in Africa maintained limits on profit remittances (such as, Angola, Somalia, and Zimbabwe), there was a trend away from such limits in the 1980s.

133. U.S. Congress, O.T.A. (1986), p. 42, reported that a frequently mentioned concern of foreigners was that foreign exchange restrictions made repatriation of profits uncertain.

134. China did not completely adopt international standards, however, such as in depreciation methods. Tam and Cheung (1988), pp. 42–43. To AMC's $300,000 dividend on 1985 returns was added a $600,000 profit repatriation on 1986 returns, paid in dollars in 1987. Mann (1989), pp. 220 and 274.

135. Income tax holidays were extended to two years of full exemption and three years of a 50% exemption, and certain types of imports were exempted from the turnover tax. See the "Decision Regarding Amendment of the JVITL" of September 1983. Exemptions from the commercial and industrial consolidated tax and customs fees were allowed for imports of machinery as part of the JV capital, and for certain imports of raw materials and auxiliary materials. (The consolidated industrial and commercial tax was a type of turnover tax that was applied to most foreign enterprises.) See Implementing Regulations, Article 71, and Cohen and Horsley (1983), p. 47.

136. After the tax holiday ran out, EOEs that exported 70% of the value of their product would have the income tax rate cut to 15%, or to 10% for such enterprises in the SEZs and certain other areas. The 1986 tax incentives are in Articles 7–11 and 13 of the 1986 Provisions. See also Cohen and Chang (1987), pp. 11–14, and NCUSCT (1987), pp. 23–46.

137. TNCs often are unwilling to license high technology directly to developing countries, but are more willing to transfer technology via joint ventures. The United States and Europe, through the Coordinating Committee (COCOM), jointly restrict technology for sale to China. Technology transfer also has been a major goal of Eastern European joint venture policies. McMillan and St. Charles (1973), p. 17.

138. These cases of fraud primarily involved industrial cooperation agreements (not specifically JVs) with enterprises in Shenzhen and Guangdong Province. Chai (1983), p. 125. Wang Yihe, et al. reflect a general suspicion that foreigners may "dupe" the Chinese in technology transfer arrangements (1984, p. 92). On the desire to develop indigenous technology, Shen Yurui (1980), p. 37.

139. General discussions of technology transfer and the results of the policy appear in Simon and Goldman (1989), and U.S. Congress, O.T.A. (1987).

140. Guangdong Province's People's Government promulgated the "Provisional Regulations of Shenzhen SEZ on Technology Introduction" (Shenzhen Jingji Tequ Jishu Yinjin Zhixing Guiding, hereafter SEZ Technology Regulations) on 8 February 1984. A Chinese language version appeared in SSZH, 8 February 1984. Wang Yihe, et al. (1984, chap. 8) discuss earlier guidelines.

141. Elimination of Japanese companies based on technology occurred with a proposed automobile JV in Shanghai, which was eventually established with Volkswagen using a lower level of technology. FEER, 23 May 1985, p. 75. F8,

F14-E, and F24-A reported that their companies were favored over others because of the type and level of technology they offered. European firms considering joint ventures hoped to compete favorably with the United States and Japan on the basis of their willingness to offer more advanced technology. *FEER*, 22 August 1985, p. 79. On Chinese examination of secret documents, F8. The case of Chinese managerial pressure was F14-C. The foreign partner consented for "political" reasons, although it was unhappy about doing so. Problems related to another joint venture in the same industry may have generated explicit or implicit pressure on the Chinese manager to press for change.

142. Legally, prices "shall be ascertained through consultation by the parties to the JV on the basis of fairness and reasonableness, or evaluated by the third party agreed upon by parties to the joint venture." Implementing Regulations, Article 25. Article 29 states that price calculations must be submitted to the approval authority as part of the approval process. On the limited proportion of technology in foreign capital contributions, A. T. Kearney (1987), p. 58. On allowance of technology as part of a foreign partner's capital contribution, Joint Venture Law, Article 5. Yugoslavia and Romania restricted such contributions to 10% of the total capital. Wang Yihe, et al. (1984), p. 108. On foreign frustration over tough Chinese negotiating over technology transfer import prices generally, Oechsli (1988), p. 36. Mann suggests that in the AMC case, however, valuation of the foreign partner's technology was not as problematic as they had anticipated, although valuation of the Chinese partner's factory and equipment was contentious (1989, pp. 77 and 136).

143. Implementing Regulations, Article 46.1, stipulate "fair and reasonable" royalties. Wang Yihe, et al. (1984, pp. 177–82) offer Chinese partners specific guidelines for figuring fair prices according to the expected rate of profit or sales, and use 3% as the "reasonable" royalty rate (*heli de ticheng feilu*). Lubman (1984), p. 90, also notes this. The Otis Elevator JV included a ten-year licensing agreement that called for technical assistance fees based on sales. *Business China*, 24 October 1984, p. 157.

144. On the belief of foreigners that valuation of their technology and royalties was inadequate, despite some increase in Chinese flexibility on this issue, see Kawai (1984), p. 13, and Yakota (1987), p. 12. F9 concurred with regard to royalties. On Chinese complaints that the royalties paid to Hitachi by their Fujian JV were too high, see Fujimura (1982).

145. Lubman (1984), p. 89. Articles 29 and 45 of the Implementing Regulations required "relevant documentation," and Article 46 provided for mutual exchange of information. This responded to arguments that most technology transfer agreements do not achieve genuine transfer because research and development is carried out in the parent's home office. Biersteker (1981), p. 11.

146. Problems subsequently arose in fulfilling the obligation to transfer known technology within the first year in the first example, however (F24-A). On the pharmaceutical venture (Squibb), see *China Trade Report*, November 1983. On the third JV, Parker-Hannifin, see *Beijing Review*, 4 November 1985, and *Business China*, 12 October 1982. Similar requirements appeared in seven other early joint ventures. Weil (1981), p. 22.

147. Implementing Regulations, Articles 46.2 and 46.6.

148. Implementing Regulations, Article 46.3, and 1984 SEZ Technology Regulations," Article 19. The SEZ limit could be extended by agreement or if the transfer was part of investment capital. Non-JV technology agreements were limited to five years, so the longer term given to JVs was an incentive. Lubman (1984), p. 91. India limited the fee period to five years (exceptions exist), and Mexico to ten years. See also Wang Yihe, et al. (1984), p. 182, and Moser (1984a), p. 131.

149. On compensation for substandard technology, Joint Venture Law, Article 5, and Lubman (1984), pp. 93–94. See also Implementing Regulations, Article 44. Responsibility for technology failures was a major issue for a large manufacturing JV (E7). No cases of such a demand for payments have been made public. See also the 1984 SEZ Technology Regulations, Articles 10 and 11. F14-B noted the common occurrence of performance clauses.

150. Hendryx (1986), p. 60. Approval for technology transfer agreements had to come from both the department in charge and the final approval authority. Implementing Regulations, Article 46.

151. A Chinese official claimed that the China Committee for the Promotion of International Trade (CCPIT) would take action (C2-A). It was unclear whether MOFERT would have a continuing oversight role (F21-A). A foreign consultant claimed there was "absolutely no ongoing supervision" over signed agreements (E1).

152. The first example is from F24. The second case is F9-D. The same authorities wanted to perform monthly checks of the imported machinery. The Chinese partner's suspicion of foreign deception in technology transfer declined over time in this JV.

153. On rotation of Chinese managers, see Chai (1983), p. 137, and Wong and Chu (1984), p. 9. F14-C reported sharing of technology provided by joint ventures.

154. The previous example, in which competitors were passed designs, was therefore an exception. U.S. Congress, O.T.A. (1987), pp. 62–63. The PRC promulgated a trademark law in 1950, but it did not meet the requirements of foreign investors. Chang and Conroy (1984), pp. 267–69.

155. Ho and Heunemann (1984), p. 104.

156. Otis' situation is reported in Hendryx (1986), p. 60. Because it was not clear whether the Chinese would continue to pay fees in the extended agreement periods, it was also unclear whether this violated the aim—to shorten the fee period—of the Chinese government in limiting transfer agreements to ten years.

157. The Shenzhen Municipal People's Government's responsibility for approval in that SEZ is in the 1984 SEZ Technology Regulations, Article 16. See generally on the decentralization in technology transfer, U.S. Congress, O.T.A. (1987), p. 47.

158. Cao Jiarui (1986), pp. K5-6. Cao, a reformer, was frustrated with the irrationalities of administrative decentralization and further complained about the lack of use of economic criteria in making technology import decisions.

159. The supposition that little technology flowed into China in the early years is supported by data on technology transfer in compensation trade and processing/assembly projects, in which the average value of connected machinery and electronic imports was only $645,000 and $8,000, respectively. (Equivalent informa-

tion on EJVs is unavailable.) Chai (1983), p. 131. The Seventh Five-Year Plan (1986–1990) called for the acceleration of new high-technology industries, especially electronics and computers.

160. On terms that China would not and would accept, see Articles 9 and 3, respectively, of the 1985 "Regulations for the Administration of Technology Import Contracts" (hereafter 1985 Technology Regulations). These regulations were promulgated by the State Council on 24 May 1985, and applied to technology transfer in JVs. Translated in *East Asian Executive Reports*, July 1985, p. 28. See also discussions in Lubman (1987), pp. 175–76, and U.S. Congress, O.T.A. (1987), pp. 49–50. Exceptions to the terms for confidentiality agreements were permitted if the supplier would provide confidential information on improvements over the term of the agreement. A Japanese trade official expressed strong discontent with China's expectation of performance standards. Yakota (1987), p. 12.

161. An example from the third phase was the "Detailed Rules for the Implementation of the Regulations on Administration of Technology Import Contracts" ("Technology Rules"), promulgated in January 1988. Although these rules did not formally apply to JVs, they were important for the issue of technology transfer to JVs because the standards applied in non-JV transfer agreements were often applied to JV technology agreements. See Oechsli (1988), p. 35.

162. See "The Patent Law of the People's Republic of China" (adopted 12 March 1984, hereafter Patent Law), translated in *CBR* (January–February 1985), pp. 54–57. This law was also designed to protect and foster innovations by Chinese technicians. For patents held by domestic units, but apparently not for patents held by foreigners, the state maintained the right to spread and apply inventions where it saw fit. Patents were justified as socialist because they do not allow patent royalties to become capital. See also Gu Ming (1985), p. 33; Eliasoph (1985), p. 50; and Tang Zongshun (1987), pp. 75–79. In 1984, China also acceded to the Paris Convention for the Protection of Intellectual Property. China had no copyright law by the end of the 1980s, although one had gone through nineteen drafts. *NYT*, 20 April 1989.

163. For example, the SEZs began to require that a worker who had trained in a JV for more than three months could not resign for another year, or else had to compensate the enterprise for the cost of training. SEZ Labor Regulations, Article 29.

164. The general definition of "appropriate" appeared in *China's Foreign Trade*, May 1982, pp. 8–9. A definition of "appropriate technology" used in the West includes notions that the labor-capital ratio of the technology fits that of the host country, and that it promotes linkages with the indigenous economy. Biersteker (1981), p. 13. Chinese analysts noted that they were willing to buy technology that was a bit out of date but not obsolete, particularly since "all of us know that other countries will not sell us the most advanced, new technology." Huan Xiang (1984), p. 7. See also Wang Yihe, et al. (1984), pp. 167–68, and Simon (1984), p. 302. Several interviewees noted the attitudinal evolution. Foreign managers frequently noted a lingering anxiety by the Chinese that the technology supplied was outdated or of insufficient quality, however (F7, F9-C, and F14-B).

165. TAEs were defined in Article 2 of the 1986 Provisions. On U.S. dominance of technologically advanced enterprises, NCUSCT (1987), p. 136. When "sophisti-

cated technology" was involved in Indian joint ventures, the foreign side could exceed 40% foreign ownership. Encarnation and Vachani (1985), p. 153.

166. This purpose was expressed repeatedly. See, for example, C4 (Shenzhen official); Yong Shan (1981); Shen Shiyi (1984), p. 144; Gu Mu (1985), p. 2; Sun Ru (1982), p. 2; and Ma Hong (1985), p. 5.

167. On the second border, *TKP*, 20 September 1982, p. W3. In the mid-1980s, some Shenzhen officials anticipated that this second border would become the primary border between Hong Kong and China, gradually erasing the Hong Kong–Shenzhen border, and thereby facilitating the political and economic reabsorption of Hong Kong into the PRC (C4). None of the other three SEZs erected second borders. The "Provisional Entry/Exit Rules for the SEZs in Guangdong Province," Article 11, implied the continuation of strict limits on the exit of Chinese citizens through Shenzhen. Translated in Chu, Moser, and Nee (1982), part 14. On the flow of goods and pornography, see Xiao An (1984), p. 4. On efforts to crush immoral activities, see Fang Zhuofen (1981), p. 54. See also Crane (1986), pp. 338–39.

168. Liang Xiang (1984), p. 17.

169. Quote is from Fang Zhuofen (1981), p. 58. On cadre education, see Shen Shi (1982); Chi Shi-ching (1982); Xu Xuehan, Mao Rongfang, and Wu Jian (1982), p. K19; Guangzhou Provincial Service (radio broadcast) (1982), p. P1; and Xiao An (1984), p. 4. On nonapplication of controls to foreigners, Xiao An (1984), p. 4. This author also suggested that the party organs in Shenzhen would need to tone down communist education if it was to be acceptable to overseas Chinese from Hong Kong and Taiwan.

170. C4. This official was educated abroad.

171. Pepper (1988), p. 16.

172. Despite the move away from SEZs, the central government never repudiated the model. On the expansion to other areas, see Pepper (1988), pp. 15–16.

173. See Liang Wensen, Shen Liren, and Tian Jianghai (1982), p. 31; Liang Xiang (Shenzhen mayor) (1985), p. 1; Xu Xuehan, Mao Rongfang, and Wu Jian (1982), p. K16; Liu Peng (1985), p. 127; Shen Shi (1982), p. 2; Liang Xiang (1985), p. 2; and Xu Luxin (1984), p. 4. On the requirement that SEZs follow the party line, Zhou Ding (1983), p. 61. The point that these regions were not special *political* zones was often stressed.

174. On the organizational similarity between SEZ municipal governments and their counterparts elsewhere, see Peter N. S. Lee (1984), p. 19. On the subjection of SEZs to Chinese law, see Wang Shouchun and Li Kanghua (1981), p. 1. The Guangdong SEZ Regulations, Article 2, required that enterprises and individuals in the zones "must abide by the laws, decrees and related regulations" of the PRC. On subordination to the socialist plan, see Chen Zhao (1982), p. 36.

175. On pressures for SEZ autonomy from those regions themselves, see, for example, Xiang Nan (Fujian first party secretary) (1983), p. 6, and Peter N. S. Lee (1984). With the 1986 Provisions, other localities outside the zones were also encouraged to pass local laws. On decentralization of authority to the zones, see Crane (1986), chap. 5.

176. By the end of 1986, thirty localities had published their own investment provisions. See NCUSCT (1987), p. 180. On SEZ laws vis-à-vis national laws, see Moser (1984a), p. 147.

177. The quote is from Sun Weixiang, director of Shenzhen Municipal Industrial Development Corporation, *WSJ*, 9 July 1985, p. 32. On disappointment of some officials, *WSJ*, 9 July 1985, p. 32. On the types of projects in the zones, Falkenheim (1986), *FEER*, 9 May 1985, p. 71; *NYT*, 28 August 1985, p. 2; *WSJ*, 9 July 1985, p. 32. On the 7% figure, see *FEER*, 1 October 1987, p. 104. According to another source, in 1981 "93% of the value of industrial production came from operations confined to technically simple assembly or packaging." Wong and Chu (1984), p. 8. The situation of the SEZs was not unusual from a comparative perspective; many Asian EPZs have had only limited success in technology transfer, particularly since enterprises in these zones are generally labor-intensive and involve technically simple assembly or packaging. Over time, however, some of the EPZs have moved further into technology intensive production (particularly in Taiwan and South Korea). Wong and Chu (1984), pp. 8–9.

178. In 1986, for example, Shenzhen's industrial output (from foreign-backed and domestic enterprises) accounted for only 30% of total output, with the less-prized construction and commerce sectors accounting for 70%. This figure was up from 18.3% in 1983, but there were doubts that it could be maintained. *FEER*, 1 October 1987, p. 104. See also "Shenzhen SEZ's Accomplishments and Prospects—A Summary" (1984), p. 91. Moreover, the money spent on capital construction as a percentage of total output in Shenzhen (80%) was extraordinarily high compared with the national expenditure (10.5%) or that spent in Shanghai (17%) and Guangzhou (7%). *FEER*, 19 September 1985, p. 63.

179. On exports, *WSJ*, 9 July 1985, p. 32. EPZs in Asia have varied greatly in terms of export contributions. Generally the contribution has been small, although contributions to exports and foreign exchange tend to increase over time. For example, Taiwan's three EPZs in 1981 contributed only 7% of total exports, and South Korea's, only 4% between 1974 and 1979. EPZs have fared better as percentage of total *manufacturing* exports or the export of domestic value added (through purchase of raw materials, labor, and so on). For example, in India's EPZ the domestic value added content of goods has been nearly 55%. Wong and Chu (1984), pp. 6–7. On the ratio of exports to imports, Falkenheim (1986), p. 366, and Crane (1986), p. 301.

180. Figures on infrastructure expenses are derived as follows: $2.2 billion was spent on infrastructure development in all four zones, and seven-eighths of this amount went to Shenzhen. (Reported figure for infrastructure was *RMB*8 million. I have converted this figure to dollars using a 3.7 *yuan*/dollar exchange rate.) Figures are from *FEER*, 1 October 1987, pp. 102 and 105. See also Crane (1986), p. 300.

181. On credit controls, Pepper (1988), pp. 15–16. State Statistical Bureau figure on 1987 export earnings was $2.74 billion. *FEER*, 24 March 1988, p. 82. This compared favorably with the 28% increase in export earnings over the same period for China as a whole. Figure on foreign exchange fees from processing is from *FEER*, 1 October 1987, p. 104. On 1988 and 1989 export earnings, *FEER*, 8 February 1990, p. 38.

182. The first governor (the former mayor of Shenzhen, Liang Xiang) also promised that the island would be exceptionally open to investment and foreigners generally: "There will be 3 freedoms. There will be the freedom of capital flow, in and out. There will be the freedom of travel to and from the island by foreigners

[without visas]. And there will be the freedom of goods to move in and out [that is, low tariffs and customs supervision]." *NYT*, 22 April 1988.

183. SEZ Regulations, Article 17, encouraged domestic sourcing. The preferential prices were based on highly subsidized export prices. Moser (1984a), p. 151. SEZ Regulations, Article 13, exempted JV imports, a practice common in Asian EPZs. Wong and Chu (1984), p. 9. In 1983, the percent of, for example, rolled steel, cement, and timber imported to the zones for construction were 66%, 47%, and 87%, respectively. Falkenheim (1986).

184. On *neilian*, see *Shenzhen Jingji Tequ Jinqi Neilian Qiye Ruogan Zhengce de Zhixing Guiding* (Provisional Regulations for Shenzhen SEZ's Recent Policies for "Internal Linkage" Enterprises). These are summarized in detail in Zhou Ding (1983), pp. 59–60. Other incentives included easier registration for Chinese workers who entered the zones to work in *neilian* enterprises, permission for some internal marketing, and greater flexibility in determining management formats. If 70% of inputs were domestically produced, the enterprises could negotiate for domestic sales. According to Crane (1986), p. 326, *neilian* enterprises of all types, including those with no foreign involvement, boomed in 1983–1984 to a level of 969 planned projects. Another *neilian* form commonly found in EPZs and also encouraged in China (especially after the problems of 1985, discussed below) included formation of JVs between inland and Chinese enterprises located in the zones to process goods from inland areas and then export them. See also Wong and Chu (1984), p. 10; Pepper (1988), p. 18; and Shen Shi (1982), p. P3.

185. Pepper (1988), p. 13, and *FEER*, 19 September 1985, p. 61. These practices also exacerbated the zones' trade deficits.

186. Interviewees who noted pressure against broadening their contacts to other regions were F14-B, F10, and F18 (CJV). On the importance of labor mobility, Simon (1989), p. 317.

187. Yu Jianxun (1987), pp. 780–84.

188. In the early 1980s, the fourteen coastal cities contained 13% of the national work force and produced 23% of the nation's industrial output. *FEER*, 20 December 1984, p. 102. The increasing concentration of foreign capital in Shanghai municipality and the surrounding coastal provinces of Jiangsu, Zhejiang, Anhui, and Jiangxi (which included five of the original fourteen coastal cities) alone contained 27% of China's industrial enterprises and produced 27% of the total industrial and agricultural output value. *FEER*, 21 March 1985, p. 76.

189. *FEER*, 6 April 1989, p. 13. Within one year of the resurgence of conservative leaders following the events at Tiananmen, the effort to concentrate foreign capital on China's eastern coast continued with the announcement of plans for the new Pudong economic zone adjacent to Shanghai.

CHAPTER FIVE
CONTROLS AT THE ENTERPRISE LEVEL

1. Schurmann (1968), part IV. Although the Soviet model never had much influence outside the northeast, despite the intention that it would spread throughout China, there was considerable suspicion of the Soviet advisors and resentment of their high salaries and comparatively luxurious lifestyles.

2. Tomlinson's study of British joint ventures in India and Pakistan showed that, in the early 1970s, foreign firms entering joint ventures usually preferred and were able to obtain managerial control. An obstacle to foreign control came where the ownership split was fifty-fifty; the host governments "jealously guarded" their equal position. The need or desirability of control by foreign parent corporations differed by industry and activity as a function of the complexity of the technology, its newness to the host market, and corporate policy. Tomlinson (1970), pp. 95–96, 124–45. On shared management generally, see Walmsley (1982), p. 32.

3. Among Eastern European joint ventures, Hungary, Poland, Romania, and Yugoslavia required at least 51% local ownership, although Bulgaria permitted foreign majority ownership. Among market economies, India limited foreign equity to 40% (except in "core" sectors, where up to 74% was permitted) and Mexico to 49%. In virtually all cases (Romania was an exception) exemptions from these ownership constraints were allowed if the JV involved high technology or created large exports or foreign exchange surpluses. See Walmsley (1982), pp. 23–24, and Encarnation and Vachani (1985), pp. 152–53. On foreign preferences for majority equity in developing countries generally, see Friedmann and Beguin (1971), pp. 368–69, and Tomlinson (1970), p. 137.

4. Minimum foreign equity requirements (Article 4) were to guarantee that the foreign side would have a significant stake in—and commitment to—the joint venture itself. See Wang Yihe, et al. (1984), pp. 151, 154.

5. On Chinese preference for majority ownership, C2-A, E1, and Wang Yihe, et al. (1984), p. 153. Arguments about China's sovereignty did occasionally enter the negotiations over equity divisions. In one early EJV negotiation, the Ministry of Petroleum would not allow the foreign side greater than 49% because it "smacked of imperialism" (E10). Several foreign interviewees also cited Chinese preference for majority or equal ownership: F4, F16-A, E23, E14, F26. Generally, problems over negotiating the equity split arose only when the foreign side assumed that majority equity translated into control, or when the foreign firm's internal policy required a certain percent equity (E4, E23).

6. Of the sample of 28 ventures, the majority had either fifty-fifty splits in equity (14) or 26%–49% foreign equity (11). Only one had 25% foreign ownership (the minimum allowed), and only two had foreign majority ownership (both between 51% and 75%). None had over 75% foreign equity. These figures are supported by those presented in table 3-L.

7. Preferences for minority shares were reported by F14 and E7. Representatives of three foreign firms indicated that 50% foreign equity was important for assuring them some degree of control (F10, F28, E6). Virtually all foreign managers and experts interviewed agreed that the issue of equity was not a contentious one in negotiations.

8. See A. T. Kearney (1987), p. 58. Several interviewees implied the Chinese valuation was not fair or was a problem in negotiations (F21-A, F28-A, E7). The 1986 Provisions, Article 4, set site use fees for "technologically advanced" and "export-oriented" enterprises, and allowed some exemptions from fees. Because the bulk of foreign equity was generally in the form of cash, the Chinese side avoided the problem of accurately valuing the foreign contribution to equity.

Technology could be the exception here, and as a result, valuation of foreign assets were sometimes the subject of dispute.

9. Wang Yihe, et al. note these criteria for majority ownership, and the need to use majority equity as an incentive (1984, p. 155). The increase of foreign majority ownership in later contracts was noted in the cases of F3-A, F4-A, F12, and confirmed by E23.

10. The figure of foreign majority-owned JVs in the MOFERT sample rose from 25 in 1985 to 78 in 1988.

11. On the separation of equity and control, see Wang Yihe, et al. (1984), pp. 153–55, C1, C7, F9-B, F12-A, F14, and E14.

12. The JV Law was silent on the board's authority. The role and composition of the board of directors (BOD) was clarified in the Implementing Regulations, Articles 33 and 34. Chinese officials in interviews added the qualification that JVs must operate within the law (C2-A, C3).

13. Even members who represented government investors (such as CITIC, which is directly under the State Council) were to represent only their own financial interests rather than to serve as a proxy for the State Council, although in practice these distinctions were highly ambiguous (C2-A).

14. The relationship between equity division and BOD representation in the sample was as follows:

Equity Splits in Joint Ventures (Sample)
(n = 25)

Representatives on the BOD	Equity Division		
	Chinese Majority	Even Division	Foreign Majority
Chinese Majority	9	1	1
Even Division	0	11	0
Foreign Majority	0	2	1

The number of representatives on boards was not expanded in practice to make representation precisely according to equity mathematically. For example, in 51% Chinese-owned joint ventures, the norm was for the Chinese to have, for example, four representatives, and the foreign side three, mathematically over-representing the Chinese side. (F4, F7, F12, F14, F16 all have foreigners slightly under-represented mathematically. F6 has the Chinese side under-represented mathematically.) I have interpreted cases of 51% Chinese equity with a one-person Chinese majority on the board as a situation where BOD representation is divided roughly according to equity split, since the BOD representation reflects a Chinese ownership majority, but by the least number of votes possible.

15. Wang Yihe, et al. (1984), p. 92. That the chair must be Chinese is in the JV Law, Article 6.

16. Voting rules were to be negotiated as part of the Articles of Association. Implementing Regulations, Article 13. Unanimous board decisions are formally required for amendments to the Articles of Association, termination and dissolu-

tion of the JV, increase in registered capital and mergers. Implementing Regulations, Article 36. Articles of Association may specify other decisions for which unanimity is required.

17. Quote is from a Foreign Investment Administration official in *JJDB*, 15 July 1985, p. 6. Other Chinese officials and publications echoed this emphasis on a consultative style (C1, C7, Wang Yihe, et al. [1984], chap. 10).

18. Twenty-four of twenty-five JVs for which data was available confirmed the existence, de facto or de jure, of unanimous decisionmaking. Foreign lawyers and consultants agreed that rules to foster unanimity and bloc voting were the norm and the veto was the most common method (E11, E15, E17). This was the case in the following JVs: F7, F8, F9-A, F12, F14-E (Chinese manager), F20, F21, F24. Seven JVs specifically mentioned bloc voting. Many foreign managers noted that decisionmaking at the board level was always unanimous or consensual (often the result of compromises), and that voting never occurred (F3A, F14-B, F16, F24, F26, F28-A). Unanimous decisionmaking and the right of veto for the minority shareholder also occurred in joint ventures in Hungary, Bulgaria, Romania, and Poland. Scriven (1982), p. 108.

19. The post-Mao desire to learn foreign management skills followed many years of fluctuation, from unity between party committees and technical management as practiced in the Soviet-inspired system of one-man management in the early 1950s, to their separation in the mid-1950s, to virtual elimination of technical management in the Great Leap Forward (1958–1959) and the Cultural Revolution (1966–1976), to greater autonomy for technical management in the early 1960s and the 1980s. Division between policy and operations of a firm existed prior to 1949. Schurmann (1968), pp. 223–24, 297. Under the post-Mao reforms, the board was to give general guidance and act directly only on major issues. Management was to run daily operations with substantial autonomy. Wang Yihe, et al. (1984, pp. 247–48) discuss the responsibilities of the general manager. Management was much more active than the board in running most joint ventures (F3-A, F4, F7, F9-A, F14-B, F21, F24-A, F26, E15, C2-A).

20. Only three of the twenty-eight JVs studied employed no expatriate managers. One of these three later sent an expatriate manager to China. C1 stated the view of the need for foreign managers early in the life of a venture. E23 confirmed this. Many foreign firms indicated that they hoped to reduce their foreign staff in order to lower expenses (F8, F9, F14-C, F21, E17). Some JVs limited expatriate tenure. For example, the general manager position was often held first by a foreigner but reverted to the Chinese side after several years (F14, F21, and Wang Yihe, et al. [1984], pp. 245–46).

21. The JV Law stated only that the general manager (president, or GM) and deputy general manager(s) (vice president, or DGM) should be appointed by the board of directors and from the various JV participants (Article 6). The Implementing Regulations said only that the general manager should represent the joint venture in outside dealings and be responsible for daily management, and that deputy general managers should assist the general manager in his or her work, and consult with the general manager on "major issues" (Articles 38–40). Although the board formally appointed top managers, in practice each side unilaterally appointed its own, sometimes over the objection of the partner (F9-B, E17).

22. F16-A, F27, E7, E14, E15, and E17 noted lack of opposition to equal management structures initiated by the Chinese side. The term "shadow" system is perhaps more precise than "deputy" (although the latter was commonly used), for there was to be virtual equality between the two managers involved, except for the GM-DGM team, in which the former sometimes held more power. Child (1990), p. 30.

23. Two of the six with even equity splits but without shadow systems had more foreign managers, four had a predominance of Chinese managers. The results of the sample were as follows:

Frequency of Shadow Management Systems
(n = 27)

	Equal Structures	Unequal Structures	No Expatriates	Total
50% equity split	7	6	0	13
Uneven equity split	7	3	4	14
Total	14	9	4	27

24. In several firms, dual signatures were required on some decisions, such as accepting complex orders (F7, F10, and E17). E15 and Wang Yihe, et al. (1984, p. 246) asserted that most JV contracts have such clauses.

25. F9-A and C1 emphasized the Chinese effort to foster the "spirit of mutual discussion."

26. E17.

27. The differential between salaries paid to Chinese and foreign managers was mentioned in interviews as a sensitive topic. A separate survey of JV management relations found that the most frequent complaint of Chinese managers was that their pay was too low compared with foreign managers. Child (1990), p. 90. The Chinese strongly resented the pay discrepancy between Chinese managers and the Soviet managers in China in the 1950s. Schurmann (1968), p. 241.

28. In one JV, at the initiative of the foreign side, all expatriates were paid by the the foreign parent. This gave the foreign side bargaining leverage and avoided the difficult issues of deciding comparability (F14-A). Equal salaries were paid in F12-A and F22, but the government took most of the Chinese managers' salaries. Another JV paid expatriates directly, but deposited the money outside of China. The high-ranking Chinese staff in this venture received 80% of their foreign counterparts' salaries, but most of this was put in a Chinese escrow account, at least until a law was established (E7). Expatriates in Hungarian JVs could also be paid by the foreign parent. Lorinczi (1982), p. 114.

29. Another JV's Chinese DGM grossed 700 *yuan* per month but only received 500 *yuan*. Department managers grossed 500 *yuan* per month and netted 400. Most lower managers received 235 *yuan* per month (figures from early 1985) (F14-C).

30. Of the twenty-three EJVs with any expatriate managers present, twenty (87%) had foreign GMs, and only three had Chinese GMs. Reflecting the shadow system, in only three of the ventures was the DGM foreign, whereas in eighteen

the DGM was Chinese. (In one there were two DGMs, one from each side.) The practice of splitting the GM and DGM positions between partners was also reported in Wang Yihe, et al. (1984), p. 246.

31. Final authority for GMs generally was asserted by C2-A and in Wang Yihe, et al. (1984, pp. 246–47), which also noted the special powers of GMs over international pricing, for example. GMs did have final authority in several JVs: F12-A, F9-B, F22 (CJV), F28.

32. The Guangdong regulations are "Regulations on Foreign Companies of the Guangdong SEZs." See Lam (1987), p. 47. For the 1990 amendments to Article 6 of the JV Law, see *China Daily*, 9 April 1990, p. 2.

33. From "Zhao Ziyang on Coastal Areas' Economic Development Strategy" (1988), p. 37.

34. On Fujian reforms, FBIS-CHI-88-019, 29 January 1988, p. 26. The MOFERT position was discussed in *China Economic News*, 1 February 1988, pp. 1–2.

35. JV autonomy in labor issues was stated in the Implementing Regulations, Article 39, and reiterated by a MOFERT official: "The state guarantees the autonomy of joint ventures in inviting applications of, hiring, dismissing, and firing employees and in determining their own wage standards, wage forms, and punishment system." Chu Baotai (1984), p. 112. A Chinese official confirmed this special decisionmaking realm, and that of social welfare, over which the Chinese retained control (C1).

36. The main additional regulations governing labor issues are the JV Labor Regulations, promulgated 26 July 1980. For an overview of wage policy in JVs, see Horsley (1984).

37. Mann's analysis of the AMC JV illustrates how in one case Chinese partners controlled personnel issues (1989, p. 252). On signatures required by the DGM on labor issues: C1; Horsley (1984), p. 24; Moser (1984a), p. 126; E17; and E19. F3-A, F7-A, and F9 noted that labor issues, particularly labor discipline, were handled by the personnel manager or DGM (who in the case of F7 was also the party secretary of the JV). On the DGM's role as representative of the workers: E15. Cases of foreign acquiescence to Chinese resistance to firing workers, or agreements to abide by Chinese labor practices, included Shanghai-Foxboro (*Beijing Review*, 17 November 1986), Peninsula Knitters' Shanghai-Uni-Wooltex (FBIS, 25 September 1986, p. K7), Hai-Ri (*China Newsletter*, No. 74, May–June 1988), and Ball International (NCUSCT [1987], p. 159). The Fujian-Hitachi JV faced outside interference when the Chinese and foreign partners together tried to establish a differential wage system to spur production. Payment to the labor organization became increasingly common, thereby giving the venture more control over distribution of wages at the expense of outside labor bureaus. *Business China*, 11 January 1988, p. 5, and NCUSCT (1987), p. 161.

38. Although the lack of labor mobility tied workers to the JV, foreign managers felt disadvantaged by the inability to fire workers or to freely hire talented workers from other enterprises, both of which also grew out of poor labor mobility. More generally, Chinese personnel managers promoted authority structures in joint ventures that were consistent with what Walder has termed the "organizational dependency" of labor-management relations in Chinese state enterprises. Walder argues that these structures create and reinforce worker subordination to avoid

threats to production and the position of the party. In addition to lack of an independent labor organization and poor labor mobility, such "organizational dependency" has been supported in state enterprises by routinized surveillance of worker activities and use of subjective evaluations of workers' personal and political behavior and attitude (*biaoxian*) in deciding worker bonuses and promotions. Walder's concept of "organized dependency" refers to the "institutional position of subordinates with regard to superiors in an organization. The greater the proportion of the subordinates' needs that is satisfied by the organization . . . [and] the fewer the alternative sources for satisfying these needs, the more dependent are subordinates." It is distinct from psychology/culture-based arguments of worker deference, for it is tied to the structure of institutions. Walder (1983), pp. 52, 53n.

39. One foreign partner succeeded in cutting the number of line workers from 260 to 60, and recommended who to keep and who to let go (F9), while the foreign side to another venture was able to set requirements such as for gender, height, and eyesight virtually unilaterally (F16). The foreign partner of the Otsuka pharmaceutical JV initiated procedures for firing or penalizing (with wage cuts) workers who deliberately breached set work standards. *FEER*, 24 April 1986, p. 77. On the foreign partner's increasing role in personnel generally, see *Business China*, 11 January 1988, pp. 4–6. Child continued to find strong Chinese influences in personnel matters, however (1990, pp. 62–63).

40. First quote is from He Xinhao (1980), p. 2. Second quote is from C1. The provision of welfare benefits in state enterprises is discussed in Walder (1983), pp. 54–55.

41. F14-E (Chinese personnel manager), E26, and C1. The trend in welfare policy to help relieve the state budget of the welfare burden was codified in the Seventh Five-Year Plan (1986–1990) and was noted by C1; F21-A; F24-A; Chu Baotai (1984), p. 112; and Wang Yihe, et al. (1984), p. 304.

42. On negotiation over welfare standards, see F16-A, F3-A, and E26. F14-E (Chinese JV personnel manager) and C1 asserted that welfare in a JV must be the same as in a state-run enterprise, although the Implementing Regulations require only the establishment of a welfare fund (discussed below). On work schedules and the like, Wang Yihe, et al. (1984), pp. 305–6. Several foreign managers noted that Chinese managers controlled social welfare decisions.

43. Article 91 of the Implementing Regulations stated that welfare matters must be handled according to the Joint Venture Labor Regulations. The "Provisions for the Implementation of the Regulations on Labor Management in Joint Ventures Using Chinese and Foreign Investment" (promulgated 19 January 1984) clarified the earlier rules somewhat. Enterprises in the SEZs paid a "labor service fee," allocated as follows: 70% went directly to the worker, 5% was retained by the JV to subsidize the welfare cost for workers (presumably through the welfare fund), and 25% paid for social labor insurance and various state subsidies (Article 8, "Provisional Regulations of the SEZs in Guangdong Province on Labor Management and Wages in Enterprises"). On basic and real wages in state enterprises and joint ventures, see Wang Yihe, et al. (1984), pp. 304ff, and Horsley (1984). Using a 1983 figure of the average annual real wage of a Chinese state-enterprise worker of 959 *yuan* ($480), the comparable joint venture real wage as suggested by the government *should* have amounted to from 1150 *yuan* to 1437 *yuan* ($575 to $718). In

fact, the actual figure for a "typical" joint venture in the same year was 2500 *yuan* to 3,000 *yuan* ($1250 to $1500). This discrepancy may indicate that joint ventures also paid subsidies previously provided directly by the state, as discussed previously.

44. First example was the Fujian-Hitachi joint venture. Imai (1984), p. 18. The second example was offered as typical in NCUSCT (1987), p. 162. When a foreign firm established a joint venture with an existing Chinese enterprise, the venture would generally take over the numerous welfare facilities already in existence. One venture established with an existing factory acquired responsibility for about thirty welfare functions and facilities, and built an additional dining area. Most of the facilities in this case were placed under the purview of the JVs Labor Organization (F14-C). In the Fujian Hitachi case, part of the Chinese side's contribution to equity was in the form of welfare installations of the existing plant. Sun Guanhua and Wang Yuan (1984), p. 40.

45. The fund was required by Implementing Regulations, Article 87. Wang Yihe, et al. give the 5%–10% figure (1984, p. 295).

46. The JV was Hai-Ri, involving a Japanese partner. *China Newsletter*, No. 74, May–June 1988, p. 22.

47. The importance of cooperation and compatible outlooks for the success of a JV is often stressed by scholars of international joint ventures. For example: Walmsley (1982), p. 12, and Lasserre (1983), p. 73. As one Chinese official put it, "consultation serves in part for the foreign side to learn from the Chinese side, but also is a way of helping the joint venture by providing [to the foreigner] knowledge of China" (C1). Wang Yihe, et al. (1984, p. 248) also cite the possibility that foreign managers can learn from Chinese managers. A Chinese official and a Chinese JV manager privately acknowledged the need for foreign managers, however (C1, F14-E).

48. Liu Zhao (1979), p. 9. A Chinese official (C1) reiterated this.

49. F4-A, F9-B, F14, F24-A, F26. Interviews with foreign JV managers conducted in 1990 revealed their perception that Chinese managers continued to take on ever greater responsibilities throughout the 1980s, but that this process was disrupted by the crackdown of 1989.

50. F14-B. This DGM was previously the general manager of the original Chinese factory that formed the JV, and had some prior management training.

51. Of twenty joint ventures for which information was available, ten indicated that some sort of joint dynamic was in effect, whereas eight (40%) felt it was not, and two (10%) indicated some mixture.

52. The reasons offered for lack of "jointness" were from F1, F8, F4, F12-A, F25, F26, F28, E6, F10, E14, E15, F9-F, F22 (CJV), E14, and *AWSJ*, 17 January 1985, p. 1.

53. These examples were from F9-B and F14, respectively, and were supported by F24-A. E11 noted that most managers were *technically* competent, though not managerially so. On general post-Mao management reforms, see Lockett and Littler (1983), pp. 691–93.

54. The examples are from F9-D, F4, and F12. F9 and F4 were among the earliest ventures, and thus had had a foreign managerial presence for a relatively long time. A strikingly harsh critique of the managerial capacities of Chinese managers came from a Japanese manager, recorded in Imai (1989), p. 12. On reluc-

tance of Chinese managers to share foreign skills, see Child (1990), p. 48. On bureaucratic problems that hinder training, see Zong Ruiyu (1987), pp. 64–65.

55. This was apparent in seven cases: F1, F4, F9-A, F11, F14-B-1, F24-A, F28-A.

56. Seventeen of twenty-one JVs with foreign managers for which sufficient information was available evidenced foreign dominance, as did two CJVs (F18, F22). Of the four joint ventures without foreign dominance, two were in textiles, where Chinese enterprises have extensive manufacturing experience. Foreign managers' preference to control production and marketing was also found by Child (1990, p. 30). Child also argues that American and Japanese managers tended to dominate their JVs more than Europeans (1990, pp. 17–18, 97, 101).

57. Quote is from F4. E23 supports this and believes Chinese acquiescence reflected the Chinese side's lack of confidence that they could take the venture through a difficult startup period.

58. In one CJV, for example, the contract granted the foreign side the right to a final say for five years.

59. On stalemates, E14, F7. Stalemates were resolved by dispute resolution methods discussed in chapter 4, or by early termination of the venture. Some support for these arguments is found in Woetzel (1989), p. 20.

60. Li Boxi (1987), p. 50.

61. Strong pressure on JVs—and Chinese managers—to show profits early was noted by F1, F9-A, F11, F12-A, F24-A, F26, E6, and E7. Ho and Huenemann note disincentives in the case of the China-Schindler JV (1984, p. 99). See also Pye (1982). Accusations of "capitalist profit-seeking" were leveled against some state enterprise managers who applied the profit motive (with official sanction) in the early 1980s. White (1983a), p. 497. For further discussion of the incentives for Chinese managers in JVs, see Child (1990).

62. On the belief that foreign managers were a necessary ingredient for success, F3-A, F7-A, F9-B, F14-E, F24-A, F26. In several cases, the Chinese partners were noted to have considered Americans of non-Chinese descent or Japanese to be superior managers to Hong Kong Chinese (C3-A, F16-A3).

63. "Tinkering" was discouraged in F9. The foreign managers in this case were particularly sensitive because they had been accused earlier of failing to ensure that the JV turned out quality goods. The case where foreign managers disagreed with Chinese managers' involvement in welfare issues was AMC, as carefully described in Mann (1989), chap. 16. Many of these issues were discussed by F1, F4, F7, F9-G, F12, and F14-B-2. Child found that, more than other foreign managers, Americans particularly tried to introduce foreign methods wholesale, an effort that often left them frustrated (1990, p. 104). He also concludes that foreigners of all origins were poor at training Chinese managers as such (p. 58). There was no evidence for a fourth possible disincentive for transfer of skills: the possibility that through effective teaching foreign managers would undermine their own position in the venture, and hence future access to the China market.

64. Some experiments in local autonomy were begun as early as the late 1970s, particularly in Sichuan Province. See Lockett and Littler (1983) and White (1983a). On how these reforms affected joint ventures, see Fischer (1989). After the early drives for increased enterprise autonomy in the late 1970s, the independ-

ent status of enterprises fluctuated greatly, and their semi-autonomy was often subverted either in implementation (by directive-minded bureaucrats) or by policy changes precipitated by economic crises (as with the tightening of enterprises' authority to spend foreign exchange).

65. The 1980 JV Labor Regulations contemplated the establishment of LOs in large-scale operations. The Implementing Regulations, Article 95, guaranteed the right of all JVs to form an LO. JV contracts usually provided for LOs (E8 and Horsley [1984], pp. 22–23). In SEZs, contracts are signed directly with staff, and labor protection is overseen at the provincial level. On financial and other support of the LO by the JV, Wang Yihe, et al. (1984), pp. 250–51.

66. On who may join a union, Wang Yihe, et al. (1984), pp. 250–51. The Fujian-Hitachi example is from Imai (1984), p. 17. The Fujian-Hitachi JV also illustrates how the foreign side was frozen out of participation in the LO. There, the LO was "an independent organization outside the official structure of the company" although it was "directly under the leadership of the [Chinese] general manager." Sun Guanhua and Wang Yuan (1984), p. 42. In general, the LO was distinct from the personnel department (F14-F, E17, and F7). In the 1983 trade union constitution, LOs were given somewhat more autonomy from direct party leadership than before, though they were responsible to the union organization at the next-higher level. Horsley (1984), p. 23.

67. According to one Chinese manager, a firing could be considered "unreasonable" if the worker had a "good attitude." If a worker was "truly bad," the LO would not offer support (F14-F). See also Wang Yihe, et al. (1984), p. 251. The LO role in signing and supervising implementation of a labor contract was stipulated in Article 97 of the Implementing Regulations.

68. The Implementing Regulations, Article 98, gave the LO participatory rights on the board, and Joint Venture Labor Regulations, Article 14, granted recourse if the LO was unhappy with a board decision. A similar right was granted to trade unions in Hungarian JVs, where unions could control the working conditions of employees and, through right of objection, could prevent the execution of measures considered detrimental. Gayer (1982), p. 134. In Romanian joint ventures, workers were by law represented on the board of directors. Business International (1973), p. 84.

69. E15 noted elimination of LO rights to attend board meetings without BOD (and given the nature of voting rules, without foreign) permission and the absence of the LO at board meetings. E4 also noted this absence, and the case of limiting the presence of the LO at board *votes* so as not to pressure the voting.

70. The quote is from Wang Yihe, et al. (1984), p. 250, and the example is from F26. On these functions, see Implementing Regulations, Article 97. C1 noted the role of the LO in retraining workers before they may be fired, although two personnel managers (F9-E, F14-F) stressed that the most technical education was done by the personnel department or by foreign experts.

71. On education, F9-E, F14-E, and F14-F (all are Chinese managers). F7 noted use of propaganda posters. Political study is discussed below.

72. F14-E, F14-F, F9-E, F12, and F14-B. Wang Yihe, et al. also suggest that Chinese investors explain to foreigners that the "primary obligation of the LO is to correctly educate the working masses, and to correctly implement the contract

provisions. Thus, the LO cannot hinder enterprise management but rather functions to promote and guarantee enterprise production" (1984, p. 249).

73. Information was available for twenty-one EJVs. In one of the ventures with no LO, workers were formally part of the LO in the Chinese partner's unit. This arrangement was not unusual, but it often separated workers from the LO representing them and led to weaker LO authority in the JV.

74. The cases reported are F24-A, F9-A, and F28. F21 noted the strategy of confining LO activities to after work hours. This was sometimes the case in state enterprises, too, and was not contrary to state policy.

75. On the growth of party authority over management starting in the mid-1950s, see Schurmann (1968), pp. 284–97.

76. E6, E7, E11, E15, and E23, all of whom had been extensively involved in negotiations, confirmed that the Chinese did not raise the issue of the party in that context. Many interviewees in the process of negotiations were not aware that the party would play a role in their JV at all. On the presence of party personnel in negotiations see, for example, F24-A. These personnel were present in that role, although others involved in the negotiations could also be party members. E15 notes the existence of internal circulars. The role of the party in JVs was clarified somewhat by the publication in 1987 of formal rules. These rules, "Interim Provisions Concerning Ideological and Political Work for Chinese Staff and Workers in Chinese-Foreign Equity and Cooperative Joint Ventures," suggested much of what is presented in the analysis here.

77. Wang Zhaozheng (1982), p. 27. Wang borrowed from Lenin's analysis of the use of foreign capital in the USSR in the 1920s. The leading role of the party was also noted by former Shenzhen mayor Liang Xiang (1985).

78. Chamberlain (1987), p. 641.

79. On party structure, F9-E (Chinese JV personnel manager), and F14-G (JV party secretary). The "Protocol Department" example was from F7-A. Party influence also could come through the Communist Youth League (CYL) branch located in the venture, but this was less influential (C1).

80. The case of the East Lake Inn (CJV) in Shenzhen was discussed in *Fahui Dang de Zuoyong, Banhao Hezi Qiye* (1984), p. 1. On cadre recruitment and supervision over implementation of the party: F14-E (Chinese manager), F14-G (JV party secretary), F16, and C1. Party observers in negotiations were noted by F12, F24-A, and E11.

81. Study was held after work in F7, F14, F28. F24-A noted that his JV lost people for several days to go for political study. Following the events at Tiananmen, Chinese managers and workers at many JVs spent many hours in political study.

82. Quotes are from F14-F (Chinese manager) and F14-E. See also F14-G (Chinese manager) and C1, p. 9. Two foreign interviewees believed that the practice of making "small reports" (particularly concerning Chinese workers' attitudes) to be placed in worker dossiers did not occur in joint ventures (F9-A, E15). However, E11 believed dossiers were kept by the party secretary on activities of foreigners.

83. This information comes from various documents in which the content of study is discussed or from which it can be inferred, as well as from interviewees.

F9-E (Chinese manager) noted the "party articles." On guarding against spiritual pollution: E6; "Strictly Observe Discipline in Domestic and Foreign Trade" (1985); Feng Sheng (1984), p. K16; Wang Zhaozheng (1982), p. 27; and *NYT*, 5 November 1982, p. A2. On building socialist spiritual civilization: Gu Mu (1985), p. 1; Xiang Nan (1983), p. 4; and *SSZH*, 5 July 1982, p. 1. On working hard and supporting the "open" policy and the reforms: F14-B; F14-F (Chinese JV manager); F14-G (JV party secretary); F24-A; F26; C1; *WSJ*, 14 March 1984, p. 17; and "Decision of the Central Committee of the Communist Party of China on Reform of the Economic Structure," part X, p. 32 (October 1984). F12 and F14-B were told that ideological study would be de-emphasized. Quote is from C1.

84. The example from Beijing is F4. The partners expected the situation to be resolved when the senior party member retired. Other JVs with vestiges of competing CCP power structures were F7-A and F14.

85. Of the nineteen JVs for which information was available, no party cell was identified by interviewees in ten. Of the nine (47%) in which party cells existed, they were said to be active in only six. It is unlikely that foreigners were not aware of a party cell that competed with the formal managerial hierarchy, or of political study that actively undermined joint venture operations.

86. F14 and F16 were the JVs with cadres who were uniquely party secretaries. In the following JVs, key CCP cadres in board or management positions in the venture were reported to hold "production" positions: F7-A, F9, F12-A, F14-G, F16-A, F24-A, F26, and Fujian-Hitachi (Imai [1984], p. 17). E8 noted that there was always one Chinese manager "clearly and overtly" from the CCP. However, according to one report, the leadership discouraged party or government cadres from concurrently holding posts in state enterprises because the state functionaries not only did not have proper training and did not have the interest of productive, competitive enterprises, or their political duties, at heart. *Dang Zheng Fuze Ganbu Buyi Jianren Qiye de Lingdao Ren* (1984).

87. F4, F16, F24-A (all three with JVs in different areas), and E14.

88. F9-B. This manager also claimed that the management staff told him that the study sessions are "more words than substance." A JV party secretary (F14-G) noted that he would cancel sessions if work was too hectic. F4 also notes that the amount of study varies from week to week.

89. Of thirteen EJVs for which information was available, foreign managers reported political study activities in seven, whereas in the remaining six no such study was evident. Study was found in some, but not all JVs, in two cities where more than one joint venture was studied, Tianjin (3 JVs) and Shanghai (3 JVs). Both JVs in Beijing had study, whereas neither in Guangdong Province did. Generalizations from this small number of cases must be regarded as highly tentative. E8 noted that provisions allowing political study were never included in contracts.

90. F9-B, F10, F28, and E15 indicated that as long as activities did not disrupt work, they did not care about the CCP activities because they posed no threat. F7 did not interfere because it was not his mandate.

91. The examples are from F28, E7, F24-A, E4, and E15, respectively.

92. F9-E. A JV party secretary also stressed that CCP activities do not "interfere with production" (F14-G). These domestic reforms of the party role went through several phases, but finally by 1984, a formal policy for a reduced role for

the party was announced, and by 1986, the government had applied this policy to most large and medium enterprises. In domestic enterprises, party influence remained stronger in some cases than the new policy implied it should. Chamberlain (1987).

93. C1. This idea was supported by F9-E, F14-F, F14-G (all three Chinese managers), F4-A, F16, and Imai (1984), p. 19.

94. He Xinhao (1980), p. 2.

95. In some cases, government "companies" (gongsi), situated in the hierarchy between the DIC and the ministry branch or MOFERT, had some jurisdiction in the early years. The authority of "companies" was reduced by the October 1984 reforms, however, and became increasingly obscure for JVs (F9-B).

96. DIC approval and supervision functions are found in Implementing Regulations, Articles 9, 46, 30, 66, 89, 56, and 103.

97. On MOFERT's role in negotiations: E17, F2, F7-A, and C1. MOFERT's supervisory authorities are found in the Implementing Regulations, Articles 8, 18, 30, 42, and 46. On MOFERT factions, E17.

98. Shirk (1985) discusses political opposition to the "open" policy and other reforms among different bureaucracies, regions, and sectors who stood to lose from it. F9-A and F28 noted opposition from local and middle-level bureaucrats.

99. Quote is from F9-E. Data on bureaucratic constraints was available for twenty EJVs in the sample. On Chinese partners' frustrations: F9-E, F11, F14-B, F14-C, F28-B, F14-B, F14-E, and E8.

100. E21.

101. Outside pressure was noted by F4, F9-D, F26, E14, and E15. The propensity of Chinese managers to pass responsibility upward in order to cover their decisions was noted by F9. See also Pye (1982).

102. These examples are from F28; F9-D; C3; F26; F28; Wei Jin (1983); WSJ, 14 March 1984; and Fujimura (1982).

103. On JV autonomy relative to state enterprises, see N. T. Wang (1984), p. 78, and C1. The Implementing Regulations stipulated departmental noninterference (Article 56), BOD authority (Article 33), and the right to do business independently (Article 7). JV autonomy was reiterated generally by Chinese officials (C1, C2-A). See also F9-A, F9-D, and F3-A. Other statements of autonomy in specific decisionmaking realms are found in Wei Yuming (1983), pp. 18–20, and Wang Yihe, et al. (1984), p. 113. Efforts to increase joint venture autonomy were not implemented uniformly, however; autonomy tended to be greater in the south and in smaller ventures, and in those approved at the local level (F4 and F21).

104. The Chinese DGM quote is F14-C. On the helpful role of DICs: C1, C7, F14-E (Chinese manager), E15, and Swindler (1984), p. 1027. F4 noted that his venture would bring members of their Beijing-based DIC to Hong Kong, put them in the best hotels, and so on. F8 noted a similar strategy; F16, F19, and F26 reiterated these views. A Chinese official acknowledged that the supervisory role was "still very abstract," weak, and "mainly procedural" (C1).

105. C7 confirmed MOFERT's authority to investigate wrongdoing in the venture: "If the JV gets in trouble it should report to [fanying] MOFERT. MOFERT can then go take a look [qu kanyikan]."

106. This "window" service did not eliminate the authority of the various gov-

ernment agencies, but did provide a government agency to coordinate the different bureaucracies. The need to improve the investment environment by improving the bureaucratic environment continued to be expressed after 1987. See, for example, Suo Qian (1987), p. 73, and Yang Aiqun (1987), p. 17.

107. See Walder's (1983) work on *guanxi* in state-run enterprises, and Solinger's treatment of *guanxi* in socialist commerce (1984, pp. 57, 125). I used both of these works, as well as interviews (especially C7), as the basis of this discussion.

108. F26. This is supported by F16. Other foreign managers felt that their *guanxi* had helped protect them during the economic retrenchment that began in 1988.

109. F9-E. The importance of *guanxi* was noted implicitly in the suggestion of Xiang Nan, writing on the SEZs: "In SEZ enterprises one person should be assigned as the 'special cadre' [*zhuan yuan*], and can be from a ministry or company's [department in charge]" (1983a, p. 16).

110. Enterprise leaders traditionally wore two "hats." Schurmann (1968), pp. 223, 259, and Solinger (1984), pp. 141–47.

111. The examples are from E21, F3-A (both on use of ties in gaining approval); F26, F9-A, F4 (all on Chinese partners handling government relations); F24 (Shanghai JV); F14-A, C2-A (both on CITIC board members); F12 and F11 (both on foreigners' ties).

112. Reliable information was available on twenty-one EJVs.

CHAPTER SIX
CONCLUSION: THE CONTROL OF
FOREIGN DIRECT INVESTMENT UNDER SOCIALISM

1. There is some conceptual overlap between these two categories of problems, implementation and the need to liberalize. In particular, when the government failed at implementing a policy—such as when the conditions of the domestic economy interfered—it sometimes later liberalized the controls.

2. Lindblom (1977) suggests that this approach characterizes planned economies.

3. See Shirk (1985).

4. See, for example, *NYT*, 21 June 1989.

5. That wide variance among socialist countries must be anticipated is established in comparative studies of Eastern European political economy. See, for example, Comisso and Tyson (1986) and Dannenbaum (1989).

6. European countries were even more willing to transfer advanced technology to China than were the United States and Japan. U.S. Congress, O.T.A. (1987), p. 118.

APPENDIX A
METHODOLOGICAL ISSUES

1. Five of the eighty-nine interviews were with foreign representatives of contractual joint ventures and two were with wholly foreign-owned firms. In several cases, one interviewee (from a foreign parent) discussed his or her firm's involvement in several EJVs, and (more often) several interviewees discussed one EJV.

2. I interviewed five Chinese managers (two of them twice each) from three ventures.

3. These organizations were CITIC, China International Economic Consultants, China Resources (a PRC investment channel located in Hong Kong), Shenzhen Municipal Industrial Development Corporation (SMIDC), Tianjin International Trade and Investment Corporation (TITIC), Tianjin Foreign Trade Ministry, and Tianjin Certified Public Accountants. With the "open" policy, many organizations adopted usage of the term "corporation," presumably to make them appear to outside investors to be independent of government control. Although some of these agencies had some degree of autonomy (and were self-funding), they usually reported directly to a government office (CITIC, SMIDC, and TITIC were directly under the State Council, Shenzhen Municipal Government, and Tianjin People's Government, respectively).

4. Because virtually all respondents requested that their names not be identified with their statements, interviews are recorded in the text by anonymous code. (See the explanation at the beginning of this Notes section.)

5. Three (11%) of the twenty-eight were located outside of the coastal areas and Beijing.

6. The most useful Chinese book is Wang Yihe, et al. (1984). A list of Chinese printed sources used in this book appears in the Bibliography.

7. Chinese-language newspapers used included *Nanfang Ribao* [*Southern Daily*] and *Shenzhen Tequ Bao* [*Shenzhen Special Zone Herald*] (daily, starting May 1982). Chinese-language economic journals used included *Guoji Maoyi Wenti* [*Problems of International Trade*] (bimonthly); *Guoji Maoyi* [*Intertrade*] (monthly); *Jingji Guanli* [*Economic Management*] (monthly); *Jingji Yanjiu* [*Economic Research*] (monthly); *Jingji Kexue* [*Economic Sciences*] (quarterly) (1980–1982); *Shijie Jingji* [*World Economics*] (1978–1982); and *Jingji Daobao* [*Economic Reporter*] (weekly, published in Hong Kong). Chinese press sources in translation included Joint Publications Research Service (JPRS), China Report (Red Flag, Economic Affairs, and Political Social and Military Affairs), and Foreign Broadcast Information Service (FBIS), Daily Report: China. Relevant articles in the Chinese editions were chosen by scanning titles and (where available) abstracts indicating contents about the following: joint ventures, foreign direct investment, joint management, the "open" policy in general, and "spiritual pollution." I did not review articles specifically on foreign trade.

8. This view is supported by Halpern (1985), p. 82.

9. See State Statistical Bureau (various years), *Statistical Yearbook for China*. Beijing: China Statistics Press; and MOFERT (all years between 1984 and 1989), *Almanac of China's Foreign Economic Relations and Trade*. Hong Kong: Joint Publishing Company.

10. The American *China Business Review* (CBR), Hong Kong–based *Far Eastern Economic Review*, (FEER), *Asian Wall Street Journal* (AWSJ), *China Newsletter* (published in Japan), and *Jingji Daobao* [*Economic Reporter, JJDB*] (noted above), provided the most thorough coverage outside of China.

11. Ho and Huenemann (1984), the chapters on FDI and the SEZs in Moser (1984 and 1987), N. T. Wang (1984), Wu (1981), and Chai (1983).

12. Praise of business and other generally anti-socialist interests found expres-

sion in the popular press and in Western business journals such as *Forbes* and *Business Week*. An example of works that rather mechanistically (that is, without concrete analysis) apply Marxian analysis to China's "open" policy to find a "capitalist restoration" is Cannon (1983).

13. NCUSCT (1987) and A. T. Kearney (1987). The latter study reports interview data on 54 manufacturing equity joint ventures. The NCUSCT study summarizes data on over 134 equity joint ventures and 55 contractual joint ventures involving American firms, using data compiled from public sources. NCUSCT discusses its sample on p. 65, and A. T. Kearney on p. 25.

APPENDIX B

NONEQUITY FORMS OF FOREIGN DIRECT INVESTMENT

1. For the descriptions of nonequity forms of investment in this section, I draw largely on N. R. Chen (1986) and Moser (1984a). FDI is more broadly defined in Chinese than in Western usage.

2. On oil contracts, see Moser (1984c). A major study of this form of investment is Oksenberg and Lieberthal (1986).

3. By September 1985, the number of compensation trade projects was 1585, or 22.5% of the total foreign-backed projects (7030). The 1600 processing and assembly arrangements established by the end of 1982 involved $197 million in equipment supplied by foreign companies. Two-thirds of the compensation trade agreements were with Hong Kong partners, and most of the rest were with Japanese firms. N. R. Chen (1986), pp. 9 (table 2) and 23–24.

4. By December 1982, China had earned $800 million in processing fees, and obtained foreign equipment valued at $197 million. Cumulative fees rose to nearly $1.3 billion by the end of 1984. N. R. Chen (1986), p. 27. On the value of this form of investment, see MOFERT, *Almanacs* from 1984 to 1987. MOFERT ceased reporting these forms as direct foreign investment in 1987.

BIBLIOGRAPHY

NON-PRC AUTHORS

A. T. Kearney and International Trade Research Institute of the PRC. 1987. *Manufacturing Equity Joint Ventures in China*. Chicago: A. T. Kearney.

Barale, Louise. 1988. "China's Investment Implementing Regulations." *China Business Review* 15, no. 2 (March–April): 19–23.

Bennett, Douglas, and Kenneth Sharpe. 1985. *Transnational Corporations versus the State: The Political Economy of the Mexican Auto Industry*. Princeton, N.J.: Princeton University Press.

Bergsten, C. Fred, Thomas Horst, and Theodore H. Moran. 1978. *American Multinationals and American Interests*. Washington, D.C.: Brookings Institution.

Biersteker, Thomas J. 1981. *Distortion or Development?: Contending Perspectives on the Multinational Corporation*. Cambridge, Mass.: MIT Press.

———. 1987. *The Political Economy of Indigenization: Multinationals, the State, and Local Capital in Nigeria*. Princeton, N.J.: Princeton University Press.

Business China. Series of short case studies on joint ventures in the PRC beginning 14 September 1983.

Business International. 1973. *Doing Business with Romania*. Geneva: Business International, S.A.

Campbell, Nigel. 1986. *China Strategies: The Inside Story*. Manchester: University of Manchester/University of Hong Kong.

Cannon, Terry. 1983. "Foreign Investment and Trade: Origins of the Modernization Policy." In *The Chinese Economic Reforms*, edited by Stephen Feuchtwang and Althar Hussein, pp. 288–345. London: Croom and Helm.

Caporaso, James. 1978. "Introduction: Dependence and Dependency in the Global System." *International Organization* 32, no. 1 (Winter): 1–12.

Cardoso, Fernando H., and Enzo Faletto. 1978 (English edition). *Dependency and Development in Latin America*. Berkeley: University of California Press.

Central Intelligence Agency. 1988. *China: Economic Policy and Performance in 1987*. Report presented to the Joint Economic Committee of Congress. Washington, D.C.: United States Congress.

Chai, Joseph. 1983. "Industrial Co-operation between China and Hong Kong." In *China and Hong Kong: The Economic Nexus*, edited by A. J. Youngson, pp. 104–55. Oxford: Oxford University Press.

Chamberlain, Heath. 1987. "Party-Management Relations in China's Industries: Some Political Dimensions of Economic Reforms." *China Quarterly* 112 (December): 631–61.

Chan, Thomas, E. K. Chen, and Steve Chin. 1986. "China's Special Economic Zones: Ideology, Policy and Practice." In *China's Special Economic Zones: Policies, Problems and Prospects*, edited by Y. C. Rao and C. K. Leung, pp. 87–104. Hong Kong: Oxford University Press.

Chang, Jesse T. H., and Charles J. Conroy. 1984. "Trade-mark Law in the People's Republic of China." In *Foreign Trade, Investment and the Law in the People's Republic of China*, edited by Michael J. Moser, pp. 267–80. Hong Kong: Oxford University Press.

Chang, Ta-kuang. 1987. "The Great Battle of the Forms." *China Business Review* 14, no. 4 (July–August): 7–10.

Chang, Ta-kuang, and Rolf Olofsson. 1989. "U.S.-Chinese Arbitrations in Stockholm." *China Business Review* 16, no. 5 (September–October): 18.

Chang, Valerie. 1989. "The New Look of China's Banks." *China Business Review* 16, no. 3 (May–June): 20–22.

Chase-Dunn, Christopher. 1982. "Socialist States in the Capitalist World Economy." In *Socialist States in the World System*, edited by C. Chase-Dunn, pp. 37–56. Beverly Hills: Sage Publications.

———, ed. 1982a. *Socialist States in the World System*. Beverly Hills: Sage Publications.

Chen, Edward K. Y. 1983. "The Impact of China's Four Modernizations on Hong Kong's Economic Development." In *China and Hong Kong: The Economic Nexus*, edited by A. J. Youngson, pp. 77–103. Hong Kong: Oxford University Press.

Chen, Nai-ruenn. 1986. *Foreign Investment in China: Current Trends*. Washington, D.C.: U.S. Department of Commerce, International Trade Administration.

Chi Shi-ching. 1982. "Zhao Ziyang Speaks on Development of Special Zones." *Wen Wei Po* in FBIS-CHI-82-109 (7 June), p. W1.

Chiang Kai-shek. 1947. *China's Destiny*, edited by Philip Jaffe. New York: Roy Publishers.

Child, John. 1990. *The Management of Equity Joint Ventures in China*. Beijing: China-European Community Management Association and China Enterprise Management Association.

Chu, Franklin. 1984. "Banking and Finance in the China Trade." In *Foreign Trade, Investment and the Law in the People's Republic of China*, edited by Michael J. Moser, pp. 29–266. Hong Kong: Oxford University Press.

Chu, Franklin, Michael J. Moser, and Owen Nee, eds. 1982. *Commercial, Business and Trade Laws: People's Republic of China*. Dobbs Ferry, N.Y.: Oceana Publications.

Cohen, Jerome A. 1982. "Equity Joint Ventures: 20 Potential Pitfalls that Every Company Should Know About." *China Business Review* 9, no. 6 (November–December): 23–30.

———. 1984. "Some Legal Aspects of Investing in China." Testimony before the U.S. House of Representatives Special Subcommittee on U.S. Trade with China, Washington, D.C. (September).

———. 1985. "The New Foreign Contract Law." *China Business Review* 12, no. 4 (July–August): 52–54.

———. 1987. "The Role of Arbitration in Economic Co-operation with China." In *Foreign Trade, Investment and the Law in the People's Republic of China*, edited by Michael J. Moser, pp. 508–53. Hong Kong: Oxford University Press.

Cohen, Jerome A., and Jamie P. Horsley. 1983. "The New JV Regulations." *China Business Review* 10, no. 6 (November–December): 44–48.

Cohen, Jerome A., and Ta-kuang Chang. 1987. "New Investment Provisions." *China Business Review* 14, no. 1 (January–February): 11.

Comisso, Ellen, and Laura D'Andrea Tyson, eds. 1986. *Power, Purpose and Collective Choice: Economic Strategy in Socialist States*. Ithaca, N.Y.: Cornell University Press.

Crane, George T. 1986. *China's SEZs: The Domestic Political Dynamics of International Economic Integration*. Ph.D. dissertation, University of Wisconsin.

Cumings, Bruce. 1984. "The Political Economy of China's Turn Outward." In *China and the World: Chinese Foreign Policy in the Post-Mao Era*, edited by Samuel Kim, pp. 235–65. Boulder, Colo.: Westview Press.

Daniels, John D., Jeffrey Krug, and Douglas Nigh. 1985. "U.S. Joint Ventures in China: Motivation and Management of Political Risk." *California Management Review* 27, no. 4 (Summer): 46–58.

Dannenbaum, Anne Henderson. 1989. "The International Monetary Fund and Eastern Europe: The Politics of Economic Stabilization and Reform." (Paper presented at the 1989 Annual Meeting of the American Political Science Association, 2 September 1989, Atlanta, Georgia.)

Dernberger, Robert F. 1975. "The Role of the Foreigner in China's Economic Development." In *China's Modern Economy in Historical Perspective*, edited by Dwight H. Perkins. Stanford: Stanford University Press.

———. 1977. "Economic Development and Modernization in Contemporary China." In *Technology and Communist Culture*, edited by Frederic Fleron, pp. 224–64. New York: Praeger Press.

———. 1982. "The Chinese Search for the Path of Self-Sustained Growth in the 1980s: An Assessment." In *China Under the Four Modernizations, Part I*, Selected Papers Submitted to the Joint Economic Committee, U.S. Congress, pp. 19–76. Washington, D.C.: U.S. Government Printing Office.

Donnithorne, Audrey. 1972. "China's Cellular Economy: Some Economic Trends Since the Cultural Revolution." *China Quarterly*, no. 52 (October–December): 605–19.

Dos Santos, Theotonio. 1970. "The Structure of Dependence." *American Economic Review* 60, pp. 232–36.

Eckstein, Harry. 1975. "Case Study and Theory in Political Science." In *Handbook of Political Science, Volume 7: Strategies of Inquiry*, edited by Fred Greenstein and Nelson Polsby, pp. 79–137. Reading, Mass.: Addison-Wesley.

Eliasoph, Ellen R. 1985. "China's Patent System Emerges." *China Business Review* 12, no. 1 (January–February): 50–54.

Encarnation, Dennis J., and Sushil Vachani. 1985. "Foreign Ownership: When Hosts Change the Rules." *Harvard Business Review* 63, no. 5 (September/October): 152–60.

Evans, Peter. 1979. *Dependent Development: The Alliance of Multinational, State and Local Capital in Brazil*. Princeton, N.J.: Princeton University Press.

———. 1987. "Class, State and Dependence in East Asia: Lessons for Latin Americanists." In *The Political Economy of the New Asian Industrialism*, edited by Frederic C. Deyo, pp. 203–26. Ithaca, N.Y.: Cornell University Press.

Falkenheim, Victor. 1986. "China's SEZs." In *China Looks to the Year 2000*, Selected Papers Submitted to the Joint Economic Committee, U.S. Congress, pp. 348–70. Washington, D.C.: U.S. Government Printing Office.

Feuchtwang, Stephen, and Althar Hussein, eds. 1983. *The Chinese Economic Reforms*. London: Croom and Helm.

Feuerwerker, Albert. 1976. *The Foreign Establishment in China in the Early Twentieth Century*. No. 29. Ann Arbor: Michigan Papers in Chinese Studies.

Fischer, William A. 1989. "China's Industrial Innovation: The Influence of Market Forces." In *Science and Technology in Post-Mao China*, edited by Denis Fred Simon and Merle Goldman, pp. 119–36. Cambridge, Mass.: Harvard Council on East Asian Studies.

Foreign Economic Trends and Their Implications for the United States. September 1985. Washington, D.C.: U.S. Department of Commerce, International Trade Administration.

Friedman, Edward. 1983. "The Societal Obstacle to China's Socialist Transition: State Capitalism or Feudal Fascism." In *State and Society in Contemporary China*, edited by Victor Nee and David Mozingo, pp. 148–71. Ithaca, N.Y.: Cornell University Press.

Friedmann, Wolfgang G., and Jean-Pierre Beguin. 1971. *Joint International Business Ventures in Developing Countries: Case Studies and Analysis of Recent Trends*. New York: Columbia University Press.

Friedrich, Carl, and Zbigniew Brzezinski. 1956. *Totalitarian Dictatorship and Autocracy*. Cambridge, Mass.: Harvard University Press.

Frisbie, John. 1988. "Balancing Foreign Exchange." *China Business Review* 15, no. 2 (March–April): 24–29.

Froebel, Folker, Jurgen Heinrichs, and Otto Kreye. 1980 (English edition). *The New International Division of Labor*. Cambridge: Cambridge University Press.

Fujimura Takayoshi. 1982. "Joint Venture for Manufacturing in China Can Face Many Troubles." *Japan Economic Journal* (22 June).

Gayer, Gyula. 1982. "Some Questions on Labour Law in Connection with Joint Ventures in Hungary." *International Business Lawyer* 10, no. 4 (April): 133–37.

Gelatt, Timothy A., and Richard D. Pomp. 1984. "China's Tax System: An Overview and Transactional Analysis." In *Foreign Trade, Investment and the Law in the People's Republic of China*, edited by Michael J. Moser, pp. 42–89. Hong Kong: Oxford University Press.

Gelatt, Timothy A., and Richard D. Pomp. 1987. "China's Tax System: An Overview and Transactional Analysis." In *Foreign Trade, Investment and the Law in the People's Republic of China*, edited by Michael J. Moser, pp. 42–89. Hong Kong: Oxford University Press.

Gereffi, Gary. 1983. *The Pharmaceutical Industry and Dependency in the Third World*. Princeton, N.J.: Princeton University Press.

Gerschenkron, Alexander. 1962. *Economic Backwardness in Historical Perspective*. Cambridge, Mass.: Harvard University Press.

Grow, Roy F. 1989. "Acquiring Foreign Technology: What Makes the Transfer Process Work?" In *Science and Technology in Post-Mao China*, edited by Denis Fred Simon and Merle Goldman, pp. 319–46. Cambridge, Mass.: Harvard Council on East Asian Studies.

Haggard, Stephan, and Tun-jen Cheng. 1987. "State and Capital in the East Asian NICs." In *The Political Economy of the New Asian Industrialism*, edited by Frederic C. Deyo, pp. 84–135. Ithaca, N.Y.: Cornell University Press.

Haley, Raymond V. 1989. "Changing Lending Practices in China." *China Business Review* 16, no. 3 (May–June): 30–31.

Halpern, Nina P. 1985. "Learning From Abroad: Chinese Views of the Eastern European Economic Experience, January, 1977–June, 1981." *Modern China* 11, no. 1 (January): 77–109.

Harding, Harry. 1987. *China's Second Revolution: Reform After Mao*. Washington, D.C.: Brookings Institution.

Harrigan, Kathryn R. 1985. *Strategies for Joint Ventures*. Lexington, Mass.: Lexington Books.

Hendryx, Steven. 1986. "Implementation of a Technology Transfer Joint Venture in the People's Republic of China." *Columbia Journal of World Business* (Spring): 57–66.

Ho, Samuel, and Ralph Huenemann. 1984. *China's Open-Door Policy: The Quest for Foreign Technology and Capital*. Vancouver: University of British Columbia Press.

Horsley, Jamie P. 1984. "Chinese Labor." *China Business Review* 11, no. 3 (May–June): 16–25.

Hou Chi-ming. 1965. *Foreign Investment and Economic Development in China*. Cambridge, Mass.: Harvard University Press.

Hsiao, Gene. 1977. *The Foreign Trade of China: Policy, Law and Practice*. Berkeley: University of California Press.

Hymer, Stephen. 1972. "The Multinational Corporation and the Law of Uneven Development." In *Economics and World Order: From the 1970s to the 1990s*, edited by Jadgish N. Bhagwati, pp. 113–40. New York: Free Press.

———. 1976. *The International Operations of National Firms: A Study of Direct Foreign Investment*. Cambridge, Mass.: MIT Press.

Imai, Satoshi. 1984. "Joint Ventures in China and Related Problems." *China Newsletter*, no. 51 (July–August): 15–20.

———. 1989. "Case Study of a Joint Venture with China (V)." *China Newsletter*, no. 79 (March–April): 11–17.

Kawai, Hiroko. 1984. "China's Open Door Policy in High Gear." *China Newsletter*, no. 53 (November–December): 11–14.

Kim, Samuel. 1989. "China and the Third World." In *China and the World* (2nd edition), edited by Samuel Kim, pp. 148–78. Boulder, Colo.: Westview Press.

Kindleberger, Charles. 1969. *American Business Abroad: Six Lectures on Direct Investment*. New Haven, Conn.: Yale University Press.

Kirby, William C. 1990. "Continuity and Change in Modern China: Economic Planning on the Mainland and on Taiwan, 1943–58." *Australian Journal of Chinese Affairs*, no. 24 (July): pp. 1–20.

Klenner, Wolfgang, and Kurt Wiesegart. 1980. "Joint Ventures in the P.R. China." *Intereconomics* (March–April): 87.

Kraus, Richard. 1983. "The Chinese State and Its Bureaucrats." In *State and Society in Contemporary China*, edited by Victor Nee and David Mozingo, pp. 132–47. Ithaca, N.Y.: Cornell University Press.

Lam, Alan. 1987. "Foreign Corporate Identity." *China Business Review* 14, no. 2 (March–April): 47.

Lampton, David M. 1987. "The Implementation Problem in Post-Mao China." In *Policy Implementation in Post-Mao China*, edited by David M. Lampton, pp. 3–24. Berkeley: University of California Press.

Lardy, Nicholas. 1987. *China's Entry into the World Economy: Implications for Northeast Asia and the US*. Lanham, Md.: University Press of America.

Lasserre, Philippe. 1983. "Strategic Assessment of International Partnership in ASEAN Countries." *Asia Pacific Journal of Management* (September): 72–78.

Lee, Hong Yung. 1986. "The Implications of Reform for Ideology, State and Society in China." *Journal of International Affairs* 39, no. 2 (Winter): 77–89.

Lee, Peter N. S. 1984. "The Changing Style of Policy-Making in Provincial Development: The Case of Guangdong in the Post-Mao Era, 1979–83." Chinese University of Hong Kong manuscript.

Lenin, Vladimir. 1966. "Imperialism: The Highest Stage of Capitalism." In *The Essential Lenin* (1916). Toronto: Bantam Books.

Liao, Kuang-sheng. 1984. *Antiforeignism and Modernization in China, 1860–1980*. Hong Kong: The Chinese University Press.

Lieberthal, Kenneth, and Michel Oksenberg. 1988. *Policy Making in China: Leaders, Structures and Processes*. Princeton, N.J.: Princeton University Press.

Lindblom, Charles. 1977. *Politics and Markets*. New York: Basic Books.

Lippit, Victor D. 1987. *The Economic Development of China*. Armonk, N.Y.: M. E. Sharpe.

Lo Ping. 1984. "Notes on a Northern Journey." *Cheng Ming*. In Summary of World Broadcasts, FE-7584-BII (6 March): 5.

Lockett, Martin, and Craig R. Littler. 1983. "Trends in Chinese Enterprise Management, 1978–1982." *World Development* 11, no. 8: 683–704.

Lorinczi, George G. 1982. "U.S.-Hungarian Joint Ventures." *International Business Lawyer* 10, no. 4 (April): 113–18.

Lubman, Stanley B. 1984. "Technology Transfer to China: Policies, Law and Practice." In *Foreign Trade, Investment and the Law in the People's Republic of China*, edited by Michael Moser, pp. 84–105. Hong Kong: Oxford University Press.

———. 1987. "Technology Transfer to China: Policies, Law and Practice." In *Foreign Trade, Investment and the Law in the People's Republic of China*, edited by Michael Moser, pp. 170–98. Hong Kong: Oxford University Press.

McCormick, Thomas. 1967. *China Market: America's Quest for Informal Empire, 1893–1901*. Chicago: Quadrangle Press.

MacDougall, Colina. 1982. "Policy Changes in China's Foreign Trade Since the Death of Mao, 1976–1980." In *China's New Development Strategy*, edited by Jack Gray and Gordon White, pp. 149–71. San Diego: Academic Press.

McMillan, Carl, and D. P. St. Charles. 1973. *Joint Ventures in Eastern Europe: A Three-Country Comparison*. Ottawa: Canadian Economic Policy Committee.

Mann, Jim. 1989. *Beijing Jeep: The Short, Unhappy Romance of American Business in China*. New York: Simon and Schuster.

Moran, Theodore. 1973. "Foreign Expansion as Institutional Necessity for U.S. Corporate Capitalism." *World Politics* 25, no. 3: 369–86.

———. 1974. *MNCs and the Politics of Dependence: Copper in Chile*. Princeton, N.J.: Princeton University Press.

Moser, Michael J., ed. 1984. *Foreign Trade, Investment and the Law in the People's Republic of China*. Hong Kong: Oxford University Press.

———. 1984a. "Foreign Investment in China: The Legal Framework." In *Foreign Trade, Investment and the Law in the People's Republic of China*, edited by Michael J. Moser, pp. 106–42. Hong Kong: Oxford University Press.

———. 1984b. "Law and Investment in the Guangdong Special Economic Zones." In *Foreign Trade, Investment and the Law in the People's Republic of China*, edited by Michael J. Moser, pp. 143–78. Hong Kong: Oxford University Press.

———. 1984c. "Offshore Oil Exploration and Development in China: The Current Regulatory Regime." In *Foreign Trade, Investment and the Law in the People's Republic of China*, edited by Michael J. Moser, pp. 179–212. Hong Kong: Oxford University Press.

———. 1987. "Law and Investment in China's Special Investment Areas." In *Foreign Trade, Investment and the Law in the People's Republic of China*, edited by Michael J. Moser, pp. 199–269. Hong Kong: Oxford University Press.

Nathan, Andrew. 1973. "A Factional Model for CCP Politics." *China Quarterly*, no. 53: 34–66.

National Council for U.S.–China Trade (NCUSCT). 1987. *U.S. Joint Ventures in China: A Progress Report*. Washington, D.C.: NCUSCT.

Nee, Owen D., Jr., and Thomas E. Jones. 1987. "Foreign Exchange Guarantees." *China Business Review* 14, no. 4 (July–August): 54–56.

Newfarmer, Richard. 1984. "International Industrial Organization and Development: A Survey." In *Profits, Progress and Poverty: Case Studies of International Industries in Latin America*, edited by Richard Newfarmer. Notre Dame: University of Notre Dame Press.

Oechsli, Christopher. 1988. "New Rules for Technology Imports." *China Business Review* 15, no. 4 (July–August): 35–36.

Oksenberg, Michel. 1982. "Economic Policy-Making in China: Summer '82." *China Quarterly*, no. 90 (June): 165–94.

Oksenberg, Michel, and Kenneth Lieberthal. 1986. *Bureaucratic Politics and Chinese Energy Development*. Washington, D.C.: U.S. Department of Commerce, International Trade Administration.

Palma, Gabriel. 1978. "Dependency: A Formal Theory of Underdevelopment or a Methodology for the Analysis of Concrete Situations of Underdevelopment?" *World Development* 6: 881–924.

Peele, Thomas, and Marsha A. Cohan. 1988. "Dispute Resolution in China." *China Business Review* 15, no. 5 (September–October): 46–48.

Pepper, Suzanne. 1988. "China's Special Economic Zones: The Current Rescue Bid for a Faltering Experiment." *Bulletin of Concerned Asian Scholars* 20, no. 3: 2–21.

Perry, Elizabeth, and Christine Wong, eds. 1985. *The Political Economy of Reform in Post-Mao China*. Cambridge, Mass.: Harvard University Council on East Asian Studies.

Pomfret, Richard. 1989. "Jiangsu's New Wave in Foreign Investment." *China Business Review* 16, no. 6 (September–October): 10–15.

Pye, Lucian. 1968. *The Spirit of Chinese Politics*. Cambridge, Mass: MIT Press.

———. 1982. *Chinese Commercial Negotiating Style*. Cambridge, Mass.: Oelge-schlager, Gunn & Hain Publishers.

Rawski, Thomas G. 1989. *Economic Growth in Prewar China*. Berkeley: University of California Press.

Ray, Dennis. 1975. "China's Perception of Social Imperialism and Economic Dependency: The Impact of Soviet Aid." *Stanford Journal of International Studies* no. 5 (Spring): 36–82.

Remer, Carl F. 1968. *Foreign Investment in China*. New York: Howard Fertig.

Reynolds, Bruce. 1984. "China in the International Economy." In *China's Foreign Policy in the 1980s*, edited by Harry Harding, pp. 71–106. New Haven, Conn.: Yale University Press.

Riskin, Carl. 1987. *China's Political Economy: The Quest for Development Since 1949*. Oxford: Oxford University Press.

Rodzinski, Witold. 1984. *The Walled Kingdom: A History of China from Antiquity to the Present*. New York: Free Press.

Schurmann, Franz. 1968 (revised edition). *Ideology and Organization in Communist China*. Berkeley: University of California Press.

Scriven, John G. 1982. "Cooperation in East-West Trade: The Equity Joint Venture." *International Business Lawyer* 10, no. 4 (April): 105–11.

Shirk, Susan. 1985. "The Politics of Industrial Reform." In *The Political Economy of Reform in Post-Mao China*, edited by Elizabeth Perry and Christine Wong, pp. 195–221. Cambridge, Mass.: Harvard University Council on East Asian Studies.

Simon, Denis Fred. 1984. "The Role of Science and Technology in China's Foreign Relations." In *China and the World* (first edition), edited by Samuel S. Kim, pp. 293–318. Boulder, Colo.: Westview Press.

———. 1989. "Technology Transfer and China's Emerging Role in the World Economy." In *Science and Technology in Post-Mao China*, edited by Denis Fred Simon and Merle Goldman. Cambridge, Mass.: Harvard Council on East Asian Studies/Harvard University.

Simon, Denis Fred, and Merle Goldman. 1989. *Science and Technology in Post-Mao China*. Cambridge, Mass.: Harvard Council on East Asian Studies.

Skilling, Gordon, and Franklyn Griffiths. 1971. *Interest Groups in Soviet Politics*. Princeton, N.J.: Princeton University Press.

Skinner, G. William, and Edwin A. Winckler. 1969. "A Compliance Succession in Rural Communist China: A Cyclical Theory." In *A Sociological Reader on Com-*

plex Organization, edited by Amitai Etzioni, pp. 410–38. New York: Holt, Rinehart and Winston.

Solinger, Dorothy J. 1984. *Chinese Business Under Socialism*. Berkeley: University of California Press.

Spence, Jonathon D. 1980 (second edition). *To Change China: Western Advisers in China, 1620–1960*. Middlesex, England: Penguin Books.

————. 1981. *The Gate of Heavenly Peace: The Chinese and Their Revolution, 1895–1980*. New York: Viking Press.

Stepan, Alfred. 1978. *The State and Society: Peru in Comparative Perspective*. Princeton, N.J.: Princeton University Press.

Stoever, William A. 1985. "The Stages of Developing Country Policy Toward Foreign Investment." *Columbia Journal of World Business* 20, no. 3 (Fall): 6–9.

Sullivan, Lawrence R. 1988. "Assault on the Reforms: Conservative Criticism of Political and Economic Liberalization in China, 1985–86." *China Quarterly*, no. 114 (June): 198–222.

Sutter, Robert. 1982. "The Political Context of the Four Modernizations." In *China After the Four Modernizations, Part I*, Selected Papers Submitted to the Joint Economic Committee, U.S. Congress, pp. 77–98. Washington, D.C.: U.S. Government Printing Office.

Swindler, Jo Anne. 1984. "The New Legal Framework for Joint Ventures in China: Guidelines for Investors." *Law and Policy in International Business* 16: 1005–50.

Szasz, Ivan. 1982. "Legal Framework of the Economic and Foreign Trade Systems of Hungary and Other CMEA Countries." *International Business Lawyer* 10, no. 4 (April): 99–105.

Tam, Terry, and Mark Cheung. 1988. "Keeping Joint Venture Accounts." *China Business Review* 15, no. 5 (September–October): 42–43.

Tan Sitong. 1954. "Excerpts from a Letter Urging Complete Westernization." In *China's Response to the West: A Documentary Survey*, edited by S. Y. Teng and John K. Fairbank. Cambridge, Mass.: Harvard University Press.

Thompson, Thomas N. 1979. *China's Nationalization of Foreign Firms: The Politics of Hostage Capitalism, 1949–1957*. Baltimore: School of Law, University of Baltimore.

Tomlinson, James W. 1970. *The Joint Venture Process in International Business: India and Pakistan*. Cambridge, Mass.: MIT Press.

Tsou Tang. 1983. "Back from the Brink of Revolutionary-'Feudal' Totalitarianism." In *State and Society in Contemporary China*, edited by Victor Nee and David Mozingo, pp. 53–88. Ithaca, N.Y.: Cornell University Press.

Uehara, Takashi. 1987. "Changes in China's Policy Regarding the Introduction of Foreign Capital." *China Newsletter*, no. 66 (January–February): 13–18.

United Nations Centre on Transnational Corporations (UNCTC). 1983. *National Legislation and Regulations Relating to Transnational Corporations: A Technical Paper*. New York: United Nations Publication.

————. 1988. *Transnational Corporations in World Development: Trends and Prospects*. New York: United Nations Publication.

United Nations Industrial Development Organization. *Manual on the Establishment of Industrial Joint Ventures in Developing Countries*. New York: United Nations Publication.

U.S. Congress, Office of Technology Assessment. 1987. *Technology Transfer to China*. OTA-ISC-340. Washington, D.C.: U.S. Government Printing Office.

Vernon, Raymond. 1977. *The Storm Over the Multinationals: The Real Issues*. Cambridge, Mass.: MIT Press.

Wakeman, Frederic. 1966. *Strangers at the Gate*. Berkeley: University of California Press.

Walder, Andrew G. 1983. "Organized Dependency and Cultures of Authority in Chinese Industry." *Journal of Asian Studies* 43, no. 1 (November): 51–76.

Wallerstein, Immanuel. 1974. *The Modern World System: Capitalist Agriculture and the Origins of the European World Economy in the Sixteenth Century*. New York: Academic Press.

Walmsley, John. 1982. *Handbook of International Joint Ventures*. London: Graham and Trotman.

Wang, N. T. 1984. *China's Modernization and Transnational Corporations*. Lexington, Mass.: Lexington Books.

Weil, Martin. 1981. "Technology Transfers." *China Business Review* 8, no. 2 (March–April): 21–25.

Westendorff, David. 1989. "Foreign Direct Investment, Technology Transfer and the International Economic System: Problems and Prospects with Reference to the Case of Shanghai." Paper Presented at the Annual Meeting of the Association for Asian Studies. Washington, D.C., 17 March 1989.

White, Gordon. 1983. "The Postrevolutionary Chinese State." In *State and Society in Contemporary China*, edited by Victor Nee and David Mozingo, pp. 27–52. Ithaca, N.Y.: Cornell University Press.

———. 1983a. "Socialist Planning and Industrial Management: Chinese Economic Reforms in the Post-Mao Era." *Development and Change* 14: 483–514.

Whiting, Allen. 1989. *China Eyes Japan*. Berkeley: University of California Press.

Woetzel, Jonathon R. 1989. *China's Economic Opening to the Outside World: The Politics of Empowerment*. New York: Praeger Publishers.

Wong, Kam C. 1984. "Commercial Dispute Resolution Process in the People's Republic of China: Continuity and Change." Paper presented at Chinese Law Conference, Chinese University of Hong Kong, 24 October 1984.

Wong, Kwan-yiu, and David K. Y. Chu. 1984. "Export Processing Zones as Generators of Economic Development: The Asian Experience." *Geografiska Annaler*, no. 66B: 1–16.

World Bank. 1985. *China: Long-Term Development Issues and Options*. Baltimore: Johns Hopkins University Press.

———. 1988. *China: External Trade and Capital*. Washington, D.C.: The World Bank.

Wu, Friedrich. 1981. "From Self-reliance to Interdependence? Developmental Strategy and Foreign Economic Policy in Post-Mao China." *Modern China* 7, no. 4 (October): 445–82.

Yakota, Takaaki. 1987. "Joint Ventures and Technology Transfer to China—The Realities." *China Newsletter*, no. 71 (November–December): 9–12.

Yowell, Diane. 1988. "Swap Center System to Expand." *China Business Review* 15, no. 5 (September–October): 10–12.

PRC AUTHORS (INCLUDING WORKS IN TRANSLATION AND
WORKS PUBLISHED OUTSIDE THE PRC)

"Build a Great Wall Ideologically." 1982. Xinhua radio report. FBIS-CHI-82-35 (22 February), p. K10.

Cao Jiarui. 1986. "The Present Condition of and Problems in China's Technological Imports." *Liaowang Overseas Edition*, no. 15 (5 May). In FBIS, 16 May 1986, pp. K5–6.

Cao Zhi. 1984. "Two Success Stories of Sino-U.S. Joint Ventures." *Interface*.

Chen Zhao. 1982. "Shilun Jingji Tequ de Shichang Tiaojie he Jiage Guanli Wenti" ["On the Question of Market Readjustment and Price Administration in the SEZs"]. *Zhongguo Jingji Wenti* [*Issues of Chinese Economy*], no. 4 (20 July): 36.

Chu Baotai. 1984. "Several Theoretical and Policy Issues Concerning the Establishment of Chinese-Foreign Joint Ventures." *GMW* no. 5, 1983. In JPRS-CEA-84-012 (30 June): 110–15.

———. 1987. "The Effectiveness of China's Absorption of Foreign Capital." In *Foreign Capital and Technology in China*, edited by Richard Robinson, pp. 21–39. New York: Praeger Publishers.

Commentator, *Hongqi*. 1982. "A Crackdown on Economic Crimes and Class Struggle." In JPRS 81911 (4 October): 44.

"Dang Zheng Fuze Ganbu Buyi Jianren Qiye de Lingdao Ren" ["It Is Inadvisable for Responsible Party and Government Cadres to Concurrently Be Enterprise Leaders"]. 1984. *SSZH* (13 July).

De Min. 1982. "It Is Not Alarmist Talk." *RMRB*. In FBIS-CHI-82-76 (20 April): K1.

"Deepen Theoretical Understanding on Reform and the Open Door Policy—Seriously Study Premier Zhao Ziyang's 'Government Work Report.'" *Hongqi*. In JPRS-CRF-84-015 (22 August): 69–77.

Deng Liqun. 1984. "Propaganda Workers Must Maintain a Clear Head." *Guangming Ribao*. In FBIS-CHI-84-10 (16 January): K5.

Deng Xiaoping. 1987. "Deng Xiaoping's Remarks on Reforms, Open Policy, Peace and Development." MOFERT, *1987 Almanac of China's Foreign Economic Relations and Trade*, p. 10. Hong Kong: Joint Publishing Company.

"Deng Xiaoping Is Concerned About Guangdong and Fujian." 1982. *Ming Pao* (HK). In FBIS, no. 104 (28 May): W1.

Dong Fureng. 1980. "Some Problems Concerning the Chinese Economy." *China Quarterly*, no. 84 (December): 727–36.

Dong Shizhong. 1985. "Potential Investors' Queries Answered." *Intertrade* (January): 53–54.

Economic Information Agency (Hong Kong). 1982. "Questions and Answers Concerning Foreign Investment in China." (Pamphlet.)

Editor of *Guoji Maoyi Wenti*. 1983. "'Shehuizhuyi Duiwai Maoyi Lilun yu Zhan-
lue Wenti' Xueshu Taolunhui Zongshu" ["Summary of Study and Discussion
Conference on 'Problems of Socialist Foreign Trade Theory and Strategy'"].
GMW, no. 2: 1–7.

Editorial Department of *Hongqi*. 1982. "On Questions Concerning China's Foreign Economic Relations." *Hongqi*. In JPRS 81062 (16 June): 1–6.

———. 1982a. "Our Banner Is Communism." *Hongqi*. In JPRS 81291 (16 July):
1–8.

———. 1982b. "On Preserving the Purity of Communism." *Hongqi*, 10 May 1982.
In FBIS-CHI-82-112, p. K5.

Editorial Department of *Jingji Ribao*. 1983. "Heighten the Consciousness for
Eliminating Spiritual Pollution." *Jingji Ribao*. In FBIS-CHI-83-219 (10 November): K5.

Editorial Department of *Red Flag*. 1987. "Opening to the Outside World, Invigo-
rating the Domestic Economy and Adhering to Socialism." In MOFERT, *1987
Almanac of China's Foreign Economic Relations and Trade*, pp. 1–6.

———. 1984. "Take China's Own Road in Building Socialism." *Red Flag*. In JPRS-
CRF-84-022 (4 December): 1–14.

Editorial Department of *Renmin Ribao*. 1982. "Protect and Develop Our National
Industry." *Renmin Ribao (People's Daily)*, (24 April). In FBIS China Report (26
April): K3–5.

"Fahui Dang de Zuoyong, Banhao Hezi Qiye" ["Bring the Party's Function Into
Play, Run Joint Ventures Well"]. 1984. *SSZH* (3 July): 1.

Fan Juyi. 1982. "The Class Struggle and Its Reflection among the Masses." *Shehui
Kexue (Social Sciences)*. In JPRS 81722 (8 September): 43–49.

Fan Kang and Wang Huaining. 1984. "The Law of History Is Irresistible—How to
Look at the Capitalist World Today." *Hongqi*. In JPRS-CRF-84-010 (31 May):
56–63.

Fang Zhuofen. 1981. "Lun Jingji Tequ de Xingzhi" ["A Discussion of the Nature of
the Special Economic Zones"]. In *JJYJ*, no. 8: 54–58.

Feng Sheng. 1984. "Several Questions Regarding Understanding of the Use of
Foreign Capital." *RMRB*. In FBIS-CHI-84-51 (14 March): K16.

"General Secretary Zhao Ziyang Calls for More Foreign-owned Ventures, Foreign
JV Managers." 1988. *China Economic News* 9 (25 January): 1–2.

GMW Special Reporter. 1983. "'Shehuizhuyi Duiwai Maoyi Lilun yu Zhanlue
Wenti' Xueshu Taolunhui Zongshu" ["Summary of Study and Discussion Conference on 'Problems of Socialist Foreign Trade Theory and Strategy'"]. *GMW*,
no. 2: 1–7.

Government Office of Shenzhen Special Economic Zone, ed. 1984. "The Coming
Shenzhen Special Economic Zone." Shenzhen, PRC.

Gu Ming. 1985. "A Socialist Patent Law with Chinese Characteristics." *Hongqi*. In
JPRS-CRF-85-007 (6 March): 33.

Gu Mu. 1985. "Zhongyang Dui Wai Kaifang Juece Da De Renxin" ["The Center's
Decision on Opening to the Outside Enjoys Great Popular Support"]. *SSZH* (18
January): 2.

"Guangzhou Municipal Party Takes Lead in Rectifying Devious Wind by Criticiz-
ing Behavior." 1979. *WWP*. In JPRS 74709 (4 December): 66.

Guangzhou Provincial Service Commentator. 1982. "Chongfen Renshi Jingji Lingyu Zibenzhuyi Sixiang Fushi de Yanzhongxing." ("Fully Understand the Gravity of Capitalist Ideological Corruption in the Economic Field"). *NFRB* (13 March): 1.

Guangzhou Provincial Service (radio broadcast). 1982. In FBIS-CHI-82-063 (1 April): P1.

He Xinhao. 1980. "Actively Use Foreign Capital to Speed Up Economic Development." *GMW*. In JPRS 76614 (14 October): 1–9.

Huan Xiang. 1984. "Have a Clear Understanding of the International Economic Situation, Usher in the New Technical Revolution." *Hongqi*, 16 May 1984. In JPRS-CRF-84-013 (31 July): 1–7.

Huang Yifeng and Jiang Duo. 1984. "How to Correctly Assess the Westernization Movement." *Hongqi*. In JPRS-CRF-84-010 (31 May): 44–50.

Ji Si. 1984. "Party Rectification Should Promote the Opening to the Outside World and Activating the Domestic Economy." *Hongqi*. In JPRS-CRF-84-014 (3 August): 76–78.

Jiang Yiguo, Wang Zumin, and Jiang Baoqi. 1978. "Jiakuai Woguo Jingji Fazhan Sudu de yigong Zhongda Zhengce" ("The Important Policy of Speeding Up Our Country's Pace of Economic Development"). *JJYJ*, no. 10: 10–15.

Juan Wenqi, Dai Lunzhang, and Wang Linsheng. 1980. "International Division of Labor, China's Economic Relations." *Social Sciences in China*. In JPRS 75578 (25 April): 1–26.

Kong Xiangyi. 1987. "A Study on Several Questions Concerning the Utilization of Foreign Capital." In *MOFERT, 1987 Almanac of China's Foreign Economic Relations and Trade*, pp. 790–91.

Li Boxi. 1987. "Prerequisites for Improving the Investment Climate in China." *Jishu Jingji yu Guanli Yanjiu* [*Research on the Economics and Management of Technology* (Taiyuan)], no. 1. In JPRS-CAR-87-027, pp. 47–57.

Li Cong. 1982. "The Strategy of Socioeconomic Development in Developing Countries." *Hongqi*. In JPRS 81665 (31 August): 79–84.

Li Qiming. 1985. "It Is Necessary to Bravely Solve the Problem of Factionalism in Leading Bodies." *Hongqi*. In JPRS-CRF-85-002 (24 January): 32–36.

Li Yanshi. 1980. "To Successfully Build Special Economic Zones, Emphasis Must Be Placed on the Word 'Special.'" *NFRB*. In JPRS 77095 (2 January): 33–36.

Liang Wensen, Shen Liren, and Tian Jianghai. 1982. "Shenzhen Teque Jingji Moshi Chutan" ["The Shenzhen Special Zone Economy's Initial Exploration Pattern"]. *JJDB* (7 June): 31.

Liang Xiang. 1984. "Strive to Make the Shenzhen Special Economic Zone a Bigger Success." *Hongqi*. In JPRS-CRF-84-014 (3 August): 11–19.

———. 1985. "Ba Shenzhen Tequ Jianshe Tigao dao Xin de Shuiping" ["Raise Shenzhen Special Zone Construction to a New Phase"]. *SSZH* (11 January): 1.

Liu Lei. 1988. "Beijing Delegates the Authority to Examine and Approve Foreign-Funded Enterprise Contracts and Articles of Association to Lower Levels." In *Guoji Shangbao (International Trade Journal)* (8 November 1988). In JPRS-CAR-89-007 (19 January 1989): 48–49.

Liu Peng. 1985. "We Must Revise Our Understanding of the Open Door Policy." *Liaowang* [*Outlook*]. In JPRS-CEA-85-038 (18 April): 126–28.

Liu Xiangdong. 1985. "Will Importing a Certain Quantity of Foreign Products Affect the Development of National Industries?" *Hongqi*. In JPRS-CRF-85-008 (3 April): 83–85.

Liu Zhao. 1979. "Zhong-Wai Heying Qiye de Jige Wenti" ["Several Problems of Chinese-Foreign Jointly Run Enterprises"]. *JJDB* (10 October): 9.

Lo Yaoqiu. 1978. "Dr. Sun Yat-sen's Views on Accelerating Development of the National Economy." *Guangming Ribao* (31 December). In FBIS-CHI-79-008 (11 January): K4–K7.

Luo Rongqu and Jiang Xiangze. 1983. "Research in American-Eastern Relations in the PRC." In *New Frontiers in American-Eastern Relations*, edited by Warren Cohen, pp. 1–16. New York: Columbia University Press.

Ma Hong. 1985. "Reading 'Building Socialism with Chinese Characteristics.'" *Hongqi*. In JPRS-CRF-85-007 (6 March): 1–9.

Mao Zedong. 1967. *On New Democracy*. Beijing: Foreign Languages Press.

———. 1974. "On the Ten Great Relationships." In *Chairman Mao Talks to the People*, edited by Stuart Schram, pp. 61–83. New York: Pantheon Press.

Ministry of Foreign Economic Relations and Trade (MOFERT). Various years. *Almanac of China's Foreign Economic Relations and Trade*. Hong Kong: Joint Publishing.

———. 1982. *Questions and Answers Concerning Foreign Investment in China*. Hong Kong: Economic Information Agency.

Qi Mingchen. 1978. "Liening Liyong Waiguo Zijin he Jishu de Sixiang Shi Dui Makesizhuyi de Zhongyao Gongxian" ("Lenin's Ideas on Using Foreign Capital and Technology are an Important Contribution to Marxism"). *JJYJ*, no. 12: 48–52.

Qian Zongqi. 1983. "Hezi Jingying shi Zhong-wai Jingji Hezuo de Zhongyao Xingshi" ["Joint Ventures Are an Important Form of Sino-Foreign Economic Cooperation"]. *JJDB* (18 May): 18–19.

Radio October Storm (clandestine). 1984. In FBIS-CHI-84-21 (31 January): K24.

Ren Zhongyi. 1982. In FBIS-CHI-82-114 (14 June): W4.

———. 1982a. *Guang Jiao Jing* (HK), no. 118 (July).

"Ren Zhongyi and Liu Tianfu Talk on Opening Up to the Outside World and Hitting at Economic Crime." 1982. *Yangcheng Wanbao*. In FBIS-CHI-82-103 (3 June): P1–P2.

"Resolution of the Central Committee of the Communist Party of China on the Guiding Principles for Building a Socialist Society with an Advanced Culture and Ideology." 1986. Resolution adopted at the 6th Session of the 12th Central Committee, 28 September 1986). In *Beijing Review* 29, no. 40 (6 November): 1–9.

"Rong Yiren Expounds Problems Concerning Joint Ventures Using Chinese and Foreign Investment." 1979. *TKP*. In JPRS 74297 (3 October): 77.

———. 1984. "Guanche Dui Wai Kaifang Zhengce Fazhan Guoji Jingji Hezuo" ["Carry Out the Policy of Opening to the Outside World to Develop International Economic Cooperation"]. *JJDB* (1 January): 73.

Shen Shi. 1982. "Views on a Number of Issues in Building Special Economic Zones." In FBIS-CHI-82-139 (20 July): P1.

Shen Shiyi. 1984. "Zhengque Chuli Jingshen Wenming Jianshezhong de Jige Guanxi" ["Correctly Handle Several Relationships in Constructing a Spiritual Civilization"]. In Zhonggong Shenzhenshi Wei Bangongting Bian, *Shenzhen Tequ Fazhan de Daolu* [CCP Shenzhen Municipal Committee General Office, *Shenzhen Special Zone's Development Road*]. Beijing: Guangming Ribao Chubanshe [Guangming Ribao Publishers].

Shen Yurui. 1980. "Balance Between Self-Reliance, Foreign Borrowing Vital," *Chuanbo Gongcheng*. In JPRS 76823 (14 November): 37.

"Shenzhen SEZ's Accomplishments and Prospects—A Summary." 1984. *GMW*, no. 5 (September–October). In JPRS-CEA-85-005, p. 91.

"Shenzhen Tequ Jingshen Wenming Jianshe de jige Wenti" ["Some Problems in the Construction of Shenzhen Special Zone's Spiritual Civilization"]. 1984. *SSZH* (11 June): 4.

State Statistical Bureau. Various years. *Statistical Yearbook of China*. Beijing: China Statistics Press.

"Strictly Observe Discipline in Domestic and Foreign Trade." 1982. In FBIS-CHI-82-266 (23 September).

Su Xing. 1984. "Several Points of Understanding About the Socialist System in Our Country." *Hongqi*. In JPRS-CRF-84-013 (31 July): 64–72.

Sun Guanhua and Wang Yuan. 1984. "We Must Attach Importance to the Summing Up of Experience Acquired From JVs." *JJGL*. In JPRS-CEA-84-30, p. 41.

Sun Ru. 1980. "The Guangdong Special Economic Zone—Its Concept and Prospects." *WWP*. In JPRS 75423 (2 April): 46–54.

———. 1982. "A Discourse on the Significance and Role of the SEZs from the Aspect of Strategic Aims." *NFRB*. In FBIS-CHI-82-114 (14 June): P1–P5.

———. 1982a. "Giving and Taking." *Yangcheng Wanbao*. In FBIS-CHI-82-37 (24 February): K5.

———. 1983. "'Shehuizhuyi Jingji Zhidu' he 'Shehuizhuyi Jingji Tizhi' Shi Liangge Butong de Gainian" ["The Socialist Economic Institution and the Socialist Economic System Are Not the Same Concept"]. *JJDB* (1 November): 14.

Suo Qian. 1987. "Several Questions and Proposals Concerning Enterprises with Foreign Investment." *Shijie Jingji Daobao (World Economic Herald)* (11 May), p. 11. In JPRS-CAR-87-010, pp. 70–74.

Tang Zongshun. 1987. "Transfer of Patented Technology to China." In *Foreign Capital and Technology in China*, edited by Richard Robinson, pp. 75–82. New York: Praeger Publishers.

Teng Weizao and Jiang Zhei. 1981. "Growth of the Multinationals." *Beijing Review*, no. 7 (16 February): 16–20.

"Vice Minister Addresses Foreigners on Investment Climate." 1987. *Xinhua* (19 June). In JPRS-CAR-87-023, p. 70.

Wang Chiwei and Liu Mindong. (1982). "Import of Foreign Technology and Economic Effectiveness." Caijing Wenti Yanjiu [*Research on Issues of Finance and Economics*] (July). In JPRS 82364 (December 1984): 23–28.

Wang Lin. 1983. *Shijie Jingji Daobao* [*World Economic Herald*] (15 August): 2.

Wang Luwen. 1987. "Foreign Investors Urged to Take Advantage of Opportunities in Shanghai." *Guoji Shangbao* [International Trade Journal] (7 May). In JPRS-CAR-87-006, pp. 91–95.

Wang Muheng and Chen Yongshan. 1981. "Taiwan de Chukou Jiagongqu" ("Taiwan's Export Processing Zones"). *GMW*, no. 3: 39–46.

Wang Shouchun and Li Kanghua. 1981. "Luelun Wo Guo Jingji Tequ de Zuoyong Wenti" ["A Brief Discussion of Problems of Our Country's Special Economic Zones"]. *GMW*, no. 1: 40–44.

Wang Yaotian. 1982. "Strategic Importance of an Open-Door Policy." *GM* (August). In JPRS 82457 (14 December): 47–54.

Wang Yihe. 1987. "Rethinking Traditional Joint Ventures." *GM*, no. 12 (27 December). In JPRS-CAR-88-13, pp. 51–52.

Wang Yihe, Xu E, and Zhou Jianping. 1984. *Zhong Wai Hezi Jingying Qiye [Chinese-Foreign Joint Venture Enterprises]*. Shanghai: Shanghai Shehui Kexue Yuan Chubanshe [Shanghai Social Sciences Institute Publishers].

Wang Zhaozheng. 1982. "Strategic Foresight and Practical Measures—A Study of Lenin's Exposition on External Economic Relations." *JFRB*. In JPRS 81755 (13 September): 25–28.

Wei Jin. 1983. In *China Market*.

Wei Yuming. 1982. "Guanyu Woguo Xishou Waiguo Zhijie Touzi de Zhengce" ["On China's Policy to Absorb Foreign Direct Investment"]. *JJDB* (14 June). In FBIS-CHI-82-112 (10 June): W3.

———. 1983. "Youguan Zhongguo Liyong Waizi de jige Wenti" ["Some Issues Concerning China's Use of Foreign Capital"]. *JJDB* (27 June): 18–20.

"Wo Guo Liyong Zhongcai Jiejue Dui Wai Jingji Jiufen ["China Uses Arbitration to Solve Foreign Economic Disputes"]. 1984. *SSZH* (25 February): 1.

Wu Shuqing. 1982. "How Do We Understand the Coexistence of Diversified Economic Forms at the Present Stage in Our Country?" *Hongqi*. In JPRS 81062 (16 June): 61–66.

Xi Wen. 1982. "Question and Answer Column." *Hongqi*. In JPRS 80980 (4 June): 69–71.

Xiang Nan. 1983. "Yiding Yao ba Xiamen Jingji Tequ Jianshe Hao" ("Definitely Must Construct Xiamen Special Economic Zone Well"). *JJGL* (5 February): 4–5.

———. 1983a. "Tequ Yao Shixing 'Si Te'" ["The Special Zones Must Put into Practice the 'Four Specials'"]. *JJDB* (19 December): 16.

———. 1984. "Spiritual Civilization and the Spirit of Reform." *Hongqi*. In JPRS-CRF-84-018 (3 October): 37.

Xiao An. 1984. "Shenzhen Tequ Jingshen Wenming Jianshe de Jige Wenti" ["A Few Issues on the Development of Shenzhen Special Zone's Spiritual Civilization"]. *SSZH* (11 June): 4.

Xie Min. 1987. "On Improving the Investment Climate—A Comprehensive Factor Influencing the Absorption of Direct Foreign Investment." *GMW*, no. 1 (January).

Xin Ren. 1982. "The Sugarcoated Bullet and Its Various Tactics." *RMRB* (6 July). In JPRS 81777 (15 September): 35–36.

Xinhua. 1979. "Socialist Road Fundamental to Chinese Modernization, Says Beijing Daily." In FBIS (7 May): L12.

Xu Daohe. 1982. "A New Question for Study." *Hongqi*. In JPRS 8129 (16 July): 28–30.

Xu Luxin. 1984. "Dui Shenzhen Tequ de Zai Renshi" ["On Understanding Shenzhen Special Zone"]. *SSZH* (23 January): 4.

Xu Xuehan, Mao Rongfang, and Wu Jian. 1982. "Several Problems Involving the Construction of the Special Economic Zones." *RMRB*. In FBIS-CHI-82-182 (20 September): K16.

Yang Aiqun. 1987. "Improve the Investment Climate to Take Advantage of Foreign Capital." *GM*, no. 10 (27 October). In JPRS-CAR-88-003 (11 February 1988): 16–18.

Yong Shan. 1981. "Tequ Zhengce Hui Suiyi Gaibian Ma?" ["Will the Special Zone Policy Change At Will?"]. *TKP* (28 August), part three.

Yu Jianxun. 1987. "Strategies of China's Inland Areas for Developing Foreign Trade." In MOFERT, *1987 Almanac of China's Economic Relations and Trade*, pp. 780–84. Hong Kong: Joint Publishing Company.

Yuan Mu. 1983. "Zhonghua Renmin Gongheguo Zhong-Wai Hezi Jingying Qiye Fa" ["The Law of the PRC on Joint Ventures Using Chinese and Foreign Investment"]. Tianjin: Tianjin Shi Dui Wai Jingji Maoyi Weiyuanhui [Tianjin Municipality Foreign Economic Relations and Trade Commission], pp. 76–77.

Zhang Hanqing. 1982. "Running SEZs on a Trial Basis Is Our Important Policy Decision for Speeding Up the Four Modernizations." *NFRB*. In FBIS-CHI-82-134 (15 July): P2.

Zhang Shangtang. 1984. "Investment in China: Practice and Theory." *International Business Lawyer* (September): 361–65.

Zhang Xinda. 1987. "On the Question of Markets for the Products of Joint Ventures in China." In *Foreign Capital and Technology in China*, edited by Richard Robinson, pp. 93–108.

Zhao Ziyang. 1987. "Advance Along the Road of Socialism with Chinese Characteristics." Report Delivered at the 13th National Congress of the Communist Party of China. *Beijing Review* (20 December): p. 18.

"Zhao Ziyang on Coastal Areas' Economic Development Strategy." 1988. In MOFERT, *1988 Almanac of China's Foreign Economic Relations and Trade*, p. 37.

Zhong Douyang and Yin Youguo. 1984. "Buduan Zengqiang yu Kuaguo Gongsi Dajiaodao de Benling" ["Continue to Strengthen Abilities in Dealing with Transnational Corporations"]. *SSZH* (9 July): 4.

Zhonggong Shenzhenshi Wei Bangongting Bian [General Office of the Shenzhen Municipal CCP Committee], ed. 1984. *Shenzhen Tequ Fazhan de Daolu* [*Shenzhen Special Zone's Development Path*]. Beijing: Guangming Ribao Chubanshe [Guangming Daily Publications].

Zhou Ding. 1983. "Gao Hao Neilian Gongzuo, Zengqiang Tequ Xiyin Waizi de Nengli" ["Do Internal Linkage Work Well, Strengthen the Special Zone's Ability to Absorb Foreign Capital"]. In *Shenzhen Tequ Fazhan de Daolu* [*Shenzhen Special Zone's Development Path*], edited by Zhonggong Shenzhenshi Wei Bangongting Bian [General Office of the Shenzhen Municipal CCP Committee]. Beijing: Guangming Ribao Chubanshe [Guangming Ribao Publications].

Zhou Shude. 1984. "Liyong Waizi yu Kongzhi Jijian Guimo" ["Use of Foreign Capital and Control of the Scale of Capital Construction"]. *GMW*, no. 3: 19.

Zhu Dingzhen. 1984. "Pay Attention to Strengthening Ideological and Political

Work Following the Shift of Work Focus." *Hongqi*, no. 11 (1 June). In JPRS-CRF-84-012, p. 72.

Zhu Shenqing. 1982. "Fire—City Gate—Disaster." *Zhejiang Ribao*. In JPRS 81871 (28 September): 48–49.

Zong Ruiyu. 1987. "Summary of a Panel Discussion by Representatives of Shanghai Joint Ventures." *GMW* (27 April): 41–43. In JPRS-CAR-87-009, pp. 63–68.

CHINESE FOREIGN INVESTMENT LAWS CITED IN THE TEXT

"Accounting Regulations for Joint Ventures Using Chinese and Foreign Investment" ("JV Accounting Regulations"). Promulgated March 1985.

"Amendments to the Law of the People's Republic of China on Joint Ventures Using Chinese and Foreign Investment." Promulgated 5 April 1990. Translated in *China Daily*, 9 April 1990.

"Detailed Rules and Regulations for the Implementation of the Income Tax Law of the PRC Concerning Joint Ventures Using Chinese and Foreign Investment." Promulgated 14 December 1980. Translated in Chu, Moser, and Nee. 1982. *Commercial, Business and Trade Laws: People's Republic of China*. Dobbs Ferry, N.Y.: Oceana Publications, part 5.

"Detailed Rules for Foreign Exchange Control for Enterprises with Overseas Chinese Capital, Enterprises with Foreign Capital and Chinese-Foreign Joint Venture Enterprises." Promulgated August 1983. Translated in *China Daily*, August 1983, p. 2. Referred to in text as "Foreign Exchange Implementation Rules."

"Detailed Rules for the Implementation of the Regulations on Administration of Technology Import Contracts." Promulgated January 1988.

"The Implementing Act for the Law of the People's Republic of China on Joint Ventures Using Chinese and Foreign Investment" ("Zhonghua Renmin Gongheguo Zhong Wai Hezi Jingying Qiye Fa Shishi Tiaoli," referred to in text as "Implementing Regulations"). Promulgated October 1983. Translated in *Beijing Review*, no. 4 (10 October 1983): 1–16.

"The Income Tax Law of the PRC Concerning Joint Ventures Using Chinese and Foreign Investment," Promulgated 10 September 1980, and translated in Chu, Moser, and Nee. 1982. *Commercial, Business and Trade Laws: People's Republic of China*. Dobbs Ferry, N.Y.: Oceana Publications, part 5. (See above for full cite.) Referred to in text as "JV Income Tax Law," or "JVITL."

"Interim Provisions Concerning Ideological and Political Work for Chinese Staff and Workers in Chinese-Foreign Equity and Cooperative Joint Ventures." Promulgated 11 August 1987.

"Law of the People's Republic of China on Economic Contracts Involving Foreign Interests." Promulgated in 1985. Translated in *China Business Review* 12, no. 4 (July–August 1985): 54–55. Referred to in text as "Economic Contract Law."

"The Law of the People's Republic of China on Joint Ventures Using Chinese and Foreign Investment" ("Zhonghua Renmin Gongheguo Zhong Wai Hezi Jingying Qiye Fa"). Promulgated 1 July 1979. Translated in Chu, Moser, and Nee. 1982. *Commercial, Business and Trade Laws: People's Republic of China*. Dobbs Ferry, N.Y.: Oceana Publications. Referred to in text as "Joint Venture Law."

"Measures on the Purchase and Export of Domestic Products by Foreign Investment Enterprises to Balance Foreign Exchange Account." Promulgated 20 January 1987. Translated in MOFERT, *1988 Almanac of China's Foreign Economic Relations and Trade*, pp. 131–32.

"The Patent Law of the People's Republic of China" (Adopted 12 March 1984. Referred to in text as "Patent Law"). Translated in *China Business Review* 12, no. 1 (January–February 1985): 54–57.

"Provisional Articles on Control of Advertising." Promulgated 17 February 1982. Translated in *East Asian Executive Reports*, May 1982, pp. 24–25.

"Provisional Entry/Exit Rules for the SEZs in Guangdong Province." Translated in Chu, Moser, and Nee. 1982. *Commercial, Business and Trade Laws: People's Republic of China*. Dobbs Ferry, N.Y.: Oceana Publications, part 14.

"Provisional Measures Guiding the Provision of Foreign Exchange Guarantees by Domestic Organizations."

"Provisional Regulations for Shenzhen SEZ on Certain Recent Policies for 'Internal Linkage' Enterprises" ("Shenzhen Jingji Tequ Jinqi Neilian Qiye Ruogan Zhengce de Zhixing Guiding"). Summarized in detail in Zhou Ding. 1983. "Gao Hao Neilian Gongzuo, Zengqiang Tequ Xiyin Waizi de Nengli" ["Do Internal Linkage Work Well, Strengthen the Special Zone's Ability to Absorb Foreign Capital"]. In *Shenzhen Tequ Fazhan de Daolu* [*Shenzhen Special Zone's Development Path*], edited by Zhonggong Shenzhenshi Wei Bangongting Bian [General Office of the Shenzhen Municipal CCP Committee]. Beijing: Guangming Ribao Chubanshe [Guangming Ribao Publications].

"Provisional Regulations of Shenzhen SEZ on Technology Introduction" ("Shenzhen Jingji Tequ Jishu Yinjin Zhixing Guiding"). Promulgated 8 February 1984. Published in Chinese in *SSZH*, 8 February 1984. Referred to in text as "SEZ Technology Regulations."

"Provisional Regulations on Foreign Exchange Control of the PRC." Promulgated December 1980. Translated in Chu, Moser, and Nee. 1982. *Commercial, Business and Trade Laws: People's Republic of China*, pp. 21–25. Dobbs Ferry, N.Y.: Oceana Publications. Referred to in text as "Foreign Exchange Regulations."

"Provisional Regulations on Wages in the Enterprises in Special Economic Zones in Guangdong Province." (Referred to in text as "SEZ Labor Regulations." Adopted by Standing Committee of the Fifth Guangdong Provincial People's Congress on 17 November 1981.) Translated in Chu, Moser and Nee. 1982. *Commercial, Business and Trade Laws: People's Republic of China*, part 9. Dobbs Ferry, N.Y.: Oceana Publications.

"Provisional Tax Regulations for 14 Open Cities, SEZs and Hainan Island." Promulgated 1 December 1984. Translated in *China Economic News*, no. 46 (3 December 1984): 1–3.

"Provisions for the Implementation of the Regulations on Labor Management in Joint Ventures Using Chinese and Foreign Investment." Promulgated 19 January 1984.

"Provisions of the State Council of the PRC for the Encouragement of Foreign Investment." Promulgated 11 October 1986. Translated in *China Business Review* 14, no. 1 (January–February 1987): 14–15.

"Regulations of the People's Republic of China on Special Economic Zones in Guangdong Province." Adopted 26 August 1980. Translated in FBIS, Daily Report: China, 28 August 1980, pp. L9–L13. Referred to in text as "SEZ Regulations."

"Regulations on Foreign Currency Balance of Equity Joint Ventures." Effective 1 February 1986.

"Regulations on Labor Management in Joint Ventures Using Chinese and Foreign Investment." Promulgated 26 July 1980. Translated in Chu, Moser, and Nee. 1982. *Commercial, Business and Trade Laws: People's Republic of China*, part 14. Dobbs Ferry, N.Y.: Oceana Publications.